GREATEST TRAGEDIES OF
SHAKESPEARE

CLASSICS

Reprint 2022

FiNGERPRINT! **CLASSICS**

An imprint of Prakash Books India Pvt. Ltd.

113/A, Darya Ganj,
New Delhi-110 002
Tel: (011) 2324 7062 – 65, Fax: (011) 2324 6975
Email: info@prakashbooks.com/sales@prakashbooks.com

facebook www.facebook.com/fingerprintpublishing
twitter www.twitter.com/FingerprintP
www.fingerprintpublishing.com

ISBN: 978 81 9489 889 4

For where love reigns, disturbing jealousy
Doth call himself affection's sentinel;
Gives false alarms, suggesteth mutiny,
And in a peaceful hour doth cry "Kill, kill!"
 Distemp'ring gentle love in his desire,
 As air and water do abate the fire.

This sour informer, this bate-breeding spy,
This canker that eats up love's tender spring,
This carry-tale, dissentious jealousy,
That sometime true news, sometime false doth bring,
 Knocks at my heart, and whispers in mine ear,
 That if I love thee, I thy death should fear.

       —Venus and Adonis

William Shakespeare was baptized on April 26, 1564. His father John engaged in various trades, and his mother Mary was the daughter of an affluent landowning farmer. John and Mary had eight children, of whom William was the third. It is believed that Shakespeare was educated at King's New School. This was a free school chartered in 1553, and was near to Shakespeare's home. This grammar school, like the others of its kind, had Latin text in its curriculum.

At the age of eighteen, William Shakespeare married Anne Hathaway and they had three children—Susanna, and twins Hamnet and Judith.

Shakespeare began his career as an actor, writer, and part owner of a playing company called the Lord Chamberlain's Men during the reign of Queen Elizabeth I, later known as King's Men when King James I took the throne and became their patron, in London. Most of his known works have been produced between 1589 and 1613. His early plays were mainly comedies and histories which are regarded as some of the best works produced in these genres. In Shakespeare's time, the plays were mainly performed at two places—the Globe, an open-roofed theatre, and Blackfriars Theatre, an indoor theatre built by James Burbage.

Shakespeare's plays are difficult to date. His early classical and Italianate comedies contain tight double plots and precise comic sequences giving way to the romantic atmosphere of his most acclaimed comedies in the mid-1590s. Playwright Ben Jonson, Shakespeare's contemporary, had believed that Shakespeare had no rival when it came to comedy. And in 1598, English writer Frances Meres declared him the greatest English writer of comedy and tragedy. *A Midsummer Night's Dream*—a witty mixture of romance, fairy magic, and comic low-life scenes—is one of his most delightful creations, shortly before he turned to *Romeo and Juliet*. Set in the kingdom of Athens and the woods nearby, revolving around the wedding preparations of Theseus and Hippolyta, *A Midsummer Night's Dream* has four interconnected plots, detailing the adventures of four young lovers—Demetrius, Lysander, Hermia, and Helena.

Romeo and Juliet is his most famous romantic tragedy of sexually charged adolescence, love, and death. It marks a departure from his earlier works and from others of the English Renaissance. Shakespeare's plays demonstrate the expansiveness of his imagination and the extent of his learning. Even so, such plays were not well-received by some of the critics. In the seventeenth century, John Dryden, in his essay 'Of Dramatic Poesie', expressed that Shakespeare may excel in imagination but he lacked judgement. He believed this was so because Shakespeare had written his plays for a poorly educated audience. It is a fact that Shakespeare had written plays keeping in mind that they were to be performed, not to be published or circulated among readers. In 1592, Robert Greene's animosity towards the Bard was apparent when he called Shakespeare 'an upstart Crow, beautified with our feathers'. Apart from some such critics, Shakespeare's work had impressed and entertained his audience and other notable writers.

His sequence of great comedies continues with The *Merchant of Venice, Much Ado About Nothing, As You Like It,* and *Twelfth Night.* One of his best-loved comedies, *Twelfth Night* is a romantic drama of confusions, comic sequences, and mistaken identities. With a perfect combination of romance and reality and excellently crafted characters, it has been amusing its audiences for more than four centuries now.

Shakespeare introduced prose comedy in the histories of the late 1590s—*Henry IV, Part I* and *Henry IV, Part II,* and *Henry V*—after the lyrical *Richard II. Julius Caesar* introduced a new kind of drama. Shakespeare wrote the so-called 'problem plays' in the early seventeenth century, *Measure for Measure, Troilus and Cressida,* and *All's Well that Ends Well* being a few of them. Until about 1608, he mainly wrote tragedies including *Hamlet, Othello, King Lear,* and *Macbeth.* The story of a brave Scottish general named Macbeth, the eponymous drama illustrates how the lust for power dooms the fate of a noble person.

Antony and Cleopatra and *Coriolanus*—his last major tragedies, contain some of his finest poetry. Shakespeare wrote tragicomedies, also known as romances, in his last phase. These include *Cymbeline*, *The Winter's Tale*, and *The Tempest*, as well as the collaboration *Pericles, Prince of Tyre*.

There is no writer, living or dead, whose reputation matches that of the beloved English bard, William Shakespeare—a man who possessed exceptional imagination and intellect, and wrote thirty-eight plays, one hundred and fifty-four sonnets, two long narrative poems, and several other verses. His works have been extensively read, analysed, and performed in many countries and translated in almost all major languages. All his works centre around human nature, which is why these works written more than four hundred years ago have withstood the test of time—because human nature never changes. Speaking of his brilliant contemporary, Ben Jonson's words were, "[Shakespeare] was not of an age but for all time." A true genius, also known as the English national poet, William Shakespeare is considered the greatest dramatist of all time.

About this Edition

A compilation of the greatest tragedies ever written by William Shakespeare, this edition comprises five plays which are immensely popular, regularly studied, frequently performed, and have inspired countless adaptations, operas, poetry, and paintings.

First published in the *First Folio* in 1623, these plays are worthy of being included in the list of the world's finest tragic literature.

Contents

Romeo and Juliet

"What's in a name? that which we call a rose
By any other name would smell as sweet;"

Characters in the Play

Escalus, PRINCE of Verona
MERCUTIO, kinsman of the Prince and friend of Romeo
PARIS, a young count, kinsman of the Prince and Mercutio, and suitor of Juliet
PAGE to Count Paris

MONTAGUE, head of a Veronese family at feud with the Capulets
LADY MONTAGUE
ROMEO, son of Montague
BENVOLIO, nephew of Montague and friend of Romeo and Mercutio
ABRAM, servant of Montague
BALTHASAR, servant of Montague attending on Romeo

CAPULET, head of a Veronese family at feud with the Montagues
LADY CAPULET
JULIET, daughter of Capulet
TYBALT, nephew of Lady Capulet
FOLLOWER
COUSIN CAPULET, an old man of the Capulet family
NURSE of Juliet, her foster-mother
PETER, servant of Capulet attending on the Nurse

SAMPSON
GREGORY
Clown, a SERVANT   } of the Capulet household
SERVINGMEN

FRIAR LAURENCE, a Franciscan
FRIAR JOHN, a Franciscan
An APOTHECARY of Mantua
FIDDLER and MUSICIANS (Simon Catling, Hugh Rebeck, James Soundpost)
Members of the WATCH
CITIZENS of Verona
Maskers, torchbearers, pages, servants

CHORUS

THE MOST EXCELLENT AND
LAMENTABLE TRAGEDY OF ROMEO AND JULIET

Prologue

Two households, both alike in dignity,
In fair Verona, where we lay our scene,
From ancient grudge break to new mutiny,
Where civil blood makes civil hands unclean.
From forth the fatal loins of these two foes
A pair of star-cross'd lovers take their life;
Whose misadventured piteous overthrows
Do with their death bury their parents' strife.
The fearful passage of their death-mark'd love,
And the continuance of their parents' rage,
Which, but their children's end, nought could remove,
Is now the two hours' traffic of our stage;
The which if you with patient ears attend,
What here shall miss, our toil shall strive to mend.

ACT

SCENE I.
VERONA. A PUBLIC PLACE.

Enter SAMPSON *and* GREGORY,
of the house of Capulet, armed with swords and bucklers

SAMPSON

    Gregory, o' my word, we'll not carry coals.

GREGORY

    No, for then we should be colliers.

SAMPSON

    I mean, an we be in choler, we'll draw.

GREGORY

    Ay, while you live, draw your neck out o' the collar.

SAMPSON

    I strike quickly, being moved.

GREGORY

    But thou art not quickly moved to strike.

SAMPSON

    A dog of the house of Montague moves me.

GREGORY

    To move is to stir; and to be valiant is to stand: therefore,
    if thou art moved, thou runn'st away.

SAMPSON

A dog of that house shall move me to stand: I will take the wall of any man or maid of Montague's.

GREGORY

That shows thee a weak slave; for the weakest goes to the wall.

SAMPSON

True; and therefore women, being the weaker vessels, are ever thrust to the wall: therefore I will push Montague's men from the wall, and thrust his maids to the wall.

GREGORY

The quarrel is between our masters and us their men.

SAMPSON

'Tis all one, I will show myself a tyrant: when I have fought with the men, I will be cruel with the maids, and cut off their heads.

GREGORY

The heads of the maids?

SAMPSON

Ay, the heads of the maids, or their maidenheads; take it in what sense thou wilt.

GREGORY

They must take it in sense that feel it.

SAMPSON

Me they shall feel while I am able to stand: and 'tis known I am a pretty piece of flesh.

GREGORY

'Tis well thou art not fish; if thou hadst, thou hadst been poor John. Draw thy tool! here comes two of the house of the Montagues.

SAMPSON

My naked weapon is out: quarrel, I will back thee.

GREGORY

How! turn thy back and run?

SAMPSON

Fear me not.

GREGORY

No, marry; I fear thee!

SAMPSON
Let us take the law of our sides; let them begin.
GREGORY
I will frown as I pass by, and let them take it as they list.
SAMPSON
Nay, as they dare. I will bite my thumb at them; which is a disgrace to them, if they bear it.

Enter ABRAHAM *and* BALTHASAR

ABRAHAM
Do you bite your thumb at us, sir?
SAMPSON
I do bite my thumb, sir.
ABRAHAM
Do you bite your thumb at us, sir?
SAMPSON
[*Aside to* GREGORY] Is the law of our side, if I say ay?
GREGORY
No.
SAMPSON
No, sir, I do not bite my thumb at you, sir, but I bite my thumb, sir.
GREGORY
Do you quarrel, sir?
ABRAHAM
Quarrel sir! no, sir.
SAMPSON
If you do, sir, I am for you: I serve as good a man as you.
ABRAHAM
No better.
SAMPSON
Well, sir.
GREGORY
Say 'better:' here comes one of my master's kinsmen.
SAMPSON
Yes, better, sir.
ABRAHAM
You lie.

SAMPSON

Draw, if you be men. Gregory, remember thy swashing blow.

They fight

Enter BENVOLIO

BENVOLIO

Part, fools!

Put up your swords; you know not what you do.

Beats down their swords

Enter TYBALT

TYBALT

What, art thou drawn among these heartless hinds?

Turn thee, Benvolio, look upon thy death.

BENVOLIO

I do but keep the peace: put up thy sword,

Or manage it to part these men with me.

TYBALT

What, drawn, and talk of peace! I hate the word,

As I hate hell, all Montagues, and thee:

Have at thee, coward!

They fight

Enter, several of both houses, who join the fray;

then enter Citizens, with clubs

FIRST CITIZEN

Clubs, bills, and partisans! strike! beat them down!

Down with the Capulets! down with the Montagues!

Enter CAPULET *in his gown,*

and LADY CAPULET

CAPULET

What noise is this? Give me my long sword, ho!

LADY CAPULET

A crutch, a crutch! why call you for a sword?

CAPULET

My sword, I say! Old Montague is come,

And flourishes his blade in spite of me.

Enter MONTAGUE *and* LADY MONTAGUE

MONTAGUE

Thou villain Capulet,—Hold me not, let me go.

LADY MONTAGUE

    Thou shalt not stir a foot to seek a foe.

Enter PRINCE, *with Attendants*

PRINCE

    Rebellious subjects, enemies to peace,
    Profaners of this neighbour-stained steel,—
    Will they not hear? What, ho! you men, you beasts,
    That quench the fire of your pernicious rage
    With purple fountains issuing from your veins,
    On pain of torture, from those bloody hands
    Throw your mistemper'd weapons to the ground,
    And hear the sentence of your moved prince.
    Three civil brawls, bred of an airy word,
    By thee, old Capulet, and Montague,
    Have thrice disturb'd the quiet of our streets,
    And made Verona's ancient citizens
    Cast by their grave beseeming ornaments,
    To wield old partisans, in hands as old,
    Canker'd with peace, to part your canker'd hate:
    If ever you disturb our streets again,
    Your lives shall pay the forfeit of the peace.
    For this time, all the rest depart away:
    You Capulet; shall go along with me:
    And, Montague, come you this afternoon,
    To know our further pleasure in this case,
    To old Free-town, our common judgment-place.
    Once more, on pain of death, all men depart.

Exeunt all but MONTAGUE,
LADY MONTAGUE, *and* BENVOLIO

MONTAGUE

    Who set this ancient quarrel new abroach?
    Speak, nephew, were you by when it began?

BENVOLIO

    Here were the servants of your adversary,
    And yours, close fighting ere I did approach:
    I drew to part them: in the instant came
    The fiery Tybalt, with his sword prepared,

Which, as he breathed defiance to my ears,
He swung about his head and cut the winds,
Who nothing hurt withal hiss'd him in scorn:
While we were interchanging thrusts and blows,
Came more and more and fought on part and part,
Till the prince came, who parted either part.

LADY MONTAGUE

O, where is Romeo? saw you him to-day?
Right glad I am he was not at this fray.

BENVOLIO

Madam, an hour before the worshipp'd sun
Peer'd forth the golden window of the east,
A troubled mind drave me to walk abroad;
Where, underneath the grove of sycamore
That westward rooteth from the city's side,
So early walking did I see your son:
Towards him I made, but he was ware of me
And stole into the covert of the wood:
I, measuring his affections by my own,
That most are busied when they're most alone,
Pursued my humour not pursuing his,
And gladly shunn'd who gladly fled from me.

MONTAGUE

Many a morning hath he there been seen,
With tears augmenting the fresh morning dew.
Adding to clouds more clouds with his deep sighs;
But all so soon as the all-cheering sun
Should in the furthest east begin to draw
The shady curtains from Aurora's bed,
Away from the light steals home my heavy son,
And private in his chamber pens himself,
Shuts up his windows, locks far daylight out
And makes himself an artificial night:
Black and portentous must this humour prove,
Unless good counsel may the cause remove.

BENVOLIO

My noble uncle, do you know the cause?

MONTAGUE
    I neither know it nor can learn of him.
BENVOLIO
    Have you importuned him by any means?
MONTAGUE
    Both by myself and many other friends:
    But he, his own affections' counsellor,
    Is to himself—I will not say how true—
    But to himself so secret and so close,
    So far from sounding and discovery,
    As is the bud bit with an envious worm,
    Ere he can spread his sweet leaves to the air,
    Or dedicate his beauty to the sun.
    Could we but learn from whence his sorrows grow.
    We would as willingly give cure as know.
Enter ROMEO
BENVOLIO
    See, where he comes: so please you, step aside;
    I'll know his grievance, or be much denied.
MONTAGUE
    I would thou wert so happy by thy stay,
    To hear true shrift. Come, madam, let's away.
Exeunt MONTAGUE *and*
LADY MONTAGUE

BENVOLIO
    Good-morrow, cousin.
ROMEO
    Is the day so young?
BENVOLIO
    But new struck nine.
ROMEO
    Ay me! sad hours seem long.
    Was that my father that went hence so fast?
BENVOLIO
    It was. What sadness lengthens Romeo's hours?
ROMEO
    Not having that, which, having, makes them short.

BENVOLIO

In love?

ROMEO

Out—

BENVOLIO

Of love?

ROMEO

Out of her favour, where I am in love.

BENVOLIO

Alas, that love, so gentle in his view,
Should be so tyrannous and rough in proof!

ROMEO

Alas, that love, whose view is muffled still,
Should, without eyes, see pathways to his will!
Where shall we dine? O me! What fray was here?
Yet tell me not, for I have heard it all.
Here's much to do with hate, but more with love.
Why, then, O brawling love! O loving hate!
O any thing, of nothing first create!
O heavy lightness! serious vanity!
Mis-shapen chaos of well-seeming forms!
Feather of lead, bright smoke, cold fire, sick health!
Still-waking sleep, that is not what it is!
This love feel I, that feel no love in this.
Dost thou not laugh?

BENVOLIO

No, coz, I rather weep.

ROMEO

Good heart, at what?

BENVOLIO

At thy good heart's oppression.

ROMEO

Why, such is love's transgression.
Griefs of mine own lie heavy in my breast,
Which thou wilt propagate, to have it prest
With more of thine: this love that thou hast shown
Doth add more grief to too much of mine own.

Love is a smoke raised with the fume of sighs;
Being purged, a fire sparkling in lovers' eyes;
Being vex'd a sea nourish'd with lovers' tears:
What is it else? a madness most discreet,
A choking gall and a preserving sweet.
Farewell, my coz.

BENVOLIO
Soft! I will go along;
An if you leave me so, you do me wrong.

ROMEO
Tut, I have lost myself; I am not here;
This is not Romeo, he's some other where.

BENVOLIO
Tell me in sadness, who is that you love.

ROMEO
What, shall I groan and tell thee?

BENVOLIO
Groan! why, no.
But sadly tell me who.

ROMEO
Bid a sick man in sadness make his will:
Ah, word ill urged to one that is so ill!
In sadness, cousin, I do love a woman.

BENVOLIO
I aim'd so near, when I supposed you loved.

ROMEO
A right good mark-man! And she's fair I love.

BENVOLIO
A right fair mark, fair coz, is soonest hit.

ROMEO
Well, in that hit you miss: she'll not be hit
With Cupid's arrow; she hath Dian's wit;
And, in strong proof of chastity well arm'd,
From love's weak childish bow she lives unharm'd.
She will not stay the siege of loving terms,
Nor bide the encounter of assailing eyes,
Nor ope her lap to saint-seducing gold:

O, she is rich in beauty, only poor,
That when she dies with beauty dies her store.

BENVOLIO
Then she hath sworn that she will still live chaste?

ROMEO
She hath, and in that sparing makes huge waste,
For beauty starved with her severity
Cuts beauty off from all posterity.
She is too fair, too wise, wisely too fair,
To merit bliss by making me despair:
She hath forsworn to love, and in that vow
Do I live dead that live to tell it now.

BENVOLIO
Be ruled by me, forget to think of her.

ROMEO
O, teach me how I should forget to think.

BENVOLIO
By giving liberty unto thine eyes;
Examine other beauties.

ROMEO
'Tis the way
To call hers exquisite, in question more:
These happy masks that kiss fair ladies' brows
Being black put us in mind they hide the fair;
He that is strucken blind cannot forget
The precious treasure of his eyesight lost:
Show me a mistress that is passing fair,
What doth her beauty serve, but as a note
Where I may read who pass'd that passing fair?
Farewell: thou canst not teach me to forget.

BENVOLIO
I'll pay that doctrine, or else die in debt.

Exeunt

SCENE II.
A STREET.

Enter CAPULET, PARIS, *and Servant*

CAPULET

But Montague is bound as well as I,
In penalty alike; and 'tis not hard, I think,
For men so old as we to keep the peace.

PARIS

Of honourable reckoning are you both;
And pity 'tis you lived at odds so long.
But now, my lord, what say you to my suit?

CAPULET

But saying o'er what I have said before:
My child is yet a stranger in the world;
She hath not seen the change of fourteen years,
Let two more summers wither in their pride,
Ere we may think her ripe to be a bride.

PARIS

Younger than she are happy mothers made.

CAPULET

And too soon marr'd are those so early made.
The earth hath swallow'd all my hopes but she,
She is the hopeful lady of my earth:
But woo her, gentle Paris, get her heart,
My will to her consent is but a part;
An she agree, within her scope of choice
Lies my consent and fair according voice.
This night I hold an old accustom'd feast,
Whereto I have invited many a guest,
Such as I love; and you, among the store,
One more, most welcome, makes my number more.
At my poor house look to behold this night
Earth-treading stars that make dark heaven light:
Such comfort as do lusty young men feel
When well-apparell'd April on the heel

Of limping winter treads, even such delight
Among fresh female buds shall you this night
Inherit at my house; hear all, all see,
And like her most whose merit most shall be:
Which on more view, of many mine being one
May stand in number, though in reckoning none,
Come, go with me.
To Servant, giving a paper
Go, sirrah, trudge about
Through fair Verona; find those persons out
Whose names are written there, and to them say,
My house and welcome on their pleasure stay.
                                        Exeunt CAPULET *and* PARIS

SERVANT
Find them out whose names are written here! It is written, that
the shoemaker should meddle with his yard, and the tailor with
his last, the fisher with his pencil, and the painter with his nets;
but I am sent to find those persons whose names are here writ,
and can never find what names the writing person hath here
writ. I must to the learned.—In good time.
                                        Enter BENVOLIO *and* ROMEO

BENVOLIO
Tut, man, one fire burns out another's burning,
One pain is lessen'd by another's anguish;
Turn giddy, and be holp by backward turning;
One desperate grief cures with another's languish:
Take thou some new infection to thy eye,
And the rank poison of the old will die.

ROMEO
Your plaintain-leaf is excellent for that.

BENVOLIO
For what, I pray thee?

ROMEO
For your broken shin.

BENVOLIO
Why, Romeo, art thou mad?

ROMEO

Not mad, but bound more than a mad-man is;
Shut up in prison, kept without my food,
Whipp'd and tormented and—God-den, good fellow.

SERVANT

God gi' god-den. I pray, sir, can you read?

ROMEO

Ay, mine own fortune in my misery.

SERVANT

Perhaps you have learned it without book: but, I
pray, can you read any thing you see?

ROMEO

Ay, if I know the letters and the language.

SERVANT

Ye say honestly: rest you merry!

ROMEO

Stay, fellow; I can read.

Reads

'Signior Martino and his wife and daughters; County Anselme
and his beauteous sisters; the lady widow of Vitravio; Signior
Placentio and his lovely nieces; Mercutio and his brother
Valentine; mine uncle Capulet, his wife and daughters; my fair
niece Rosaline; Livia; Signior Valentio and his cousin Tybalt,
Lucio and the lively Helena.' A fair assembly: whither should
they come?

SERVANT

Up.

ROMEO

Whither?

SERVANT

To supper; to our house.

ROMEO

Whose house?

SERVANT

My master's.

ROMEO

Indeed, I should have ask'd you that before.

SERVANT

Now I'll tell you without asking: my master is the great rich
Capulet; and if you be not of the house of Montagues, I pray,
come and crush a cup of wine. Rest you merry!

Exit

BENVOLIO

At this same ancient feast of Capulet's
Sups the fair Rosaline whom thou so lovest,
With all the admired beauties of Verona:
Go thither; and, with unattainted eye,
Compare her face with some that I shall show,
And I will make thee think thy swan a crow.

ROMEO

When the devout religion of mine eye
Maintains such falsehood, then turn tears to fires;
And these, who often drown'd could never die,
Transparent heretics, be burnt for liars!
One fairer than my love! the all-seeing sun
Ne'er saw her match since first the world begun.

BENVOLIO

Tut, you saw her fair, none else being by,
Herself poised with herself in either eye:
But in that crystal scales let there be weigh'd
Your lady's love against some other maid
That I will show you shining at this feast,
And she shall scant show well that now shows best.

ROMEO

I'll go along, no such sight to be shown,
But to rejoice in splendor of mine own.

Exeunt

SCENE III.
A ROOM IN CAPULET'S HOUSE.

Enter LADY CAPULET *and Nurse*

LADY CAPULET

Nurse, where's my daughter? call her forth to me.

NURSE

    Now, by my maidenhead, at twelve year old,

    I bade her come. What, lamb! what, ladybird!

    God forbid! Where's this girl? What, Juliet!

Enter JULIET

JULIET

    How now! who calls?

NURSE

    Your mother.

JULIET

    Madam, I am here.

    What is your will?

LADY CAPULET

    This is the matter:—Nurse, give leave awhile,

    We must talk in secret:—nurse, come back again;

    I have remember'd me, thou's hear our counsel.

    Thou know'st my daughter's of a pretty age.

NURSE

    Faith, I can tell her age unto an hour.

LADY CAPULET

    She's not fourteen.

NURSE

    I'll lay fourteen of my teeth,—

    And yet, to my teeth be it spoken, I have but four—

    She is not fourteen. How long is it now

    To Lammas-tide?

LADY CAPULET

    A fortnight and odd days.

NURSE

    Even or odd, of all days in the year,

    Come Lammas-eve at night shall she be fourteen.

    Susan and she—God rest all Christian souls!—

    Were of an age: well, Susan is with God;

    She was too good for me: but, as I said,

    On Lammas-eve at night shall she be fourteen;

    That shall she, marry; I remember it well.

    'Tis since the earthquake now eleven years;

And she was wean'd,—I never shall forget it,—
Of all the days of the year, upon that day:
For I had then laid wormwood to my dug,
Sitting in the sun under the dove-house wall;
My lord and you were then at Mantua:—
Nay, I do bear a brain:—but, as I said,
When it did taste the wormwood on the nipple
Of my dug and felt it bitter, pretty fool,
To see it tetchy and fall out with the dug!
Shake quoth the dove-house: 'twas no need, I trow,
To bid me trudge:
And since that time it is eleven years;
For then she could stand alone; nay, by the rood,
She could have run and waddled all about;
For even the day before, she broke her brow:
And then my husband—God be with his soul!
A' was a merry man—took up the child:
'Yea,' quoth he, 'dost thou fall upon thy face?
Thou wilt fall backward when thou hast more wit;
Wilt thou not, Jule?' and, by my holidame,
The pretty wretch left crying and said 'Ay.'
To see, now, how a jest shall come about!
I warrant, an I should live a thousand years,
I never should forget it: 'Wilt thou not, Jule?' quoth he;
And, pretty fool, it stinted and said 'Ay.'

LADY CAPULET

Enough of this; I pray thee, hold thy peace.

NURSE

Yes, madam: yet I cannot choose but laugh,
To think it should leave crying and say 'Ay.'
And yet, I warrant, it had upon its brow
A bump as big as a young cockerel's stone;
A parlous knock; and it cried bitterly:
'Yea,' quoth my husband, 'fall'st upon thy face?
Thou wilt fall backward when thou comest to age;
Wilt thou not, Jule?' it stinted and said 'Ay.'

JULIET

> And stint thou too, I pray thee, nurse, say I.

NURSE

> Peace, I have done. God mark thee to his grace!
> Thou wast the prettiest babe that e'er I nursed:
> An I might live to see thee married once,
> I have my wish.

LADY CAPULET

> Marry, that 'marry' is the very theme
> I came to talk of. Tell me, daughter Juliet,
> How stands your disposition to be married?

JULIET

> It is an honour that I dream not of.

NURSE

> An honour! were not I thine only nurse,
> I would say thou hadst suck'd wisdom from thy teat.

LADY CAPULET

> Well, think of marriage now; younger than you,
> Here in Verona, ladies of esteem,
> Are made already mothers: by my count,
> I was your mother much upon these years
> That you are now a maid. Thus then in brief:
> The valiant Paris seeks you for his love.

NURSE

> A man, young lady! lady, such a man
> As all the world—why, he's a man of wax.

LADY CAPULET

> Verona's summer hath not such a flower.

NURSE

> Nay, he's a flower; in faith, a very flower.

LADY CAPULET

> What say you? can you love the gentleman?
> This night you shall behold him at our feast;
> Read o'er the volume of young Paris' face,
> And find delight writ there with beauty's pen;
> Examine every married lineament,
> And see how one another lends content

And what obscured in this fair volume lies
Find written in the margent of his eyes.
This precious book of love, this unbound lover,
To beautify him, only lacks a cover:
The fish lives in the sea, and 'tis much pride
For fair without the fair within to hide:
That book in many's eyes doth share the glory,
That in gold clasps locks in the golden story;
So shall you share all that he doth possess,
By having him, making yourself no less.

NURSE

No less! nay, bigger; women grow by men.

LADY CAPULET

Speak briefly, can you like of Paris' love?

JULIET

I'll look to like, if looking liking move:
But no more deep will I endart mine eye
Than your consent gives strength to make it fly.

Enter a Servant

SERVANT

Madam, the guests are come, supper served up, you called, my young lady asked for, the nurse cursed in the pantry, and every thing in extremity. I must hence to wait; I beseech you, follow straight.

LADY CAPULET

We follow thee.

Exit Servant

Juliet, the county stays.

NURSE

Go, girl, seek happy nights to happy days.

Exeunt

SCENE IV.
A STREET.

Enter ROMEO, MERCUTIO, BENVOLIO,
with five or six Maskers, Torch-bearers, and others

ROMEO

What, shall this speech be spoke for our excuse?
Or shall we on without a apology?

BENVOLIO

The date is out of such prolixity:
We'll have no Cupid hoodwink'd with a scarf,
Bearing a Tartar's painted bow of lath,
Scaring the ladies like a crow-keeper;
Nor no without-book prologue, faintly spoke
After the prompter, for our entrance:
But let them measure us by what they will;
We'll measure them a measure, and be gone.

ROMEO

Give me a torch: I am not for this ambling;
Being but heavy, I will bear the light.

MERCUTIO

Nay, gentle Romeo, we must have you dance.

ROMEO

Not I, believe me: you have dancing shoes
With nimble soles: I have a soul of lead
So stakes me to the ground I cannot move.

MERCUTIO

You are a lover; borrow Cupid's wings,
And soar with them above a common bound.

ROMEO

I am too sore enpierced with his shaft
To soar with his light feathers, and so bound,
I cannot bound a pitch above dull woe:
Under love's heavy burden do I sink.

MERCUTIO

And, to sink in it, should you burden love;
Too great oppression for a tender thing.

ROMEO

Is love a tender thing? it is too rough,
Too rude, too boisterous, and it pricks like thorn.

MERCUTIO

If love be rough with you, be rough with love;
Prick love for pricking, and you beat love down.
Give me a case to put my visage in:
A visor for a visor! what care I
What curious eye doth quote deformities?
Here are the beetle brows shall blush for me.

BENVOLIO

Come, knock and enter; and no sooner in,
But every man betake him to his legs.

ROMEO

A torch for me: let wantons light of heart
Tickle the senseless rushes with their heels,
For I am proverb'd with a grandsire phrase;
I'll be a candle-holder, and look on.
The game was ne'er so fair, and I am done.

MERCUTIO

Tut, dun's the mouse, the constable's own word:
If thou art dun, we'll draw thee from the mire
Of this sir-reverence love, wherein thou stick'st
Up to the ears. Come, we burn daylight, ho!

ROMEO

Nay, that's not so.

MERCUTIO

I mean, sir, in delay
We waste our lights in vain, like lamps by day.
Take our good meaning, for our judgment sits
Five times in that ere once in our five wits.

ROMEO

And we mean well in going to this mask;
But 'tis no wit to go.

MERCUTIO

Why, may one ask?

ROMEO
    I dream'd a dream to-night.
MERCUTIO
    And so did I.
ROMEO
    Well, what was yours?
MERCUTIO
    That dreamers often lie.
ROMEO
    In bed asleep, while they do dream things true.
MERCUTIO
    O, then, I see Queen Mab hath been with you.
    She is the fairies' midwife, and she comes
    In shape no bigger than an agate-stone
    On the fore-finger of an alderman,
    Drawn with a team of little atomies
    Athwart men's noses as they lie asleep;
    Her wagon-spokes made of long spiders' legs,
    The cover of the wings of grasshoppers,
    The traces of the smallest spider's web,
    The collars of the moonshine's watery beams,
    Her whip of cricket's bone, the lash of film,
    Her wagoner a small grey-coated gnat,
    Not so big as a round little worm
    Prick'd from the lazy finger of a maid;
    Her chariot is an empty hazel-nut
    Made by the joiner squirrel or old grub,
    Time out o' mind the fairies' coachmakers.
    And in this state she gallops night by night
    Through lovers' brains, and then they dream of love;
    O'er courtiers' knees, that dream on court'sies straight,
    O'er lawyers' fingers, who straight dream on fees,
    O'er ladies' lips, who straight on kisses dream,
    Which oft the angry Mab with blisters plagues,
    Because their breaths with sweetmeats tainted are:
    Sometime she gallops o'er a courtier's nose,

And then dreams he of smelling out a suit;
And sometime comes she with a tithe-pig's tail
Tickling a parson's nose as a' lies asleep,
Then dreams, he of another benefice:
Sometime she driveth o'er a soldier's neck,
And then dreams he of cutting foreign throats,
Of breaches, ambuscadoes, Spanish blades,
Of healths five-fathom deep; and then anon
Drums in his ear, at which he starts and wakes,
And being thus frighted swears a prayer or two
And sleeps again. This is that very Mab
That plats the manes of horses in the night,
And bakes the elflocks in foul sluttish hairs,
Which once untangled, much misfortune bodes:
This is the hag, when maids lie on their backs,
That presses them and learns them first to bear,
Making them women of good carriage:
This is she—

ROMEO

Peace, peace, Mercutio, peace!
Thou talk'st of nothing.

MERCUTIO

True, I talk of dreams,
Which are the children of an idle brain,
Begot of nothing but vain fantasy,
Which is as thin of substance as the air
And more inconstant than the wind, who wooes
Even now the frozen bosom of the north,
And, being anger'd, puffs away from thence,
Turning his face to the dew-dropping south.

BENVOLIO

This wind, you talk of, blows us from ourselves;
Supper is done, and we shall come too late.

ROMEO

I fear, too early: for my mind misgives
Some consequence yet hanging in the stars
Shall bitterly begin his fearful date

With this night's revels and expire the term
Of a despised life closed in my breast
By some vile forfeit of untimely death.
But He, that hath the steerage of my course,
Direct my sail! On, lusty gentlemen.

BENVOLIO
Strike, drum.

Exeunt

SCENE V.
A HALL IN CAPULET'S HOUSE.

Musicians waiting.
Enter Servingmen with napkins

FIRST SERVANT
Where's Potpan, that he helps not to take away? He shift a trencher? he scrape a trencher!

SECOND SERVANT
When good manners shall lie all in one or two men's hands and they unwashed too, 'tis a foul thing.

FIRST SERVANT
Away with the joint-stools, remove the court-cupboard, look to the plate. Good thou, save me a piece of marchpane; and, as thou lovest me, let the porter let in Susan Grindstone and Nell. Antony, and Potpan!

SECOND SERVANT
Ay, boy, ready.

FIRST SERVANT
You are looked for and called for, asked for and sought for, in the great chamber.

SECOND SERVANT
We cannot be here and there too. Cheerly, boys; be brisk awhile, and the longer liver take all.

Enter CAPULET, *with* JULIET *and*
others of his house, meeting the Guests and Maskers

CAPULET
Welcome, gentlemen! ladies that have their toes

Unplagued with corns will have a bout with you.
Ah ha, my mistresses! which of you all
Will now deny to dance? she that makes dainty,
She, I'll swear, hath corns; am I come near ye now?
Welcome, gentlemen! I have seen the day
That I have worn a visor and could tell
A whispering tale in a fair lady's ear,
Such as would please: 'tis gone, 'tis gone, 'tis gone:
You are welcome, gentlemen! come, musicians, play.
A hall, a hall! give room! and foot it, girls.
Music plays, and they dance
More light, you knaves; and turn the tables up,
And quench the fire, the room is grown too hot.
Ah, sirrah, this unlook'd-for sport comes well.
Nay, sit, nay, sit, good cousin Capulet;
For you and I are past our dancing days:
How long is't now since last yourself and I
Were in a mask?

SECOND CAPULET
By'r lady, thirty years.

CAPULET
What, man! 'tis not so much, 'tis not so much:
'Tis since the nuptials of Lucentio,
Come pentecost as quickly as it will,
Some five and twenty years; and then we mask'd.

SECOND CAPULET
'Tis more, 'tis more, his son is elder, sir;
His son is thirty.

CAPULET
Will you tell me that?
His son was but a ward two years ago.

ROMEO
[*To a Servingman*] What lady is that, which doth enrich the hand
Of yonder knight?

SERVANT
I know not, sir.

ROMEO

    O, she doth teach the torches to burn bright!
    It seems she hangs upon the cheek of night
    Like a rich jewel in an Ethiope's ear;
    Beauty too rich for use, for earth too dear!
    So shows a snowy dove trooping with crows,
    As yonder lady o'er her fellows shows.
    The measure done, I'll watch her place of stand,
    And, touching hers, make blessed my rude hand.
    Did my heart love till now? forswear it, sight!
    For I ne'er saw true beauty till this night.

TYBALT

    This, by his voice, should be a Montague.
    Fetch me my rapier, boy. What dares the slave
    Come hither, cover'd with an antic face,
    To fleer and scorn at our solemnity?
    Now, by the stock and honour of my kin,
    To strike him dead, I hold it not a sin.

CAPULET

    Why, how now, kinsman! wherefore storm you so?

TYBALT

    Uncle, this is a Montague, our foe,
    A villain that is hither come in spite,
    To scorn at our solemnity this night.

CAPULET

    Young Romeo is it?

TYBALT

    'Tis he, that villain Romeo.

CAPULET

    Content thee, gentle coz, let him alone;
    He bears him like a portly gentleman;
    And, to say truth, Verona brags of him
    To be a virtuous and well-govern'd youth:
    I would not for the wealth of all the town
    Here in my house do him disparagement:
    Therefore be patient, take no note of him:

It is my will, the which if thou respect,
Show a fair presence and put off these frowns,
And ill-beseeming semblance for a feast.

TYBALT

It fits, when such a villain is a guest:
I'll not endure him.

CAPULET

He shall be endured:
What, goodman boy! I say, he shall: go to;
Am I the master here, or you? go to.
You'll not endure him! God shall mend my soul!
You'll make a mutiny among my guests!
You will set cock-a-hoop! you'll be the man!

TYBALT

Why, uncle, 'tis a shame.

CAPULET

Go to, go to;
You are a saucy boy: is't so, indeed?
This trick may chance to scathe you, I know what:
You must contrary me! marry, 'tis time.
Well said, my hearts! You are a princox; go:
Be quiet, or—More light, more light! For shame!
I'll make you quiet. What, cheerly, my hearts!

TYBALT

Patience perforce with wilful choler meeting
Makes my flesh tremble in their different greeting.
I will withdraw: but this intrusion shall
Now seeming sweet convert to bitter gall.

Exit

ROMEO

[*To* JULIET] If I profane with my unworthiest hand
This holy shrine, the gentle fine is this:
My lips, two blushing pilgrims, ready stand
To smooth that rough touch with a tender kiss.

JULIET

Good pilgrim, you do wrong your hand too much,
Which mannerly devotion shows in this;

For saints have hands that pilgrims' hands do touch,
And palm to palm is holy palmers' kiss.

ROMEO

O, then, dear saint, let lips do what hands do;
Have not saints lips, and holy palmers too?

JULIET

Ay, pilgrim, lips that they must use in prayer.

ROMEO

O, then, dear saint, let lips do what hands do;
They pray, grant thou, lest faith turn to despair.

JULIET

Saints do not move, though grant for prayers' sake.

ROMEO

Then move not, while my prayer's effect I take.
Thus from my lips, by yours, my sin is purged.

JULIET

Then have my lips the sin that they have took.

ROMEO

Sin from thy lips? O trespass sweetly urged!
Give me my sin again.

JULIET

You kiss by the book.

NURSE

Madam, your mother craves a word with you.

ROMEO

What is her mother?

NURSE

Marry, bachelor,
Her mother is the lady of the house,
And a good lady, and a wise and virtuous
I nursed her daughter, that you talk'd withal;
I tell you, he that can lay hold of her
Shall have the chinks.

ROMEO

Is she a Capulet?
O dear account! my life is my foe's debt.

BENVOLIO

Away, begone; the sport is at the best.

ROMEO

Ay, so I fear; the more is my unrest.

CAPULET

Nay, gentlemen, prepare not to be gone;
We have a trifling foolish banquet towards.
Is it e'en so? why, then, I thank you all
I thank you, honest gentlemen; good night.
More torches here! Come on then, let's to bed.
Ah, sirrah, by my fay, it waxes late:
I'll to my rest.

Exeunt all but JULIET *and Nurse*

JULIET

Come hither, nurse. What is yond gentleman?

NURSE

The son and heir of old Tiberio.

JULIET

What's he that now is going out of door?

NURSE

Marry, that, I think, be young Petrucio.

JULIET

What's he that follows there, that would not dance?

NURSE

I know not.

JULIET

Go ask his name: if he be married.
My grave is like to be my wedding bed.

NURSE

His name is Romeo, and a Montague;
The only son of your great enemy.

JULIET

My only love sprung from my only hate!
Too early seen unknown, and known too late!
Prodigious birth of love it is to me,
That I must love a loathed enemy.

NURSE

What's this? what's this?

JULIET
A rhyme I learn'd even now
Of one I danced withal.
One calls within 'Juliet.'
NURSE
Anon, anon!
Come, let's away; the strangers all are gone.

Exeunt

ACT

II

Enter Chorus

CHORUS
　　Now old desire doth in his death-bed lie,
　　And young affection gapes to be his heir;
　　That fair for which love groan'd for and would die,
　　With tender Juliet match'd, is now not fair.
　　Now Romeo is beloved and loves again,
　　Alike betwitched by the charm of looks,
　　But to his foe supposed he must complain,
　　And she steal love's sweet bait from fearful hooks:
　　Being held a foe, he may not have access
　　To breathe such vows as lovers use to swear;
　　And she as much in love, her means much less
　　To meet her new-beloved any where:
　　But passion lends them power, time means, to meet
　　Tempering extremities with extreme sweet.

Exit

SCENE I.
A LANE BY THE WALL
OF CAPULET'S ORCHARD.

Enter ROMEO

ROMEO

　　Can I go forward when my heart is here?
　　Turn back, dull earth, and find thy centre out.
　　He climbs the wall, and leaps down within it
　　　　　　　Enter BENVOLIO *and* MERCUTIO

BENVOLIO

　　Romeo! my cousin Romeo!

MERCUTIO

　　He is wise;
　　And, on my lie, hath stol'n him home to bed.

BENVOLIO

　　He ran this way, and leap'd this orchard wall: Call, good Mercutio.

MERCUTIO

　　Nay, I'll conjure too.
　　Romeo! humours! madman! passion! lover!
　　Appear thou in the likeness of a sigh:
　　Speak but one rhyme, and I am satisfied;
　　Cry but 'Ay me!' pronounce but 'love' and 'dove;'
　　Speak to my gossip Venus one fair word,
　　One nick-name for her purblind son and heir,
　　Young Adam Cupid, he that shot so trim,
　　When King Cophetua loved the beggar-maid!
　　He heareth not, he stirreth not, he moveth not;
　　The ape is dead, and I must conjure him.
　　I conjure thee by Rosaline's bright eyes,
　　By her high forehead and her scarlet lip,
　　By her fine foot, straight leg and quivering thigh
　　And the demesnes that there adjacent lie,
　　That in thy likeness thou appear to us!

BENVOLIO

　　And if he hear thee, thou wilt anger him.

MERCUTIO

    This cannot anger him: 'twould anger him
    To raise a spirit in his mistress' circle
    Of some strange nature, letting it there stand
    Till she had laid it and conjured it down;
    That were some spite: my invocation
    Is fair and honest, and in his mistress' name
    I conjure only but to raise up him.

BENVOLIO

    Come, he hath hid himself among these trees,
    To be consorted with the humorous night:
    Blind is his love and best befits the dark.

MERCUTIO

    If love be blind, love cannot hit the mark.
    Now will he sit under a medlar tree,
    And wish his mistress were that kind of fruit
    As maids call medlars, when they laugh alone.
    Romeo, that she were, O, that she were
    An open et caetera, thou a poperin pear!
    Romeo, good night: I'll to my truckle-bed;
    This field-bed is too cold for me to sleep:
    Come, shall we go?

BENVOLIO

    Go, then; for 'tis in vain
    To seek him here that means not to be found.

Exeunt

SCENE II.
CAPULET'S ORCHARD.

Enter ROMEO

ROMEO

    He jests at scars that never felt a wound.
    JULIET appears above at a window
    But, soft! what light through yonder window breaks?
    It is the east, and Juliet is the sun.
    Arise, fair sun, and kill the envious moon,

Who is already sick and pale with grief,
That thou her maid art far more fair than she:
Be not her maid, since she is envious;
Her vestal livery is but sick and green
And none but fools do wear it; cast it off.
It is my lady, O, it is my love!
O, that she knew she were!
She speaks yet she says nothing: what of that?
Her eye discourses; I will answer it.
I am too bold, 'tis not to me she speaks:
Two of the fairest stars in all the heaven,
Having some business, do entreat her eyes
To twinkle in their spheres till they return.
What if her eyes were there, they in her head?
The brightness of her cheek would shame those stars,
As daylight doth a lamp; her eyes in heaven
Would through the airy region stream so bright
That birds would sing and think it were not night.
See, how she leans her cheek upon her hand!
O, that I were a glove upon that hand,
That I might touch that cheek!

JULIET

Ay me!

ROMEO

She speaks:
O, speak again, bright angel! for thou art
As glorious to this night, being o'er my head
As is a winged messenger of heaven
Unto the white-upturned wondering eyes
Of mortals that fall back to gaze on him
When he bestrides the lazy-pacing clouds
And sails upon the bosom of the air.

JULIET

O Romeo, Romeo! wherefore art thou Romeo?
Deny thy father and refuse thy name;
Or, if thou wilt not, be but sworn my love,
And I'll no longer be a Capulet.

ROMEO

    [*Aside*] Shall I hear more, or shall I speak at this?

JULIET

    'Tis but thy name that is my enemy;

    Thou art thyself, though not a Montague.

    What's Montague? it is nor hand, nor foot,

    Nor arm, nor face, nor any other part

    Belonging to a man. O, be some other name!

    What's in a name? that which we call a rose

    By any other name would smell as sweet;

    So Romeo would, were he not Romeo call'd,

    Retain that dear perfection which he owes

    Without that title. Romeo, doff thy name,

    And for that name which is no part of thee

    Take all myself.

ROMEO

    I take thee at thy word:

    Call me but love, and I'll be new baptized;

    Henceforth I never will be Romeo.

JULIET

    What man art thou that thus bescreen'd in night So stumblest

    on my counsel?

ROMEO

    By a name

    I know not how to tell thee who I am:

    My name, dear saint, is hateful to myself,

    Because it is an enemy to thee;

    Had I it written, I would tear the word.

JULIET

    My ears have not yet drunk a hundred words

    Of that tongue's utterance, yet I know the sound:

    Art thou not Romeo and a Montague?

ROMEO

    Neither, fair saint, if either thee dislike.

JULIET

    How camest thou hither, tell me, and wherefore?

    The orchard walls are high and hard to climb,

And the place death, considering who thou art,
If any of my kinsmen find thee here.

ROMEO

With love's light wings did I o'er-perch these walls;
For stony limits cannot hold love out,
And what love can do that dares love attempt;
Therefore thy kinsmen are no let to me.

JULIET

If they do see thee, they will murder thee.

ROMEO

Alack, there lies more peril in thine eye
Than twenty of their swords: look thou but sweet,
And I am proof against their enmity.

JULIET

I would not for the world they saw thee here.

ROMEO

I have night's cloak to hide me from their sight;
And but thou love me, let them find me here:
My life were better ended by their hate,
Than death prorogued, wanting of thy love.

JULIET

By whose direction found'st thou out this place?

ROMEO

By love, who first did prompt me to inquire;
He lent me counsel and I lent him eyes.
I am no pilot; yet, wert thou as far
As that vast shore wash'd with the farthest sea,
I would adventure for such merchandise.

JULIET

Thou know'st the mask of night is on my face,
Else would a maiden blush bepaint my cheek
For that which thou hast heard me speak to-night
Fain would I dwell on form, fain, fain deny
What I have spoke: but farewell compliment!
Dost thou love me? I know thou wilt say 'Ay,'
And I will take thy word: yet if thou swear'st,
Thou mayst prove false; at lovers' perjuries

Then say, Jove laughs. O gentle Romeo,
If thou dost love, pronounce it faithfully:
Or if thou think'st I am too quickly won,
I'll frown and be perverse an say thee nay,
So thou wilt woo; but else, not for the world.
In truth, fair Montague, I am too fond,
And therefore thou mayst think my 'havior light:
But trust me, gentleman, I'll prove more true
Than those that have more cunning to be strange.
I should have been more strange, I must confess,
But that thou overheard'st, ere I was ware,
My true love's passion: therefore pardon me,
And not impute this yielding to light love,
Which the dark night hath so discovered.

ROMEO

Lady, by yonder blessed moon I swear
That tips with silver all these fruit-tree tops—

JULIET

O, swear not by the moon, the inconstant moon,
That monthly changes in her circled orb,
Lest that thy love prove likewise variable.

ROMEO

What shall I swear by?

JULIET

Do not swear at all;
Or, if thou wilt, swear by thy gracious self,
Which is the god of my idolatry,
And I'll believe thee.

ROMEO

If my heart's dear love—

JULIET

Well, do not swear: although I joy in thee,
I have no joy of this contract to-night:
It is too rash, too unadvised, too sudden;
Too like the lightning, which doth cease to be
Ere one can say 'It lightens.' Sweet, good night!

This bud of love, by summer's ripening breath,
May prove a beauteous flower when next we meet.
Good night, good night! as sweet repose and rest
Come to thy heart as that within my breast!

ROMEO

O, wilt thou leave me so unsatisfied?

JULIET

What satisfaction canst thou have to-night?

ROMEO

The exchange of thy love's faithful vow for mine.

JULIET

I gave thee mine before thou didst request it:
And yet I would it were to give again.

ROMEO

Wouldst thou withdraw it? for what purpose, love?

JULIET

But to be frank, and give it thee again.
And yet I wish but for the thing I have:
My bounty is as boundless as the sea,
My love as deep; the more I give to thee,
The more I have, for both are infinite.

Nurse calls within

I hear some noise within; dear love, adieu!
Anon, good nurse! Sweet Montague, be true.
Stay but a little, I will come again.

Exit, above

ROMEO

O blessed, blessed night! I am afeard.
Being in night, all this is but a dream,
Too flattering-sweet to be substantial.

Re-enter JULIET, *above*

JULIET

Three words, dear Romeo, and good night indeed.
If that thy bent of love be honourable,
Thy purpose marriage, send me word to-morrow,
By one that I'll procure to come to thee,

Where and what time thou wilt perform the rite;
And all my fortunes at thy foot I'll lay
And follow thee my lord throughout the world.

NURSE
[*Within*] Madam!

JULIET
I come, anon.—But if thou mean'st not well,
I do beseech thee—

NURSE
[*Within*] Madam!

JULIET
By and by, I come:—
To cease thy suit, and leave me to my grief:
To-morrow will I send.

ROMEO
So thrive my soul—

JULIET
A thousand times good night!

Exit, above

ROMEO
A thousand times the worse, to want thy light.
Love goes toward love, as schoolboys from their books,
But love from love, toward school with heavy looks.
Retiring

Re-enter JULIET, *above*

JULIET
Hist! Romeo, hist! O, for a falconer's voice,
To lure this tassel-gentle back again!
Bondage is hoarse, and may not speak aloud;
Else would I tear the cave where Echo lies,
And make her airy tongue more hoarse than mine,
With repetition of my Romeo's name.

ROMEO
It is my soul that calls upon my name:
How silver-sweet sound lovers' tongues by night,
Like softest music to attending ears!

JULIET

Romeo!

ROMEO

My dear?

JULIET

At what o'clock to-morrow
Shall I send to thee?

ROMEO

At the hour of nine.

JULIET

I will not fail: 'tis twenty years till then.
I have forgot why I did call thee back.

ROMEO

Let me stand here till thou remember it.

JULIET

I shall forget, to have thee still stand there,
Remembering how I love thy company.

ROMEO

And I'll still stay, to have thee still forget,
Forgetting any other home but this.

JULIET

'Tis almost morning; I would have thee gone:
And yet no further than a wanton's bird;
Who lets it hop a little from her hand,
Like a poor prisoner in his twisted gyves,
And with a silk thread plucks it back again,
So loving-jealous of his liberty.

ROMEO

I would I were thy bird.

JULIET

Sweet, so would I:
Yet I should kill thee with much cherishing.
Good night, good night! parting is such sweet sorrow,
That I shall say good night till it be morrow.

Exit above

ROMEO

Sleep dwell upon thine eyes, peace in thy breast!

Would I were sleep and peace, so sweet to rest!
Hence will I to my ghostly father's cell,
His help to crave, and my dear hap to tell.

Exit

SCENE III.
FRIAR LAURENCE'S CELL.

Enter FRIAR LAURENCE, *with a basket*

FRIAR LAURENCE

The grey-eyed morn smiles on the frowning night,
Chequering the eastern clouds with streaks of light,
And flecked darkness like a drunkard reels
From forth day's path and Titan's fiery wheels:
Now, ere the sun advance his burning eye,
The day to cheer and night's dank dew to dry,
I must up-fill this osier cage of ours
With baleful weeds and precious-juiced flowers.
The earth that's nature's mother is her tomb;
What is her burying grave that is her womb,
And from her womb children of divers kind
We sucking on her natural bosom find,
Many for many virtues excellent,
None but for some and yet all different.
O, mickle is the powerful grace that lies
In herbs, plants, stones, and their true qualities:
For nought so vile that on the earth doth live
But to the earth some special good doth give,
Nor aught so good but strain'd from that fair use
Revolts from true birth, stumbling on abuse:
Virtue itself turns vice, being misapplied;
And vice sometimes by action dignified.
Within the infant rind of this small flower
Poison hath residence and medicine power:
For this, being smelt, with that part cheers each part;
Being tasted, slays all senses with the heart.
Two such opposed kings encamp them still

In man as well as herbs, grace and rude will;
And where the worser is predominant,
Full soon the canker death eats up that plant.

Enter ROMEO

ROMEO
Good morrow, father.

FRIAR LAURENCE
Benedicite!
What early tongue so sweet saluteth me?
Young son, it argues a distemper'd head
So soon to bid good morrow to thy bed:
Care keeps his watch in every old man's eye,
And where care lodges, sleep will never lie;
But where unbruised youth with unstuff'd brain
Doth couch his limbs, there golden sleep doth reign:
Therefore thy earliness doth me assure
Thou art up-roused by some distemperature;
Or if not so, then here I hit it right,
Our Romeo hath not been in bed to-night.

ROMEO
That last is true; the sweeter rest was mine.

FRIAR LAURENCE
God pardon sin! wast thou with Rosaline?

ROMEO
With Rosaline, my ghostly father? no;
I have forgot that name, and that name's woe.

FRIAR LAURENCE
That's my good son: but where hast thou been, then?

ROMEO
I'll tell thee, ere thou ask it me again.
I have been feasting with mine enemy,
Where on a sudden one hath wounded me,
That's by me wounded: both our remedies
Within thy help and holy physic lies:
I bear no hatred, blessed man, for, lo,
My intercession likewise steads my foe.

FRIAR LAURENCE

    Be plain, good son, and homely in thy drift;
    Riddling confession finds but riddling shrift.

ROMEO

    Then plainly know my heart's dear love is set
    On the fair daughter of rich Capulet:
    As mine on hers, so hers is set on mine;
    And all combined, save what thou must combine
    By holy marriage: when and where and how
    We met, we woo'd and made exchange of vow,
    I'll tell thee as we pass; but this I pray,
    That thou consent to marry us to-day.

FRIAR LAURENCE

    Holy Saint Francis, what a change is here!
    Is Rosaline, whom thou didst love so dear,
    So soon forsaken? young men's love then lies
    Not truly in their hearts, but in their eyes.
    Jesu Maria, what a deal of brine
    Hath wash'd thy sallow cheeks for Rosaline!
    How much salt water thrown away in waste,
    To season love, that of it doth not taste!
    The sun not yet thy sighs from heaven clears,
    Thy old groans ring yet in my ancient ears;
    Lo, here upon thy cheek the stain doth sit
    Of an old tear that is not wash'd off yet:
    If e'er thou wast thyself and these woes thine,
    Thou and these woes were all for Rosaline:
    And art thou changed? pronounce this sentence then,
    Women may fall, when there's no strength in men.

ROMEO

    Thou chid'st me oft for loving Rosaline.

FRIAR LAURENCE

    For doting, not for loving, pupil mine.

ROMEO

    And bad'st me bury love.

FRIAR LAURENCE
    Not in a grave,
    To lay one in, another out to have.
ROMEO
    I pray thee, chide not; she whom I love now
    Doth grace for grace and love for love allow;
    The other did not so.
FRIAR LAURENCE
    O, she knew well
    Thy love did read by rote and could not spell.
    But come, young waverer, come, go with me,
    In one respect I'll thy assistant be;
    For this alliance may so happy prove,
    To turn your households' rancour to pure love.
ROMEO
    O, let us hence; I stand on sudden haste.
FRIAR LAURENCE
    Wisely and slow; they stumble that run fast.

Exeunt

SCENE IV.
A STREET.

Enter BENVOLIO *and* MERCUTIO

MERCUTIO
    Where the devil should this Romeo be?
    Came he not home to-night?
BENVOLIO
    Not to his father's; I spoke with his man.
MERCUTIO
    Ah, that same pale hard-hearted wench, that Rosaline.
    Torments him so, that he will sure run mad.
BENVOLIO
    Tybalt, the kinsman of old Capulet,
    Hath sent a letter to his father's house.

MERCUTIO

A challenge, on my life.

BENVOLIO

Romeo will answer it.

MERCUTIO

Any man that can write may answer a letter.

BENVOLIO

Nay, he will answer the letter's master, how he dares, being dared.

MERCUTIO

Alas poor Romeo! he is already dead; stabbed with a white wench's black eye; shot through the ear with a love-song; the very pin of his heart cleft with the blind bow-boy's butt-shaft: and is he a man to encounter Tybalt?

BENVOLIO

Why, what is Tybalt?

MERCUTIO

More than prince of cats, I can tell you. O, he is the courageous captain of compliments. He fights as you sing prick-song, keeps time, distance, and proportion; rests me his minim rest, one, two, and the third in your bosom: the very butcher of a silk button, a duellist, a duellist; a gentleman of the very first house, of the first and second cause: ah, the immortal passado! the punto reverso! the hai!

BENVOLIO

The what?

MERCUTIO

The pox of such antic, lisping, affecting fantasticoes; these new tuners of accents! 'By Jesu, a very good blade! a very tall man! a very good whore!' Why, is not this a lamentable thing, grandsire, that we should be thus afflicted with these strange flies, these fashion-mongers, these perdona-mi's, who stand so much on the new form, that they cannot at ease on the old bench? O, their bones, their bones!

Enter ROMEO

BENVOLIO

Here comes Romeo, here comes Romeo.

MERCUTIO

Without his roe, like a dried herring: flesh, flesh, how art thou
fishified! Now is he for the numbers that Petrarch flowed in:
Laura to his lady was but a kitchen-wench; marry, she had a
better love to be-rhyme her; Dido a dowdy; Cleopatra a gipsy;
Helen and Hero hildings and harlots; Thisbe a grey eye or so, but
not to the purpose. Signior Romeo, bon jour! there's a French
salutation to your French slop. You gave us the counterfeit fairly
last night.

ROMEO

Good morrow to you both. What counterfeit did I give you?

MERCUTIO

The ship, sir, the slip; can you not conceive?

ROMEO

Pardon, good Mercutio, my business was great; and in such a
case as mine a man may strain courtesy.

MERCUTIO

That's as much as to say, such a case as yours constrains a man
to bow in the hams.

ROMEO

Meaning, to court'sy.

MERCUTIO

Thou hast most kindly hit it.

ROMEO

A most courteous exposition.

MERCUTIO

Nay, I am the very pink of courtesy.

ROMEO

Pink for flower.

MERCUTIO

Right.

ROMEO

Why, then is my pump well flowered.

MERCUTIO

Well said: follow me this jest now till thou hast worn out thy
pump, that when the single sole of it is worn, the jest may remain
after the wearing sole singular.

ROMEO

O single-soled jest, solely singular for the singleness.

MERCUTIO

Come between us, good Benvolio; my wits faint.

ROMEO

Switch and spurs, switch and spurs; or I'll cry a match.

MERCUTIO

Nay, if thy wits run the wild-goose chase, I have done, for thou hast more of the wild-goose in one of thy wits than, I am sure, I have in my whole five: was I with you there for the goose?

ROMEO

Thou wast never with me for any thing when thou wast not there for the goose.

MERCUTIO

I will bite thee by the ear for that jest.

ROMEO

Nay, good goose, bite not.

MERCUTIO

Thy wit is a very bitter sweeting; it is a most sharp sauce.

ROMEO

And is it not well served in to a sweet goose?

MERCUTIO

O here's a wit of cheveril, that stretches from an inch narrow to an ell broad!

ROMEO

I stretch it out for that word 'broad;' which added to the goose, proves thee far and wide a broad goose.

MERCUTIO

Why, is not this better now than groaning for love? now art thou sociable, now art thou Romeo; now art thou what thou art, by art as well as by nature: for this drivelling love is like a great natural, that runs lolling up and down to hide his bauble in a hole.

BENVOLIO

Stop there, stop there.

MERCUTIO

Thou desirest me to stop in my tale against the hair.

BENVOLIO

Thou wouldst else have made thy tale large.

MERCUTIO

O, thou art deceived; I would have made it short: for I was come to the whole depth of my tale; and meant, indeed, to occupy the argument no longer.

ROMEO

Here's goodly gear!

Enter Nurse and PETER

MERCUTIO

A sail, a sail!

BENVOLIO

Two, two; a shirt and a smock.

NURSE

Peter!

PETER

Anon!

NURSE

My fan, Peter.

MERCUTIO

Good Peter, to hide her face; for her fan's the fairer face.

NURSE

God ye good morrow, gentlemen.

MERCUTIO

God ye good den, fair gentlewoman.

NURSE

Is it good den?

MERCUTIO

'Tis no less, I tell you, for the bawdy hand of the dial is now upon the prick of noon.

NURSE

Out upon you! what a man are you!

ROMEO

One, gentlewoman, that God hath made for himself to mar.

NURSE

By my troth, it is well said; 'for himself to mar,' quoth a'? Gentlemen, can any of you tell me where I may find the young Romeo?

ROMEO

I can tell you; but young Romeo will be older when you have
found him than he was when you sought him: I am the youngest
of that name, for fault of a worse.

NURSE

You say well.

MERCUTIO

Yea, is the worst well? very well took, i' faith; wisely, wisely.

NURSE

If you be he, sir, I desire some confidence with you.

BENVOLIO

She will indite him to some supper.

MERCUTIO

A bawd, a bawd, a bawd! so ho!

ROMEO

What hast thou found?

MERCUTIO

No hare, sir; unless a hare, sir, in a lenten pie, that is something
stale and hoar ere it be spent.

Sings

An old hare hoar,
And an old hare hoar,
Is very good meat in lent
But a hare that is hoar
Is too much for a score,
When it hoars ere it be spent.
Romeo, will you come to your father's? We'll to dinner, thither.

ROMEO

I will follow you.

MERCUTIO

Farewell, ancient lady; farewell,
Singing
'lady, lady, lady.'

Exeunt MERCUTIO *and* BENVOLIO

NURSE

Marry, farewell! I pray you, sir, what saucy merchant was this,
that was so full of his ropery?

ROMEO

A gentleman, nurse, that loves to hear himself talk, and will speak more in a minute than he will stand to in a month.

NURSE

An a' speak any thing against me, I'll take him down, an a' were lustier than he is, and twenty such Jacks; and if I cannot, I'll find those that shall. Scurvy knave! I am none of his flirt-gills; I am none of his skains-mates. And thou must stand by too, and suffer every knave to use me at his pleasure?

PETER

I saw no man use you a pleasure; if I had, my weapon should quickly have been out, I warrant you: I dare draw as soon as another man, if I see occasion in a good quarrel, and the law on my side.

NURSE

Now, afore God, I am so vexed, that every part about me quivers. Scurvy knave! Pray you, sir, a word: and as I told you, my young lady bade me inquire you out; what she bade me say, I will keep to myself: but first let me tell ye, if ye should lead her into a fool's paradise, as they say, it were a very gross kind of behavior, as they say: for the gentlewoman is young; and, therefore, if you should deal double with her, truly it were an ill thing to be offered to any gentlewoman, and very weak dealing.

ROMEO

Nurse, commend me to thy lady and mistress. I protest unto thee—

NURSE

Good heart, and, i' faith, I will tell her as much:
Lord, Lord, she will be a joyful woman.

ROMEO

What wilt thou tell her, nurse? thou dost not mark me.

NURSE

I will tell her, sir, that you do protest; which, as I take it, is a gentlemanlike offer.

ROMEO

Bid her devise
Some means to come to shrift this afternoon;

And there she shall at Friar Laurence' cell
Be shrived and married. Here is for thy pains.

NURSE

No truly sir; not a penny.

ROMEO

Go to; I say you shall.

NURSE

This afternoon, sir? well, she shall be there.

ROMEO

And stay, good nurse, behind the abbey wall:
Within this hour my man shall be with thee
And bring thee cords made like a tackled stair;
Which to the high top-gallant of my joy
Must be my convoy in the secret night.
Farewell; be trusty, and I'll quit thy pains:
Farewell; commend me to thy mistress.

NURSE

Now God in heaven bless thee! Hark you, sir.

ROMEO

What say'st thou, my dear nurse?

NURSE

Is your man secret? Did you ne'er hear say,
Two may keep counsel, putting one away?

ROMEO

I warrant thee, my man's as true as steel.

NURSE

Well, sir; my mistress is the sweetest lady—Lord, Lord! when
'twas a little prating thing:—O, there is a nobleman in town, one
Paris, that would fain lay knife aboard; but she, good soul, had
as lief see a toad, a very toad, as see him. I anger her sometimes
and tell her that Paris is the properer man; but, I'll warrant you,
when I say so, she looks as pale as any clout in the versal world.
Doth not rosemary and Romeo begin both with a letter?

ROMEO

Ay, nurse; what of that? both with an R.

NURSE

Ah. mocker! that's the dog's name; R is for the—No; I know

it begins with some other letter:—and she hath the prettiest sententious of it, of you and rosemary, that it would do you good to hear it.

ROMEO

Commend me to thy lady.

NURSE

Ay, a thousand times.

Exit Romeo

Peter!

PETER

Anon!

NURSE

Peter, take my fan, and go before and apace.

Exeunt

SCENE V.
CAPULET'S ORCHARD.

Enter JULIET

JULIET

The clock struck nine when I did send the nurse;
In half an hour she promised to return.
Perchance she cannot meet him: that's not so.
O, she is lame! love's heralds should be thoughts,
Which ten times faster glide than the sun's beams,
Driving back shadows over louring hills:
Therefore do nimble-pinion'd doves draw love,
And therefore hath the wind-swift Cupid wings.
Now is the sun upon the highmost hill
Of this day's journey, and from nine till twelve
Is three long hours, yet she is not come.
Had she affections and warm youthful blood,
She would be as swift in motion as a ball;
My words would bandy her to my sweet love,
And his to me:
But old folks, many feign as they were dead;
Unwieldy, slow, heavy and pale as lead.

O God, she comes!

Enter Nurse and PETER

O honey nurse, what news?

Hast thou met with him? Send thy man away.

NURSE

Peter, stay at the gate.

Exit PETER

JULIET

Now, good sweet nurse,—O Lord, why look'st thou sad?

Though news be sad, yet tell them merrily;

If good, thou shamest the music of sweet news

By playing it to me with so sour a face.

NURSE

I am a-weary, give me leave awhile:

Fie, how my bones ache! what a jaunt have I had!

JULIET

I would thou hadst my bones, and I thy news:

Nay, come, I pray thee, speak; good, good nurse, speak.

NURSE

Jesu, what haste? can you not stay awhile?

Do you not see that I am out of breath?

JULIET

How art thou out of breath, when thou hast breath

To say to me that thou art out of breath?

The excuse that thou dost make in this delay

Is longer than the tale thou dost excuse.

Is thy news good, or bad? answer to that;

Say either, and I'll stay the circumstance:

Let me be satisfied, is't good or bad?

NURSE

Well, you have made a simple choice; you know not

how to choose a man: Romeo! no, not he; though his

face be better than any man's, yet his leg excels all men's; and

for a hand, and a foot, and a body, though they be not to be

talked on, yet they are past compare: he is not the flower of

courtesy, but, I'll warrant him, as gentle as a lamb. Go thy

ways, wench; serve God. What, have you dined at home?

JULIET

No, no: but all this did I know before.
What says he of our marriage? what of that?

NURSE

Lord, how my head aches! what a head have I!
It beats as it would fall in twenty pieces.
My back o' t' other side,—O, my back, my back!
Beshrew your heart for sending me about,
To catch my death with jaunting up and down!

JULIET

I' faith, I am sorry that thou art not well.
Sweet, sweet, sweet nurse, tell me, what says my love?

NURSE

Your love says, like an honest gentleman, and a courteous, and
a kind, and a handsome, and, I warrant, a virtuous,—Where is
your mother?

JULIET

Where is my mother! why, she is within;
Where should she be? How oddly thou repliest!
'Your love says, like an honest gentleman,
Where is your mother?'

NURSE

O God's lady dear!
Are you so hot? marry, come up, I trow;
Is this the poultice for my aching bones?
Henceforward do your messages yourself.

JULIET

Here's such a coil! come, what says Romeo?

NURSE

Have you got leave to go to shrift to-day?

JULIET

I have.

NURSE

Then hie you hence to Friar Laurence' cell;
There stays a husband to make you a wife:
Now comes the wanton blood up in your cheeks,
They'll be in scarlet straight at any news.

Hie you to church; I must another way,
To fetch a ladder, by the which your love
Must climb a bird's nest soon when it is dark:
I am the drudge and toil in your delight,
But you shall bear the burden soon at night.
Go; I'll to dinner: hie you to the cell.

JULIET

Hie to high fortune! Honest nurse, farewell.

Exeunt

SCENE VI.
FRIAR LAURENCE'S CELL.

Enter FRIAR LAURENCE *and* ROMEO

FRIAR LAURENCE

So smile the heavens upon this holy act,
That after hours with sorrow chide us not!

ROMEO

Amen, amen! but come what sorrow can,
It cannot countervail the exchange of joy
That one short minute gives me in her sight:
Do thou but close our hands with holy words,
Then love-devouring death do what he dare;
It is enough I may but call her mine.

FRIAR LAURENCE

These violent delights have violent ends
And in their triumph die, like fire and powder,
Which as they kiss consume: the sweetest honey
Is loathsome in his own deliciousness
And in the taste confounds the appetite:
Therefore love moderately; long love doth so;
Too swift arrives as tardy as too slow.

Enter JULIET

Here comes the lady: O, so light a foot
Will ne'er wear out the everlasting flint:
A lover may bestride the gossamer

That idles in the wanton summer air,
And yet not fall; so light is vanity.

JULIET

Good even to my ghostly confessor.

FRIAR LAURENCE

Romeo shall thank thee, daughter, for us both.

JULIET

As much to him, else is his thanks too much.

ROMEO

Ah, Juliet, if the measure of thy joy
Be heap'd like mine and that thy skill be more
To blazon it, then sweeten with thy breath
This neighbour air, and let rich music's tongue
Unfold the imagined happiness that both
Receive in either by this dear encounter.

JULIET

Conceit, more rich in matter than in words,
Brags of his substance, not of ornament:
They are but beggars that can count their worth;
But my true love is grown to such excess
I cannot sum up sum of half my wealth.

FRIAR LAURENCE

Come, come with me, and we will make short work;
For, by your leaves, you shall not stay alone
Till holy church incorporate two in one.

Exeunt

ACT

III

SCENE I.
A PUBLIC PLACE.

Enter MERCUTIO, BENVOLIO, *Page, and Servants*

BENVOLIO

    I pray thee, good Mercutio, let's retire:

    The day is hot, the Capulets abroad,

    And, if we meet, we shall not scape a brawl;

    For now, these hot days, is the mad blood stirring.

MERCUTIO

    Thou art like one of those fellows that when he enters the
confines of a tavern claps me his sword upon the table and
says 'God send me no need of thee!' and by the operation
of the second cup draws it on the drawer, when indeed
there is no need.

BENVOLIO

    Am I like such a fellow?

MERCUTIO

    Come, come, thou art as hot a Jack in thy mood as any in
Italy, and as soon moved to be moody, and as soon moody
to be moved.

BENVOLIO

And what to?

MERCUTIO

Nay, an there were two such, we should have none shortly, for one would kill the other. Thou! why, thou wilt quarrel with a man that hath a hair more, or a hair less, in his beard, than thou hast: thou wilt quarrel with a man for cracking nuts, having no other reason but because thou hast hazel eyes: what eye but such an eye would spy out such a quarrel? Thy head is as fun of quarrels as an egg is full of meat, and yet thy head hath been beaten as addle as an egg for quarrelling: thou hast quarrelled with a man for coughing in the street, because he hath wakened thy dog that hath lain asleep in the sun: didst thou not fall out with a tailor for wearing his new doublet before Easter? with another, for tying his new shoes with old riband? and yet thou wilt tutor me from quarrelling!

BENVOLIO

An I were so apt to quarrel as thou art, any man should buy the fee-simple of my life for an hour and a quarter.

MERCUTIO

The fee-simple! O simple!

BENVOLIO

By my head, here come the Capulets.

MERCUTIO

By my heel, I care not.

Enter TYBALT *and others*

TYBALT

Follow me close, for I will speak to them.

Gentlemen, good den: a word with one of you.

MERCUTIO

And but one word with one of us? Couple it with something; make it a word and a blow.

TYBALT

You shall find me apt enough to that, sir, an you will give me occasion.

MERCUTIO

Could you not take some occasion without giving?

TYBALT

    Mercutio, thou consort'st with Romeo,—

MERCUTIO

    Consort! what, dost thou make us minstrels? an thou make
    minstrels of us, look to hear nothing but discords: here's my
    fiddlestick; here's that shall make you dance. 'Zounds, consort!

BENVOLIO

    We talk here in the public haunt of men:
    Either withdraw unto some private place,
    And reason coldly of your grievances,
    Or else depart; here all eyes gaze on us.

MERCUTIO

    Men's eyes were made to look, and let them gaze;
    I will not budge for no man's pleasure, I.

Enter ROMEO

TYBALT

    Well, peace be with you, sir: here comes my man.

MERCUTIO

    But I'll be hanged, sir, if he wear your livery:
    Marry, go before to field, he'll be your follower;
    Your worship in that sense may call him 'man.'

TYBALT

    Romeo, the hate I bear thee can afford
    No better term than this,—thou art a villain.

ROMEO

    Tybalt, the reason that I have to love thee
    Doth much excuse the appertaining rage
    To such a greeting: villain am I none;
    Therefore farewell; I see thou know'st me not.

TYBALT

    Boy, this shall not excuse the injuries
    That thou hast done me; therefore turn and draw.

ROMEO

    I do protest, I never injured thee,
    But love thee better than thou canst devise,
    Till thou shalt know the reason of my love:

And so, good Capulet,—which name I tender
As dearly as my own,—be satisfied.

MERCUTIO

O calm, dishonourable, vile submission!
Alla stoccata carries it away.

Draws

Tybalt, you rat-catcher, will you walk?

TYBALT

What wouldst thou have with me?

MERCUTIO

Good king of cats, nothing but one of your nine lives; that I
mean to make bold withal, and as you shall use me hereafter,
drybeat the rest of the eight. Will you pluck your sword out of
his pitcher by the ears? make haste, lest mine be about your ears
ere it be out.

TYBALT

I am for you.

Drawing

ROMEO

Gentle Mercutio, put thy rapier up.

MERCUTIO

Come, sir, your passado.

They fight

ROMEO

Draw, Benvolio; beat down their weapons.
Gentlemen, for shame, forbear this outrage!
Tybalt, Mercutio, the prince expressly hath
Forbidden bandying in Verona streets:
Hold, Tybalt! good Mercutio!

TYBALT *under* ROMEO'S *arm stabs* MERCUTIO,
and flies with his followers

MERCUTIO

I am hurt.
A plague o' both your houses! I am sped.
Is he gone, and hath nothing?

BENVOLIO

What, art thou hurt?

MERCUTIO

Ay, ay, a scratch, a scratch; marry, 'tis enough.
Where is my page? Go, villain, fetch a surgeon.

Exit Page

ROMEO

Courage, man; the hurt cannot be much.

MERCUTIO

No, 'tis not so deep as a well, nor so wide as a church-door; but
'tis enough, 'twill serve: ask for me to-morrow, and you shall
find me a grave man. I am peppered, I warrant, for this world.
A plague o' both your houses! 'Zounds, a dog, a rat, a mouse,
a cat, to scratch a man to death! a braggart, a rogue, a villain,
that fights by the book of arithmetic! Why the devil came you
between us? I was hurt under your arm.

ROMEO

I thought all for the best.

MERCUTIO

Help me into some house, Benvolio,
Or I shall faint. A plague o' both your houses!
They have made worms' meat of me: I have it,
And soundly too: your houses!

Exeunt MERCUTIO
and BENVOLIO

ROMEO

This gentleman, the prince's near ally,
My very friend, hath got his mortal hurt
In my behalf; my reputation stain'd
With Tybalt's slander,—Tybalt, that an hour
Hath been my kinsman! O sweet Juliet,
Thy beauty hath made me effeminate
And in my temper soften'd valour's steel!

Re-enter BENVOLIO

BENVOLIO

O Romeo, Romeo, brave Mercutio's dead!
That gallant spirit hath aspired the clouds,
Which too untimely here did scorn the earth.

ROMEO

    This day's black fate on more days doth depend;

    This but begins the woe, others must end.

BENVOLIO

    Here comes the furious Tybalt back again.

ROMEO

    Alive, in triumph! and Mercutio slain!

    Away to heaven, respective lenity,

    And fire-eyed fury be my conduct now!

                     Re-enter TYBALT

    Now, Tybalt, take the villain back again,

    That late thou gavest me; for Mercutio's soul

    Is but a little way above our heads,

    Staying for thine to keep him company:

    Either thou, or I, or both, must go with him.

TYBALT

    Thou, wretched boy, that didst consort him here, Shalt with him

    hence.

ROMEO

    This shall determine that.

    They fight; TYBALT *falls*

BENVOLIO

    Romeo, away, be gone!

    The citizens are up, and Tybalt slain.

    Stand not amazed: the prince will doom thee death,

    If thou art taken: hence, be gone, away!

ROMEO

    O, I am fortune's fool!

BENVOLIO

    Why dost thou stay?

                           Exit ROMEO

            Enter Citizens, & c

FIRST CITIZEN

    Which way ran he that kill'd Mercutio?

    Tybalt, that murderer, which way ran he?

BENVOLIO

    There lies that Tybalt.

FIRST CITIZEN

    Up, sir, go with me;

    I charge thee in the princes name, obey.

                Enter PRINCE, *attended;* MONTAGUE,

               CAPULET, *their Wives, and others*

PRINCE

    Where are the vile beginners of this fray?

BENVOLIO

    O noble prince, I can discover all

    The unlucky manage of this fatal brawl:

    There lies the man, slain by young Romeo,

    That slew thy kinsman, brave Mercutio.

LADY CAPULET

    Tybalt, my cousin! O my brother's child!

    O prince! O cousin! husband! O, the blood is spilt

    O my dear kinsman! Prince, as thou art true,

    For blood of ours, shed blood of Montague.

    O cousin, cousin!

PRINCE

    Benvolio, who began this bloody fray?

BENVOLIO

    Tybalt, here slain, whom Romeo's hand did slay;

    Romeo that spoke him fair, bade him bethink

    How nice the quarrel was, and urged withal

    Your high displeasure: all this uttered

    With gentle breath, calm look, knees humbly bow'd,

    Could not take truce with the unruly spleen

    Of Tybalt deaf to peace, but that he tilts

    With piercing steel at bold Mercutio's breast,

    Who all as hot, turns deadly point to point,

    And, with a martial scorn, with one hand beats

    Cold death aside, and with the other sends

    It back to Tybalt, whose dexterity,

    Retorts it: Romeo he cries aloud,

    'Hold, friends! friends, part!' and, swifter than his tongue,

    His agile arm beats down their fatal points,

    And 'twixt them rushes; underneath whose arm

An envious thrust from Tybalt hit the life
Of stout Mercutio, and then Tybalt fled;
But by and by comes back to Romeo,
Who had but newly entertain'd revenge,
And to't they go like lightning, for, ere I
Could draw to part them, was stout Tybalt slain.
And, as he fell, did Romeo turn and fly.
This is the truth, or let Benvolio die.

LADY CAPULET

He is a kinsman to the Montague;
Affection makes him false; he speaks not true:
Some twenty of them fought in this black strife,
And all those twenty could but kill one life.
I beg for justice, which thou, prince, must give;
Romeo slew Tybalt, Romeo must not live.

PRINCE

Romeo slew him, he slew Mercutio;
Who now the price of his dear blood doth owe?

MONTAGUE

Not Romeo, prince, he was Mercutio's friend;
His fault concludes but what the law should end,
The life of Tybalt.

PRINCE

And for that offence
Immediately we do exile him hence:
I have an interest in your hate's proceeding,
My blood for your rude brawls doth lie a-bleeding;
But I'll amerce you with so strong a fine
That you shall all repent the loss of mine:
I will be deaf to pleading and excuses;
Nor tears nor prayers shall purchase out abuses:
Therefore use none: let Romeo hence in haste,
Else, when he's found, that hour is his last.
Bear hence this body and attend our will:
Mercy but murders, pardoning those that kill.

Exeunt

SCENE II.
CAPULET'S ORCHARD.

Enter JULIET

JULIET
    Gallop apace, you fiery-footed steeds,
    Towards Phoebus' lodging: such a wagoner
    As Phaethon would whip you to the west,
    And bring in cloudy night immediately.
    Spread thy close curtain, love-performing night,
    That runaway's eyes may wink and Romeo
    Leap to these arms, untalk'd of and unseen.
    Lovers can see to do their amorous rites
    By their own beauties; or, if love be blind,
    It best agrees with night. Come, civil night,
    Thou sober-suited matron, all in black,
    And learn me how to lose a winning match,
    Play'd for a pair of stainless maidenhoods:
    Hood my unmann'd blood, bating in my cheeks,
    With thy black mantle; till strange love, grown bold,
    Think true love acted simple modesty.
    Come, night; come, Romeo; come, thou day in night;
    For thou wilt lie upon the wings of night
    Whiter than new snow on a raven's back.
    Come, gentle night, come, loving, black-brow'd night,
    Give me my Romeo; and, when he shall die,
    Take him and cut him out in little stars,
    And he will make the face of heaven so fine
    That all the world will be in love with night
    And pay no worship to the garish sun.
    O, I have bought the mansion of a love,
    But not possess'd it, and, though I am sold,
    Not yet enjoy'd: so tedious is this day
    As is the night before some festival
    To an impatient child that hath new robes
    And may not wear them. O, here comes my nurse,

And she brings news; and every tongue that speaks
But Romeo's name speaks heavenly eloquence.

Enter Nurse, with cords

Now, nurse, what news? What hast thou there? the cords
That Romeo bid thee fetch?

NURSE

Ay, ay, the cords.

Throws them down

JULIET

Ay me! what news? why dost thou wring thy hands?

NURSE

Ah, well-a-day! he's dead, he's dead, he's dead!
We are undone, lady, we are undone!
Alack the day! he's gone, he's kill'd, he's dead!

JULIET

Can heaven be so envious?

NURSE

Romeo can,
Though heaven cannot: O Romeo, Romeo!
Who ever would have thought it? Romeo!

JULIET

What devil art thou, that dost torment me thus?
This torture should be roar'd in dismal hell.
Hath Romeo slain himself? say thou but 'I,'
And that bare vowel 'I' shall poison more
Than the death-darting eye of cockatrice:
I am not I, if there be such an I;
Or those eyes shut, that make thee answer 'I.'
If he be slain, say 'I'; or if not, no:
Brief sounds determine of my weal or woe.

NURSE

I saw the wound, I saw it with mine eyes,—
God save the mark!—here on his manly breast:
A piteous corse, a bloody piteous corse;
Pale, pale as ashes, all bedaub'd in blood,
All in gore-blood; I swounded at the sight.

JULIET

O, break, my heart! poor bankrupt, break at once!
To prison, eyes, ne'er look on liberty!
Vile earth, to earth resign; end motion here;
And thou and Romeo press one heavy bier!

NURSE

O Tybalt, Tybalt, the best friend I had!
O courteous Tybalt! honest gentleman!
That ever I should live to see thee dead!

JULIET

What storm is this that blows so contrary?
Is Romeo slaughter'd, and is Tybalt dead?
My dear-loved cousin, and my dearer lord?
Then, dreadful trumpet, sound the general doom!
For who is living, if those two are gone?

NURSE

Tybalt is gone, and Romeo banished;
Romeo that kill'd him, he is banished.

JULIET

O God! did Romeo's hand shed Tybalt's blood?

NURSE

It did, it did; alas the day, it did!

JULIET

O serpent heart, hid with a flowering face!
Did ever dragon keep so fair a cave?
Beautiful tyrant! fiend angelical!
Dove-feather'd raven! wolvish-ravening lamb!
Despised substance of divinest show!
Just opposite to what thou justly seem'st,
A damned saint, an honourable villain!
O nature, what hadst thou to do in hell,
When thou didst bower the spirit of a fiend
In moral paradise of such sweet flesh?
Was ever book containing such vile matter
So fairly bound? O that deceit should dwell
In such a gorgeous palace!

NURSE

There's no trust,
No faith, no honesty in men; all perjured,
All forsworn, all naught, all dissemblers.
Ah, where's my man? give me some aqua vitae:
These griefs, these woes, these sorrows make me old.
Shame come to Romeo!

JULIET

Blister'd be thy tongue
For such a wish! he was not born to shame:
Upon his brow shame is ashamed to sit;
For 'tis a throne where honour may be crown'd
Sole monarch of the universal earth.
O, what a beast was I to chide at him!

NURSE

Will you speak well of him that kill'd your cousin?

JULIET

Shall I speak ill of him that is my husband?
Ah, poor my lord, what tongue shall smooth thy name,
When I, thy three-hours wife, have mangled it?
But, wherefore, villain, didst thou kill my cousin?
That villain cousin would have kill'd my husband:
Back, foolish tears, back to your native spring;
Your tributary drops belong to woe,
Which you, mistaking, offer up to joy.
My husband lives, that Tybalt would have slain;
And Tybalt's dead, that would have slain my husband:
All this is comfort; wherefore weep I then?
Some word there was, worser than Tybalt's death,
That murder'd me: I would forget it fain;
But, O, it presses to my memory,
Like damned guilty deeds to sinners' minds:
'Tybalt is dead, and Romeo—banished;'
That 'banished,' that one word 'banished,'
Hath slain ten thousand Tybalts. Tybalt's death
Was woe enough, if it had ended there:

Or, if sour woe delights in fellowship
And needly will be rank'd with other griefs,
Why follow'd not, when she said 'Tybalt's dead,'
Thy father, or thy mother, nay, or both,
Which modern lamentations might have moved?
But with a rear-ward following Tybalt's death,
'Romeo is banished,' to speak that word,
Is father, mother, Tybalt, Romeo, Juliet,
All slain, all dead. 'Romeo is banished!'
There is no end, no limit, measure, bound,
In that word's death; no words can that woe sound.
Where is my father, and my mother, nurse?

NURSE

Weeping and wailing over Tybalt's corse:
Will you go to them? I will bring you thither.

JULIET

Wash they his wounds with tears: mine shall be spent,
When theirs are dry, for Romeo's banishment.
Take up those cords: poor ropes, you are beguiled,
Both you and I; for Romeo is exiled:
He made you for a highway to my bed;
But I, a maid, die maiden-widowed.
Come, cords, come, nurse; I'll to my wedding-bed;
And death, not Romeo, take my maidenhead!

NURSE

Hie to your chamber: I'll find Romeo
To comfort you: I wot well where he is.
Hark ye, your Romeo will be here at night:
I'll to him; he is hid at Laurence' cell.

JULIET

O, find him! give this ring to my true knight,
And bid him come to take his last farewell.

Exeunt

Romeo and Juliet

SCENE III.
FRIAR LAURENCE'S CELL.

Enter FRIAR LAURENCE

FRIAR LAURENCE
>Romeo, come forth; come forth, thou fearful man:
>Affliction is enamour'd of thy parts,
>And thou art wedded to calamity.
>> *Enter* ROMEO

ROMEO
>Father, what news? what is the prince's doom?
>What sorrow craves acquaintance at my hand,
>That I yet know not?

FRIAR LAURENCE
>Too familiar
>Is my dear son with such sour company:
>I bring thee tidings of the prince's doom.

ROMEO
>What less than dooms-day is the prince's doom?

FRIAR LAURENCE
>A gentler judgment vanish'd from his lips,
>Not body's death, but body's banishment.

ROMEO
>Ha, banishment! be merciful, say 'death;'
>For exile hath more terror in his look,
>Much more than death: do not say 'banishment.'

FRIAR LAURENCE
>Hence from Verona art thou banished:
>Be patient, for the world is broad and wide.

ROMEO
>There is no world without Verona walls,
>But purgatory, torture, hell itself.
>Hence-banished is banish'd from the world,
>And world's exile is death: then banished,
>Is death mis-term'd: calling death banishment,
>Thou cutt'st my head off with a golden axe,
>And smilest upon the stroke that murders me.

• 89 •

FRIAR LAURENCE
> O deadly sin! O rude unthankfulness!
> Thy fault our law calls death; but the kind prince,
> Taking thy part, hath rush'd aside the law,
> And turn'd that black word death to banishment:
> This is dear mercy, and thou seest it not.

ROMEO
> 'Tis torture, and not mercy: heaven is here,
> Where Juliet lives; and every cat and dog
> And little mouse, every unworthy thing,
> Live here in heaven and may look on her;
> But Romeo may not: more validity,
> More honourable state, more courtship lives
> In carrion-flies than Romeo: they my seize
> On the white wonder of dear Juliet's hand
> And steal immortal blessing from her lips,
> Who even in pure and vestal modesty,
> Still blush, as thinking their own kisses sin;
> But Romeo may not; he is banished:
> Flies may do this, but I from this must fly:
> They are free men, but I am banished.
> And say'st thou yet that exile is not death?
> Hadst thou no poison mix'd, no sharp-ground knife,
> No sudden mean of death, though ne'er so mean,
> But 'banished' to kill me?—'banished'?
> O friar, the damned use that word in hell;
> Howlings attend it: how hast thou the heart,
> Being a divine, a ghostly confessor,
> A sin-absolver, and my friend profess'd,
> To mangle me with that word 'banished'?

FRIAR LAURENCE
> Thou fond mad man, hear me but speak a word.

ROMEO
> O, thou wilt speak again of banishment.

FRIAR LAURENCE
> I'll give thee armour to keep off that word:

Adversity's sweet milk, philosophy,
To comfort thee, though thou art banished.

ROMEO

Yet 'banished'? Hang up philosophy!
Unless philosophy can make a Juliet,
Displant a town, reverse a prince's doom,
It helps not, it prevails not: talk no more.

FRIAR LAURENCE

O, then I see that madmen have no ears.

ROMEO

How should they, when that wise men have no eyes?

FRIAR LAURENCE

Let me dispute with thee of thy estate.

ROMEO

Thou canst not speak of that thou dost not feel:
Wert thou as young as I, Juliet thy love,
An hour but married, Tybalt murdered,
Doting like me and like me banished,
Then mightst thou speak, then mightst thou tear thy hair,
And fall upon the ground, as I do now,
Taking the measure of an unmade grave.

Knocking within

FRIAR LAURENCE

Arise; one knocks; good Romeo, hide thyself.

ROMEO

Not I; unless the breath of heartsick groans,
Mist-like, infold me from the search of eyes.

Knocking

FRIAR LAURENCE

Hark, how they knock! Who's there? Romeo, arise;
Thou wilt be taken. Stay awhile! Stand up;

Knocking

Run to my study. By and by! God's will,
What simpleness is this! I come, I come!

Knocking

Who knocks so hard? whence come you? what's your will?

NURSE

[*Within*] Let me come in, and you shall know my errand;
I come from Lady Juliet.

FRIAR LAURENCE

Welcome, then.

Enter Nurse

NURSE

O holy friar, O, tell me, holy friar,
Where is my lady's lord, where's Romeo?

FRIAR LAURENCE

There on the ground, with his own tears made drunk.

NURSE

O, he is even in my mistress' case,
Just in her case! O woful sympathy!
Piteous predicament! Even so lies she,
Blubbering and weeping, weeping and blubbering.
Stand up, stand up; stand, and you be a man:
For Juliet's sake, for her sake, rise and stand;
Why should you fall into so deep an O?

ROMEO

Nurse!

NURSE

Ah sir! ah sir! Well, death's the end of all.

ROMEO

Spakest thou of Juliet? how is it with her?
Doth she not think me an old murderer,
Now I have stain'd the childhood of our joy
With blood removed but little from her own?
Where is she? and how doth she? and what says
My conceal'd lady to our cancell'd love?

NURSE

O, she says nothing, sir, but weeps and weeps;
And now falls on her bed; and then starts up,
And Tybalt calls; and then on Romeo cries,
And then down falls again.

ROMEO

As if that name,

Shot from the deadly level of a gun,
Did murder her; as that name's cursed hand
Murder'd her kinsman. O, tell me, friar, tell me,
In what vile part of this anatomy
Doth my name lodge? tell me, that I may sack
The hateful mansion.
Drawing his sword

FRIAR LAURENCE
Hold thy desperate hand:
Art thou a man? thy form cries out thou art:
Thy tears are womanish; thy wild acts denote
The unreasonable fury of a beast:
Unseemly woman in a seeming man!
Or ill-beseeming beast in seeming both!
Thou hast amazed me: by my holy order,
I thought thy disposition better temper'd.
Hast thou slain Tybalt? wilt thou slay thyself?
And stay thy lady too that lives in thee,
By doing damned hate upon thyself?
Why rail'st thou on thy birth, the heaven, and earth?
Since birth, and heaven, and earth, all three do meet
In thee at once; which thou at once wouldst lose.
Fie, fie, thou shamest thy shape, thy love, thy wit;
Which, like a usurer, abound'st in all,
And usest none in that true use indeed
Which should bedeck thy shape, thy love, thy wit:
Thy noble shape is but a form of wax,
Digressing from the valour of a man;
Thy dear love sworn but hollow perjury,
Killing that love which thou hast vow'd to cherish;
Thy wit, that ornament to shape and love,
Misshapen in the conduct of them both,
Like powder in a skitless soldier's flask,
Is set afire by thine own ignorance,
And thou dismember'd with thine own defence.
What, rouse thee, man! thy Juliet is alive,
For whose dear sake thou wast but lately dead;

There art thou happy: Tybalt would kill thee,
But thou slew'st Tybalt; there are thou happy too:
The law that threaten'd death becomes thy friend
And turns it to exile; there art thou happy:
A pack of blessings lights up upon thy back;
Happiness courts thee in her best array;
But, like a misbehaved and sullen wench,
Thou pout'st upon thy fortune and thy love:
Take heed, take heed, for such die miserable.
Go, get thee to thy love, as was decreed,
Ascend her chamber, hence and comfort her:
But look thou stay not till the watch be set,
For then thou canst not pass to Mantua;
Where thou shalt live, till we can find a time
To blaze your marriage, reconcile your friends,
Beg pardon of the prince, and call thee back
With twenty hundred thousand times more joy
Than thou went'st forth in lamentation.
Go before, nurse: commend me to thy lady;
And bid her hasten all the house to bed,
Which heavy sorrow makes them apt unto:
Romeo is coming.

NURSE

O Lord, I could have stay'd here all the night
To hear good counsel: O, what learning is!
My lord, I'll tell my lady you will come.

ROMEO

Do so, and bid my sweet prepare to chide.

NURSE

Here, sir, a ring she bid me give you, sir:
Hie you, make haste, for it grows very late.

Exit

ROMEO

How well my comfort is revived by this!

FRIAR LAURENCE

Go hence; good night; and here stands all your state:
Either be gone before the watch be set,

Or by the break of day disguised from hence:
Sojourn in Mantua; I'll find out your man,
And he shall signify from time to time
Every good hap to you that chances here:
Give me thy hand; 'tis late: farewell; good night.

ROMEO

But that a joy past joy calls out on me,
It were a grief, so brief to part with thee: Farewell.

Exeunt

SCENE IV.
A ROOM IN CAPULET'S HOUSE.

Enter CAPULET, LADY CAPULET, *and* PARIS

CAPULET

Things have fall'n out, sir, so unluckily,
That we have had no time to move our daughter:
Look you, she loved her kinsman Tybalt dearly,
And so did I:—Well, we were born to die.
'Tis very late, she'll not come down to-night:
I promise you, but for your company,
I would have been a-bed an hour ago.

PARIS

These times of woe afford no time to woo.
Madam, good night: commend me to your daughter.

LADY CAPULET

I will, and know her mind early to-morrow;
To-night she is mew'd up to her heaviness.

CAPULET

Sir Paris, I will make a desperate tender
Of my child's love: I think she will be ruled
In all respects by me; nay, more, I doubt it not.
Wife, go you to her ere you go to bed;
Acquaint her here of my son Paris' love;
And bid her, mark you me, on Wednesday next—
But, soft! what day is this?

PARIS

Monday, my lord,

CAPULET

Monday! ha, ha! Well, Wednesday is too soon,
O' Thursday let it be: o' Thursday, tell her,
She shall be married to this noble earl.
Will you be ready? do you like this haste?
We'll keep no great ado,—a friend or two;
For, hark you, Tybalt being slain so late,
It may be thought we held him carelessly,
Being our kinsman, if we revel much:
Therefore we'll have some half a dozen friends,
And there an end. But what say you to Thursday?

PARIS

My lord, I would that Thursday were to-morrow.

CAPULET

Well get you gone: o' Thursday be it, then.
Go you to Juliet ere you go to bed,
Prepare her, wife, against this wedding-day.
Farewell, my lord. Light to my chamber, ho!
Afore me! it is so very very late,
That we may call it early by and by.
Good night.

Exeunt

SCENE V.
CAPULET'S ORCHARD.

Enter ROMEO *and* JULIET *above, at the window*

JULIET

Wilt thou be gone? it is not yet near day:
It was the nightingale, and not the lark,
That pierced the fearful hollow of thine ear;
Nightly she sings on yon pomegranate-tree:
Believe me, love, it was the nightingale.

ROMEO

It was the lark, the herald of the morn,

No nightingale: look, love, what envious streaks
Do lace the severing clouds in yonder east:
Night's candles are burnt out, and jocund day
Stands tiptoe on the misty mountain tops.
I must be gone and live, or stay and die.

JULIET

Yon light is not day-light, I know it, I:
It is some meteor that the sun exhales,
To be to thee this night a torch-bearer,
And light thee on thy way to Mantua:
Therefore stay yet; thou need'st not to be gone.

ROMEO

Let me be ta'en, let me be put to death;
I am content, so thou wilt have it so.
I'll say yon grey is not the morning's eye,
'Tis but the pale reflex of Cynthia's brow;
Nor that is not the lark, whose notes do beat
The vaulty heaven so high above our heads:
I have more care to stay than will to go:
Come, death, and welcome! Juliet wills it so.
How is't, my soul? let's talk; it is not day.

JULIET

It is, it is: hie hence, be gone, away!
It is the lark that sings so out of tune,
Straining harsh discords and unpleasing sharps.
Some say the lark makes sweet division;
This doth not so, for she divideth us:
Some say the lark and loathed toad change eyes,
O, now I would they had changed voices too!
Since arm from arm that voice doth us affray,
Hunting thee hence with hunt's-up to the day,
O, now be gone; more light and light it grows.

ROMEO

More light and light; more dark and dark our woes!

Enter Nurse, to the chamber

NURSE

Madam!

JULIET

    Nurse?

NURSE

    Your lady mother is coming to your chamber:

    The day is broke; be wary, look about.

Exit

JULIET

    Then, window, let day in, and let life out.

ROMEO

    Farewell, farewell! one kiss, and I'll descend.

    He goeth down

JULIET

    Art thou gone so? love, lord, ay, husband, friend!

    I must hear from thee every day in the hour,

    For in a minute there are many days:

    O, by this count I shall be much in years

    Ere I again behold my Romeo!

ROMEO

    Farewell!

    I will omit no opportunity

    That may convey my greetings, love, to thee.

JULIET

    O think'st thou we shall ever meet again?

ROMEO

    I doubt it not; and all these woes shall serve

    For sweet discourses in our time to come.

JULIET

    O God, I have an ill-divining soul!

    Methinks I see thee, now thou art below,

    As one dead in the bottom of a tomb:

    Either my eyesight fails, or thou look'st pale.

ROMEO

    And trust me, love, in my eye so do you:

    Dry sorrow drinks our blood. Adieu, adieu!

Exit

JULIET

    O fortune, fortune! all men call thee fickle:

If thou art fickle, what dost thou with him.
That is renown'd for faith? Be fickle, fortune;
For then, I hope, thou wilt not keep him long,
But send him back.

LADY CAPULET
[*Within*] Ho, daughter! are you up?

JULIET
Who is't that calls? is it my lady mother?
Is she not down so late, or up so early?
What unaccustom'd cause procures her hither?
                        Enter LADY CAPULET

LADY CAPULET
Why, how now, Juliet!

JULIET
Madam, I am not well.

LADY CAPULET
Evermore weeping for your cousin's death?
What, wilt thou wash him from his grave with tears?
An if thou couldst, thou couldst not make him live;
Therefore, have done: some grief shows much of love;
But much of grief shows still some want of wit.

JULIET
Yet let me weep for such a feeling loss.

LADY CAPULET
So shall you feel the loss, but not the friend
Which you weep for.

JULIET
Feeling so the loss,
Cannot choose but ever weep the friend.

LADY CAPULET
Well, girl, thou weep'st not so much for his death,
As that the villain lives which slaughter'd him.

JULIET
What villain madam?

LADY CAPULET
That same villain, Romeo.

JULIET

    [*Aside*] Villain and he be many miles asunder.—

    God Pardon him! I do, with all my heart;

    And yet no man like he doth grieve my heart.

LADY CAPULET

    That is, because the traitor murderer lives.

JULIET

    Ay, madam, from the reach of these my hands:

    Would none but I might venge my cousin's death!

LADY CAPULET

    We will have vengeance for it, fear thou not:

    Then weep no more. I'll send to one in Mantua,

    Where that same banish'd runagate doth live,

    Shall give him such an unaccustom'd dram,

    That he shall soon keep Tybalt company:

    And then, I hope, thou wilt be satisfied.

JULIET

    Indeed, I never shall be satisfied

    With Romeo, till I behold him—dead—

    Is my poor heart for a kinsman vex'd.

    Madam, if you could find out but a man

    To bear a poison, I would temper it;

    That Romeo should, upon receipt thereof,

    Soon sleep in quiet. O, how my heart abhors

    To hear him named, and cannot come to him.

    To wreak the love I bore my cousin

    Upon his body that slaughter'd him!

LADY CAPULET

    Find thou the means, and I'll find such a man.

    But now I'll tell thee joyful tidings, girl.

JULIET

    And joy comes well in such a needy time:

    What are they, I beseech your ladyship?

LADY CAPULET

    Well, well, thou hast a careful father, child;

    One who, to put thee from thy heaviness,

Hath sorted out a sudden day of joy,
That thou expect'st not nor I look'd not for.

JULIET

Madam, in happy time, what day is that?

LADY CAPULET

Marry, my child, early next Thursday morn,
The gallant, young and noble gentleman,
The County Paris, at Saint Peter's Church,
Shall happily make thee there a joyful bride.

JULIET

Now, by Saint Peter's Church and Peter too,
He shall not make me there a joyful bride.
I wonder at this haste; that I must wed
Ere he, that should be husband, comes to woo.
I pray you, tell my lord and father, madam,
I will not marry yet; and, when I do, I swear,
It shall be Romeo, whom you know I hate,
Rather than Paris. These are news indeed!

LADY CAPULET

Here comes your father; tell him so yourself,
And see how he will take it at your hands.

Enter CAPULET *and Nurse*

CAPULET

When the sun sets, the air doth drizzle dew;
But for the sunset of my brother's son
It rains downright.
How now! a conduit, girl? what, still in tears?
Evermore showering? In one little body
Thou counterfeit'st a bark, a sea, a wind;
For still thy eyes, which I may call the sea,
Do ebb and flow with tears; the bark thy body is,
Sailing in this salt flood; the winds, thy sighs;
Who, raging with thy tears, and they with them,
Without a sudden calm, will overset
Thy tempest-tossed body. How now, wife!
Have you deliver'd to her our decree?

LADY CAPULET

Ay, sir; but she will none, she gives you thanks.
I would the fool were married to her grave!

CAPULET

Soft! take me with you, take me with you, wife.
How! will she none? doth she not give us thanks?
Is she not proud? doth she not count her blest,
Unworthy as she is, that we have wrought
So worthy a gentleman to be her bridegroom?

JULIET

Not proud, you have; but thankful, that you have:
Proud can I never be of what I hate;
But thankful even for hate, that is meant love.

CAPULET

How now, how now, chop-logic! What is this?
'Proud,' and 'I thank you,' and 'I thank you not;'
And yet 'not proud,' mistress minion, you,
Thank me no thankings, nor, proud me no prouds,
But fettle your fine joints 'gainst Thursday next,
To go with Paris to Saint Peter's Church,
Or I will drag thee on a hurdle thither.
Out, you green-sickness carrion! out, you baggage!
You tallow-face!

LADY CAPULET

Fie, fie! what, are you mad?

JULIET

Good father, I beseech you on my knees,
Hear me with patience but to speak a word.

CAPULET

Hang thee, young baggage! disobedient wretch!
I tell thee what: get thee to church o' Thursday,
Or never after look me in the face:
Speak not, reply not, do not answer me;
My fingers itch. Wife, we scarce thought us blest
That God had lent us but this only child;
But now I see this one is one too much,

And that we have a curse in having her:
Out on her, hilding!

NURSE

God in heaven bless her!
You are to blame, my lord, to rate her so.

CAPULET

And why, my lady wisdom? hold your tongue,
Good prudence; smatter with your gossips, go.

NURSE

I speak no treason.

CAPULET

O, God ye god-den.

NURSE

May not one speak?

CAPULET

Peace, you mumbling fool!
Utter your gravity o'er a gossip's bowl;
For here we need it not.

LADY CAPULET

You are too hot.

CAPULET

God's bread! it makes me mad:
Day, night, hour, tide, time, work, play,
Alone, in company, still my care hath been
To have her match'd: and having now provided
A gentleman of noble parentage,
Of fair demesnes, youthful, and nobly train'd,
Stuff'd, as they say, with honourable parts,
Proportion'd as one's thought would wish a man;
And then to have a wretched puling fool,
A whining mammet, in her fortune's tender,
To answer 'I'll not wed; I cannot love,
I am too young; I pray you, pardon me.'
But, as you will not wed, I'll pardon you:
Graze where you will you shall not house with me:
Look to't, think on't, I do not use to jest.

Thursday is near; lay hand on heart, advise:
An you be mine, I'll give you to my friend;
And you be not, hang, beg, starve, die in the streets,
For, by my soul, I'll ne'er acknowledge thee,
Nor what is mine shall never do thee good:
Trust to't, bethink you; I'll not be forsworn.

Exit

JULIET

Is there no pity sitting in the clouds,
That sees into the bottom of my grief?
O, sweet my mother, cast me not away!
Delay this marriage for a month, a week;
Or, if you do not, make the bridal bed
In that dim monument where Tybalt lies.

LADY CAPULET

Talk not to me, for I'll not speak a word:
Do as thou wilt, for I have done with thee.

Exit

JULIET

O God!—O nurse, how shall this be prevented?
My husband is on earth, my faith in heaven;
How shall that faith return again to earth,
Unless that husband send it me from heaven
By leaving earth? comfort me, counsel me.
Alack, alack, that heaven should practise stratagems
Upon so soft a subject as myself!
What say'st thou? hast thou not a word of joy?
Some comfort, nurse.

NURSE

Faith, here it is.
Romeo is banish'd; and all the world to nothing,
That he dares ne'er come back to challenge you;
Or, if he do, it needs must be by stealth.
Then, since the case so stands as now it doth,
I think it best you married with the county.
O, he's a lovely gentleman!
Romeo's a dishclout to him: an eagle, madam,

Hath not so green, so quick, so fair an eye
As Paris hath. Beshrew my very heart,
I think you are happy in this second match,
For it excels your first: or if it did not,
Your first is dead; or 'twere as good he were,
As living here and you no use of him.

JULIET
Speakest thou from thy heart?

NURSE
And from my soul too;
Or else beshrew them both.

JULIET
Amen!

NURSE
What?

JULIET
Well, thou hast comforted me marvellous much.
Go in: and tell my lady I am gone,
Having displeased my father, to Laurence' cell,
To make confession and to be absolved.

NURSE
Marry, I will; and this is wisely done.

Exit

JULIET
Ancient damnation! O most wicked fiend!
Is it more sin to wish me thus forsworn,
Or to dispraise my lord with that same tongue
Which she hath praised him with above compare
So many thousand times? Go, counsellor;
Thou and my bosom henceforth shall be twain.
I'll to the friar, to know his remedy:
If all else fail, myself have power to die.

Exit

ACT

IV

SCENE I.
FRIAR LAURENCE'S CELL.

Enter FRIAR LAURENCE *and* PARIS

FRIAR LAURENCE

    On Thursday, sir? the time is very short.

PARIS

    My father Capulet will have it so;
    And I am nothing slow to slack his haste.

FRIAR LAURENCE

    You say you do not know the lady's mind:
    Uneven is the course, I like it not.

PARIS

    Immoderately she weeps for Tybalt's death,
    And therefore have I little talk'd of love;
    For Venus smiles not in a house of tears.
    Now, sir, her father counts it dangerous
    That she doth give her sorrow so much sway,
    And in his wisdom hastes our marriage,
    To stop the inundation of her tears;
    Which, too much minded by herself alone,

May be put from her by society:
Now do you know the reason of this haste.

FRIAR LAURENCE
[*Aside*] I would I knew not why it should be slow'd.
Look, sir, here comes the lady towards my cell.

Enter JULIET

PARIS
Happily met, my lady and my wife!

JULIET
That may be, sir, when I may be a wife.

PARIS
That may be must be, love, on Thursday next.

JULIET
What must be shall be.

FRIAR LAURENCE
That's a certain text.

PARIS
Come you to make confession to this father?

JULIET
To answer that, I should confess to you.

PARIS
Do not deny to him that you love me.

JULIET
I will confess to you that I love him.

PARIS
So will ye, I am sure, that you love me.

JULIET
If I do so, it will be of more price,
Being spoke behind your back, than to your face.

PARIS
Poor soul, thy face is much abused with tears.

JULIET
The tears have got small victory by that;
For it was bad enough before their spite.

PARIS
Thou wrong'st it, more than tears, with that report.

JULIET

That is no slander, sir, which is a truth;

And what I spake, I spake it to my face.

PARIS

Thy face is mine, and thou hast slander'd it.

JULIET

It may be so, for it is not mine own.

Are you at leisure, holy father, now;

Or shall I come to you at evening mass?

FRIAR LAURENCE

My leisure serves me, pensive daughter, now.

My lord, we must entreat the time alone.

PARIS

God shield I should disturb devotion!

Juliet, on Thursday early will I rouse ye:

Till then, adieu; and keep this holy kiss.

Exit

JULIET

O shut the door! and when thou hast done so,

Come weep with me; past hope, past cure, past help!

FRIAR LAURENCE

Ah, Juliet, I already know thy grief;

It strains me past the compass of my wits:

I hear thou must, and nothing may prorogue it,

On Thursday next be married to this county.

JULIET

Tell me not, friar, that thou hear'st of this,

Unless thou tell me how I may prevent it:

If, in thy wisdom, thou canst give no help,

Do thou but call my resolution wise,

And with this knife I'll help it presently.

God join'd my heart and Romeo's, thou our hands;

And ere this hand, by thee to Romeo seal'd,

Shall be the label to another deed,

Or my true heart with treacherous revolt

Turn to another, this shall slay them both:

Therefore, out of thy long-experienced time,

Give me some present counsel, or, behold,
'Twixt my extremes and me this bloody knife
Shall play the umpire, arbitrating that
Which the commission of thy years and art
Could to no issue of true honour bring.
Be not so long to speak; I long to die,
If what thou speak'st speak not of remedy.

FRIAR LAURENCE

Hold, daughter: I do spy a kind of hope,
Which craves as desperate an execution.
As that is desperate which we would prevent.
If, rather than to marry County Paris,
Thou hast the strength of will to slay thyself,
Then is it likely thou wilt undertake
A thing like death to chide away this shame,
That copest with death himself to scape from it:
And, if thou darest, I'll give thee remedy.

JULIET

O, bid me leap, rather than marry Paris,
From off the battlements of yonder tower;
Or walk in thievish ways; or bid me lurk
Where serpents are; chain me with roaring bears;
Or shut me nightly in a charnel-house,
O'er-cover'd quite with dead men's rattling bones,
With reeky shanks and yellow chapless skulls;
Or bid me go into a new-made grave
And hide me with a dead man in his shroud;
Things that, to hear them told, have made me tremble;
And I will do it without fear or doubt,
To live an unstain'd wife to my sweet love.

FRIAR LAURENCE

Hold, then; go home, be merry, give consent
To marry Paris: Wednesday is to-morrow:
To-morrow night look that thou lie alone;
Let not thy nurse lie with thee in thy chamber:
Take thou this vial, being then in bed,
And this distilled liquor drink thou off;

When presently through all thy veins shall run
A cold and drowsy humour, for no pulse
Shall keep his native progress, but surcease:
No warmth, no breath, shall testify thou livest;
The roses in thy lips and cheeks shall fade
To paly ashes, thy eyes' windows fall,
Like death, when he shuts up the day of life;
Each part, deprived of supple government,
Shall, stiff and stark and cold, appear like death:
And in this borrow'd likeness of shrunk death
Thou shalt continue two and forty hours,
And then awake as from a pleasant sleep.
Now, when the bridegroom in the morning comes
To rouse thee from thy bed, there art thou dead:
Then, as the manner of our country is,
In thy best robes uncover'd on the bier
Thou shalt be borne to that same ancient vault
Where all the kindred of the Capulets lie.
In the mean time, against thou shalt awake,
Shall Romeo by my letters know our drift,
And hither shall he come: and he and I
Will watch thy waking, and that very night
Shall Romeo bear thee hence to Mantua.
And this shall free thee from this present shame;
If no inconstant toy, nor womanish fear,
Abate thy valour in the acting it.

JULIET

Give me, give me! O, tell not me of fear!

FRIAR LAURENCE

Hold; get you gone, be strong and prosperous
In this resolve: I'll send a friar with speed
To Mantua, with my letters to thy lord.

JULIET

Love give me strength! and strength shall help afford.
Farewell, dear father!

Exeunt

SCENE II.
HALL IN CAPULET'S HOUSE.

Enter CAPULET, LADY CAPULET,
Nurse, and two Servingmen

CAPULET

So many guests invite as here are writ.

Exit First Servant

Sirrah, go hire me twenty cunning cooks.

SECOND SERVANT

You shall have none ill, sir; for I'll try if they can lick their fingers.

CAPULET

How canst thou try them so?

SECOND SERVANT

Marry, sir, 'tis an ill cook that cannot lick his own fingers:
therefore he that cannot lick his fingers goes not with me.

CAPULET

Go, be gone.

Exit Second Servant

We shall be much unfurnished for this time.
What, is my daughter gone to Friar Laurence?

NURSE

Ay, forsooth.

CAPULET

Well, he may chance to do some good on her:
A peevish self-will'd harlotry it is.

NURSE

See where she comes from shrift with merry look.

Enter JULIET

CAPULET

How now, my headstrong! where have you been gadding?

JULIET

Where I have learn'd me to repent the sin
Of disobedient opposition
To you and your behests, and am enjoin'd
By holy Laurence to fall prostrate here,

And beg your pardon: pardon, I beseech you!
Henceforward I am ever ruled by you.

CAPULET

Send for the county; go tell him of this:
I'll have this knot knit up to-morrow morning.

JULIET

I met the youthful lord at Laurence' cell;
And gave him what becomed love I might,
Not step o'er the bounds of modesty.

CAPULET

Why, I am glad on't; this is well: stand up:
This is as't should be. Let me see the county;
Ay, marry, go, I say, and fetch him hither.
Now, afore God! this reverend holy friar,
Our whole city is much bound to him.

JULIET

Nurse, will you go with me into my closet,
To help me sort such needful ornaments
As you think fit to furnish me to-morrow?

LADY CAPULET

No, not till Thursday; there is time enough.

CAPULET

Go, nurse, go with her: we'll to church to-morrow.

Exeunt JULIET
and Nurse

LADY CAPULET

We shall be short in our provision:
'Tis now near night.

CAPULET

Tush, I will stir about,
And all things shall be well, I warrant thee, wife:
Go thou to Juliet, help to deck up her;
I'll not to bed to-night; let me alone;
I'll play the housewife for this once. What, ho!
They are all forth. Well, I will walk myself
To County Paris, to prepare him up

Against to-morrow: my heart is wondrous light,
Since this same wayward girl is so reclaim'd.

Exeunt

SCENE III.
JULIET'S CHAMBER.

Enter JULIET *and Nurse*

JULIET
Ay, those attires are best: but, gentle nurse,
I pray thee, leave me to my self to-night,
For I have need of many orisons
To move the heavens to smile upon my state,
Which, well thou know'st, is cross, and full of sin.

Enter LADY CAPULET

LADY CAPULET
What, are you busy, ho? need you my help?

JULIET
No, madam; we have cull'd such necessaries
As are behoveful for our state to-morrow:
So please you, let me now be left alone,
And let the nurse this night sit up with you;
For, I am sure, you have your hands full all,
In this so sudden business.

LADY CAPULET
Good night:
Get thee to bed, and rest; for thou hast need.

Exeunt LADY CAPULET
and Nurse

JULIET
Farewell! God knows when we shall meet again.
I have a faint cold fear thrills through my veins,
That almost freezes up the heat of life:
I'll call them back again to comfort me:
Nurse! What should she do here?
My dismal scene I needs must act alone. Come, vial.

What if this mixture do not work at all?
Shall I be married then to-morrow morning?
No, no: this shall forbid it: lie thou there.

Laying down her dagger

What if it be a poison, which the friar
Subtly hath minister'd to have me dead,
Lest in this marriage he should be dishonour'd,
Because he married me before to Romeo?
I fear it is: and yet, methinks, it should not,
For he hath still been tried a holy man.
How if, when I am laid into the tomb,
I wake before the time that Romeo
Come to redeem me? there's a fearful point!
Shall I not, then, be stifled in the vault,
To whose foul mouth no healthsome air breathes in,
And there die strangled ere my Romeo comes?
Or, if I live, is it not very like,
The horrible conceit of death and night,
Together with the terror of the place,—
As in a vault, an ancient receptacle,
Where, for these many hundred years, the bones
Of all my buried ancestors are packed:
Where bloody Tybalt, yet but green in earth,
Lies festering in his shroud; where, as they say,
At some hours in the night spirits resort;—
Alack, alack, is it not like that I,
So early waking, what with loathsome smells,
And shrieks like mandrakes' torn out of the earth,
That living mortals, hearing them, run mad:—
O, if I wake, shall I not be distraught,
Environed with all these hideous fears?
And madly play with my forefather's joints?
And pluck the mangled Tybalt from his shroud?
And, in this rage, with some great kinsman's bone,
As with a club, dash out my desperate brains?
O, look! methinks I see my cousin's ghost
Seeking out Romeo, that did spit his body

Upon a rapier's point: stay, Tybalt, stay!
Romeo, I come! this do I drink to thee.
She falls upon her bed, within the curtains

SCENE IV.
HALL IN CAPULET'S HOUSE.

Enter LADY CAPULET *and Nurse*

LADY CAPULET

Hold, take these keys, and fetch more spices, nurse.

NURSE

They call for dates and quinces in the pastry.

Enter CAPULET

CAPULET

Come, stir, stir, stir! the second cock hath crow'd,
The curfew-bell hath rung, 'tis three o'clock:
Look to the baked meats, good Angelica:
Spare not for the cost.

NURSE

Go, you cot-quean, go,
Get you to bed; faith, You'll be sick to-morrow
For this night's watching.

CAPULET

No, not a whit: what! I have watch'd ere now
All night for lesser cause, and ne'er been sick.

LADY CAPULET

Ay, you have been a mouse-hunt in your time;
But I will watch you from such watching now.

Exeunt LADY CAPULET *and Nurse*

CAPULET

A jealous hood, a jealous hood!

Enter three or four Servingmen,
with spits, logs, and baskets

Now, fellow,
What's there?

FIRST SERVANT

Things for the cook, sir; but I know not what.

CAPULET

Make haste, make haste.

Sirrah, fetch drier logs:
Call Peter, he will show thee where they are.

SECOND SERVANT

I have a head, sir, that will find out logs,
And never trouble Peter for the matter.

Exit

CAPULET

Mass, and well said; a merry whoreson, ha!
Thou shalt be logger-head. Good faith, 'tis day:
The county will be here with music straight,
For so he said he would: I hear him near.

Music within

Nurse! Wife! What, ho! What, nurse, I say!

Re-enter Nurse

Go waken Juliet, go and trim her up;
I'll go and chat with Paris: hie, make haste,
Make haste; the bridegroom he is come already:
Make haste, I say.

Exeunt

SCENE V.
JULIET'S CHAMBER.

Enter Nurse

NURSE

Mistress! what, mistress! Juliet! fast, I warrant her, she:
Why, lamb! why, lady! fie, you slug-a-bed!
Why, love, I say! madam! sweet-heart! why, bride!
What, not a word? you take your pennyworths now;
Sleep for a week; for the next night, I warrant,
The County Paris hath set up his rest,
That you shall rest but little. God forgive me,
Marry, and amen, how sound is she asleep!
I must needs wake her. Madam, madam, madam!

Ay, let the county take you in your bed;
He'll fright you up, i' faith. Will it not be?
Undraws the curtains
What, dress'd! and in your clothes! and down again!
I must needs wake you; Lady! lady! lady!
Alas, alas! Help, help! my lady's dead!
O, well-a-day, that ever I was born!
Some aqua vitae, ho! My lord! my lady!
                    Enter LADY CAPULET

LADY CAPULET
    What noise is here?
NURSE
    O lamentable day!
LADY CAPULET
    What is the matter?
NURSE
    Look, look! O heavy day!
LADY CAPULET
    O me, O me! My child, my only life,
    Revive, look up, or I will die with thee!
    Help, help! Call help.
                    Enter CAPULET

CAPULET
    For shame, bring Juliet forth; her lord is come.
NURSE
    She's dead, deceased, she's dead; alack the day!
LADY CAPULET
    Alack the day, she's dead, she's dead, she's dead!
CAPULET
    Ha! let me see her: out, alas! she's cold:
    Her blood is settled, and her joints are stiff;
    Life and these lips have long been separated:
    Death lies on her like an untimely frost
    Upon the sweetest flower of all the field.
NURSE
    O lamentable day!

LADY CAPULET
     O woful time!
CAPULET
     Death, that hath ta'en her hence to make me wail,
     Ties up my tongue, and will not let me speak.

                    Enter FRIAR LAURENCE *and*
                    PARIS, *with Musicians*

FRIAR LAURENCE
     Come, is the bride ready to go to church?
CAPULET
     Ready to go, but never to return.
     O son! the night before thy wedding-day
     Hath Death lain with thy wife. There she lies,
     Flower as she was, deflowered by him.
     Death is my son-in-law, Death is my heir;
     My daughter he hath wedded: I will die,
     And leave him all; life, living, all is Death's.
PARIS
     Have I thought long to see this morning's face,
     And doth it give me such a sight as this?
LADY CAPULET
     Accursed, unhappy, wretched, hateful day!
     Most miserable hour that e'er time saw
     In lasting labour of his pilgrimage!
     But one, poor one, one poor and loving child,
     But one thing to rejoice and solace in,
     And cruel death hath catch'd it from my sight!
NURSE
     O woe! O woful, woful, woful day!
     Most lamentable day, most woful day,
     That ever, ever, I did yet behold!
     O day! O day! O day! O hateful day!
     Never was seen so black a day as this:
     O woful day, O woful day!
PARIS
     Beguiled, divorced, wronged, spited, slain!
     Most detestable death, by thee beguil'd,

By cruel cruel thee quite overthrown!
O love! O life! not life, but love in death!

CAPULET

Despised, distressed, hated, martyr'd, kill'd!
Uncomfortable time, why camest thou now
To murder, murder our solemnity?
O child! O child! my soul, and not my child!
Dead art thou! Alack! my child is dead;
And with my child my joys are buried.

FRIAR LAURENCE

Peace, ho, for shame! confusion's cure lives not
In these confusions. Heaven and yourself
Had part in this fair maid; now heaven hath all,
And all the better is it for the maid:
Your part in her you could not keep from death,
But heaven keeps his part in eternal life.
The most you sought was her promotion;
For 'twas your heaven she should be advanced:
And weep ye now, seeing she is advanced
Above the clouds, as high as heaven itself?
O, in this love, you love your child so ill,
That you run mad, seeing that she is well:
She's not well married that lives married long;
But she's best married that dies married young.
Dry up your tears, and stick your rosemary
On this fair corse; and, as the custom is,
In all her best array bear her to church:
For though fond nature bids us an lament,
Yet nature's tears are reason's merriment.

CAPULET

All things that we ordained festival,
Turn from their office to black funeral;
Our instruments to melancholy bells,
Our wedding cheer to a sad burial feast,
Our solemn hymns to sullen dirges change,
Our bridal flowers serve for a buried corse,
And all things change them to the contrary.

FRIAR LAURENCE
    Sir, go you in; and, madam, go with him;
    And go, Sir Paris; every one prepare
    To follow this fair corse unto her grave:
    The heavens do lour upon you for some ill;
    Move them no more by crossing their high will.
                    Exeunt CAPULET, LADY CAPULET,
                    PARIS, *and* FRIAR LAURENCE

FIRST MUSICIAN
    Faith, we may put up our pipes, and be gone.
NURSE
    Honest goodfellows, ah, put up, put up;
    For, well you know, this is a pitiful case.
                                            Exit

FIRST MUSICIAN
    Ay, by my troth, the case may be amended.
                    Enter PETER
PETER
    Musicians, O, musicians, 'Heart's ease, Heart's ease:' O, an you
    will have me live, play 'Heart's ease.'
FIRST MUSICIAN
    Why 'Heart's ease?'
PETER
    O, musicians, because my heart itself plays 'My heart is full of
    woe:' O, play me some merry dump, to comfort me.
FIRST MUSICIAN
    Not a dump we; 'tis no time to play now.
PETER
    You will not, then?
FIRST MUSICIAN
    No.
PETER
    I will then give it you soundly.
FIRST MUSICIAN
    What will you give us?

PETER

No money, on my faith, but the gleek;
I will give you the minstrel.

FIRST MUSICIAN

Then I will give you the serving-creature.

PETER

Then will I lay the serving-creature's dagger on your pate. I will
carry no crotchets: I'll re you, I'll fa you; do you note me?

FIRST MUSICIAN

An you re us and fa us, you note us.

SECOND MUSICIAN

Pray you, put up your dagger, and put out your wit.

PETER

Then have at you with my wit! I will dry-beat you with an iron
wit, and put up my iron dagger.
Answer me like men:
'When griping grief the heart doth wound,
And doleful dumps the mind oppress,
Then music with her silver sound'—
why 'silver sound'? why 'music with her silver
sound'? What say you, Simon Catling?

MUSICIAN

Marry, sir, because silver hath a sweet sound.

PETER

Pretty! What say you, Hugh Rebeck?

SECOND MUSICIAN

I say 'silver sound,' because musicians sound for silver.

PETER

Pretty too! What say you, James Soundpost?

THIRD MUSICIAN

Faith, I know not what to say.

PETER

O, I cry you mercy; you are the singer: I will say
for you. It is 'music with her silver sound,'
because musicians have no gold for sounding:
'Then music with her silver sound

With speedy help doth lend redress.'

Exit

FIRST MUSICIAN
   What a pestilent knave is this same!
SECOND MUSICIAN
   Hang him, Jack! Come, we'll in here; tarry for the mourners, and
   stay dinner.

Exeunt

ACT

V

SCENE I.
MANTUA. A STREET.

Enter ROMEO

ROMEO

If I may trust the flattering truth of sleep,
My dreams presage some joyful news at hand:
My bosom's lord sits lightly in his throne;
And all this day an unaccustom'd spirit
Lifts me above the ground with cheerful thoughts.
I dreamt my lady came and found me dead—
Strange dream, that gives a dead man leave to think!—
And breathed such life with kisses in my lips,
That I revived, and was an emperor.
Ah me! how sweet is love itself possess'd,
When but love's shadows are so rich in joy!
          Enter BALTHASAR, *booted*
News from Verona!—How now, Balthasar!
Dost thou not bring me letters from the friar?
How doth my lady? Is my father well?
How fares my Juliet? that I ask again;
For nothing can be ill, if she be well.

BALTHASAR
    Then she is well, and nothing can be ill:
    Her body sleeps in Capel's monument,
    And her immortal part with angels lives.
    I saw her laid low in her kindred's vault,
    And presently took post to tell it you:
    O, pardon me for bringing these ill news,
    Since you did leave it for my office, sir.
ROMEO
    Is it even so? then I defy you, stars!
    Thou know'st my lodging: get me ink and paper,
    And hire post-horses; I will hence to-night.
BALTHASAR
    I do beseech you, sir, have patience:
    Your looks are pale and wild, and do import
    Some misadventure.
ROMEO
    Tush, thou art deceived:
    Leave me, and do the thing I bid thee do.
    Hast thou no letters to me from the friar?
BALTHASAR
    No, my good lord.
ROMEO
    No matter: get thee gone,
    And hire those horses; I'll be with thee straight.

                                    Exit BALTHASAR

    Well, Juliet, I will lie with thee to-night.
    Let's see for means: O mischief, thou art swift
    To enter in the thoughts of desperate men!
    I do remember an apothecary,—
    And hereabouts he dwells,—which late I noted
    In tatter'd weeds, with overwhelming brows,
    Culling of simples; meagre were his looks,
    Sharp misery had worn him to the bones:
    And in his needy shop a tortoise hung,
    An alligator stuff'd, and other skins
    Of ill-shaped fishes; and about his shelves

A beggarly account of empty boxes,
Green earthen pots, bladders and musty seeds,
Remnants of packthread and old cakes of roses,
Were thinly scatter'd, to make up a show.
Noting this penury, to myself I said
'An if a man did need a poison now,
Whose sale is present death in Mantua,
Here lives a caitiff wretch would sell it him.'
O, this same thought did but forerun my need;
And this same needy man must sell it me.
As I remember, this should be the house.
Being holiday, the beggar's shop is shut.
What, ho! apothecary!

Enter Apothecary

APOTHECARY
Who calls so loud?

ROMEO
Come hither, man. I see that thou art poor:
Hold, there is forty ducats: let me have
A dram of poison, such soon-speeding gear
As will disperse itself through all the veins
That the life-weary taker may fall dead
And that the trunk may be discharged of breath
As violently as hasty powder fired
Doth hurry from the fatal cannon's womb.

APOTHECARY
Such mortal drugs I have; but Mantua's law
Is death to any he that utters them.

ROMEO
Art thou so bare and full of wretchedness,
And fear'st to die? famine is in thy cheeks,
Need and oppression starveth in thine eyes,
Contempt and beggary hangs upon thy back;
The world is not thy friend nor the world's law;
The world affords no law to make thee rich;
Then be not poor, but break it, and take this.

APOTHECARY
>My poverty, but not my will, consents.

ROMEO
>I pay thy poverty, and not thy will.

APOTHECARY
>Put this in any liquid thing you will,
>And drink it off; and, if you had the strength
>Of twenty men, it would dispatch you straight.

ROMEO
>There is thy gold, worse poison to men's souls,
>Doing more murders in this loathsome world,
>Than these poor compounds that thou mayst not sell.
>I sell thee poison; thou hast sold me none.
>Farewell: buy food, and get thyself in flesh.
>Come, cordial and not poison, go with me
>To Juliet's grave; for there must I use thee.

>>>>>>>>>>>>>>>>>>*Exeunt*

SCENE II.
FRIAR LAURENCE'S CELL.

>>*Enter* FRIAR JOHN

FRIAR JOHN
>Holy Franciscan friar! brother, ho!
>>>>>>>*Enter* FRIAR LAURENCE

FRIAR LAURENCE
>This same should be the voice of Friar John.
>Welcome from Mantua: what says Romeo?
>Or, if his mind be writ, give me his letter.

FRIAR JOHN
>Going to find a bare-foot brother out
>One of our order, to associate me,
>Here in this city visiting the sick,
>And finding him, the searchers of the town,
>Suspecting that we both were in a house
>Where the infectious pestilence did reign,

Seal'd up the doors, and would not let us forth;
So that my speed to Mantua there was stay'd.

FRIAR LAURENCE
Who bare my letter, then, to Romeo?

FRIAR JOHN
I could not send it,—here it is again,—
Nor get a messenger to bring it thee,
So fearful were they of infection.

FRIAR LAURENCE
Unhappy fortune! by my brotherhood,
The letter was not nice but full of charge
Of dear import, and the neglecting it
May do much danger. Friar John, go hence;
Get me an iron crow, and bring it straight
Unto my cell.

FRIAR JOHN
Brother, I'll go and bring it thee.

Exit

FRIAR LAURENCE
Now must I to the monument alone;
Within three hours will fair Juliet wake:
She will beshrew me much that Romeo
Hath had no notice of these accidents;
But I will write again to Mantua,
And keep her at my cell till Romeo come;
Poor living corse, closed in a dead man's tomb!

Exit

SCENE III.
A CHURCHYARD; IN IT A TOMB
BELONGING TO THE CAPULETS.

Enter PARIS, *and his Page bearing flowers and a torch*

PARIS
Give me thy torch, boy: hence, and stand aloof:
Yet put it out, for I would not be seen.

Under yond yew-trees lay thee all along,
Holding thine ear close to the hollow ground;
So shall no foot upon the churchyard tread,
Being loose, unfirm, with digging up of graves,
But thou shalt hear it: whistle then to me,
As signal that thou hear'st something approach.
Give me those flowers. Do as I bid thee, go.

PAGE [*Aside*]

I am almost afraid to stand alone
Here in the churchyard; yet I will adventure.
Retires

PARIS

Sweet flower, with flowers thy bridal bed I strew,—
O woe! thy canopy is dust and stones;—
Which with sweet water nightly I will dew,
Or, wanting that, with tears distill'd by moans:
The obsequies that I for thee will keep
Nightly shall be to strew thy grave and weep.
The Page whistles
The boy gives warning something doth approach.
What cursed foot wanders this way to-night,
To cross my obsequies and true love's rite?
What with a torch! muffle me, night, awhile.
Retires

Enter ROMEO *and* BALTHASAR,
with a torch, mattock, &c

ROMEO

Give me that mattock and the wrenching iron.
Hold, take this letter; early in the morning
See thou deliver it to my lord and father.
Give me the light: upon thy life, I charge thee,
Whate'er thou hear'st or seest, stand all aloof,
And do not interrupt me in my course.
Why I descend into this bed of death,
Is partly to behold my lady's face;
But chiefly to take thence from her dead finger
A precious ring, a ring that I must use

In dear employment: therefore hence, be gone:
But if thou, jealous, dost return to pry
In what I further shall intend to do,
By heaven, I will tear thee joint by joint
And strew this hungry churchyard with thy limbs:
The time and my intents are savage-wild,
More fierce and more inexorable far
Than empty tigers or the roaring sea.

BALTHASAR

I will be gone, sir, and not trouble you.

ROMEO

So shalt thou show me friendship. Take thou that:
Live, and be prosperous: and farewell, good fellow.

BALTHASAR

[*Aside*] For all this same, I'll hide me hereabout:
His looks I fear, and his intents I doubt.
Retires

ROMEO

Thou detestable maw, thou womb of death,
Gorged with the dearest morsel of the earth,
Thus I enforce thy rotten jaws to open,
And, in despite, I'll cram thee with more food!
Opens the tomb

PARIS

This is that banish'd haughty Montague,
That murder'd my love's cousin, with which grief,
It is supposed, the fair creature died;
And here is come to do some villanous shame
To the dead bodies: I will apprehend him.
Comes forward
Stop thy unhallow'd toil, vile Montague!
Can vengeance be pursued further than death?
Condemned villain, I do apprehend thee:
Obey, and go with me; for thou must die.

ROMEO

I must indeed; and therefore came I hither.
Good gentle youth, tempt not a desperate man;

Fly hence, and leave me: think upon these gone;
Let them affright thee. I beseech thee, youth,
Put not another sin upon my head,
By urging me to fury: O, be gone!
By heaven, I love thee better than myself;
For I come hither arm'd against myself:
Stay not, be gone; live, and hereafter say,
A madman's mercy bade thee run away.

PARIS

I do defy thy conjurations,
And apprehend thee for a felon here.

ROMEO

Wilt thou provoke me? then have at thee, boy!
They fight

PAGE

O Lord, they fight! I will go call the watch.

Exit

PARIS

O, I am slain!
Falls
If thou be merciful,
Open the tomb, lay me with Juliet.

Dies

ROMEO

In faith, I will. Let me peruse this face.
Mercutio's kinsman, noble County Paris!
What said my man, when my betossed soul
Did not attend him as we rode? I think
He told me Paris should have married Juliet:
Said he not so? or did I dream it so?
Or am I mad, hearing him talk of Juliet,
To think it was so? O, give me thy hand,
One writ with me in sour misfortune's book!
I'll bury thee in a triumphant grave;
A grave? O no! a lantern, slaughter'd youth,
For here lies Juliet, and her beauty makes

This vault a feasting presence full of light.
Death, lie thou there, by a dead man interr'd.
Laying PARIS *in the tomb*
How oft when men are at the point of death
Have they been merry! which their keepers call
A lightning before death: O, how may I
Call this a lightning? O my love! my wife!
Death, that hath suck'd the honey of thy breath,
Hath had no power yet upon thy beauty:
Thou art not conquer'd; beauty's ensign yet
Is crimson in thy lips and in thy cheeks,
And death's pale flag is not advanced there.
Tybalt, liest thou there in thy bloody sheet?
O, what more favour can I do to thee,
Than with that hand that cut thy youth in twain
To sunder his that was thine enemy?
Forgive me, cousin! Ah, dear Juliet,
Why art thou yet so fair? shall I believe
That unsubstantial death is amorous,
And that the lean abhorred monster keeps
Thee here in dark to be his paramour?
For fear of that, I still will stay with thee;
And never from this palace of dim night
Depart again: here, here will I remain
With worms that are thy chamber-maids; O, here
Will I set up my everlasting rest,
And shake the yoke of inauspicious stars
From this world-wearied flesh. Eyes, look your last!
Arms, take your last embrace! and, lips, O you
The doors of breath, seal with a righteous kiss
A dateless bargain to engrossing death!
Come, bitter conduct, come, unsavoury guide!
Thou desperate pilot, now at once run on
The dashing rocks thy sea-sick weary bark!
Here's to my love!
Drinks

O true apothecary!
Thy drugs are quick. Thus with a kiss I die.

Dies

Enter, at the other end of the churchyard,
FRIAR LAURENCE, *with a lantern, crow, and spade*

FRIAR LAURENCE
Saint Francis be my speed! how oft to-night
Have my old feet stumbled at graves! Who's there?

BALTHASAR
Here's one, a friend, and one that knows you well.

FRIAR LAURENCE
Bliss be upon you! Tell me, good my friend,
What torch is yond, that vainly lends his light
To grubs and eyeless skulls? as I discern,
It burneth in the Capel's monument.

BALTHASAR
It doth so, holy sir; and there's my master,
One that you love.

FRIAR LAURENCE
Who is it?

BALTHASAR
Romeo.

FRIAR LAURENCE
How long hath he been there?

BALTHASAR
Full half an hour.

FRIAR LAURENCE
Go with me to the vault.

BALTHASAR
I dare not, sir
My master knows not but I am gone hence;
And fearfully did menace me with death,
If I did stay to look on his intents.

FRIAR LAURENCE
Stay, then; I'll go alone. Fear comes upon me:
O, much I fear some ill unlucky thing.

BALTHASAR

    As I did sleep under this yew-tree here,
    I dreamt my master and another fought,
    And that my master slew him.

FRIAR LAURENCE

    Romeo!
    Advances
    Alack, alack, what blood is this, which stains
    The stony entrance of this sepulchre?
    What mean these masterless and gory swords
    To lie discolour'd by this place of peace?
                      Enters the tomb
    Romeo! O, pale! Who else? what, Paris too?
    And steep'd in blood? Ah, what an unkind hour
    Is guilty of this lamentable chance!
    The lady stirs.
    JULIET *wakes*

JULIET

    O comfortable friar! where is my lord?
    I do remember well where I should be,
    And there I am. Where is my Romeo?
    Noise within

FRIAR LAURENCE

    I hear some noise. Lady, come from that nest
    Of death, contagion, and unnatural sleep:
    A greater power than we can contradict
    Hath thwarted our intents. Come, come away.
    Thy husband in thy bosom there lies dead;
    And Paris too. Come, I'll dispose of thee
    Among a sisterhood of holy nuns:
    Stay not to question, for the watch is coming;
    Come, go, good Juliet,
    Noise again
    I dare no longer stay.

JULIET

    Go, get thee hence, for I will not away.
                       Exit FRIAR LAURENCE

What's here? a cup, closed in my true love's hand?
Poison, I see, hath been his timeless end:
O churl! drunk all, and left no friendly drop
To help me after? I will kiss thy lips;
Haply some poison yet doth hang on them,
To make die with a restorative.
Kisses him
Thy lips are warm.

FIRST WATCHMAN
[*Within*] Lead, boy: which way?

JULIET
Yea, noise? then I'll be brief. O happy dagger!
Snatching ROMEO'S *dagger*
This is thy sheath;
Stabs herself
there rust, and let me die.
Falls on ROMEO'S *body, and dies*
                    Enter Watch, with the Page of PARIS

PAGE
This is the place; there, where the torch doth burn.

FIRST WATCHMAN
The ground is bloody; search about the churchyard:
Go, some of you, whoe'er you find attach.
Pitiful sight! here lies the county slain,
And Juliet bleeding, warm, and newly dead,
Who here hath lain these two days buried.
Go, tell the prince: run to the Capulets:
Raise up the Montagues: some others search:
We see the ground whereon these woes do lie;
But the true ground of all these piteous woes
We cannot without circumstance descry.
                    Re-enter some of the Watch, with BALTHASAR

SECOND WATCHMAN
Here's Romeo's man; we found him in the churchyard.

FIRST WATCHMAN
Hold him in safety, till the prince come hither.
                    Re-enter others of the Watch, with FRIAR LAURENCE

THIRD WATCHMAN

>Here is a friar, that trembles, sighs and weeps:
>We took this mattock and this spade from him,
>As he was coming from this churchyard side.

FIRST WATCHMAN

>A great suspicion: stay the friar too.

Enter the PRINCE *and Attendants*

PRINCE

>What misadventure is so early up,
>That calls our person from our morning's rest?

Enter CAPULET, LADY CAPULET, *and others*

CAPULET

>What should it be, that they so shriek abroad?

LADY CAPULET

>The people in the street cry Romeo,
>Some Juliet, and some Paris; and all run,
>With open outcry toward our monument.

PRINCE

>What fear is this which startles in our ears?

FIRST WATCHMAN

>Sovereign, here lies the County Paris slain;
>And Romeo dead; and Juliet, dead before,
>Warm and new kill'd.

PRINCE

>Search, seek, and know how this foul murder comes.

FIRST WATCHMAN

>Here is a friar, and slaughter'd Romeo's man;
>With instruments upon them, fit to open
>These dead men's tombs.

CAPULET

>O heavens! O wife, look how our daughter bleeds!
>This dagger hath mista'en—for, lo, his house
>Is empty on the back of Montague,—
>And it mis-sheathed in my daughter's bosom!

LADY CAPULET

>O me! this sight of death is as a bell,
>That warns my old age to a sepulchre.

Enter MONTAGUE *and others*

PRINCE

    Come, Montague; for thou art early up,

    To see thy son and heir more early down.

MONTAGUE

    Alas, my liege, my wife is dead to-night;

    Grief of my son's exile hath stopp'd her breath:

    What further woe conspires against mine age?

PRINCE

    Look, and thou shalt see.

MONTAGUE

    O thou untaught! what manners is in this? To press before thy

    father to a grave?

PRINCE

    Seal up the mouth of outrage for a while,

    Till we can clear these ambiguities,

    And know their spring, their head, their true descent;

    And then will I be general of your woes,

    And lead you even to death: meantime forbear,

    And let mischance be slave to patience.

    Bring forth the parties of suspicion.

FRIAR LAURENCE

    I am the greatest, able to do least,

    Yet most suspected, as the time and place

    Doth make against me of this direful murder;

    And here I stand, both to impeach and purge

    Myself condemned and myself excused.

PRINCE

    Then say at once what thou dost know in this.

FRIAR LAURENCE

    I will be brief, for my short date of breath

    Is not so long as is a tedious tale.

    Romeo, there dead, was husband to that Juliet;

    And she, there dead, that Romeo's faithful wife:

    I married them; and their stol'n marriage-day

    Was Tybalt's dooms-day, whose untimely death

    Banish'd the new-made bridegroom from the city,

For whom, and not for Tybalt, Juliet pined.
You, to remove that siege of grief from her,
Betroth'd and would have married her perforce
To County Paris: then comes she to me,
And, with wild looks, bid me devise some mean
To rid her from this second marriage,
Or in my cell there would she kill herself.
Then gave I her, so tutor'd by my art,
A sleeping potion; which so took effect
As I intended, for it wrought on her
The form of death: meantime I writ to Romeo,
That he should hither come as this dire night,
To help to take her from her borrow'd grave,
Being the time the potion's force should cease.
But he which bore my letter, Friar John,
Was stay'd by accident, and yesternight
Return'd my letter back. Then all alone
At the prefixed hour of her waking,
Came I to take her from her kindred's vault;
Meaning to keep her closely at my cell,
Till I conveniently could send to Romeo:
But when I came, some minute ere the time
Of her awaking, here untimely lay
The noble Paris and true Romeo dead.
She wakes; and I entreated her come forth,
And bear this work of heaven with patience:
But then a noise did scare me from the tomb;
And she, too desperate, would not go with me,
But, as it seems, did violence on herself.
All this I know; and to the marriage
Her nurse is privy: and, if aught in this
Miscarried by my fault, let my old life
Be sacrificed, some hour before his time,
Unto the rigour of severest law.

PRINCE

We still have known thee for a holy man. Where's Romeo's man?
what can he say in this?

BALTHASAR

    I brought my master news of Juliet's death;
    And then in post he came from Mantua
    To this same place, to this same monument.
    This letter he early bid me give his father,
    And threatened me with death, going in the vault,
    I departed not and left him there.

PRINCE

    Give me the letter; I will look on it.
    Where is the county's page, that raised the watch?
    Sirrah, what made your master in this place?

PAGE

    He came with flowers to strew his lady's grave;
    And bid me stand aloof, and so I did:
    Anon comes one with light to ope the tomb;
    And by and by my master drew on him;
    And then I ran away to call the watch.

PRINCE

    This letter doth make good the friar's words,
    Their course of love, the tidings of her death:
    And here he writes that he did buy a poison
    Of a poor 'pothecary, and therewithal
    Came to this vault to die, and lie with Juliet.
    Where be these enemies? Capulet! Montague!
    See, what a scourge is laid upon your hate,
    That heaven finds means to kill your joys with love.
    And I for winking at your discords too
    Have lost a brace of kinsmen: all are punish'd.

CAPULET

    O brother Montague, give me thy hand:
    This is my daughter's jointure, for no more
    Can I demand.

MONTAGUE

    But I can give thee more:
    For I will raise her statue in pure gold;
    That while Verona by that name is known,

There shall no figure at such rate be set
As that of true and faithful Juliet.

CAPULET

As rich shall Romeo's by his lady's lie;
Poor sacrifices of our enmity!

PRINCE

A glooming peace this morning with it brings;
The sun, for sorrow, will not show his head:
Go hence, to have more talk of these sad things;
Some shall be pardon'd, and some punished:
For never was a story of more woe
Than this of Juliet and her Romeo.

Exeunt

Hamlet

"To be, or not to be: that is the question:"

CONTEXT

The earliest of the great tragedies, *Hamlet* was written in the early seventeenth century. It was entered in the Register of the Stationers' Company in July 1602 and was first published in printed form in 1603 followed by an enlarged edition in 1604. Always writing for the contemporary theatre, Shakespeare manipulated the Elizabethan stage with great resources and invention. He derived his ideas and stories from earlier literary works, a common practise during the sixteenth and seventeenth centuries. The legend of Amleth, preserved in *Gesta Danorum* by a twelfth-century chronicler Saxo Grammaticus, and a prose work by the French writer François de Belleforest, entitled *Histoires Tragiques*, are the possible sources from where the story of *Hamlet* was derived.

A play in which verse is used with great skill, *Hamlet* is a story of murder, suicide, madness—to those who call for melodrama—but for others it is a most subtle analysis of character. The raw material that Shakespeare appropriated in writing this play is the story of a Danish prince whose uncle murders the King, marries the Queen, and claims the throne. The prince pretends to be feeble-minded to throw his uncle off guard and manages to take revenge by killing him. Shakespeare changed the emphasis of this story entirely. His primary purpose was to satisfy his audience, but this was not enough, for he had to satisfy himself. His Hamlet was a philosophically minded prince who delays action because his knowledge of his uncle's crime is uncertain. Shakespeare went far beyond making uncertainty a personal quirk of Hamlet's and introduced a number of important ambiguities into the play that even the audience cannot resolve with certainty. For instance, whether Hamlet's mother, Gertrude, shares in Claudius's guilt; whether Hamlet continues to love Ophelia even as he spurns her, in Act III; whether Ophelia's death is suicide or accident; whether the ghost offers reliable knowledge, or seeks to deceive and tempt Hamlet; and, perhaps most importantly, whether Hamlet would be morally justified in taking revenge on his uncle. Shakespeare makes it clear that the stakes riding on some of these questions are enormous—the actions of these characters bring disaster upon an entire kingdom. At the play's end it is not even clear whether justice has been achieved.

Hamlet—a play about indecisiveness, and Hamlet's failure to act appropriately—is the most self-conscious tragedy. Shakespeare made it resonate with the most fundamental themes and problems of the Renaissance—a vast cultural phenomenon that began in the fifteenth-century Italy with the recovery of classical Greek and Latin texts that had been lost to the Middle Ages. The play is governed by the Renaissance atmosphere of art, ostentation, learning, and crime. The eponymous character himself is a renaissance scholar-prince— clever, melancholic, and introspective. Like a character in life itself, Hamlet may not be capable of full interpretation, though it is clear that through him Shakespeare explored the whole problem of action and reflective mind.

Renaissance humanism, as the movement is now called, generated a new interest in human experience, and also an enormous optimism about the potential scope of human understanding. Hamlet's famous speech in Act II, "What a piece of work is a man! How noble in reason, how infinite in faculty, in form and moving how express and admirable, in action how like an angel, in apprehension how like a god—the beauty of the world, the paragon of animals!" is directly based upon one of the major texts of the Italian humanists, Pico della Mirandola's *Oration on the Dignity of Man*. For the humanists, the purpose of cultivating reason was to lead to a better understanding of how to act, and their fondest hope was that the coordination of action and understanding would lead to great benefits for society as a whole.

Shakespeare allowed his characters a freedom to live their own lives to the uttermost confines of good and evil, but he was ever conscious that they existed in a moral world. The speeches in which Hamlet addresses the players show that Shakespeare felt the restriction of the actor's ability to interpret, and of the audience's intelligence in appreciation. He faced his contemporary audience, answered its needs, and contrived a drama which the Court could appreciate and the public enjoy. He wrote out the play fully as his own genius directed, knowing that deletion would be imperative when his script reached the theatre.

The world of other people is a world of appearances, and *Hamlet*, is fundamentally a play about the difficulty of living in that world.

Characters in the Play

CLAUDIUS, King of Denmark

HAMLET, son to the late, and nephew to the present King

POLONIUS, Lord Chamberlain

HORATIO, friend to Hamlet

LAERTES, son to Polonius

VOLTIMAND, CORNELIUS, ROSENCRANTZ, GUILDENSTERN, OSRIC, a Gentleman, courtiers

A Priest

MARCELLUS, BARNARDO, officers

FRANCISCO, a soldier

REYNALDO, servant to Polonius

Players

Two Clowns, grave-diggers

FORTINBRAS, Prince of Norway

A Captain

English Ambassadors

GERTRUDE, Queen of Denmark and mother to Hamlet

OPHELIA, daughter to Polonius

Lords, Ladies, Officers, Soldiers, Sailors, Messengers, and other Attendants

Ghost of Hamlet's Father

SCENE: Denmark.

ACT

SCENE I.
ELSINORE. A PLATFORM
BEFORE THE CASTLE.

FRANCISCO *at his post. Enter to him* BERNARDO

BERNARDO
   Who's there?

FRANCISCO
   Nay, answer me: stand, and unfold yourself.

BERNARDO
   Long live the king!

FRANCISCO
   Bernardo?

BERNARDO
   He.

FRANCISCO
   You come most carefully upon your hour.

BERNARDO
   'Tis now struck twelve; get thee to bed, Francisco.

FRANCISCO
   For this relief much thanks: 'tis bitter cold,
   And I am sick at heart.

BERNARDO

    Have you had quiet guard?

FRANCISCO

    Not a mouse stirring.

BERNARDO

    Well, good night. If you do meet Horatio and Marcellus,
    The rivals of my watch, bid them make haste.

FRANCISCO

    I think I hear them. Stand, ho! Who's there?

               Enter HORATIO *and* MARCELLUS

HORATIO

    Friends to this ground.

MARCELLUS

    And liegemen to the Dane.

FRANCISCO

    Give you good night.

MARCELLUS

    O, farewell, honest soldier:
    Who hath relieved you?

FRANCISCO

    Bernardo has my place.
    Give you good night.

                                                 Exit

MARCELLUS

    Holla! Bernardo!

BERNARDO

    Say, what, is Horatio there?

HORATIO

    A piece of him.

BERNARDO

    Welcome, Horatio, welcome, good Marcellus.

MARCELLUS

    What, has this thing appear'd again to-night?

BERNARDO

    I have seen nothing.

MARCELLUS

    Horatio says 'tis but our fantasy,

And will not let belief take hold of him
Touching this dreaded sight, twice seen of us:
Therefore I have entreated him along
With us to watch the minutes of this night;
That if again this apparition come,
He may approve our eyes and speak to it.

HORATIO

Tush, tush, 'twill not appear.

BERNARDO

Sit down awhile;
And let us once again assail your ears,
That are so fortified against our story
What we have two nights seen.

HORATIO

Well, sit we down,
And let us hear Bernardo speak of this.

BERNARDO

Last night of all,
When yond same star that's westward from the pole
Had made his course to illume that part of heaven
Where now it burns, Marcellus and myself,
The bell then beating one—

Enter Ghost

MARCELLUS

Peace, break thee off; look, where it comes again!

BERNARDO

In the same figure, like the king that's dead.

MARCELLUS

Thou art a scholar; speak to it, Horatio.

BERNARDO

Looks it not like the king? Mark it, Horatio.

HORATIO

Most like: it harrows me with fear and wonder.

BERNARDO

It would be spoke to.

MARCELLUS

Question it, Horatio.

HORATIO

What art thou that usurp'st this time of night,
Together with that fair and warlike form
In which the majesty of buried Denmark
Did sometimes march? by heaven I charge thee, speak!

MARCELLUS

It is offended.

BERNARDO

See, it stalks away!

HORATIO

Stay! speak, speak! I charge thee, speak!

Exit Ghost

MARCELLUS

'Tis gone, and will not answer.

BERNARDO

How now, Horatio? You tremble and look pale:
Is not this something more than fantasy?
What think you on't?

HORATIO

Before my God, I might not this believe
Without the sensible and true avouch
Of mine own eyes.

MARCELLUS

Is it not like the king?

HORATIO

As thou art to thyself:
Such was the very armour he had on
When he the ambitious Norway combated;
So frown'd he once, when in an angry parle,
He smote the sledded Polacks on the ice.
'Tis strange.

MARCELLUS

Thus twice before, and jump at this dead hour,
With martial stalk hath he gone by our watch.

HORATIO

In what particular thought to work I know not;

But in the gross and scope of my opinion,
This bodes some strange eruption to our state.

MARCELLUS

Good now, sit down, and tell me, he that knows,
Why this same strict and most observant watch
So nightly toils the subject of the land,
And why such daily cast of brazen cannon,
And foreign mart for implements of war;
Why such impress of shipwrights, whose sore task
Does not divide the Sunday from the week;
What might be toward, that this sweaty haste
Doth make the night joint-labourer with the day:
Who is't that can inform me?

HORATIO

That can I;
At least, the whisper goes so. Our last king,
Whose image even but now appear'd to us,
Was, as you know, by Fortinbras of Norway,
Thereto prick'd on by a most emulate pride,
Dared to the combat; in which our valiant Hamlet—
For so this side of our known world esteem'd him—
Did slay this Fortinbras; who by a seal'd compact,
Well ratified by law and heraldry,
Did forfeit, with his life, all those his lands
Which he stood seized of, to the conqueror:
Against the which, a moiety competent
Was gaged by our king; which had return'd
To the inheritance of Fortinbras,
Had he been vanquisher; as, by the same covenant,
And carriage of the article design'd,
His fell to Hamlet. Now, sir, young Fortinbras,
Of unimproved mettle hot and full,
Hath in the skirts of Norway here and there
Shark'd up a list of lawless resolutes,
For food and diet, to some enterprise
That hath a stomach in't; which is no other—

As it doth well appear unto our state—
But to recover of us, by strong hand
And terms compulsatory, those foresaid lands
So by his father lost: and this, I take it,
Is the main motive of our preparations,
The source of this our watch and the chief head
Of this post-haste and romage in the land.

BERNARDO

I think it be no other but e'en so:
Well may it sort that this portentous figure
Comes armed through our watch; so like the king
That was and is the question of these wars.

HORATIO

A mote it is to trouble the mind's eye.
In the most high and palmy state of Rome,
A little ere the mightiest Julius fell,
The graves stood tenantless and the sheeted dead
Did squeak and gibber in the Roman streets:
As stars with trains of fire and dews of blood,
Disasters in the sun; and the moist star
Upon whose influence Neptune's empire stands
Was sick almost to doomsday with eclipse:
And even the like precurse of fierce events,
As harbingers preceding still the fates
And prologue to the omen coming on,
Have heaven and earth together demonstrated
Unto our climatures and countrymen.
But soft, behold! lo, where it comes again!

Re-enter Ghost

I'll cross it, though it blast me. Stay, illusion!
If thou hast any sound, or use of voice,
Speak to me:
If there be any good thing to be done,
That may to thee do ease and grace to me,
Speak to me:

Cock crows

If thou art privy to thy country's fate,

Which, happily, foreknowing may avoid, O, speak!
Or if thou hast uphoarded in thy life
Extorted treasure in the womb of earth,
For which, they say, you spirits oft walk in death,
Speak of it: stay, and speak! Stop it, Marcellus.

MARCELLUS

Shall I strike at it with my partisan?

HORATIO

Do, if it will not stand.

BERNARDO

'Tis here!

HORATIO

'Tis here!

MARCELLUS

'Tis gone!

Exit Ghost

We do it wrong, being so majestical,
To offer it the show of violence;
For it is, as the air, invulnerable,
And our vain blows malicious mockery.

BERNARDO

It was about to speak, when the cock crew.

HORATIO

And then it started like a guilty thing
Upon a fearful summons. I have heard,
The cock, that is the trumpet to the morn,
Doth with his lofty and shrill-sounding throat
Awake the god of day; and, at his warning,
Whether in sea or fire, in earth or air,
The extravagant and erring spirit hies
To his confine: and of the truth herein
This present object made probation.

MARCELLUS

It faded on the crowing of the cock.
Some say that ever 'gainst that season comes
Wherein our Saviour's birth is celebrated,
The bird of dawning singeth all night long:

And then, they say, no spirit dares stir abroad;
The nights are wholesome; then no planets strike,
No fairy takes, nor witch hath power to charm,
So hallow'd and so gracious is the time.

HORATIO

So have I heard and do in part believe it.
But, look, the morn, in russet mantle clad,
Walks o'er the dew of yon high eastward hill:
Break we our watch up; and by my advice,
Let us impart what we have seen to-night
Unto young Hamlet; for, upon my life,
This spirit, dumb to us, will speak to him.
Do you consent we shall acquaint him with it,
As needful in our loves, fitting our duty?

MARCELLUS

Let's do't, I pray; and I this morning know
Where we shall find him most conveniently.

Exeunt

SCENE II.
A ROOM OF STATE IN THE CASTLE.

Enter KING CLAUDIUS, QUEEN GERTRUDE,
HAMLET, POLONIUS, LAERTES, VOLTIMAND,
CORNELIUS, *Lords, and Attendants*

KING CLAUDIUS

Though yet of Hamlet our dear brother's death
The memory be green, and that it us befitted
To bear our hearts in grief and our whole kingdom
To be contracted in one brow of woe,
Yet so far hath discretion fought with nature
That we with wisest sorrow think on him,
Together with remembrance of ourselves.
Therefore our sometime sister, now our queen,
The imperial jointress to this warlike state,
Have we, as 'twere with a defeated joy,
With an auspicious and a dropping eye,

With mirth in funeral and with dirge in marriage,
In equal scale weighing delight and dole,
Taken to wife: nor have we herein barr'd
Your better wisdoms, which have freely gone
With this affair along. For all, our thanks.
Now follows, that you know, young Fortinbras,
Holding a weak supposal of our worth,
Or thinking by our late dear brother's death
Our state to be disjoint and out of frame,
Colleagued with the dream of his advantage,
He hath not fail'd to pester us with message,
Importing the surrender of those lands
Lost by his father, with all bonds of law,
To our most valiant brother. So much for him.
Now for ourself and for this time of meeting:
Thus much the business is: we have here writ
To Norway, uncle of young Fortinbras,
Who, impotent and bed-rid, scarcely hears
Of this his nephew's purpose, to suppress
His further gait herein; in that the levies,
The lists and full proportions, are all made
Out of his subject: and we here dispatch
You, good Cornelius, and you, Voltimand,
For bearers of this greeting to old Norway;
Giving to you no further personal power
To business with the king, more than the scope
Of these delated articles allow.
Farewell, and let your haste commend your duty.

CORNELIUS VOLTIMAND
In that and all things will we show our duty.

KING CLAUDIUS
We doubt it nothing: heartily farewell.

Exeunt VOLTIMAND *and* CORNELIUS
And now, Laertes, what's the news with you?
You told us of some suit; what is't, Laertes?
You cannot speak of reason to the Dane,
And loose your voice: what wouldst thou beg, Laertes,

That shall not be my offer, not thy asking?
The head is not more native to the heart,
The hand more instrumental to the mouth,
Than is the throne of Denmark to thy father.
What wouldst thou have, Laertes?

LAERTES

My dread lord,
Your leave and favour to return to France;
From whence though willingly I came to Denmark,
To show my duty in your coronation,
Yet now, I must confess, that duty done,
My thoughts and wishes bend again toward France
And bow them to your gracious leave and pardon.

KING CLAUDIUS

Have you your father's leave? What says Polonius?

LORD POLONIUS

He hath, my lord, wrung from me my slow leave
By laboursome petition, and at last
Upon his will I seal'd my hard consent:
I do beseech you, give him leave to go.

KING CLAUDIUS

Take thy fair hour, Laertes; time be thine,
And thy best graces spend it at thy will!
But now, my cousin Hamlet, and my son?

HAMLET

[*Aside*] A little more than kin, and less than kind.

KING CLAUDIUS

How is it that the clouds still hang on you?

HAMLET

Not so, my lord; I am too much i' the sun.

QUEEN GERTRUDE

Good Hamlet, cast thy nighted colour off,
And let thine eye look like a friend on Denmark.
Do not for ever with thy vailed lids
Seek for thy noble father in the dust:
Thou know'st 'tis common; all that lives must die,
Passing through nature to eternity.

HAMLET
    Ay, madam, it is common.
QUEEN GERTRUDE
    If it be,
    Why seems it so particular with thee?
HAMLET
    Seems, madam! nay it is; I know not 'seems.'
    'Tis not alone my inky cloak, good mother,
    Nor customary suits of solemn black,
    Nor windy suspiration of forced breath,
    No, nor the fruitful river in the eye,
    Nor the dejected 'havior of the visage,
    Together with all forms, moods, shapes of grief,
    That can denote me truly: these indeed seem,
    For they are actions that a man might play:
    But I have that within which passeth show;
    These but the trappings and the suits of woe.
KING CLAUDIUS
    'Tis sweet and commendable in your nature, Hamlet,
    To give these mourning duties to your father:
    But, you must know, your father lost a father;
    That father lost, lost his, and the survivor bound
    In filial obligation for some term
    To do obsequious sorrow: but to persever
    In obstinate condolement is a course
    Of impious stubbornness; 'tis unmanly grief;
    It shows a will most incorrect to heaven,
    A heart unfortified, a mind impatient,
    An understanding simple and unschool'd:
    For what we know must be and is as common
    As any the most vulgar thing to sense,
    Why should we in our peevish opposition
    Take it to heart? Fie! 'tis a fault to heaven,
    A fault against the dead, a fault to nature,
    To reason most absurd: whose common theme
    Is death of fathers, and who still hath cried,
    From the first corse till he that died to-day,

'This must be so.' We pray you, throw to earth
This unprevailing woe, and think of us
As of a father: for let the world take note,
You are the most immediate to our throne;
And with no less nobility of love
Than that which dearest father bears his son,
Do I impart toward you. For your intent
In going back to school in Wittenberg,
It is most retrograde to our desire:
And we beseech you, bend you to remain
Here, in the cheer and comfort of our eye,
Our chiefest courtier, cousin, and our son.

QUEEN GERTRUDE

Let not thy mother lose her prayers, Hamlet:
I pray thee, stay with us; go not to Wittenberg.

HAMLET

I shall in all my best obey you, madam.

KING CLAUDIUS

Why, 'tis a loving and a fair reply:
Be as ourself in Denmark. Madam, come;
This gentle and unforced accord of Hamlet
Sits smiling to my heart: in grace whereof,
No jocund health that Denmark drinks to-day,
But the great cannon to the clouds shall tell,
And the king's rouse the heavens all bruit again,
Re-speaking earthly thunder. Come away.

Exeunt all but HAMLET

HAMLET

O, that this too too solid flesh would melt,
Thaw and resolve itself into a dew!
Or that the Everlasting had not fix'd
His canon 'gainst self-slaughter! O God! God!
How weary, stale, flat and unprofitable,
Seem to me all the uses of this world!
Fie on't! ah fie! 'tis an unweeded garden,
That grows to seed; things rank and gross in nature

Possess it merely. That it should come to this!
But two months dead: nay, not so much, not two:
So excellent a king; that was, to this,
Hyperion to a satyr; so loving to my mother
That he might not beteem the winds of heaven
Visit her face too roughly. Heaven and earth!
Must I remember? why, she would hang on him,
As if increase of appetite had grown
By what it fed on: and yet, within a month—
Let me not think on't—Frailty, thy name is woman!
A little month, or ere those shoes were old
With which she follow'd my poor father's body,
Like Niobe, all tears: why she, even she—
O, God! A beast that wants discourse of reason,
Would have mourn'd longer—married with my uncle,
My father's brother, but no more like my father
Than I to Hercules: within a month:
Ere yet the salt of most unrighteous tears
Had left the flushing in her galled eyes,
She married. O, most wicked speed, to post
With such dexterity to incestuous sheets!
It is not nor it cannot come to good:
But break, my heart; for I must hold my tongue.

Enter HORATIO, MARCELLUS, *and* BERNARDO

HORATIO

Hail to your lordship!

HAMLET

I am glad to see you well:
Horatio, or I do forget myself.

HORATIO

The same, my lord, and your poor servant ever.

HAMLET

Sir, my good friend; I'll change that name with you:
And what make you from Wittenberg, Horatio? Marcellus?

MARCELLUS

My good lord—

HAMLET

I am very glad to see you. Good even, sir.

But what, in faith, make you from Wittenberg?

HORATIO

A truant disposition, good my lord.

HAMLET

I would not hear your enemy say so,

Nor shall you do mine ear that violence,

To make it truster of your own report

Against yourself: I know you are no truant.

But what is your affair in Elsinore?

We'll teach you to drink deep ere you depart.

HORATIO

My lord, I came to see your father's funeral.

HAMLET

I pray thee, do not mock me, fellow-student;

I think it was to see my mother's wedding.

HORATIO

Indeed, my lord, it follow'd hard upon.

HAMLET

Thrift, thrift, Horatio! the funeral baked meats

Did coldly furnish forth the marriage tables.

Would I had met my dearest foe in heaven

Or ever I had seen that day, Horatio!

My father! methinks I see my father.

HORATIO

Where, my lord?

HAMLET

In my mind's eye, Horatio.

HORATIO

I saw him once; he was a goodly king.

HAMLET

He was a man, take him for all in all,

I shall not look upon his like again.

HORATIO

My lord, I think I saw him yesternight.

HAMLET
Saw? who?
HORATIO
My lord, the king your father.
HAMLET
The king my father!
HORATIO
Season your admiration for awhile
With an attent ear, till I may deliver,
Upon the witness of these gentlemen,
This marvel to you.
HAMLET
For God's love, let me hear.
HORATIO
Two nights together had these gentlemen,
Marcellus and Bernardo, on their watch,
In the dead vast and middle of the night,
Been thus encounter'd. A figure like your father,
Armed at point exactly, cap-a-pe,
Appears before them, and with solemn march
Goes slow and stately by them: thrice he walk'd
By their oppress'd and fear-surprised eyes,
Within his truncheon's length; whilst they, distilled
Almost to jelly with the act of fear,
Stand dumb and speak not to him. This to me
In dreadful secrecy impart they did;
And I with them the third night kept the watch;
Where, as they had deliver'd, both in time,
Form of the thing, each word made true and good,
The apparition comes: I knew your father;
These hands are not more like.
HAMLET
But where was this?
MARCELLUS
My lord, upon the platform where we watch'd.
HAMLET
Did you not speak to it?

HORATIO
    My lord, I did;
    But answer made it none: yet once methought
    It lifted up its head and did address
    Itself to motion, like as it would speak;
    But even then the morning cock crew loud,
    And at the sound it shrunk in haste away,
    And vanish'd from our sight.
HAMLET
    'Tis very strange.
HORATIO
    As I do live, my honour'd lord, 'tis true;
    And we did think it writ down in our duty
    To let you know of it.
HAMLET
    Indeed, indeed, sirs, but this troubles me.
    Hold you the watch to-night?
MARCELLUS BERNARDO
    We do, my lord.
HAMLET
    Arm'd, say you?
MARCELLUS BERNARDO
    Arm'd, my lord.
HAMLET
    From top to toe?
MARCELLUS BERNARDO
    My lord, from head to foot.
HAMLET
    Then saw you not his face?
HORATIO
    O, yes, my lord; he wore his beaver up.
HAMLET
    What, look'd he frowningly?
HORATIO
    A countenance more in sorrow than in anger.
HAMLET
    Pale or red?

HORATIO
    Nay, very pale.
HAMLET
    And fix'd his eyes upon you?
HORATIO
    Most constantly.
HAMLET
    I would I had been there.
HORATIO
    It would have much amazed you.
HAMLET
    Very like, very like. Stay'd it long?
HORATIO
    While one with moderate haste might tell a hundred.
MARCELLUS BERNARDO
    Longer, longer.
HORATIO
    Not when I saw't.
HAMLET
    His beard was grizzled—no?
HORATIO
    It was, as I have seen it in his life,
    A sable silver'd.
HAMLET
    I will watch to-night;
    Perchance 'twill walk again.
HORATIO
    I warrant it will.
HAMLET
    If it assume my noble father's person,
    I'll speak to it, though hell itself should gape
    And bid me hold my peace. I pray you all,
    If you have hitherto conceal'd this sight,
    Let it be tenable in your silence still;
    And whatsoever else shall hap to-night,
    Give it an understanding, but no tongue:
    I will requite your loves. So, fare you well:

Upon the platform, 'twixt eleven and twelve,
I'll visit you.

ALL

Our duty to your honour.

HAMLET

Your loves, as mine to you: farewell.

Exeunt all but HAMLET

My father's spirit in arms! all is not well;
I doubt some foul play: would the night were come!
Till then sit still, my soul: foul deeds will rise,
Though all the earth o'erwhelm them, to men's eyes.

Exit

SCENE III.
A ROOM IN POLONIUS' HOUSE.

Enter LAERTES *and* OPHELIA

LAERTES

My necessaries are embark'd: farewell:
And, sister, as the winds give benefit
And convoy is assistant, do not sleep,
But let me hear from you.

OPHELIA

Do you doubt that?

LAERTES

For Hamlet and the trifling of his favour,
Hold it a fashion and a toy in blood,
A violet in the youth of primy nature,
Forward, not permanent, sweet, not lasting,
The perfume and suppliance of a minute; No more.

OPHELIA

No more but so?

LAERTES

Think it no more;
For nature, crescent, does not grow alone
In thews and bulk, but, as this temple waxes,

The inward service of the mind and soul
Grows wide withal. Perhaps he loves you now,
And now no soil nor cautel doth besmirch
The virtue of his will: but you must fear,
His greatness weigh'd, his will is not his own;
For he himself is subject to his birth:
He may not, as unvalued persons do,
Carve for himself; for on his choice depends
The safety and health of this whole state;
And therefore must his choice be circumscribed
Unto the voice and yielding of that body
Whereof he is the head. Then if he says he loves you,
It fits your wisdom so far to believe it
As he in his particular act and place
May give his saying deed; which is no further
Than the main voice of Denmark goes withal.
Then weigh what loss your honour may sustain,
If with too credent ear you list his songs,
Or lose your heart, or your chaste treasure open
To his unmaster'd importunity.
Fear it, Ophelia, fear it, my dear sister,
And keep you in the rear of your affection,
Out of the shot and danger of desire.
The chariest maid is prodigal enough,
If she unmask her beauty to the moon:
Virtue itself 'scapes not calumnious strokes:
The canker galls the infants of the spring,
Too oft before their buttons be disclosed,
And in the morn and liquid dew of youth
Contagious blastments are most imminent.
Be wary then; best safety lies in fear:
Youth to itself rebels, though none else near.

OPHELIA
I shall the effect of this good lesson keep,
As watchman to my heart. But, good my brother,
Do not, as some ungracious pastors do,

Show me the steep and thorny way to heaven;
Whiles, like a puff'd and reckless libertine,
Himself the primrose path of dalliance treads,
And recks not his own rede.

LAERTES

O, fear me not.
I stay too long: but here my father comes.

Enter POLONIUS

A double blessing is a double grace,
Occasion smiles upon a second leave.

LORD POLONIUS

Yet here, Laertes! aboard, aboard, for shame!
The wind sits in the shoulder of your sail,
And you are stay'd for. There; my blessing with thee!
And these few precepts in thy memory
See thou character. Give thy thoughts no tongue,
Nor any unproportioned thought his act.
Be thou familiar, but by no means vulgar.
Those friends thou hast, and their adoption tried,
Grapple them to thy soul with hoops of steel;
But do not dull thy palm with entertainment
Of each new-hatch'd, unfledged comrade. Beware
Of entrance to a quarrel, but being in,
Bear't that the opposed may beware of thee.
Give every man thy ear, but few thy voice;
Take each man's censure, but reserve thy judgment.
Costly thy habit as thy purse can buy,
But not express'd in fancy; rich, not gaudy;
For the apparel oft proclaims the man,
And they in France of the best rank and station
Are of a most select and generous chief in that.
Neither a borrower nor a lender be;
For loan oft loses both itself and friend,
And borrowing dulls the edge of husbandry.
This above all: to thine ownself be true,
And it must follow, as the night the day,

Thou canst not then be false to any man.
Farewell: my blessing season this in thee!

LAERTES

Most humbly do I take my leave, my lord.

LORD POLONIUS

The time invites you; go; your servants tend.

LAERTES

Farewell, Ophelia; and remember well
What I have said to you.

OPHELIA

'Tis in my memory lock'd,
And you yourself shall keep the key of it.

LAERTES

Farewell.

Exit

LORD POLONIUS

What is't, Ophelia, be hath said to you?

OPHELIA

So please you, something touching the Lord Hamlet.

LORD POLONIUS

Marry, well bethought:
'Tis told me, he hath very oft of late
Given private time to you; and you yourself
Have of your audience been most free and bounteous:
If it be so, as so 'tis put on me,
And that in way of caution, I must tell you,
You do not understand yourself so clearly
As it behoves my daughter and your honour.
What is between you? give me up the truth.

OPHELIA

He hath, my lord, of late made many tenders
Of his affection to me.

LORD POLONIUS

Affection! pooh! you speak like a green girl,
Unsifted in such perilous circumstance.
Do you believe his tenders, as you call them?

OPHELIA
    I do not know, my lord, what I should think.
LORD POLONIUS
    Marry, I'll teach you: think yourself a baby;
    That you have ta'en these tenders for true pay,
    Which are not sterling. Tender yourself more dearly;
    Or—not to crack the wind of the poor phrase,
    Running it thus—you'll tender me a fool.
OPHELIA
    My lord, he hath importuned me with love
    In honourable fashion.
LORD POLONIUS
    Ay, fashion you may call it; go to, go to.
OPHELIA
    And hath given countenance to his speech, my lord,
    With almost all the holy vows of heaven.
LORD POLONIUS
    Ay, springes to catch woodcocks. I do know,
    When the blood burns, how prodigal the soul
    Lends the tongue vows: these blazes, daughter,
    Giving more light than heat, extinct in both,
    Even in their promise, as it is a-making,
    You must not take for fire. From this time
    Be somewhat scanter of your maiden presence;
    Set your entreatments at a higher rate
    Than a command to parley. For Lord Hamlet,
    Believe so much in him, that he is young
    And with a larger tether may he walk
    Than may be given you: in few, Ophelia,
    Do not believe his vows; for they are brokers,
    Not of that dye which their investments show,
    But mere implorators of unholy suits,
    Breathing like sanctified and pious bawds,
    The better to beguile. This is for all:
    I would not, in plain terms, from this time forth,
    Have you so slander any moment leisure,

As to give words or talk with the Lord Hamlet.
Look to't, I charge you: come your ways.
OPHELIA
I shall obey, my lord.

Exeunt

SCENE IV.
THE PLATFORM.

Enter HAMLET, HORATIO, *and* MARCELLUS
HAMLET
The air bites shrewdly; it is very cold.
HORATIO
It is a nipping and an eager air.
HAMLET
What hour now?
HORATIO
I think it lacks of twelve.
HAMLET
No, it is struck.
HORATIO
Indeed? I heard it not: then it draws near the season
Wherein the spirit held his wont to walk.
A flourish of trumpets, and ordnance shot off, within
What does this mean, my lord?
HAMLET
The king doth wake to-night and takes his rouse,
Keeps wassail, and the swaggering up-spring reels;
And, as he drains his draughts of Rhenish down,
The kettle-drum and trumpet thus bray out
The triumph of his pledge.
HORATIO
Is it a custom?
HAMLET
Ay, marry, is't:
But to my mind, though I am native here

And to the manner born, it is a custom
More honour'd in the breach than the observance.
This heavy-headed revel east and west
Makes us traduced and tax'd of other nations:
They clepe us drunkards, and with swinish phrase
Soil our addition; and indeed it takes
From our achievements, though perform'd at height,
The pith and marrow of our attribute.
So, oft it chances in particular men,
That for some vicious mole of nature in them,
As, in their birth—wherein they are not guilty,
Since nature cannot choose his origin—
By the o'ergrowth of some complexion,
Oft breaking down the pales and forts of reason,
Or by some habit that too much o'er-leavens
The form of plausive manners, that these men,
Carrying, I say, the stamp of one defect,
Being nature's livery, or fortune's star,
Their virtues else be they as pure as grace,
As infinite as man may undergo—
Shall in the general censure take corruption
From that particular fault: the dram of eale
Doth all the noble substance of a doubt
To his own scandal.

HORATIO

Look, my lord, it comes!

Enter Ghost

HAMLET

Angels and ministers of grace defend us!
Be thou a spirit of health or goblin damn'd,
Bring with thee airs from heaven or blasts from hell,
Be thy intents wicked or charitable,
Thou comest in such a questionable shape
That I will speak to thee: I'll call thee Hamlet,
King, father, royal Dane: O, answer me!
Let me not burst in ignorance; but tell
Why thy canonized bones, hearsed in death,

Have burst their cerements; why the sepulchre,
Wherein we saw thee quietly inurn'd,
Hath oped his ponderous and marble jaws,
To cast thee up again. What may this mean,
That thou, dead corse, again in complete steel
Revisit'st thus the glimpses of the moon,
Making night hideous; and we fools of nature
So horridly to shake our disposition
With thoughts beyond the reaches of our souls?
Say, why is this? wherefore? what should we do?
                    Ghost beckons HAMLET

HORATIO
    It beckons you to go away with it,
    As if it some impartment did desire
    To you alone.
MARCELLUS
    Look, with what courteous action
    It waves you to a more removed ground:
    But do not go with it.
HORATIO
    No, by no means.
HAMLET
    It will not speak; then I will follow it.
HORATIO
    Do not, my lord.
HAMLET
    Why, what should be the fear?
    I do not set my life in a pin's fee;
    And for my soul, what can it do to that,
    Being a thing immortal as itself?
    It waves me forth again: I'll follow it.
HORATIO
    What if it tempt you toward the flood, my lord,
    Or to the dreadful summit of the cliff
    That beetles o'er his base into the sea,
    And there assume some other horrible form,
    Which might deprive your sovereignty of reason

And draw you into madness? think of it:
The very place puts toys of desperation,
Without more motive, into every brain
That looks so many fathoms to the sea
And hears it roar beneath.

HAMLET

It waves me still.
Go on; I'll follow thee.

MARCELLUS

You shall not go, my lord.

HAMLET

Hold off your hands.

HORATIO

Be ruled; you shall not go.

HAMLET

My fate cries out,
And makes each petty artery in this body
As hardy as the Nemean lion's nerve.
Still am I call'd. Unhand me, gentlemen.
By heaven, I'll make a ghost of him that lets me!
I say, away! Go on; I'll follow thee.

Exeunt Ghost and HAMLET

HORATIO

He waxes desperate with imagination.

MARCELLUS

Let's follow; 'tis not fit thus to obey him.

HORATIO

Have after. To what issue will this come?

MARCELLUS

Something is rotten in the state of Denmark.

HORATIO

Heaven will direct it.

MARCELLUS

Nay, let's follow him.

Exeunt

SCENE V.
ANOTHER PART OF THE PLATFORM.

Enter Ghost and HAMLET

HAMLET

Where wilt thou lead me? speak; I'll go no further.

GHOST

Mark me.

HAMLET

I will.

GHOST

My hour is almost come,
When I to sulphurous and tormenting flames
Must render up myself.

HAMLET

Alas, poor ghost!

GHOST

Pity me not, but lend thy serious hearing
To what I shall unfold.

HAMLET

Speak; I am bound to hear.

GHOST

So art thou to revenge, when thou shalt hear.

HAMLET

What?

GHOST

I am thy father's spirit,
Doom'd for a certain term to walk the night,
And for the day confined to fast in fires,
Till the foul crimes done in my days of nature
Are burnt and purged away. But that I am forbid
To tell the secrets of my prison-house,
I could a tale unfold whose lightest word
Would harrow up thy soul, freeze thy young blood,
Make thy two eyes, like stars, start from their spheres,
Thy knotted and combined locks to part
And each particular hair to stand on end,

Like quills upon the fretful porpentine:
But this eternal blazon must not be
To ears of flesh and blood. List, list, O, list!
If thou didst ever thy dear father love—

HAMLET

O God!

GHOST

Revenge his foul and most unnatural murder.

HAMLET

Murder!

GHOST

Murder most foul, as in the best it is;
But this most foul, strange and unnatural.

HAMLET

Haste me to know't, that I, with wings as swift
As meditation or the thoughts of love,
May sweep to my revenge.

GHOST

I find thee apt;
And duller shouldst thou be than the fat weed
That roots itself in ease on Lethe wharf,
Wouldst thou not stir in this. Now, Hamlet, hear:
'Tis given out that, sleeping in my orchard,
A serpent stung me; so the whole ear of Denmark
Is by a forged process of my death
Rankly abused: but know, thou noble youth,
The serpent that did sting thy father's life
Now wears his crown.

HAMLET

O my prophetic soul! My uncle!

GHOST

Ay, that incestuous, that adulterate beast,
With witchcraft of his wit, with traitorous gifts—
O wicked wit and gifts, that have the power
So to seduce!—won to his shameful lust
The will of my most seeming-virtuous queen:
O Hamlet, what a falling-off was there!

From me, whose love was of that dignity
That it went hand in hand even with the vow
I made to her in marriage, and to decline
Upon a wretch whose natural gifts were poor
To those of mine!
But virtue, as it never will be moved,
Though lewdness court it in a shape of heaven,
So lust, though to a radiant angel link'd,
Will sate itself in a celestial bed,
And prey on garbage.
But, soft! methinks I scent the morning air;
Brief let me be. Sleeping within my orchard,
My custom always of the afternoon,
Upon my secure hour thy uncle stole,
With juice of cursed hebenon in a vial,
And in the porches of my ears did pour
The leperous distilment; whose effect
Holds such an enmity with blood of man
That swift as quicksilver it courses through
The natural gates and alleys of the body,
And with a sudden vigour doth posset
And curd, like eager droppings into milk,
The thin and wholesome blood: so did it mine;
And a most instant tetter bark'd about,
Most lazar-like, with vile and loathsome crust,
All my smooth body.
Thus was I, sleeping, by a brother's hand
Of life, of crown, of queen, at once dispatch'd:
Cut off even in the blossoms of my sin,
Unhousel'd, disappointed, unanel'd,
No reckoning made, but sent to my account
With all my imperfections on my head:
O, horrible! O, horrible! most horrible!
If thou hast nature in thee, bear it not;
Let not the royal bed of Denmark be
A couch for luxury and damned incest.
But, howsoever thou pursuest this act,

Taint not thy mind, nor let thy soul contrive
Against thy mother aught: leave her to heaven
And to those thorns that in her bosom lodge,
To prick and sting her. Fare thee well at once!
The glow-worm shows the matin to be near,
And 'gins to pale his uneffectual fire:
Adieu, adieu! Hamlet, remember me.

Exit

HAMLET
O all you host of heaven! O earth! what else?
And shall I couple hell? O, fie! Hold, hold, my heart;
And you, my sinews, grow not instant old,
But bear me stiffly up. Remember thee!
Ay, thou poor ghost, while memory holds a seat
In this distracted globe. Remember thee!
Yea, from the table of my memory
I'll wipe away all trivial fond records,
All saws of books, all forms, all pressures past,
That youth and observation copied there;
And thy commandment all alone shall live
Within the book and volume of my brain,
Unmix'd with baser matter: yes, by heaven!
O most pernicious woman!
O villain, villain, smiling, damned villain!
My tables, meet it is I set it down,
That one may smile, and smile, and be a villain;
At least I'm sure it may be so in Denmark:
Writing
So, uncle, there you are. Now to my word;
It is 'Adieu, adieu! remember me.'
I have sworn 't.

MARCELLUS HORATIO
[*Within*] My lord, my lord—
MARCELLUS
[*Within*] Lord Hamlet—
HORATIO
[*Within*] Heaven secure him!

HAMLET
    So be it!
HORATIO
    [*Within*] Hillo, ho, ho, my lord!
HAMLET
    Hillo, ho, ho, boy! come, bird, come.

                    Enter HORATIO *and* MARCELLUS

MARCELLUS
    How is't, my noble lord?
HORATIO
    What news, my lord?
HAMLET
    O, wonderful!
HORATIO
    Good my lord, tell it.
HAMLET
    No; you'll reveal it.
HORATIO
    Not I, my lord, by heaven.
MARCELLUS
    Nor I, my lord.
HAMLET
    How say you, then; would heart of man once think it?
    But you'll be secret?
HORATIO MARCELLUS
    Ay, by heaven, my lord.
HAMLET
    There's ne'er a villain dwelling in all Denmark
    But he's an arrant knave.
HORATIO
    There needs no ghost, my lord, come from the grave
    To tell us this.
HAMLET
    Why, right; you are i' the right;
    And so, without more circumstance at all,
    I hold it fit that we shake hands and part:
    You, as your business and desire shall point you;

For every man has business and desire,
Such as it is; and for mine own poor part,
Look you, I'll go pray.

HORATIO

These are but wild and whirling words, my lord.

HAMLET

I'm sorry they offend you, heartily;
Yes, faith heartily.

HORATIO

There's no offence, my lord.

HAMLET

Yes, by Saint Patrick, but there is, Horatio,
And much offence too. Touching this vision here,
It is an honest ghost, that let me tell you:
For your desire to know what is between us,
O'ermaster 't as you may. And now, good friends,
As you are friends, scholars and soldiers,
Give me one poor request.

HORATIO

What is't, my lord? we will.

HAMLET

Never make known what you have seen to-night.

HORATIO MARCELLUS

My lord, we will not.

HAMLET

Nay, but swear't.

HORATIO

In faith,
My lord, not I.

MARCELLUS

Nor I, my lord, in faith.

HAMLET

Upon my sword.

MARCELLUS

We have sworn, my lord, already.

HAMLET

Indeed, upon my sword, indeed.

GHOST
    [*Beneath*] Swear.
HAMLET
    Ah, ha, boy! say'st thou so?
    art thou there, truepenny?
    Come on—you hear this fellow in the cellarage—
    Consent to swear.
HORATIO
    Propose the oath, my lord.
HAMLET
    Never to speak of this that you have seen,
    Swear by my sword.
GHOST
    [*Beneath*] Swear.
HAMLET
    Hic et ubique? Then we'll shift our ground.
    Come hither, gentlemen,
    And lay your hands again upon my sword:
    Never to speak of this that you have heard,
    Swear by my sword.
GHOST
    [*Beneath*] Swear.
HAMLET
    Well said, old mole! canst work i' the earth so fast?
    A worthy pioner! Once more remove, good friends.
HORATIO
    O day and night, but this is wondrous strange!
HAMLET
    And therefore as a stranger give it welcome.
    There are more things in heaven and earth, Horatio,
    Than are dreamt of in your philosophy. But come;
    Here, as before, never, so help you mercy,
    How strange or odd soe'er I bear myself,
    As I perchance hereafter shall think meet
    To put an antic disposition on,
    That you, at such times seeing me, never shall,
    With arms encumber'd thus, or this headshake,

Or by pronouncing of some doubtful phrase,
As 'Well, well, we know,' or 'We could, an if we would,'
Or 'If we list to speak,' or 'There be, an if they might,'
Or such ambiguous giving out, to note
That you know aught of me: this not to do,
So grace and mercy at your most need help you, Swear.

GHOST

[*Beneath*] Swear.

HAMLET

Rest, rest, perturbed spirit!
They swear
So, gentlemen,
With all my love I do commend me to you:
And what so poor a man as Hamlet is
May do, to express his love and friending to you,
God willing, shall not lack. Let us go in together;
And still your fingers on your lips, I pray.
The time is out of joint: O cursed spite,
That ever I was born to set it right!
Nay, come, let's go together.

Exeunt

ACT

SCENE I.
A ROOM IN POLONIUS' HOUSE.

Enter POLONIUS *and* REYNALDO

LORD POLONIUS
Give him this money and these notes, Reynaldo.

REYNALDO
I will, my lord.

LORD POLONIUS
You shall do marvellous wisely, good Reynaldo,
Before you visit him, to make inquire
Of his behavior.

REYNALDO
My lord, I did intend it.

LORD POLONIUS
Marry, well said; very well said. Look you, sir,
Inquire me first what Danskers are in Paris;
And how, and who, what means, and where they keep,
What company, at what expense; and finding
By this encompassment and drift of question
That they do know my son, come you more nearer

Than your particular demands will touch it:
Take you, as 'twere, some distant knowledge of him;
As thus, 'I know his father and his friends,
And in part him.' Do you mark this, Reynaldo?

REYNALDO

Ay, very well, my lord.

LORD POLONIUS

'And in part him; but' you may say 'not well:
But, if't be he I mean, he's very wild;
Addicted so and so:' and there put on him
What forgeries you please; marry, none so rank
As may dishonour him; take heed of that;
But, sir, such wanton, wild and usual slips
As are companions noted and most known
To youth and liberty.

REYNALDO

As gaming, my lord.

LORD POLONIUS

Ay, or drinking, fencing, swearing, quarrelling,
Drabbing: you may go so far.

REYNALDO

My lord, that would dishonour him.

LORD POLONIUS

Faith, no; as you may season it in the charge
You must not put another scandal on him,
That he is open to incontinency;
That's not my meaning:
but breathe his faults so quaintly
That they may seem the taints of liberty,
The flash and outbreak of a fiery mind,
A savageness in unreclaimed blood,
Of general assault.

REYNALDO

But, my good lord—

LORD POLONIUS

Wherefore should you do this?

REYNALDO
     Ay, my lord,
     I would know that.
LORD POLONIUS
     Marry, sir, here's my drift;
     And I believe, it is a fetch of wit:
     You laying these slight sullies on my son,
     As 'twere a thing a little soil'd i' the working, Mark you,
     Your party in converse, him you would sound,
     Having ever seen in the prenominate crimes
     The youth you breathe of guilty, be assured
     He closes with you in this consequence;
     'Good sir,' or so, or 'friend,' or 'gentleman,'
     According to the phrase or the addition
     Of man and country.
REYNALDO
     Very good, my lord.
LORD POLONIUS
     And then, sir, does he this—he does—what was I about to say?
     By the mass, I was about to say something: where did I leave?
REYNALDO
     At 'closes in the consequence,'
     at 'friend or so,' and 'gentleman.'
LORD POLONIUS
     At 'closes in the consequence,' ay, marry;
     He closes thus: 'I know the gentleman;
     I saw him yesterday, or t' other day,
     Or then, or then; with such, or such; and, as you say,
     There was a' gaming; there o'ertook in's rouse;
     There falling out at tennis:' or perchance,
     'I saw him enter such a house of sale,'
     Videlicet, a brothel, or so forth.
     See you now;
     Your bait of falsehood takes this carp of truth:
     And thus do we of wisdom and of reach,
     With windlasses and with assays of bias,

By indirections find directions out:
So by my former lecture and advice,
Shall you my son. You have me, have you not?

REYNALDO
My lord, I have.

LORD POLONIUS
God be wi' you; fare you well.

REYNALDO
Good my lord!

LORD POLONIUS
Observe his inclination in yourself.

REYNALDO
I shall, my lord.

LORD POLONIUS
And let him ply his music.

REYNALDO
Well, my lord.

LORD POLONIUS
Farewell!

Exit REYNALDO

Enter OPHELIA
How now, Ophelia! What's the matter?

OPHELIA
O, my lord, my lord, I have been so affrighted!

LORD POLONIUS
With what, i' the name of God?

OPHELIA
My lord, as I was sewing in my closet,
Lord Hamlet, with his doublet all unbraced;
No hat upon his head; his stockings foul'd,
Ungarter'd, and down-gyved to his ancle;
Pale as his shirt; his knees knocking each other;
And with a look so piteous in purport
As if he had been loosed out of hell
To speak of horrors—he comes before me.

LORD POLONIUS
Mad for thy love?

OPHELIA

    My lord, I do not know;
    But truly, I do fear it.

LORD POLONIUS

    What said he?

OPHELIA

    He took me by the wrist and held me hard;
    Then goes he to the length of all his arm;
    And, with his other hand thus o'er his brow,
    He falls to such perusal of my face
    As he would draw it. Long stay'd he so;
    At last, a little shaking of mine arm
    And thrice his head thus waving up and down,
    He raised a sigh so piteous and profound
    As it did seem to shatter all his bulk
    And end his being: that done, he lets me go:
    And, with his head over his shoulder turn'd,
    He seem'd to find his way without his eyes;
    For out o' doors he went without their helps,
    And, to the last, bended their light on me.

LORD POLONIUS

    Come, go with me: I will go seek the king.
    This is the very ecstasy of love,
    Whose violent property fordoes itself
    And leads the will to desperate undertakings
    As oft as any passion under heaven
    That does afflict our natures. I am sorry.
    What, have you given him any hard words of late?

OPHELIA

    No, my good lord, but, as you did command,
    I did repel his fetters and denied
    His access to me.

LORD POLONIUS

    That hath made him mad.
    I am sorry that with better heed and judgment
    I had not quoted him: I fear'd he did but trifle,
    And meant to wreck thee; but, beshrew my jealousy!

By heaven, it is as proper to our age
To cast beyond ourselves in our opinions
As it is common for the younger sort
To lack discretion. Come, go we to the king:
This must be known; which,
being kept close, might move
More grief to hide than hate to utter love.

Exeunt

SCENE II.
A ROOM IN THE CASTLE.

Enter KING CLAUDIUS, QUEEN GERTRUDE,
ROSENCRANTZ, GUILDENSTERN, *and Attendants*

KING CLAUDIUS

Welcome, dear Rosencrantz and Guildenstern!
Moreover that we much did long to see you,
The need we have to use you did provoke
Our hasty sending. Something have you heard
Of Hamlet's transformation; so call it,
Sith nor the exterior nor the inward man
Resembles that it was. What it should be,
More than his father's death, that thus hath put him
So much from the understanding of himself,
I cannot dream of: I entreat you both,
That, being of so young days brought up with him,
And sith so neighbour'd to his youth and havior,
That you vouchsafe your rest here in our court
Some little time: so by your companies
To draw him on to pleasures, and to gather,
So much as from occasion you may glean,
Whether aught, to us unknown, afflicts him thus,
That, open'd, lies within our remedy.

QUEEN GERTRUDE

Good gentlemen, he hath much talk'd of you;
And sure I am two men there are not living
To whom he more adheres. If it will please you

To show us so much gentry and good will
As to expend your time with us awhile,
For the supply and profit of our hope,
Your visitation shall receive such thanks
As fits a king's remembrance.

ROSENCRANTZ

Both your majesties
Might, by the sovereign power you have of us,
Put your dread pleasures more into command
Than to entreaty.

GUILDENSTERN

But we both obey,
And here give up ourselves, in the full bent
To lay our service freely at your feet,
To be commanded.

KING CLAUDIUS

Thanks, Rosencrantz and gentle Guildenstern.

QUEEN GERTRUDE

Thanks, Guildenstern and gentle Rosencrantz:
And I beseech you instantly to visit
My too much changed son. Go, some of you,
And bring these gentlemen where Hamlet is.

GUILDENSTERN

Heavens make our presence and our practises
Pleasant and helpful to him!

QUEEN GERTRUDE

Ay, amen!

Exeunt ROSENCRANTZ, GUILDENSTERN,
and some Attendants

Enter POLONIUS

LORD POLONIUS

The ambassadors from Norway, my good lord,
Are joyfully return'd.

KING CLAUDIUS

Thou still hast been the father of good news.

LORD POLONIUS

Have I, my lord? I assure my good liege,

I hold my duty, as I hold my soul,
Both to my God and to my gracious king:
And I do think, or else this brain of mine
Hunts not the trail of policy so sure
As it hath used to do, that I have found
The very cause of Hamlet's lunacy.

KING CLAUDIUS

O, speak of that; that do I long to hear.

LORD POLONIUS

Give first admittance to the ambassadors;
My news shall be the fruit to that great feast.

KING CLAUDIUS

Thyself do grace to them, and bring them in.

Exit POLONIUS

He tells me, my dear Gertrude, he hath found
The head and source of all your son's distemper.

QUEEN GERTRUDE

I doubt it is no other but the main;
His father's death, and our o'erhasty marriage.

KING CLAUDIUS

Well, we shall sift him.

Re-enter POLONIUS, *with* VOLTIMAND *and* CORNELIUS

Welcome, my good friends!
Say, Voltimand, what from our brother Norway?

VOLTIMAND

Most fair return of greetings and desires.
Upon our first, he sent out to suppress
His nephew's levies; which to him appear'd
To be a preparation 'gainst the Polack;
But, better look'd into, he truly found
It was against your highness: whereat grieved,
That so his sickness, age and impotence
Was falsely borne in hand, sends out arrests
On Fortinbras; which he, in brief, obeys;
Receives rebuke from Norway, and in fine
Makes vow before his uncle never more
To give the assay of arms against your majesty.

Whereon old Norway, overcome with joy,
Gives him three thousand crowns in annual fee,
And his commission to employ those soldiers,
So levied as before, against the Polack:
With an entreaty, herein further shown,
Giving a paper
That it might please you to give quiet pass
Through your dominions for this enterprise,
On such regards of safety and allowance
As therein are set down.

KING CLAUDIUS
It likes us well;
And at our more consider'd time well read,
Answer, and think upon this business.
Meantime we thank you for your well-took labour:
Go to your rest; at night we'll feast together:
Most welcome home!

Exeunt VOLTIMAND *and* CORNELIUS

LORD POLONIUS
This business is well ended.
My liege, and madam, to expostulate
What majesty should be, what duty is,
Why day is day, night night, and time is time,
Were nothing but to waste night, day and time.
Therefore, since brevity is the soul of wit,
And tediousness the limbs and outward flourishes,
I will be brief: your noble son is mad:
Mad call I it; for, to define true madness,
What is't but to be nothing else but mad?
But let that go.

QUEEN GERTRUDE
More matter, with less art.

LORD POLONIUS
Madam, I swear I use no art at all.
That he is mad, 'tis true: 'tis true 'tis pity;
And pity 'tis 'tis true: a foolish figure;
But farewell it, for I will use no art.

Mad let us grant him, then: and now remains
That we find out the cause of this effect,
Or rather say, the cause of this defect,
For this effect defective comes by cause:
Thus it remains, and the remainder thus. Perpend.
I have a daughter—have while she is mine—
Who, in her duty and obedience, mark,
Hath given me this: now gather, and surmise.
Reads
'To the celestial and my soul's idol, the most beautified
Ophelia,'—
That's an ill phrase, a vile phrase; 'beautified' is a vile phrase: but
you shall hear. Thus:
Reads
'In her excellent white bosom, these, & c.'

QUEEN GERTRUDE
Came this from Hamlet to her?

LORD POLONIUS
Good madam, stay awhile; I will be faithful.
Reads
'Doubt thou the stars are fire;
Doubt that the sun doth move;
Doubt truth to be a liar;
But never doubt I love.
'O dear Ophelia, I am ill at these numbers;
I have not art to reckon my groans: but that
I love thee best, O most best, believe it. Adieu.
'Thine evermore most dear lady, whilst
this machine is to him, HAMLET.'
This, in obedience, hath my daughter shown me,
And more above, hath his solicitings,
As they fell out by time, by means and place,
All given to mine ear.

KING CLAUDIUS
But how hath she
Received his love?

LORD POLONIUS
What do you think of me?
KING CLAUDIUS
As of a man faithful and honourable.
LORD POLONIUS
I would fain prove so. But what might you think,
When I had seen this hot love on the wing—
As I perceived it, I must tell you that,
Before my daughter told me—what might you,
Or my dear majesty your queen here, think,
If I had play'd the desk or table-book,
Or given my heart a winking, mute and dumb,
Or look'd upon this love with idle sight;
What might you think? No, I went round to work,
And my young mistress thus I did bespeak:
'Lord Hamlet is a prince, out of thy star;
This must not be:' and then I precepts gave her,
That she should lock herself from his resort,
Admit no messengers, receive no tokens.
Which done, she took the fruits of my advice;
And he, repulsed—a short tale to make—
Fell into a sadness, then into a fast,
Thence to a watch, thence into a weakness,
Thence to a lightness, and, by this declension,
Into the madness wherein now he raves,
And all we mourn for.
KING CLAUDIUS
Do you think 'tis this?
QUEEN GERTRUDE
It may be, very likely.
LORD POLONIUS
Hath there been such a time—I'd fain know that—
That I have positively said 'Tis so,
When it proved otherwise?
KING CLAUDIUS
Not that I know.

LORD POLONIUS
  [*Pointing to his head and shoulder*]
  Take this from this, if this be otherwise:
  If circumstances lead me, I will find
  Where truth is hid, though it were hid indeed
  Within the centre.
KING CLAUDIUS
  How may we try it further?
LORD POLONIUS
  You know, sometimes he walks four hours together
  Here in the lobby.
QUEEN GERTRUDE
  So he does indeed.
LORD POLONIUS
  At such a time I'll loose my daughter to him:
  Be you and I behind an arras then;
  Mark the encounter: if he love her not
  And be not from his reason fall'n thereon,
  Let me be no assistant for a state,
  But keep a farm and carters.
KING CLAUDIUS
  We will try it.
QUEEN GERTRUDE
  But, look, where sadly the poor wretch comes reading.
LORD POLONIUS
  Away, I do beseech you, both away:
  I'll board him presently.

> *Exeunt* KING CLAUDIUS,
> QUEEN GERTRUDE, *and Attendants*
> *Enter* HAMLET, *reading*

  O, give me leave:
  How does my good Lord Hamlet?
HAMLET
  Well, God-a-mercy.
LORD POLONIUS
  Do you know me, my lord?

HAMLET

Excellent well; you are a fishmonger.

LORD POLONIUS

Not I, my lord.

HAMLET

Then I would you were so honest a man.

LORD POLONIUS

Honest, my lord!

HAMLET

Ay, sir; to be honest, as this world goes, is to be one man picked out of ten thousand.

LORD POLONIUS

That's very true, my lord.

HAMLET

For if the sun breed maggots in a dead dog, being a god kissing carrion,—Have you a daughter?

LORD POLONIUS

I have, my lord.

HAMLET

Let her not walk i' the sun: conception is a blessing: but not as your daughter may conceive. Friend, look to 't.

LORD POLONIUS

[*Aside*] How say you by that? Still harping on my daughter: yet he knew me not at first; he said I was a fishmonger: he is far gone, far gone: and truly in my youth I suffered much extremity for love; very near this. I'll speak to him again. What do you read, my lord?

HAMLET

Words, words, words.

LORD POLONIUS

What is the matter, my lord?

HAMLET

Between who?

LORD POLONIUS

I mean, the matter that you read, my lord.

HAMLET

Slanders, sir: for the satirical rogue says here that old men have grey beards, that their faces are wrinkled, their eyes purging thick amber and plum tree gum and that they have a plentiful lack of wit, together with most weak hams: all which, sir, though I most powerfully and potently believe, yet I hold it not honesty to have it thus set down, for yourself, sir, should be old as I am, if like a crab you could go backward.

LORD POLONIUS

[*Aside*] Though this be madness, yet there is method in 't. Will you walk out of the air, my lord?

HAMLET

Into my grave.

LORD POLONIUS

Indeed, that is out o' the air.

[*Aside*]

How pregnant sometimes his replies are! a happiness that often madness hits on, which reason and sanity could not so prosperously be delivered of. I will leave him, and suddenly contrive the means of meeting between him and my daughter. My honourable lord, I will most humbly take my leave of you.

HAMLET

You cannot, sir, take from me any thing that I will more willingly part withal: except my life, except my life, except my life.

LORD POLONIUS

Fare you well, my lord.

HAMLET

These tedious old fools!

Enter ROSENCRANTZ *and* GUILDENSTERN

LORD POLONIUS

You go to seek the Lord Hamlet; there he is.

ROSENCRANTZ

[*To* POLONIUS] God save you, sir!

Exit POLONIUS

GUILDENSTERN

My honoured lord!

ROSENCRANTZ

My most dear lord!

HAMLET

My excellent good friends! How dost thou, Guildenstern? Ah, Rosencrantz! Good lads, how do ye both?

ROSENCRANTZ

As the indifferent children of the earth.

GUILDENSTERN

Happy, in that we are not over-happy;
On fortune's cap we are not the very button.

HAMLET

Nor the soles of her shoe?

ROSENCRANTZ

Neither, my lord.

HAMLET

Then you live about her waist,
or in the middle of her favours?

GUILDENSTERN

Faith, her privates we.

HAMLET

In the secret parts of fortune? O, most true; she is a strumpet. What's the news?

ROSENCRANTZ

None, my lord, but that the world's grown honest.

HAMLET

Then is doomsday near: but your news is not true. Let me question more in particular: what have you, my good friends, deserved at the hands of fortune, that she sends you to prison hither?

GUILDENSTERN

Prison, my lord!

HAMLET

Denmark's a prison.

ROSENCRANTZ

Then is the world one.

HAMLET

A goodly one; in which there are many confines, wards and dungeons, Denmark being one o' the worst.

ROSENCRANTZ

We think not so, my lord.

HAMLET

Why, then, 'tis none to you; for there is nothing either good or bad, but thinking makes it so: to me it is a prison.

ROSENCRANTZ

Why then, your ambition makes it one; 'tis too narrow for your mind.

HAMLET

O God, I could be bounded in a nut shell and count myself a king of infinite space, were it not that I have bad dreams.

GUILDENSTERN

Which dreams indeed are ambition, for the very substance of the ambitious is merely the shadow of a dream.

HAMLET

A dream itself is but a shadow.

ROSENCRANTZ

Truly, and I hold ambition of so airy and light a quality that it is but a shadow's shadow.

HAMLET

Then are our beggars bodies, and our monarchs and outstretched heroes the beggars' shadows. Shall we to the court? for, by my fay, I cannot reason.

ROSENCRANTZ GUILDENSTERN

We'll wait upon you.

HAMLET

No such matter: I will not sort you with the rest of my servants, for, to speak to you like an honest man, I am most dreadfully attended. But, in the beaten way of friendship, what make you at Elsinore?

ROSENCRANTZ

To visit you, my lord; no other occasion.

HAMLET

Beggar that I am, I am even poor in thanks; but I thank you: and sure, dear friends, my thanks are too dear a halfpenny. Were you not sent for? Is it your own inclining? Is it a free visitation? Come, deal justly with me: come, come; nay, speak.

GUILDENSTERN
　　What should we say, my lord?

HAMLET
　　Why, any thing, but to the purpose. You were sent for; and there
　　is a kind of confession in your looks which your modesties have
　　not craft enough to colour: I know the good king and queen
　　have sent for you.

ROSENCRANTZ
　　To what end, my lord?

HAMLET
　　That you must teach me. But let me conjure you, by the rights
　　of our fellowship, by the consonancy of our youth, by the
　　obligation of our ever-preserved love, and by what more dear a
　　better proposer could charge you withal, be even and direct with
　　me, whether you were sent for, or no?

ROSENCRANTZ
　　[*Aside to* GUILDENSTERN] What say you?

HAMLET
　　[*Aside*] Nay, then, I have an eye of you. If you love me, hold not
　　off.

GUILDENSTERN
　　My lord, we were sent for.

HAMLET
　　I will tell you why; so shall my anticipation prevent your
　　discovery, and your secrecy to the king and queen moult no
　　feather. I have of late—but wherefore I know not—lost all
　　my mirth, forgone all custom of exercises; and indeed it goes
　　so heavily with my disposition that this goodly frame, the
　　earth, seems to me a sterile promontory, this most excellent
　　canopy, the air, look you, this brave o'erhanging firmament,
　　this majestical roof fretted with golden fire, why, it appears no
　　other thing to me than a foul and pestilent congregation of
　　vapours. What a piece of work is a man! how noble in reason!
　　how infinite in faculty! in form and moving how express and
　　admirable! in action how like an angel! in apprehension how
　　like a god! the beauty of the world! the paragon of animals!
　　And yet, to me, what is this quintessence of dust? man delights

not me: no, nor woman neither, though by your smiling you seem to say so.

ROSENCRANTZ

My lord, there was no such stuff in my thoughts.

HAMLET

Why did you laugh then, when I said 'man delights not me'?

ROSENCRANTZ

To think, my lord, if you delight not in man, what lenten entertainment the players shall receive from you: we coted them on the way; and hither are they coming, to offer you service.

HAMLET

He that plays the king shall be welcome; his majesty shall have tribute of me; the adventurous knight shall use his foil and target; the lover shall not sigh gratis; the humourous man shall end his part in peace; the clown shall make those laugh whose lungs are tickled o' the sere; and the lady shall say her mind freely, or the blank verse shall halt for't. What players are they?

ROSENCRANTZ

Even those you were wont to take delight in, the tragedians of the city.

HAMLET

How chances it they travel? their residence, both in reputation and profit, was better both ways.

ROSENCRANTZ

I think their inhibition comes by the means of the late innovation.

HAMLET

Do they hold the same estimation they did when I was in the city? are they so followed?

ROSENCRANTZ

No, indeed, are they not.

HAMLET

How comes it? do they grow rusty?

ROSENCRANTZ

Nay, their endeavour keeps in the wonted pace: but there is, sir, an aery of children, little eyases, that cry out on the top of question, and are most tyrannically clapped for't: these are now

the fashion, and so berattle the common stages—so they call
them—that many wearing rapiers are afraid of goose-quills and
dare scarce come thither.

HAMLET

What, are they children? Who maintains 'em? How are they
escoted? Will they pursue the quality no longer than they can
sing? Will they not say afterwards, if they should grow themselves
to common players—as it is most like, if their means are no
better—their writers do them wrong, to make them exclaim
against their own succession?

ROSENCRANTZ

Faith, there has been much to do on both sides; and the nation
holds it no sin to tarre them to controversy: there was, for a
while, no money bid for argument, unless the poet and the
player went to cuffs in the question.

HAMLET

Is't possible?

GUILDENSTERN

O, there has been much throwing about of brains.

HAMLET

Do the boys carry it away?

ROSENCRANTZ

Ay, that they do, my lord; Hercules and his load too.

HAMLET

It is not very strange; for mine uncle is king of Denmark, and
those that would make mows at him while my father lived, give
twenty, forty, fifty, an hundred ducats a-piece for his picture in
little. 'Sblood, there is something in this more than natural, if
philosophy could find it out.

Flourish of trumpets within

GUILDENSTERN

There are the players.

HAMLET

Gentlemen, you are welcome to Elsinore. Your hands, come
then: the appurtenance of welcome is fashion and ceremony: let
me comply with you in this garb, lest my extent to the players,

which, I tell you, must show fairly outward, should more appear like entertainment than yours. You are welcome: but my uncle-father and aunt-mother are deceived.

GUILDENSTERN

In what, my dear lord?

HAMLET

I am but mad north-north-west: when the wind is southerly I know a hawk from a handsaw.

Enter POLONIUS

LORD POLONIUS

Well be with you, gentlemen!

HAMLET

Hark you, Guildenstern; and you too: at each ear a hearer: that great baby you see there is not yet out of his swaddling-clouts.

ROSENCRANTZ

Happily he's the second time come to them; for they say an old man is twice a child.

HAMLET

I will prophesy he comes to tell me of the players; mark it. You say right, sir: o' Monday morning; 'twas so indeed.

LORD POLONIUS

My lord, I have news to tell you.

HAMLET

My lord, I have news to tell you.
When Roscius was an actor in Rome—

LORD POLONIUS

The actors are come hither, my lord.

HAMLET

Buz, buz!

LORD POLONIUS

Upon mine honour—

HAMLET

Then came each actor on his ass—

LORD POLONIUS

The best actors in the world, either for tragedy, comedy, history, pastoral, pastoral-comical, historical-pastoral, tragical-historical, tragical-comical-historical-pastoral, scene individable, or poem unlimited: Seneca cannot be too heavy, nor Plautus too light. For the law of writ and the liberty, these are the only men.

HAMLET

O Jephthah, judge of Israel, what a treasure hadst thou!

LORD POLONIUS

What a treasure had he, my lord?

HAMLET

Why,
'One fair daughter and no more,
The which he loved passing well.'

LORD POLONIUS

[*Aside*] Still on my daughter.

HAMLET

Am I not i' the right, old Jephthah?

LORD POLONIUS

If you call me Jephthah, my lord, I have a daughter that I love passing well.

HAMLET

Nay, that follows not.

LORD POLONIUS

What follows, then, my lord?

HAMLET

Why, 'As by lot, God wot,' and then, you know, 'It came to pass, as most like it was,'—the first row of the pious chanson will show you more; for look, where my abridgement comes.

Enter four or five Players

You are welcome, masters; welcome, all. I am glad to see thee well. Welcome, good friends. O, my old friend! thy face is valenced since I saw thee last: comest thou to beard me in Denmark? What, my young lady and mistress! By'r lady, your ladyship is nearer to heaven than when I saw you last, by the altitude of a chopine. Pray God, your voice, like a piece of uncurrent gold, be not cracked within the ring. Masters, you are all welcome. We'll e'en to't like French falconers, fly at any thing we see: we'll have a speech straight: come, give us a taste of your quality; come, a passionate speech.

FIRST PLAYER

What speech, my lord?

HAMLET

I heard thee speak me a speech once, but it was never acted; or, if it was, not above once; for the play, I remember, pleased not the million; 'twas caviare to the general: but it was—as I received it, and others, whose judgments in such matters cried in the top of mine—an excellent play, well digested in the scenes, set down with as much modesty as cunning. I remember, one said there were no sallets in the lines to make the matter savoury, nor no matter in the phrase that might indict the author of affectation; but called it an honest method, as wholesome as sweet, and by very much more handsome than fine. One speech in it I chiefly loved: 'twas Aeneas' tale to Dido; and thereabout of it especially, where he speaks of Priam's slaughter: if it live in your memory, begin at this line: let me see, let me see—'The rugged Pyrrhus, like the Hyrcanian beast,'— it is not so:—it begins with Pyrrhus:—'The rugged Pyrrhus, he whose sable arms, Black as his purpose, did the night resemble When he lay couched in the ominous horse, Hath now this dread and black complexion smear'd With heraldry more dismal; head to foot Now is he total gules; horridly trick'd With blood of fathers, mothers, daughters, sons, Baked and impasted with the parching streets, That lend a tyrannous and damned light To their lord's murder: roasted in wrath and fire, And thus o'er-sized with coagulate gore, With eyes like carbuncles, the hellish Pyrrhus Old grandsire Priam seeks.' So, proceed you.

LORD POLONIUS

Fore God, my lord, well spoken, with good accent and good discretion.

FIRST PLAYER

'Anon he finds him
Striking too short at Greeks; his antique sword,
Rebellious to his arm, lies where it falls,
Repugnant to command: unequal match'd,
Pyrrhus at Priam drives; in rage strikes wide;
But with the whiff and wind of his fell sword

The unnerved father falls. Then senseless Ilium,
Seeming to feel this blow, with flaming top
Stoops to his base, and with a hideous crash
Takes prisoner Pyrrhus' ear: for, lo! his sword,
Which was declining on the milky head
Of reverend Priam, seem'd i' the air to stick:
So, as a painted tyrant, Pyrrhus stood,
And like a neutral to his will and matter,
Did nothing.
But, as we often see, against some storm,
A silence in the heavens, the rack stand still,
The bold winds speechless and the orb below
As hush as death, anon the dreadful thunder
Doth rend the region, so, after Pyrrhus' pause,
Aroused vengeance sets him new a-work;
And never did the Cyclops' hammers fall
On Mars's armour forged for proof eterne
With less remorse than Pyrrhus' bleeding sword
Now falls on Priam.
Out, out, thou strumpet, Fortune! All you gods,
In general synod take away her power;
Break all the spokes and fellies from her wheel,
And bowl the round nave down the hill of heaven,
As low as to the fiends!'

LORD POLONIUS
    This is too long.

HAMLET
    It shall to the barber's, with your beard. Prithee, say on: he's for
    a jig or a tale of bawdry, or he sleeps: say on: come to Hecuba.

FIRST PLAYER
    'But who, O, who had seen the mobled queen—'

HAMLET
    'The mobled queen?'

LORD POLONIUS
    That's good; 'mobled queen' is good.

FIRST PLAYER
    'Run barefoot up and down, threatening the flames

With bisson rheum; a clout upon that head
Where late the diadem stood, and for a robe,
About her lank and all o'er-teemed loins,
A blanket, in the alarm of fear caught up;
Who this had seen, with tongue in venom steep'd,
'Gainst Fortune's state would treason have pronounced:
But if the gods themselves did see her then
When she saw Pyrrhus make malicious sport
In mincing with his sword her husband's limbs,
The instant burst of clamour that she made,
Unless things mortal move them not at all,
Would have made milch the burning eyes of heaven,
And passion in the gods.'

LORD POLONIUS

Look, whether he has not turned his colour and has tears in's
eyes. Pray you, no more.

HAMLET

'Tis well: I'll have thee speak out the rest soon. Good my lord,
will you see the players well bestowed? Do you hear, let them be
well used; for they are the abstract and brief chronicles of the
time: after your death you were better have a bad epitaph than
their ill report while you live.

LORD POLONIUS

My lord, I will use them according to their desert.

HAMLET

God's bodykins, man, much better: use every man after his
desert, and who should 'scape whipping? Use them after your
own honour and dignity: the less they deserve, the more merit is
in your bounty. Take them in.

LORD POLONIUS

Come, sirs.

HAMLET

Follow him, friends: we'll hear a play to-morrow.

Exit POLONIUS *with*
all the Players but the First

Dost thou hear me, old friend; can you play the Murder of
Gonzago?

FIRST PLAYER
    Ay, my lord.
HAMLET
    We'll ha't to-morrow night. You could, for a need, study a speech
    of some dozen or sixteen lines, which I would set down and
    insert in't, could you not?
FIRST PLAYER
    Ay, my lord.
HAMLET
    Very well. Follow that lord; and look you mock him not.

                                        Exit First Player
    My good friends, I'll leave you till night: you are welcome to
    Elsinore.
ROSENCRANTZ
    Good, my lord!
HAMLET
    Ay, so, God be wi' ye;

                                        Exeunt ROSENCRANTZ
                                        and GUILDENSTERN

    Now I am alone.
    O, what a rogue and peasant slave am I!
    Is it not monstrous that this player here,
    But in a fiction, in a dream of passion,
    Could force his soul so to his own conceit
    That from her working all his visage wann'd,
    Tears in his eyes, distraction in's aspect,
    A broken voice, and his whole function suiting
    With forms to his conceit? and all for nothing!
    For Hecuba!
    What's Hecuba to him, or he to Hecuba,
    That he should weep for her? What would he do,
    Had he the motive and the cue for passion
    That I have? He would drown the stage with tears
    And cleave the general ear with horrid speech,
    Make mad the guilty and appal the free,
    Confound the ignorant, and amaze indeed
    The very faculties of eyes and ears. Yet I,

A dull and muddy-mettled rascal, peak,
Like John-a-dreams, unpregnant of my cause,
And can say nothing; no, not for a king,
Upon whose property and most dear life
A damn'd defeat was made. Am I a coward?
Who calls me villain? breaks my pate across?
Plucks off my beard, and blows it in my face?
Tweaks me by the nose? gives me the lie i' the throat,
As deep as to the lungs? who does me this?
Ha!
'Swounds, I should take it: for it cannot be
But I am pigeon-liver'd and lack gall
To make oppression bitter, or ere this
I should have fatted all the region kites
With this slave's offal: bloody, bawdy villain!
Remorseless, treacherous, lecherous, kindless villain!
O, vengeance!
Why, what an ass am I! This is most brave,
That I, the son of a dear father murder'd,
Prompted to my revenge by heaven and hell,
Must, like a whore, unpack my heart with words,
And fall a-cursing, like a very drab,
A scullion!
Fie upon't! foh! About, my brain! I have heard
That guilty creatures sitting at a play
Have by the very cunning of the scene
Been struck so to the soul that presently
They have proclaim'd their malefactions;
For murder, though it have no tongue, will speak
With most miraculous organ. I'll have these players
Play something like the murder of my father
Before mine uncle: I'll observe his looks;
I'll tent him to the quick: if he but blench,
I know my course. The spirit that I have seen
May be the devil: and the devil hath power
To assume a pleasing shape; yea, and perhaps
Out of my weakness and my melancholy,

As he is very potent with such spirits,
Abuses me to damn me: I'll have grounds
More relative than this: the play 's the thing
Wherein I'll catch the conscience of the king.

Exit

ACT

III

SCENE I.
A ROOM IN THE CASTLE.

Enter KING CLAUDIUS,
QUEEN GERTRUDE, POLONIUS,
OPHELIA, ROSENCRANTZ,
and GUILDENSTERN

KING CLAUDIUS

    And can you, by no drift of circumstance,
    Get from him why he puts on this confusion,
    Grating so harshly all his days of quiet
    With turbulent and dangerous lunacy?

ROSENCRANTZ

    He does confess he feels himself distracted;
    But from what cause he will by no means speak.

GUILDENSTERN

    Nor do we find him forward to be sounded,
    But, with a crafty madness, keeps aloof,
    When we would bring him on to some confession
    Of his true state.

QUEEN GERTRUDE

    Did he receive you well?

ROSENCRANTZ
  Most like a gentleman.
GUILDENSTERN
  But with much forcing of his disposition.
ROSENCRANTZ
  Niggard of question; but, of our demands,
  Most free in his reply.
QUEEN GERTRUDE
  Did you assay him?
  To any pastime?
ROSENCRANTZ
  Madam, it so fell out, that certain players
  We o'er-raught on the way: of these we told him;
  And there did seem in him a kind of joy
  To hear of it: they are about the court,
  And, as I think, they have already order
  This night to play before him.
LORD POLONIUS
  'Tis most true:
  And he beseech'd me to entreat your majesties
  To hear and see the matter.
KING CLAUDIUS
  With all my heart; and it doth much content me
  To hear him so inclined.
  Good gentlemen, give him a further edge,
  And drive his purpose on to these delights.
ROSENCRANTZ
  We shall, my lord.

Exeunt ROSENCRANTZ
and GUILDENSTERN

KING CLAUDIUS
  Sweet Gertrude, leave us too;
  For we have closely sent for Hamlet hither,
  That he, as 'twere by accident, may here
  Affront Ophelia:
  Her father and myself, lawful espials,
  Will so bestow ourselves that, seeing, unseen,

We may of their encounter frankly judge,
And gather by him, as he is behaved,
If 't be the affliction of his love or no
That thus he suffers for.

QUEEN GERTRUDE

I shall obey you.
And for your part, Ophelia, I do wish
That your good beauties be the happy cause
Of Hamlet's wildness: so shall I hope your virtues
Will bring him to his wonted way again,
To both your honours.

OPHELIA

Madam, I wish it may.

Exit QUEEN GERTRUDE

LORD POLONIUS

Ophelia, walk you here. Gracious, so please you,
We will bestow ourselves.

To OPHELIA

Read on this book;
That show of such an exercise may colour
Your loneliness. We are oft to blame in this—
'Tis too much proved—that with devotion's visage
And pious action we do sugar o'er
The devil himself.

KING CLAUDIUS

[*Aside*] O, 'tis too true!
How smart a lash that speech doth give my conscience!
The harlot's cheek, beautied with plastering art,
Is not more ugly to the thing that helps it
Than is my deed to my most painted word:
O heavy burthen!

LORD POLONIUS

I hear him coming: let's withdraw, my lord.

Exeunt KING CLAUDIUS
and POLONIUS

Enter HAMLET

HAMLET
    To be, or not to be: that is the question:
    Whether 'tis nobler in the mind to suffer
    The slings and arrows of outrageous fortune,
    Or to take arms against a sea of troubles,
    And by opposing end them? To die: to sleep;
    No more; and by a sleep to say we end
    The heart-ache and the thousand natural shocks
    That flesh is heir to, 'tis a consummation
    Devoutly to be wish'd. To die, to sleep;
    To sleep: perchance to dream: ay, there's the rub;
    For in that sleep of death what dreams may come
    When we have shuffled off this mortal coil,
    Must give us pause: there's the respect
    That makes calamity of so long life;
    For who would bear the whips and scorns of time,
    The oppressor's wrong, the proud man's contumely,
    The pangs of despised love, the law's delay,
    The insolence of office and the spurns
    That patient merit of the unworthy takes,
    When he himself might his quietus make
    With a bare bodkin? who would fardels bear,
    To grunt and sweat under a weary life,
    But that the dread of something after death,
    The undiscover'd country from whose bourn
    No traveller returns, puzzles the will
    And makes us rather bear those ills we have
    Than fly to others that we know not of?
    Thus conscience does make cowards of us all;
    And thus the native hue of resolution
    Is sicklied o'er with the pale cast of thought,
    And enterprises of great pith and moment
    With this regard their currents turn awry,
    And lose the name of action. Soft you now!
    The fair Ophelia! Nymph, in thy orisons
    Be all my sins remember'd.

OPHELIA

Good my lord,

How does your honour for this many a day?

HAMLET

I humbly thank you; well, well, well.

OPHELIA

My lord, I have remembrances of yours,

That I have longed long to re-deliver;

I pray you, now receive them.

HAMLET

No, not I;

I never gave you aught.

OPHELIA

My honour'd lord, you know right well you did;

And, with them, words of so sweet breath composed

As made the things more rich: their perfume lost,

Take these again; for to the noble mind

Rich gifts wax poor when givers prove unkind.

There, my lord.

HAMLET

Ha, ha! are you honest?

OPHELIA

My lord?

HAMLET

Are you fair?

OPHELIA

What means your lordship?

HAMLET

That if you be honest and fair, your honesty should admit no discourse to your beauty.

OPHELIA

Could beauty, my lord, have better commerce than with honesty?

HAMLET

Ay, truly; for the power of beauty will sooner transform honesty from what it is to a bawd than the force of honesty can translate beauty into his likeness: this was sometime a paradox, but now the time gives it proof. I did love you once.

OPHELIA

Indeed, my lord, you made me believe so.

HAMLET

You should not have believed me; for virtue cannot so inoculate our old stock but we shall relish of it: I loved you not.

OPHELIA

I was the more deceived.

HAMLET

Get thee to a nunnery: why wouldst thou be a breeder of sinners? I am myself indifferent honest; but yet I could accuse me of such things that it were better my mother had not borne me: I am very proud, revengeful, ambitious, with more offences at my beck than I have thoughts to put them in, imagination to give them shape, or time to act them in. What should such fellows as I do crawling between earth and heaven? We are arrant knaves, all; believe none of us. Go thy ways to a nunnery. Where's your father?

OPHELIA

At home, my lord.

HAMLET

Let the doors be shut upon him, that he may play the fool no where but in's own house. Farewell.

OPHELIA

O, help him, you sweet heavens!

HAMLET

If thou dost marry, I'll give thee this plague for thy dowry: be thou as chaste as ice, as pure as snow, thou shalt not escape calumny. Get thee to a nunnery, go: farewell. Or, if thou wilt needs marry, marry a fool; for wise men know well enough what monsters you make of them. To a nunnery, go, and quickly too. Farewell.

OPHELIA

O heavenly powers, restore him!

HAMLET

I have heard of your paintings too, well enough; God has given you one face, and you make yourselves another: you jig, you amble, and you lisp, and nick name God's creatures, and make

your wantonness your ignorance. Go to, I'll no more on't; it hath
made me mad. I say, we will have no more marriages: those that
are married already, all but one, shall live; the rest shall keep as
they are. To a nunnery, go.

Exit

OPHELIA
    O, what a noble mind is here o'erthrown!
    The courtier's, soldier's, scholar's, eye, tongue, sword;
    The expectancy and rose of the fair state,
    The glass of fashion and the mould of form,
    The observed of all observers, quite, quite down!
    And I, of ladies most deject and wretched,
    That suck'd the honey of his music vows,
    Now see that noble and most sovereign reason,
    Like sweet bells jangled, out of tune and harsh;
    That unmatch'd form and feature of blown youth
    Blasted with ecstasy: O, woe is me,
    To have seen what I have seen, see what I see!

Re-enter KING CLAUDIUS *and* POLONIUS

KING CLAUDIUS
    Love! his affections do not that way tend;
    Nor what he spake, though it lack'd form a little,
    Was not like madness. There's something in his soul,
    O'er which his melancholy sits on brood;
    And I do doubt the hatch and the disclose
    Will be some danger: which for to prevent,
    I have in quick determination
    Thus set it down: he shall with speed to England,
    For the demand of our neglected tribute
    Haply the seas and countries different
    With variable objects shall expel
    This something-settled matter in his heart,
    Whereon his brains still beating puts him thus
    From fashion of himself. What think you on't?

LORD POLONIUS
    It shall do well: but yet do I believe
    The origin and commencement of his grief

Sprung from neglected love. How now, Ophelia!
You need not tell us what Lord Hamlet said;
We heard it all. My lord, do as you please;
But, if you hold it fit, after the play
Let his queen mother all alone entreat him
To show his grief: let her be round with him;
And I'll be placed, so please you, in the ear
Of all their conference. If she find him not,
To England send him, or confine him where
Your wisdom best shall think.

KING CLAUDIUS

It shall be so:
Madness in great ones must not unwatch'd go.

Exeunt

SCENE II.
A HALL IN THE CASTLE.

Enter HAMLET *and Players*

HAMLET

Speak the speech, I pray you, as I pronounced it to you, trippingly on the tongue: but if you mouth it, as many of your players do, I had as lief the town-crier spoke my lines. Nor do not saw the air too much with your hand, thus, but use all gently; for in the very torrent, tempest, and, as I may say, the whirlwind of passion, you must acquire and beget a temperance that may give it smoothness. O, it offends me to the soul to hear a robustious periwig-pated fellow tear a passion to tatters, to very rags, to split the ears of the groundlings, who for the most part are capable of nothing but inexplicable dumbshows and noise: I would have such a fellow whipped for o'erdoing Termagant; it out-herods Herod: pray you, avoid it.

FIRST PLAYER

I warrant your honour.

HAMLET

Be not too tame neither, but let your own discretion be your tutor: suit the action to the word, the word to the action; with this special o'erstep not the modesty of nature: for any thing so overdone is from the purpose of playing, whose end, both at the first and now, was and is, to hold, as 'twere, the mirror up to nature; to show virtue her own feature, scorn her own image, and the very age and body of the time his form and pressure. Now this overdone, or come tardy off, though it make the unskilful laugh, cannot but make the judicious grieve; the censure of the which one must in your allowance o'erweigh a whole theatre of others. O, there be players that I have seen play, and heard others praise, and that highly, not to speak it profanely, that, neither having the accent of Christians nor the gait of Christian, pagan, nor man, have so strutted and bellowed that I have thought some of nature's journeymen had made men and not made them well, they imitated humanity so abominably.

FIRST PLAYER

I hope we have reformed that indifferently with us, sir.

HAMLET

O, reform it altogether. And let those that play your clowns speak no more than is set down for them; for there be of them that will themselves laugh, to set on some quantity of barren spectators to laugh too; though, in the mean time, some necessary question of the play be then to be considered: that's villanous, and shows a most pitiful ambition in the fool that uses it. Go, make you ready.

Exeunt Players

Enter POLONIUS,
ROSENCRANTZ, *and* GUILDENSTERN

How now, my lord! I will the king hear this piece of work?

LORD POLONIUS

And the queen too, and that presently.

HAMLET

Bid the players make haste.

Exit POLONIUS

Will you two help to hasten them?

ROSENCRANTZ GUILDENSTERN

We will, my lord.

Exeunt ROSENCRANTZ *and* GUILDENSTERN

HAMLET
 What ho! Horatio!

Enter HORATIO

HORATIO
 Here, sweet lord, at your service.
HAMLET
 Horatio, thou art e'en as just a man
 As e'er my conversation coped withal.
HORATIO
 O, my dear lord—
HAMLET
 Nay, do not think I flatter;
 For what advancement may I hope from thee
 That no revenue hast but thy good spirits,
 To feed and clothe thee? Why should the poor be flatter'd?
 No, let the candied tongue lick absurd pomp,
 And crook the pregnant hinges of the knee
 Where thrift may follow fawning. Dost thou hear?
 Since my dear soul was mistress of her choice
 And could of men distinguish, her election
 Hath seal'd thee for herself; for thou hast been
 As one, in suffering all, that suffers nothing,
 A man that fortune's buffets and rewards
 Hast ta'en with equal thanks: and blest are those
 Whose blood and judgment are so well commingled,
 That they are not a pipe for fortune's finger
 To sound what stop she please. Give me that man
 That is not passion's slave, and I will wear him
 In my heart's core, ay, in my heart of heart,
 As I do thee. Something too much of this.
 There is a play to-night before the king;
 One scene of it comes near the circumstance
 Which I have told thee of my father's death:
 I prithee, when thou seest that act afoot,
 Even with the very comment of thy soul
 Observe mine uncle: if his occulted guilt
 Do not itself unkennel in one speech,

It is a damned ghost that we have seen,
And my imaginations are as foul
As Vulcan's stithy. Give him heedful note;
For I mine eyes will rivet to his face,
And after we will both our judgments join
In censure of his seeming.

HORATIO

Well, my lord:
If he steal aught the whilst this play is playing,
And 'scape detecting, I will pay the theft.

HAMLET

They are coming to the play; I must be idle:
Get you a place.

Danish march. A flourish.
Enter KING CLAUDIUS, QUEEN GERTRUDE,
POLONIUS, OPHELIA, ROSENCRANTZ,
GUILDENSTERN, *and others*

KING CLAUDIUS

How fares our cousin Hamlet?

HAMLET

Excellent, i' faith; of the chameleon's dish: I eat the air, promise-crammed: you cannot feed capons so.

KING CLAUDIUS

I have nothing with this answer, Hamlet; these words are not mine.

HAMLET

No, nor mine now.
To POLONIUS
My lord, you played once i' the university, you say?

LORD POLONIUS

That did I, my lord; and was accounted a good actor.

HAMLET

What did you enact?

LORD POLONIUS

I did enact Julius Caesar: I was killed i' the Capitol; Brutus killed me.

HAMLET

It was a brute part of him to kill so capital a calf there. Be the players ready?

ROSENCRANTZ

Ay, my lord; they stay upon your patience.

QUEEN GERTRUDE

Come hither, my dear Hamlet, sit by me.

HAMLET

No, good mother, here's metal more attractive.

LORD POLONIUS

[*To* KING CLAUDIUS] O, ho! do you mark that?

HAMLET

Lady, shall I lie in your lap?

Lying down at OPHELIA's *feet*

OPHELIA

No, my lord.

HAMLET

I mean, my head upon your lap?

OPHELIA

Ay, my lord.

HAMLET

Do you think I meant country matters?

OPHELIA

I think nothing, my lord.

HAMLET

That's a fair thought to lie between maids' legs.

OPHELIA

What is, my lord?

HAMLET

Nothing.

OPHELIA

You are merry, my lord.

HAMLET

Who, I?

OPHELIA

Ay, my lord.

HAMLET

O God, your only jig-maker. What should a man do but be merry? for, look you, how cheerfully my mother looks, and my father died within these two hours.

OPHELIA

Nay, 'tis twice two months, my lord.

HAMLET

So long? Nay then, let the devil wear black, for I'll have a suit of sables. O heavens! die two months ago, and not forgotten yet? Then there's hope a great man's memory may outlive his life half a year: but, by'r lady, he must build churches, then; or else shall he suffer not thinking on, with the hobby-horse, whose epitaph is 'For, O, for, O, the hobby-horse is forgot.'

Hautboys play. The dumb-show enters Enter a King and a Queen very lovingly; the Queen embracing him, and he her. She kneels, and makes show of protestation unto him. He takes her up, and declines his head upon her neck: lays him down upon a bank of flowers: she, seeing him asleep, leaves him. Anon comes in a fellow, takes off his crown, kisses it, and pours poison in the King's ears, and exit. The Queen returns; finds the King dead, and makes passionate action. The Poisoner, with some two or three Mutes, comes in again, seeming to lament with her. The dead body is carried away. The Poisoner wooes the Queen with gifts: she seems loath and unwilling awhile, but in the end accepts his love.

Exeunt

OPHELIA

What means this, my lord?

HAMLET

Marry, this is miching mallecho; it means mischief.

OPHELIA

Belike this show imports the argument of the play.

Enter Prologue

HAMLET

We shall know by this fellow: the players cannot keep counsel; they'll tell all.

OPHELIA

Will he tell us what this show meant?

HAMLET

Ay, or any show that you'll show him: be not you ashamed to
show, he'll not shame to tell you what it means.

OPHELIA

You are naught, you are naught: I'll mark the play.

PROLOGUE

For us, and for our tragedy,
Here stooping to your clemency,
We beg your hearing patiently.

Exit

HAMLET

Is this a prologue, or the posy of a ring?

OPHELIA

'Tis brief, my lord.

HAMLET

As woman's love.

Enter two Players, King and Queen

PLAYER KING

Full thirty times hath Phoebus' cart gone round
Neptune's salt wash and Tellus' orbed ground,
And thirty dozen moons with borrow'd sheen
About the world have times twelve thirties been,
Since love our hearts and Hymen did our hands
Unite commutual in most sacred bands.

PLAYER QUEEN

So many journeys may the sun and moon
Make us again count o'er ere love be done!
But, woe is me, you are so sick of late,
So far from cheer and from your former state,
That I distrust you. Yet, though I distrust,
Discomfort you, my lord, it nothing must:
For women's fear and love holds quantity;
In neither aught, or in extremity.
Now, what my love is, proof hath made you know;
And as my love is sized, my fear is so:
Where love is great, the littlest doubts are fear;
Where little fears grow great, great love grows there.

PLAYER KING
　　'Faith, I must leave thee, love, and shortly too;
　　My operant powers their functions leave to do:
　　And thou shalt live in this fair world behind,
　　Honour'd, beloved; and haply one as kind
　　For husband shalt thou—
PLAYER QUEEN
　　O, confound the rest!
　　Such love must needs be treason in my breast:
　　In second husband let me be accurst!
　　None wed the second but who kill'd the first.
HAMLET
　　[*Aside*] Wormwood, wormwood.
PLAYER QUEEN
　　The instances that second marriage move
　　Are base respects of thrift, but none of love:
　　A second time I kill my husband dead,
　　When second husband kisses me in bed.
PLAYER KING
　　I do believe you think what now you speak;
　　But what we do determine oft we break.
　　Purpose is but the slave to memory,
　　Of violent birth, but poor validity;
　　Which now, like fruit unripe, sticks on the tree;
　　But fall, unshaken, when they mellow be.
　　Most necessary 'tis that we forget
　　To pay ourselves what to ourselves is debt:
　　What to ourselves in passion we propose,
　　The passion ending, doth the purpose lose.
　　The violence of either grief or joy
　　Their own enactures with themselves destroy:
　　Where joy most revels, grief doth most lament;
　　Grief joys, joy grieves, on slender accident.
　　This world is not for aye, nor 'tis not strange
　　That even our loves should with our fortunes change;
　　For 'tis a question left us yet to prove,
　　Whether love lead fortune, or else fortune love.

The great man down, you mark his favourite flies;
The poor advanced makes friends of enemies.
And hitherto doth love on fortune tend;
For who not needs shall never lack a friend,
And who in want a hollow friend doth try,
Directly seasons him his enemy.
But, orderly to end where I begun,
Our wills and fates do so contrary run
That our devices still are overthrown;
Our thoughts are ours, their ends none of our own:
So think thou wilt no second husband wed;
But die thy thoughts when thy first lord is dead.

PLAYER QUEEN

Nor earth to me give food, nor heaven light!
Sport and repose lock from me day and night!
To desperation turn my trust and hope!
An anchor's cheer in prison be my scope!
Each opposite that blanks the face of joy
Meet what I would have well and it destroy!
Both here and hence pursue me lasting strife,
If, once a widow, ever I be wife!

HAMLET

If she should break it now!

PLAYER KING

'Tis deeply sworn. Sweet, leave me here awhile;
My spirits grow dull, and fain I would beguile
The tedious day with sleep.

Sleeps

PLAYER QUEEN

Sleep rock thy brain,
And never come mischance between us twain!

Exit

HAMLET

Madam, how like you this play?

QUEEN GERTRUDE

The lady protests too much, methinks.

HAMLET

O, but she'll keep her word.

KING CLAUDIUS

Have you heard the argument? Is there no offence in 't?

HAMLET

No, no, they do but jest, poison in jest; no offence i' the world.

KING CLAUDIUS

What do you call the play?

HAMLET

The Mouse-trap. Marry, how? Tropically. This play is the image of a murder done in Vienna: Gonzago is the duke's name; his wife, Baptista: you shall see anon; 'tis a knavish piece of work: but what o' that? your majesty and we that have free souls, it touches us not: let the galled jade wince, our withers are unwrung.

Enter LUCIANUS

This is one Lucianus, nephew to the king.

OPHELIA

You are as good as a chorus, my lord.

HAMLET

I could interpret between you and your love, if I could see the puppets dallying.

OPHELIA

You are keen, my lord, you are keen.

HAMLET

It would cost you a groaning to take off my edge.

OPHELIA

Still better, and worse.

HAMLET

So you must take your husbands. Begin, murderer; pox, leave thy damnable faces, and begin. Come: 'the croaking raven doth bellow for revenge.'

LUCIANUS

Thoughts black, hands apt, drugs fit, and time agreeing;
Confederate season, else no creature seeing;
Thou mixture rank, of midnight weeds collected,
With Hecate's ban thrice blasted, thrice infected,
Thy natural magic and dire property,

On wholesome life usurp immediately.
Pours the poison into the sleeper's ears

HAMLET

He poisons him i' the garden for's estate. His name's Gonzago: the story is extant, and writ in choice Italian: you shall see anon how the murderer gets the love of Gonzago's wife.

OPHELIA

The king rises.

HAMLET

What, frighted with false fire!

QUEEN GERTRUDE

How fares my lord?

LORD POLONIUS

Give o'er the play.

KING CLAUDIUS

Give me some light: away!

ALL

Lights, lights, lights!

Exeunt all but HAMLET
and HORATIO

HAMLET

Why, let the stricken deer go weep,
The hart ungalled play;
For some must watch, while some must sleep:
So runs the world away.
Would not this, sir, and a forest of feathers—if
the rest of my fortunes turn Turk with me—with two
Provincial roses on my razed shoes, get me a
fellowship in a cry of players, sir?

HORATIO

Half a share.

HAMLET

A whole one, I.
For thou dost know, O Damon dear,
This realm dismantled was
Of Jove himself; and now reigns here
A very, very—pajock.

HORATIO

You might have rhymed.

HAMLET

O good Horatio, I'll take the ghost's word for a thousand pound. Didst perceive?

HORATIO

Very well, my lord.

HAMLET

Upon the talk of the poisoning?

HORATIO

I did very well note him.

HAMLET

Ah, ha! Come, some music! come, the recorders!
For if the king like not the comedy,
Why then, belike, he likes it not, perdy.
Come, some music!

Re-enter ROSENCRANTZ
and GUILDENSTERN

GUILDENSTERN

Good my lord, vouchsafe me a word with you.

HAMLET

Sir, a whole history.

GUILDENSTERN

The king, sir—

HAMLET

Ay, sir, what of him?

GUILDENSTERN

Is in his retirement marvellous distempered.

HAMLET

With drink, sir?

GUILDENSTERN

No, my lord, rather with choler.

HAMLET

Your wisdom should show itself more richer to signify this to his doctor; for, for me to put him to his purgation would perhaps plunge him into far more choler.

GUILDENSTERN
>Good my lord, put your discourse into some frame and start not so wildly from my affair.

HAMLET
>I am tame, sir: pronounce.

GUILDENSTERN
>The queen, your mother, in most great affliction of spirit, hath sent me to you.

HAMLET
>You are welcome.

GUILDENSTERN
>Nay, good my lord, this courtesy is not of the right breed. If it shall please you to make me a wholesome answer, I will do your mother's commandment: if not, your pardon and my return shall be the end of my business.

HAMLET
>Sir, I cannot.

GUILDENSTERN
>What, my lord?

HAMLET
>Make you a wholesome answer; my wit's diseased: but, sir, such answer as I can make, you shall command; or, rather, as you say, my mother: therefore no more, but to the matter: my mother, you say—

ROSENCRANTZ
>Then thus she says; your behavior hath struck her into amazement and admiration.

HAMLET
>O wonderful son, that can so astonish a mother! But is there no sequel at the heels of this mother's admiration? Impart.

ROSENCRANTZ
>She desires to speak with you in her closet, ere you go to bed.

HAMLET
>We shall obey, were she ten times our mother. Have you any further trade with us?

ROSENCRANTZ
>My lord, you once did love me.

HAMLET

So I do still, by these pickers and stealers.

ROSENCRANTZ

Good my lord, what is your cause of distemper? you do, surely, bar the door upon your own liberty, if you deny your griefs to your friend.

HAMLET

Sir, I lack advancement.

ROSENCRANTZ

How can that be, when you have the voice of the king himself for your succession in Denmark?

HAMLET

Ay, but sir, 'While the grass grows,'—the proverb is something musty.

Re-enter Players with recorders

O, the recorders! let me see one. To withdraw with you: why do you go about to recover the wind of me, as if you would drive me into a toil?

GUILDENSTERN

O, my lord, if my duty be too bold, my love is too unmannerly.

HAMLET

I do not well understand that. Will you play upon this pipe?

GUILDENSTERN

My lord, I cannot.

HAMLET

I pray you.

GUILDENSTERN

Believe me, I cannot.

HAMLET

I do beseech you.

GUILDENSTERN

I know no touch of it, my lord.

HAMLET

'Tis as easy as lying: govern these ventages with your lingers and thumb, give it breath with your mouth, and it will discourse most eloquent music. Look you, these are the stops.

GUILDENSTERN

But these cannot I command to any utterance of harmony; I have not the skill.

HAMLET

Why, look you now, how unworthy a thing you make of me! You would play upon me; you would seem to know my stops; you would pluck out the heart of my mystery; you would sound me from my lowest note to the top of my compass: and there is much music, excellent voice, in this little organ; yet cannot you make it speak. 'Sblood, do you think I am easier to be played on than a pipe? Call me what instrument you will, though you can fret me, yet you cannot play upon me.

Enter POLONIUS

God bless you, sir!

LORD POLONIUS

My lord, the queen would speak with you, and presently.

HAMLET

Do you see yonder cloud that's almost in shape of a camel?

LORD POLONIUS

By the mass, and 'tis like a camel, indeed.

HAMLET

Methinks it is like a weasel.

LORD POLONIUS

It is backed like a weasel.

HAMLET

Or like a whale?

LORD POLONIUS

Very like a whale.

HAMLET

Then I will come to my mother by and by. They fool me to the top of my bent. I will come by and by.

LORD POLONIUS

I will say so.

HAMLET

By and by is easily said.

Exit POLONIUS

Leave me, friends.

'Tis now the very witching time of night,
When churchyards yawn and hell itself breathes out
Contagion to this world: now could I drink hot blood,
And do such bitter business as the day
Would quake to look on. Soft! now to my mother.
O heart, lose not thy nature; let not ever
The soul of Nero enter this firm bosom:
Let me be cruel, not unnatural:
I will speak daggers to her, but use none;
My tongue and soul in this be hypocrites;
How in my words soever she be shent,
To give them seals never, my soul, consent!

Exit

SCENE III.
A ROOM IN THE CASTLE.

Enter KING CLAUDIUS, ROSENCRANTZ, *and* GUILDENSTERN

KING CLAUDIUS

I like him not, nor stands it safe with us
To let his madness range. Therefore prepare you;
I your commission will forthwith dispatch,
And he to England shall along with you:
The terms of our estate may not endure
Hazard so dangerous as doth hourly grow
Out of his lunacies.

GUILDENSTERN

We will ourselves provide:
Most holy and religious fear it is
To keep those many many bodies safe
That live and feed upon your majesty.

ROSENCRANTZ

The single and peculiar life is bound,
With all the strength and armour of the mind,
To keep itself from noyance; but much more
That spirit upon whose weal depend and rest

The lives of many. The cease of majesty
Dies not alone; but, like a gulf, doth draw
What's near it with it: it is a massy wheel,
Fix'd on the summit of the highest mount,
To whose huge spokes ten thousand lesser things
Are mortised and adjoin'd; which, when it falls,
Each small annexment, petty consequence,
Attends the boisterous ruin. Never alone
Did the king sigh, but with a general groan.

KING CLAUDIUS

Arm you, I pray you, to this speedy voyage;
For we will fetters put upon this fear,
Which now goes too free-footed.

ROSENCRANTZ GUILDENSTERN

We will haste us.

Exeunt ROSENCRANTZ *and*
GUILDENSTERN

Enter POLONIUS

LORD POLONIUS

My lord, he's going to his mother's closet:
Behind the arras I'll convey myself,
To hear the process; and warrant she'll tax him home:
And, as you said, and wisely was it said,
'Tis meet that some more audience than a mother,
Since nature makes them partial, should o'erhear
The speech, of vantage. Fare you well, my liege:
I'll call upon you ere you go to bed,
And tell you what I know.

KING CLAUDIUS

Thanks, dear my lord.

Exit POLONIUS

O, my offence is rank it smells to heaven;
It hath the primal eldest curse upon't,
A brother's murder. Pray can I not,
Though inclination be as sharp as will:
My stronger guilt defeats my strong intent;
And, like a man to double business bound,

I stand in pause where I shall first begin,
And both neglect. What if this cursed hand
Were thicker than itself with brother's blood,
Is there not rain enough in the sweet heavens
To wash it white as snow? Whereto serves mercy
But to confront the visage of offence?
And what's in prayer but this two-fold force,
To be forestalled ere we come to fall,
Or pardon'd being down? Then I'll look up;
My fault is past. But, O, what form of prayer
Can serve my turn? 'Forgive me my foul murder'?
That cannot be; since I am still possess'd
Of those effects for which I did the murder,
My crown, mine own ambition and my queen.
May one be pardon'd and retain the offence?
In the corrupted currents of this world
Offence's gilded hand may shove by justice,
And oft 'tis seen the wicked prize itself
Buys out the law: but 'tis not so above;
There is no shuffling, there the action lies
In his true nature; and we ourselves compell'd,
Even to the teeth and forehead of our faults,
To give in evidence. What then? what rests?
Try what repentance can: what can it not?
Yet what can it when one can not repent?
O wretched state! O bosom black as death!
O limed soul, that, struggling to be free,
Art more engaged! Help, angels! Make assay!
Bow, stubborn knees; and, heart with strings of steel,
Be soft as sinews of the newborn babe!
All may be well.
Retires and kneels

Enter HAMLET

HAMLET
　　Now might I do it pat, now he is praying;
　　And now I'll do't. And so he goes to heaven;
　　And so am I revenged. That would be scann'd:

A villain kills my father; and for that,
I, his sole son, do this same villain send
To heaven.
O, this is hire and salary, not revenge.
He took my father grossly, full of bread;
With all his crimes broad blown, as flush as May;
And how his audit stands who knows save heaven?
But in our circumstance and course of thought,
'Tis heavy with him: and am I then revenged,
To take him in the purging of his soul,
When he is fit and season'd for his passage?
No!
Up, sword; and know thou a more horrid hent:
When he is drunk asleep, or in his rage,
Or in the incestuous pleasure of his bed;
At gaming, swearing, or about some act
That has no relish of salvation in't;
Then trip him, that his heels may kick at heaven,
And that his soul may be as damn'd and black
As hell, whereto it goes. My mother stays:
This physic but prolongs thy sickly days.

Exit

KING CLAUDIUS
    [*Rising*] My words fly up, my thoughts remain below:
    Words without thoughts never to heaven go.

Exit

SCENE IV.
THE QUEEN'S CLOSET.

Enter QUEEN GERTRUDE *and* POLONIUS

LORD POLONIUS
    He will come straight. Look you lay home to him:
    Tell him his pranks have been too broad to bear with,
    And that your grace hath screen'd and stood between
    Much heat and him. I'll sconce me even here.
    Pray you, be round with him.

HAMLET

[*Within*] Mother, mother, mother!

QUEEN GERTRUDE

I'll warrant you,

Fear me not: withdraw, I hear him coming.

POLONIUS *hides behind the arras*

Enter HAMLET

HAMLET

Now, mother, what's the matter?

QUEEN GERTRUDE

Hamlet, thou hast thy father much offended.

HAMLET

Mother, you have my father much offended.

QUEEN GERTRUDE

Come, come, you answer with an idle tongue.

HAMLET

Go, go, you question with a wicked tongue.

QUEEN GERTRUDE

Why, how now, Hamlet!

HAMLET

What's the matter now?

QUEEN GERTRUDE

Have you forgot me?

HAMLET

No, by the rood, not so:

You are the queen, your husband's brother's wife;

And—would it were not so!—you are my mother.

QUEEN GERTRUDE

Nay, then, I'll set those to you that can speak.

HAMLET

Come, come, and sit you down; you shall not budge;

You go not till I set you up a glass

Where you may see the inmost part of you.

QUEEN GERTRUDE

What wilt thou do? thou wilt not murder me?

Help, help, ho!

LORD POLONIUS

    [*Behind*] What, ho! help, help, help!

HAMLET

    [*Drawing*] How now! a rat? Dead, for a ducat, dead!

    Makes a pass through the arras

LORD POLONIUS

    [*Behind*] O, I am slain!

    Falls and dies

QUEEN GERTRUDE

    O me, what hast thou done?

HAMLET

    Nay, I know not:

    Is it the king?

QUEEN GERTRUDE

    O, what a rash and bloody deed is this!

HAMLET

    A bloody deed! almost as bad, good mother,

    As kill a king, and marry with his brother.

QUEEN GERTRUDE

    As kill a king!

HAMLET

    Ay, lady, 'twas my word.

    Lifts up the array and discovers POLONIUS

    Thou wretched, rash, intruding fool, farewell!

    I took thee for thy better: take thy fortune;

    Thou find'st to be too busy is some danger.

    Leave wringing of your hands: peace! sit you down,

    And let me wring your heart; for so I shall,

    If it be made of penetrable stuff,

    If damned custom have not brass'd it so

    That it is proof and bulwark against sense.

QUEEN GERTRUDE

    What have I done, that thou darest wag thy tongue

    In noise so rude against me?

HAMLET

    Such an act

    That blurs the grace and blush of modesty,

Calls virtue hypocrite, takes off the rose
From the fair forehead of an innocent love
And sets a blister there, makes marriage-vows
As false as dicers' oaths: O, such a deed
As from the body of contraction plucks
The very soul, and sweet religion makes
A rhapsody of words: heaven's face doth glow:
Yea, this solidity and compound mass,
With tristful visage, as against the doom,
Is thought-sick at the act.

QUEEN GERTRUDE
Ay me, what act,
That roars so loud, and thunders in the index?

HAMLET
Look here, upon this picture, and on this,
The counterfeit presentment of two brothers.
See, what a grace was seated on this brow;
Hyperion's curls; the front of Jove himself;
An eye like Mars, to threaten and command;
A station like the herald Mercury
New-lighted on a heaven-kissing hill;
A combination and a form indeed,
Where every god did seem to set his seal,
To give the world assurance of a man:
This was your husband. Look you now, what follows:
Here is your husband; like a mildew'd ear,
Blasting his wholesome brother. Have you eyes?
Could you on this fair mountain leave to feed,
And batten on this moor? Ha! have you eyes?
You cannot call it love; for at your age
The hey-day in the blood is tame, it's humble,
And waits upon the judgment: and what judgment
Would step from this to this? Sense, sure, you have,
Else could you not have motion; but sure, that sense
Is apoplex'd; for madness would not err,
Nor sense to ecstasy was ne'er so thrall'd
But it reserved some quantity of choice,

To serve in such a difference. What devil was't
That thus hath cozen'd you at hoodman-blind?
Eyes without feeling, feeling without sight,
Ears without hands or eyes, smelling sans all,
Or but a sickly part of one true sense
Could not so mope.
O shame! where is thy blush? Rebellious hell,
If thou canst mutine in a matron's bones,
To flaming youth let virtue be as wax,
And melt in her own fire: proclaim no shame
When the compulsive ardour gives the charge,
Since frost itself as actively doth burn
And reason panders will.
QUEEN GERTRUDE
    O Hamlet, speak no more:
    Thou turn'st mine eyes into my very soul;
    And there I see such black and grained spots
    As will not leave their tinct.
HAMLET
    Nay, but to live
    In the rank sweat of an enseamed bed,
    Stew'd in corruption, honeying and making love
    Over the nasty sty.—
QUEEN GERTRUDE
    O, speak to me no more;
    These words, like daggers, enter in mine ears;
    No more, sweet Hamlet!
HAMLET
    A murderer and a villain;
    A slave that is not twentieth part the tithe
    Of your precedent lord; a vice of kings;
    A cutpurse of the empire and the rule,
    That from a shelf the precious diadem stole,
    And put it in his pocket!
QUEEN GERTRUDE
    No more!

HAMLET

    A king of shreds and patches,—

                        Enter Ghost

    Save me, and hover o'er me with your wings,

    You heavenly guards! What would your gracious figure?

QUEEN GERTRUDE

    Alas, he's mad!

HAMLET

    Do you not come your tardy son to chide,

    That, lapsed in time and passion, lets go by

    The important acting of your dread command? O, say!

GHOST

    Do not forget: this visitation

    Is but to whet thy almost blunted purpose.

    But, look, amazement on thy mother sits:

    O, step between her and her fighting soul:

    Conceit in weakest bodies strongest works:

    Speak to her, Hamlet.

HAMLET

    How is it with you, lady?

QUEEN GERTRUDE

    Alas, how is't with you,

    That you do bend your eye on vacancy

    And with the incorporal air do hold discourse?

    Forth at your eyes your spirits wildly peep;

    And, as the sleeping soldiers in the alarm,

    Your bedded hair, like life in excrements,

    Starts up, and stands on end. O gentle son,

    Upon the heat and flame of thy distemper

    Sprinkle cool patience. Whereon do you look?

HAMLET

    On him, on him! Look you, how pale he glares!

    His form and cause conjoin'd, preaching to stones,

    Would make them capable. Do not look upon me;

    Lest with this piteous action you convert

    My stern effects: then what I have to do

    Will want true colour; tears perchance for blood.

QUEEN GERTRUDE

To whom do you speak this?

HAMLET

Do you see nothing there?

QUEEN GERTRUDE

Nothing at all; yet all that is I see.

HAMLET

Nor did you nothing hear?

QUEEN GERTRUDE

No, nothing but ourselves.

HAMLET

Why, look you there! look, how it steals away!

My father, in his habit as he lived!

Look, where he goes, even now, out at the portal!

Exit Ghost

QUEEN GERTRUDE

This the very coinage of your brain:

This bodiless creation ecstasy

Is very cunning in.

HAMLET

Ecstasy!

My pulse, as yours, doth temperately keep time,

And makes as healthful music: it is not madness

That I have utter'd: bring me to the test,

And I the matter will re-word; which madness

Would gambol from. Mother, for love of grace,

Lay not that mattering unction to your soul,

That not your trespass, but my madness speaks:

It will but skin and film the ulcerous place,

Whilst rank corruption, mining all within,

Infects unseen. Confess yourself to heaven;

Repent what's past; avoid what is to come;

And do not spread the compost on the weeds,

To make them ranker. Forgive me this my virtue;

For in the fatness of these pursy times

Virtue itself of vice must pardon beg,

Yea, curb and woo for leave to do him good.

QUEEN GERTRUDE
    O Hamlet, thou hast cleft my heart in twain.
HAMLET
    O, throw away the worser part of it,
    And live the purer with the other half.
    Good night: but go not to mine uncle's bed;
    Assume a virtue, if you have it not.
    That monster, custom, who all sense doth eat,
    Of habits devil, is angel yet in this,
    That to the use of actions fair and good
    He likewise gives a frock or livery,
    That aptly is put on. Refrain to-night,
    And that shall lend a kind of easiness
    To the next abstinence: the next more easy;
    For use almost can change the stamp of nature,
    And either the devil, or throw him out
    With wondrous potency. Once more, good night:
    And when you are desirous to be bless'd,
    I'll blessing beg of you. For this same lord,
    Pointing to POLONIUS
    I do repent: but heaven hath pleased it so,
    To punish me with this and this with me,
    That I must be their scourge and minister.
    I will bestow him, and will answer well
    The death I gave him. So, again, good night.
    I must be cruel, only to be kind:
    Thus bad begins and worse remains behind.
    One word more, good lady.
QUEEN GERTRUDE
    What shall I do?
HAMLET
    Not this, by no means, that I bid you do:
    Let the bloat king tempt you again to bed;
    Pinch wanton on your cheek; call you his mouse;
    And let him, for a pair of reechy kisses,
    Or paddling in your neck with his damn'd fingers,
    Make you to ravel all this matter out,

That I essentially am not in madness,
But mad in craft. 'Twere good you let him know;
For who, that's but a queen, fair, sober, wise,
Would from a paddock, from a bat, a gib,
Such dear concernings hide? who would do so?
No, in despite of sense and secrecy,
Unpeg the basket on the house's top.
Let the birds fly, and, like the famous ape,
To try conclusions, in the basket creep,
And break your own neck down.

QUEEN GERTRUDE
Be thou assured, if words be made of breath,
And breath of life, I have no life to breathe
What thou hast said to me.

HAMLET
I must to England; you know that?

QUEEN GERTRUDE
Alack,
I had forgot: 'tis so concluded on.

HAMLET
There's letters seal'd: and my two schoolfellows,
Whom I will trust as I will adders fang'd,
They bear the mandate; they must sweep my way,
And marshal me to knavery. Let it work;
For 'tis the sport to have the engineer
Hoist with his own petard: and 't shall go hard
But I will delve one yard below their mines,
And blow them at the moon: O, 'tis most sweet,
When in one line two crafts directly meet.
This man shall set me packing:
I'll lug the guts into the neighbour room.
Mother, good night. Indeed this counsellor
Is now most still, most secret and most grave,
Who was in life a foolish prating knave.
Come, sir, to draw toward an end with you.
Good night, mother.

Exeunt severally; HAMLET *dragging in* POLONIUS

ACT

IV

SCENE I.
A ROOM IN THE CASTLE.

Enter KING CLAUDIUS, QUEEN GERTRUDE,
ROSENCRANTZ, *and* GUILDENSTERN

KING CLAUDIUS

 There's matter in these sighs, these profound heaves:
 You must translate: 'tis fit we understand them.
 Where is your son?

QUEEN GERTRUDE

 Bestow this place on us a little while.
       Exeunt ROSENCRANTZ *and* GUILDENSTERN
 Ah, my good lord, what have I seen to-night!

KING CLAUDIUS

 What, Gertrude? How does Hamlet?

QUEEN GERTRUDE

 Mad as the sea and wind, when both contend
 Which is the mightier: in his lawless fit,
 Behind the arras hearing something stir,
 Whips out his rapier, cries, 'A rat, a rat!'
 And, in this brainish apprehension, kills
 The unseen good old man.

KING CLAUDIUS

O heavy deed!
It had been so with us, had we been there:
His liberty is full of threats to all;
To you yourself, to us, to every one.
Alas, how shall this bloody deed be answer'd?
It will be laid to us, whose providence
Should have kept short, restrain'd and out of haunt,
This mad young man: but so much was our love,
We would not understand what was most fit;
But, like the owner of a foul disease,
To keep it from divulging, let it feed
Even on the pith of Life. Where is he gone?

QUEEN GERTRUDE

To draw apart the body he hath kill'd:
O'er whom his very madness, like some ore
Among a mineral of metals base,
Shows itself pure; he weeps for what is done.

KING CLAUDIUS

O Gertrude, come away!
The sun no sooner shall the mountains touch,
But we will ship him hence: and this vile deed
We must, with all our majesty and skill,
Both countenance and excuse. Ho, Guildenstern!

Re-enter ROSENCRANTZ *and* GUILDENSTERN

Friends both, go join you with some further aid:
Hamlet in madness hath Polonius slain,
And from his mother's closet hath he dragg'd him:
Go seek him out; speak fair, and bring the body
Into the chapel. I pray you, haste in this.

Exeunt ROSENCRANTZ *and* GUILDENSTERN

Come, Gertrude, we'll call up our wisest friends;
And let them know, both what we mean to do,
And what's untimely done. O, come away!
My soul is full of discord and dismay.

Exeunt

SCENE II.
ANOTHER ROOM IN THE CASTLE.

Enter HAMLET

HAMLET

Safely stowed.

ROSENCRANTZ: GUILDENSTERN:

[*Within*] Hamlet! Lord Hamlet!

HAMLET

What noise? who calls on Hamlet?

O, here they come.

Enter ROSENCRANTZ *and* GUILDENSTERN

ROSENCRANTZ

What have you done, my lord, with the dead body?

HAMLET

Compounded it with dust, whereto 'tis kin.

ROSENCRANTZ

Tell us where 'tis, that we may take it thence

And bear it to the chapel.

HAMLET

Do not believe it.

ROSENCRANTZ

Believe what?

HAMLET

That I can keep your counsel and not mine own.

Besides, to be demanded of a sponge! what replication should be
made by the son of a king?

ROSENCRANTZ

Take you me for a sponge, my lord?

HAMLET

Ay, sir, that soaks up the king's countenance, his rewards, his
authorities. But such officers do the king best service in the end:
he keeps them, like an ape, in the corner of his jaw; first mouthed,
to be last swallowed: when he needs what you have gleaned, it is
but squeezing you, and, sponge, you shall be dry again.

ROSENCRANTZ

I understand you not, my lord.

HAMLET

I am glad of it: a knavish speech sleeps in a foolish ear.

ROSENCRANTZ

My lord, you must tell us where the body is, and go with us to the king.

HAMLET

The body is with the king, but the king is not with the body. The king is a thing—

GUILDENSTERN

A thing, my lord!

HAMLET

Of nothing: bring me to him. Hide fox, and all after.

Exeunt

SCENE III.
ANOTHER ROOM IN THE CASTLE.

Enter KING CLAUDIUS, *attended*

KING CLAUDIUS

I have sent to seek him, and to find the body.
How dangerous is it that this man goes loose!
Yet must not we put the strong law on him:
He's loved of the distracted multitude,
Who like not in their judgment, but their eyes;
And where 'tis so, the offender's scourge is weigh'd,
But never the offence. To bear all smooth and even,
This sudden sending him away must seem
Deliberate pause: diseases desperate grown
By desperate appliance are relieved,
Or not at all.

Enter ROSENCRANTZ

How now! what hath befall'n?

ROSENCRANTZ

Where the dead body is bestow'd, my lord,
We cannot get from him.

KING CLAUDIUS

But where is he?

ROSENCRANTZ

Without, my lord; guarded, to know your pleasure.

KING CLAUDIUS

Bring him before us.

ROSENCRANTZ

Ho, Guildenstern! bring in my lord.

Enter HAMLET *and* GUILDENSTERN

KING CLAUDIUS

Now, Hamlet, where's Polonius?

HAMLET

At supper.

KING CLAUDIUS

At supper! where?

HAMLET

Not where he eats, but where he is eaten: a certain convocation of politic worms are e'en at him. Your worm is your only emperor for diet: we fat all creatures else to fat us, and we fat ourselves for maggots: your fat king and your lean beggar is but variable service, two dishes, but to one table: that's the end.

KING CLAUDIUS

Alas, alas!

HAMLET

A man may fish with the worm that hath eat of a king, and eat of the fish that hath fed of that worm.

KING CLAUDIUS

What dost you mean by this?

HAMLET

Nothing but to show you how a king may go a progress through the guts of a beggar.

KING CLAUDIUS

Where is Polonius?

HAMLET

In heaven; send hither to see: if your messenger find him not there, seek him i' the other place yourself. But indeed, if you find him not within this month, you shall nose him as you go up the stairs into the lobby.

KING CLAUDIUS
Go seek him there.

To some Attendants

HAMLET
He will stay till ye come.

Exeunt Attendants

KING CLAUDIUS
Hamlet, this deed, for thine especial safety—
Which we do tender, as we dearly grieve
For that which thou hast done—must send thee hence
With fiery quickness: therefore prepare thyself;
The bark is ready, and the wind at help,
The associates tend, and every thing is bent
For England.

HAMLET
For England!

KING CLAUDIUS
Ay, Hamlet.

HAMLET
Good.

KING CLAUDIUS
So is it, if thou knew'st our purposes.

HAMLET
I see a cherub that sees them. But, come; for England! Farewell,
dear mother.

KING CLAUDIUS
Thy loving father, Hamlet.

HAMLET
My mother: father and mother is man and wife; man and wife is
one flesh; and so, my mother. Come, for England!

Exit

KING CLAUDIUS
Follow him at foot; tempt him with speed aboard;
Delay it not; I'll have him hence to-night:
Away! for every thing is seal'd and done
That else leans on the affair: pray you, make haste.

Exeunt ROSENCRANTZ *and* GUILDENSTERN

And, England, if my love thou hold'st at aught—
As my great power thereof may give thee sense,
Since yet thy cicatrice looks raw and red
After the Danish sword, and thy free awe
Pays homage to us—thou mayst not coldly set
Our sovereign process; which imports at full,
By letters congruing to that effect,
The present death of Hamlet. Do it, England;
For like the hectic in my blood he rages,
And thou must cure me: till I know 'tis done,
Howe'er my haps, my joys were ne'er begun.

Exit

SCENE IV.
A PLAIN IN DENMARK.

Enter FORTINBRAS, *a Captain, and Soldiers, marching*

PRINCE FORTINBRAS

Go, captain, from me greet the Danish king;
Tell him that, by his licence, Fortinbras
Craves the conveyance of a promised march
Over his kingdom. You know the rendezvous.
If that his majesty would aught with us,
We shall express our duty in his eye;
And let him know so.

CAPTAIN

I will do't, my lord.

PRINCE FORTINBRAS

Go softly on.

Exeunt FORTINBRAS *and Soldiers*

Enter HAMLET, ROSENCRANTZ,
GUILDENSTERN, *and others*

HAMLET

Good sir, whose powers are these?

CAPTAIN

They are of Norway, sir.

HAMLET
How purposed, sir, I pray you?
CAPTAIN
Against some part of Poland.
HAMLET
Who commands them, sir?
CAPTAIN
The nephews to old Norway, Fortinbras.
HAMLET
Goes it against the main of Poland, sir,
Or for some frontier?
CAPTAIN
Truly to speak, and with no addition,
We go to gain a little patch of ground
That hath in it no profit but the name.
To pay five ducats, five, I would not farm it;
Nor will it yield to Norway or the Pole
A ranker rate, should it be sold in fee.
HAMLET
Why, then the Polack never will defend it.
CAPTAIN
Yes, it is already garrison'd.
HAMLET
Two thousand souls and twenty thousand ducats
Will not debate the question of this straw:
This is the imposthume of much wealth and peace,
That inward breaks, and shows no cause without
Why the man dies. I humbly thank you, sir.
CAPTAIN
God be wi' you, sir.

Exit

ROSENCRANTZ
Wilt please you go, my lord?
HAMLET
I'll be with you straight go a little before.

Exeunt all except HAMLET

How all occasions do inform against me,

And spur my dull revenge! What is a man,
If his chief good and market of his time
Be but to sleep and feed? a beast, no more.
Sure, he that made us with such large discourse,
Looking before and after, gave us not
That capability and god-like reason
To fust in us unused. Now, whether it be
Bestial oblivion, or some craven scruple
Of thinking too precisely on the event,
A thought which, quarter'd, hath but one part wisdom
And ever three parts coward, I do not know
Why yet I live to say 'This thing's to do;'
Sith I have cause and will and strength and means
To do't. Examples gross as earth exhort me:
Witness this army of such mass and charge
Led by a delicate and tender prince,
Whose spirit with divine ambition puff'd
Makes mouths at the invisible event,
Exposing what is mortal and unsure
To all that fortune, death and danger dare,
Even for an egg-shell. Rightly to be great
Is not to stir without great argument,
But greatly to find quarrel in a straw
When honour's at the stake. How stand I then,
That have a father kill'd, a mother stain'd,
Excitements of my reason and my blood,
And let all sleep? while, to my shame, I see
The imminent death of twenty thousand men,
That, for a fantasy and trick of fame,
Go to their graves like beds, fight for a plot
Whereon the numbers cannot try the cause,
Which is not tomb enough and continent
To hide the slain? O, from this time forth,
My thoughts be bloody, or be nothing worth!

Exit

SCENE V.
ELSINORE. A ROOM IN THE CASTLE.

Enter QUEEN GERTRUDE, HORATIO, *and a Gentleman*

QUEEN GERTRUDE

I will not speak with her.

GENTLEMAN

She is importunate, indeed distract:
Her mood will needs be pitied.

QUEEN GERTRUDE

What would she have?

GENTLEMAN

She speaks much of her father; says she hears
There's tricks i' the world; and hems,
and beats her heart;
Spurns enviously at straws; speaks things in doubt,
That carry but half sense: her speech is nothing,
Yet the unshaped use of it doth move
The hearers to collection; they aim at it,
And botch the words up fit to their own thoughts;
Which, as her winks, and nods,
and gestures yield them,
Indeed would make one think there might be thought,
Though nothing sure, yet much unhappily.

HORATIO

'Twere good she were spoken with; for she may strew
Dangerous conjectures in ill-breeding minds.

QUEEN GERTRUDE

Let her come in.

Exit HORATIO

To my sick soul, as sin's true nature is,
Each toy seems prologue to some great amiss:
So full of artless jealousy is guilt,
It spills itself in fearing to be spilt.

Re-enter HORATIO, *with* OPHELIA

OPHELIA

Where is the beauteous majesty of Denmark?

QUEEN GERTRUDE

How now, Ophelia!

OPHELIA

[*Sings*]

How should I your true love know
From another one?
By his cockle hat and staff,
And his sandal shoon.

QUEEN GERTRUDE

Alas, sweet lady, what imports this song?

OPHELIA

Say you? nay, pray you, mark.

[*Sings*]

He is dead and gone, lady,
He is dead and gone;
At his head a grass-green turf,
At his heels a stone.

QUEEN GERTRUDE

Nay, but, Ophelia—

OPHELIA

Pray you, mark.

[*Sings*]

White his shroud as the mountain snow—

Enter KING CLAUDIUS

QUEEN GERTRUDE

Alas, look here, my lord.

OPHELIA

[*Sings*]

Larded with sweet flowers
Which bewept to the grave did go
With true-love showers.

KING CLAUDIUS

How do you, pretty lady?

OPHELIA

Well, God 'ild you! They say the owl was a baker's daughter.
Lord, we know what we are, but know not what we may be. God
be at your table!

KING CLAUDIUS

    Conceit upon her father.

OPHELIA

    Pray you, let's have no words of this; but when they ask you what
    it means, say you this:

    [*Sings*]

    To-morrow is Saint Valentine's day,

    All in the morning betime,

    And I a maid at your window,

    To be your Valentine.

    Then up he rose, and donn'd his clothes,

    And dupp'd the chamber-door;

    Let in the maid, that out a maid

    Never departed more.

KING CLAUDIUS

    Pretty Ophelia!

OPHELIA

    Indeed, la, without an oath, I'll make an end on't:

    [*Sings*]

    By Gis and by Saint Charity,

    Alack, and fie for shame!

    Young men will do't, if they come to't;

    By cock, they are to blame.

    Quoth she, before you tumbled me,

    You promised me to wed.

    So would I ha' done, by yonder sun,

    An thou hadst not come to my bed.

KING CLAUDIUS

    How long hath she been thus?

OPHELIA

    I hope all will be well. We must be patient: but I cannot choose
    but weep, to think they should lay him i' the cold ground. My
    brother shall know of it: and so I thank you for your good
    counsel. Come, my coach! Good night, ladies; good night, sweet
    ladies; good night, good night.

Exit

KING CLAUDIUS

Follow her close; give her good watch,
I pray you.

Exit HORATIO

O, this is the poison of deep grief; it springs
All from her father's death. O Gertrude, Gertrude,
When sorrows come, they come not single spies
But in battalions. First, her father slain:
Next, your son gone; and he most violent author
Of his own just remove: the people muddied,
Thick and unwholesome in their thoughts and whispers,
For good Polonius' death;
and we have done but greenly,
In hugger-mugger to inter him: poor Ophelia
Divided from herself and her fair judgment,
Without the which we are pictures, or mere beasts:
Last, and as much containing as all these,
Her brother is in secret come from France;
Feeds on his wonder, keeps himself in clouds,
And wants not buzzers to infect his ear
With pestilent speeches of his father's death;
Wherein necessity, of matter beggar'd,
Will nothing stick our person to arraign
In ear and ear. O my dear Gertrude, this,
Like to a murdering-piece, in many places
Gives me superfluous death.

A noise within

QUEEN GERTRUDE

Alack, what noise is this?

KING CLAUDIUS

Where are my Switzers? Let them guard the door.

Enter another Gentleman

What is the matter?

GENTLEMAN

Save yourself, my lord:
The ocean, overpeering of his list,

Eats not the flats with more impetuous haste
Than young Laertes, in a riotous head,
O'erbears your officers. The rabble call him lord;
And, as the world were now but to begin,
Antiquity forgot, custom not known,
The ratifiers and props of every word,
They cry 'Choose we: Laertes shall be king:'
Caps, hands, and tongues, applaud it to the clouds:
'Laertes shall be king, Laertes king!'

QUEEN GERTRUDE

How cheerfully on the false trail they cry!
O, this is counter, you false Danish dogs!

KING CLAUDIUS

The doors are broke.

Noise within

        Enter LAERTES, *armed; Danes following*

LAERTES

Where is this king? Sirs, stand you all without.

DANES

No, let's come in.

LAERTES

I pray you, give me leave.

DANES

We will, we will.

They retire without the door

LAERTES

I thank you: keep the door. O thou vile king,
Give me my father!

QUEEN GERTRUDE

Calmly, good Laertes.

LAERTES

That drop of blood that's calm proclaims me bastard,
Cries cuckold to my father, brands the harlot
Even here, between the chaste unsmirched brow
Of my true mother.

KING CLAUDIUS

    What is the cause, Laertes,

    That thy rebellion looks so giant-like?

    Let him go, Gertrude; do not fear our person:

    There's such divinity doth hedge a king,

    That treason can but peep to what it would,

    Acts little of his will. Tell me, Laertes,

    Why thou art thus incensed. Let him go, Gertrude.

    Speak, man.

LAERTES

    Where is my father?

KING CLAUDIUS

    Dead.

QUEEN GERTRUDE

    But not by him.

KING CLAUDIUS

    Let him demand his fill.

LAERTES

    How came he dead? I'll not be juggled with:

    To hell, allegiance! vows, to the blackest devil!

    Conscience and grace, to the profoundest pit!

    I dare damnation. To this point I stand,

    That both the worlds I give to negligence,

    Let come what comes; only I'll be revenged

    Most thoroughly for my father.

KING CLAUDIUS

    Who shall stay you?

LAERTES

    My will, not all the world:

    And for my means, I'll husband them so well,

    They shall go far with little.

KING CLAUDIUS

    Good Laertes,

    If you desire to know the certainty

    Of your dear father's death, is't writ in your revenge,

    That, swoopstake, you will draw both friend and foe,

    Winner and loser?

LAERTES

    None but his enemies.

KING CLAUDIUS

    Will you know them then?

LAERTES

    To his good friends thus wide I'll ope my arms;
    And like the kind life-rendering pelican,
    Repast them with my blood.

KING CLAUDIUS

    Why, now you speak
    Like a good child and a true gentleman.
    That I am guiltless of your father's death,
    And am most sensible in grief for it,
    It shall as level to your judgment pierce
    As day does to your eye.

DANES

    [*Within*] Let her come in.

LAERTES

    How now! what noise is that?

                 Re-enter OPHELIA

    O heat, dry up my brains! tears seven times salt,
    Burn out the sense and virtue of mine eye!
    By heaven, thy madness shall be paid by weight,
    Till our scale turn the beam. O rose of May!
    Dear maid, kind sister, sweet Ophelia!
    O heavens! is't possible, a young maid's wits
    Should be as moral as an old man's life?
    Nature is fine in love, and where 'tis fine,
    It sends some precious instance of itself
    After the thing it loves.

OPHELIA

    [*Sings*]
    They bore him barefaced on the bier;
    Hey non nonny, nonny, hey nonny;
    And in his grave rain'd many a tear:—
    Fare you well, my dove!

LAERTES

Hadst thou thy wits, and didst persuade revenge,
It could not move thus.

OPHELIA

[*Sings*]
You must sing a-down a-down,
An you call him a-down-a.
O, how the wheel becomes it! It is the false
steward, that stole his master's daughter.

LAERTES

This nothing's more than matter.

OPHELIA

There's rosemary, that's for remembrance; pray, love, remember:
and there is pansies. that's for thoughts.

LAERTES

A document in madness, thoughts and remembrance fitted.

OPHELIA

There's fennel for you, and columbines: there's rue for you; and
here's some for me: we may call it herb-grace o' Sundays: O you
must wear your rue with a difference. There's a daisy: I would
give you some violets, but they withered all when my father died:
they say he made a good end—
[*Sings*]
For bonny sweet Robin is all my joy.

LAERTES

Thought and affliction, passion, hell itself,
She turns to favour and to prettiness.

OPHELIA

[*Sings*]
And will he not come again?
And will he not come again?
No, no, he is dead:
Go to thy death-bed:
He never will come again.
His beard was as white as snow,
All flaxen was his poll:
He is gone, he is gone,

And we cast away moan:
God ha' mercy on his soul!
And of all Christian souls, I pray God. God be wi' ye.

Exit

LAERTES

Do you see this, O God?

KING CLAUDIUS

Laertes, I must commune with your grief,
Or you deny me right. Go but apart,
Make choice of whom your wisest friends you will.
And they shall hear and judge 'twixt you and me:
If by direct or by collateral hand
They find us touch'd, we will our kingdom give,
Our crown, our life, and all that we can ours,
To you in satisfaction; but if not,
Be you content to lend your patience to us,
And we shall jointly labour with your soul
To give it due content.

LAERTES

Let this be so;
His means of death, his obscure funeral—
No trophy, sword, nor hatchment o'er his bones,
No noble rite nor formal ostentation—
Cry to be heard, as 'twere from heaven to earth,
That I must call't in question.

KING CLAUDIUS

So you shall;
And where the offence is let the great axe fall.
I pray you, go with me.

Exeunt

SCENE VI.
ANOTHER ROOM IN THE CASTLE.

Enter HORATIO *and a Servant*

HORATIO

What are they that would speak with me?

SERVANT

Sailors, sir: they say they have letters for you.

HORATIO

Let them come in.

Exit Servant

I do not know from what part of the world
I should be greeted, if not from Lord Hamlet.

Enter Sailors

FIRST SAILOR

God bless you, sir.

HORATIO

Let him bless thee too.

FIRST SAILOR

He shall, sir, an't please him. There's a letter for you, sir; it comes from the ambassador that was bound for England; if your name be Horatio, as I am let to know it is.

HORATIO

[*Reads*] 'Horatio, when thou shalt have overlooked this, give these fellows some means to the king: they have letters for him. Ere we were two days old at sea, a pirate of very warlike appointment gave us chase. Finding ourselves too slow of sail, we put on a compelled valour, and in the grapple I boarded them: on the instant they got clear of our ship; so I alone became their prisoner. They have dealt with me like thieves of mercy: but they knew what they did; I am to do a good turn for them. Let the king have the letters I have sent; and repair thou to me with as much speed as thou wouldst fly death. I have words to speak in thine ear will make thee dumb; yet are they much too light for the bore of the matter. These good fellows will bring thee where I am. Rosencrantz and Guildenstern hold their course for England: of them I have much to tell thee. Farewell.

'He that thou knowest thine, HAMLET.' Come, I will make you way for these your letters; And do't the speedier, that you may direct me To him from whom you brought them.

Exeunt

SCENE VII.
ANOTHER ROOM IN THE CASTLE.

Enter KING CLAUDIUS *and* LAERTES

KING CLAUDIUS

    Now must your conscience my acquaintance seal,
    And you must put me in your heart for friend,
    Sith you have heard, and with a knowing ear,
    That he which hath your noble father slain
    Pursued my life.

LAERTES

    It well appears: but tell me
    Why you proceeded not against these feats,
    So crimeful and so capital in nature,
    As by your safety, wisdom, all things else,
    You mainly were stirr'd up.

KING CLAUDIUS

    O, for two special reasons;
    Which may to you, perhaps, seem much unsinew'd,
    But yet to me they are strong. The queen his mother
    Lives almost by his looks; and for myself—
    My virtue or my plague, be it either which—
    She's so conjunctive to my life and soul,
    That, as the star moves not but in his sphere,
    I could not but by her. The other motive,
    Why to a public count I might not go,
    Is the great love the general gender bear him;
    Who, dipping all his faults in their affection,
    Would, like the spring that turneth wood to stone,
    Convert his gyves to graces; so that my arrows,
    Too slightly timber'd for so loud a wind,
    Would have reverted to my bow again,
    And not where I had aim'd them.

LAERTES

    And so have I a noble father lost;
    A sister driven into desperate terms,

Whose worth, if praises may go back again,
Stood challenger on mount of all the age
For her perfections: but my revenge will come.

KING CLAUDIUS

Break not your sleeps for that: you must not think
That we are made of stuff so flat and dull
That we can let our beard be shook with danger
And think it pastime. You shortly shall hear more:
I loved your father, and we love ourself;
And that, I hope, will teach you to imagine—

Enter a Messenger

How now! what news?

MESSENGER

Letters, my lord, from Hamlet:
This to your majesty; this to the queen.

KING CLAUDIUS

From Hamlet! who brought them?

MESSENGER

Sailors, my lord, they say; I saw them not:
They were given me by Claudio; he received them
Of him that brought them.

KING CLAUDIUS

Laertes, you shall hear them. Leave us.

Exit Messenger

Reads

'High and mighty, You shall know I am set naked on your
kingdom. To-morrow shall I beg leave to see your kingly eyes:
when I shall, first asking your pardon thereunto, recount the
occasion of my sudden and more strange return. 'HAMLET.'
What should this mean? Are all the rest come back?
Or is it some abuse, and no such thing?

LAERTES

Know you the hand?

KING CLAUDIUS

'Tis Hamlets character. 'Naked!
And in a postscript here, he says 'alone.'
Can you advise me?

LAERTES

    I'm lost in it, my lord. But let him come;
    It warms the very sickness in my heart,
    That I shall live and tell him to his teeth,
    'Thus didest thou.'

KING CLAUDIUS

    If it be so, Laertes—
    As how should it be so? how otherwise?—
    Will you be ruled by me?

LAERTES

    Ay, my lord;
    So you will not o'errule me to a peace.

KING CLAUDIUS

    To thine own peace. If he be now return'd,
    As checking at his voyage, and that he means
    No more to undertake it, I will work him
    To an exploit, now ripe in my device,
    Under the which he shall not choose but fall:
    And for his death no wind of blame shall breathe,
    But even his mother shall uncharge the practise
    And call it accident.

LAERTES

    My lord, I will be ruled;
    The rather, if you could devise it so
    That I might be the organ.

KING CLAUDIUS

    It falls right.
    You have been talk'd of since your travel much,
    And that in Hamlet's hearing, for a quality
    Wherein, they say, you shine: your sum of parts
    Did not together pluck such envy from him
    As did that one, and that, in my regard,
    Of the unworthiest siege.

LAERTES

    What part is that, my lord?

KING CLAUDIUS

    A very riband in the cap of youth,

Yet needful too; for youth no less becomes
The light and careless livery that it wears
Than settled age his sables and his weeds,
Importing health and graveness. Two months since,
Here was a gentleman of Normandy:—
I've seen myself, and served against, the French,
And they can well on horseback: but this gallant
Had witchcraft in't; he grew unto his seat;
And to such wondrous doing brought his horse,
As he had been incorpsed and demi-natured
With the brave beast: so far he topp'd my thought,
That I, in forgery of shapes and tricks,
Come short of what he did.

LAERTES

A Norman was't?

KING CLAUDIUS

A Norman.

LAERTES

Upon my life, Lamond.

KING CLAUDIUS

The very same.

LAERTES

I know him well: he is the brooch indeed
And gem of all the nation.

KING CLAUDIUS

He made confession of you,
And gave you such a masterly report
For art and exercise in your defence
And for your rapier most especially,
That he cried out, 'twould be a sight indeed,
If one could match you: the scrimers of their nation,
He swore, had had neither motion, guard, nor eye,
If you opposed them. Sir, this report of his
Did Hamlet so envenom with his envy
That he could nothing do but wish and beg
Your sudden coming o'er, to play with him.
Now, out of this—

LAERTES
>What out of this, my lord?

KING CLAUDIUS
>Laertes, was your father dear to you?
>Or are you like the painting of a sorrow,
>A face without a heart?

LAERTES
>Why ask you this?

KING CLAUDIUS
>Not that I think you did not love your father;
>But that I know love is begun by time;
>And that I see, in passages of proof,
>Time qualifies the spark and fire of it.
>There lives within the very flame of love
>A kind of wick or snuff that will abate it;
>And nothing is at a like goodness still;
>For goodness, growing to a plurisy,
>Dies in his own too much: that we would do
>We should do when we would; for this 'would' changes
>And hath abatements and delays as many
>As there are tongues, are hands, are accidents;
>And then this 'should' is like a spendthrift sigh,
>That hurts by easing. But, to the quick o' the ulcer:—
>Hamlet comes back: what would you undertake,
>To show yourself your father's son in deed
>More than in words?

LAERTES
>To cut his throat i' the church.

KING CLAUDIUS
>No place, indeed, should murder sanctuarize;
>Revenge should have no bounds. But, good Laertes,
>Will you do this, keep close within your chamber.
>Hamlet return'd shall know you are come home:
>We'll put on those shall praise your excellence
>And set a double varnish on the fame
>The Frenchman gave you, bring you in fine together
>And wager on your heads: he, being remiss,

Most generous and free from all contriving,
Will not peruse the foils; so that, with ease,
Or with a little shuffling, you may choose
A sword unbated, and in a pass of practise
Requite him for your father.

LAERTES
I will do't:
And, for that purpose, I'll anoint my sword.
I bought an unction of a mountebank,
So mortal that, but dip a knife in it,
Where it draws blood no cataplasm so rare,
Collected from all simples that have virtue
Under the moon, can save the thing from death
That is but scratch'd withal: I'll touch my point
With this contagion, that, if I gall him slightly,
It may be death.

KING CLAUDIUS
Let's further think of this;
Weigh what convenience both of time and means
May fit us to our shape: if this should fail,
And that our drift look through our bad performance,
'Twere better not assay'd: therefore this project
Should have a back or second, that might hold,
If this should blast in proof. Soft! let me see:
We'll make a solemn wager on your cunnings: I ha't.
When in your motion you are hot and dry—
As make your bouts more violent to that end—
And that he calls for drink, I'll have prepared him
A chalice for the nonce, whereon but sipping,
If he by chance escape your venom'd stuck,
Our purpose may hold there.

Enter QUEEN GERTRUDE
How now, sweet queen!

QUEEN GERTRUDE
One woe doth tread upon another's heel,
So fast they follow; your sister's drown'd, Laertes.

LAERTES

Drown'd! O, where?

QUEEN GERTRUDE

There is a willow grows aslant a brook,
That shows his hoar leaves in the glassy stream;
There with fantastic garlands did she come
Of crow-flowers, nettles, daisies, and long purples
That liberal shepherds give a grosser name,
But our cold maids do dead men's fingers call them:
There, on the pendent boughs her coronet weeds
Clambering to hang, an envious sliver broke;
When down her weedy trophies and herself
Fell in the weeping brook. Her clothes spread wide;
And, mermaid-like, awhile they bore her up:
Which time she chanted snatches of old tunes;
As one incapable of her own distress,
Or like a creature native and indued
Unto that element: but long it could not be
Till that her garments, heavy with their drink,
Pull'd the poor wretch from her melodious lay
To muddy death.

LAERTES

Alas, then, she is drown'd?

QUEEN GERTRUDE

Drown'd, drown'd.

LAERTES

Too much of water hast thou, poor Ophelia,
And therefore I forbid my tears: but yet
It is our trick; nature her custom holds,
Let shame say what it will: when these are gone,
The woman will be out. Adieu, my lord:
I have a speech of fire, that fain would blaze,
But that this folly douts it.

Exit

KING CLAUDIUS

Let's follow, Gertrude:

How much I had to do to calm his rage!
Now fear I this will give it start again;
Therefore let's follow.

Exeunt

ACT

V

SCENE I.
A CHURCHYARD.

Enter two Clowns, with spades, & c

FIRST CLOWN

Is she to be buried in Christian burial that wilfully seeks
her own salvation?

SECOND CLOWN

I tell thee she is: and therefore make her grave straight:
the crowner hath sat on her, and finds it Christian burial.

FIRST CLOWN

How can that be, unless she drowned herself in her own
defence?

SECOND CLOWN

Why, 'tis found so.

FIRST CLOWN

It must be 'se offendendo;' it cannot be else. For here lies
the point: if I drown myself wittingly, it argues an act: and
an act hath three branches: it is, to act, to do, to perform:
argal, she drowned herself wittingly.

SECOND CLOWN

Nay, but hear you, goodman delver—

FIRST CLOWN

Give me leave. Here lies the water; good: here stands the man; good; if the man go to this water, and drown himself, it is, will he, nill he, he goes—mark you that; but if the water come to him and drown him, he drowns not himself: argal, he that is not guilty of his own death shortens not his own life.

SECOND CLOWN

But is this law?

FIRST CLOWN

Ay, marry, is't; crowner's quest law.

SECOND CLOWN

Will you ha' the truth on't? If this had not been a gentlewoman, she should have been buried out o' Christian burial.

FIRST CLOWN

Why, there thou say'st: and the more pity that great folk should have countenance in this world to drown or hang themselves, more than their even Christian. Come, my spade. There is no ancient gentleman but gardeners, ditchers, and grave-makers: they hold up Adam's profession.

SECOND CLOWN

Was he a gentleman?

FIRST CLOWN

He was the first that ever bore arms.

SECOND CLOWN

Why, he had none.

FIRST CLOWN

What, art a heathen? How dost thou understand the Scripture? The Scripture says 'Adam digged:' could he dig without arms? I'll put another question to thee: if thou answerest me not to the purpose, confess thyself—

SECOND CLOWN

Go to.

FIRST CLOWN

What is he that builds stronger than either the mason, the shipwright, or the carpenter?

SECOND CLOWN

The gallows-maker; for that frame outlives a thousand tenants.

FIRST CLOWN

I like thy wit well, in good faith: the gallows does well; but how does it well? it does well to those that do in: now thou dost ill to say the gallows is built stronger than the church: argal, the gallows may do well to thee. To't again, come.

SECOND CLOWN

'Who builds stronger than a mason, a shipwright, or a carpenter?'

FIRST CLOWN

Ay, tell me that, and unyoke.

SECOND CLOWN

Marry, now I can tell.

FIRST CLOWN

To't.

SECOND CLOWN

Mass, I cannot tell.

Enter HAMLET *and* HORATIO, *at a distance*

FIRST CLOWN

Cudgel thy brains no more about it, for your dull ass will not mend his pace with beating; and, when you are asked this question next, say 'a grave-maker': the houses that he makes last till doomsday. Go, get thee to Yaughan: fetch me a stoup of liquor.

Exit Second Clown

He digs and sings

In youth, when I did love, did love,
Methought it was very sweet,
To contract, O, the time, for, ah, my behove,
O, methought, there was nothing meet.

HAMLET

Has this fellow no feeling of his business, that he sings at grave-making?

HORATIO

Custom hath made it in him a property of easiness.

HAMLET

'Tis e'en so: the hand of little employment hath the daintier sense.

FIRST CLOWN

[*Sings*]

But age, with his stealing steps,

Hath claw'd me in his clutch,

And hath shipped me intil the land,

As if I had never been such.

Throws up a skull

HAMLET

That skull had a tongue in it, and could sing once: how the knave jowls it to the ground, as if it were Cain's jaw-bone, that did the first murder! It might be the pate of a politician, which this ass now o'er-reaches; one that would circumvent God, might it not?

HORATIO

It might, my lord.

HAMLET

Or of a courtier; which could say 'Good morrow, sweet lord! How dost thou, good lord?' This might be my lord such-a-one, that praised my lord such-a-one's horse, when he meant to beg it; might it not?

HORATIO

Ay, my lord.

HAMLET

Why, e'en so: and now my Lady Worm's; chapless, and knocked about the mazzard with a sexton's spade: here's fine revolution, an we had the trick to see't. Did these bones cost no more the breeding, but to play at loggats with 'em? mine ache to think on't.

FIRST CLOWN

[*Sings*]

A pick-axe, and a spade, a spade,

For and a shrouding sheet:

O, a pit of clay for to be made

For such a guest is meet.

Throws up another skull

HAMLET

There's another: why may not that be the skull of a lawyer? Where be his quiddities now, his quillets, his cases, his tenures, and his tricks? why does he suffer this rude knave now to knock him about the sconce with a dirty shovel, and will not tell him of his action of battery? Hum! This fellow might be in's time a great buyer of land, with his statutes, his recognizances, his fines, his double vouchers, his recoveries: is this the fine of his fines, and the recovery of his recoveries, to have his fine pate full of fine dirt? will his vouchers vouch him no more of his purchases, and double ones too, than the length and breadth of a pair of indentures? The very conveyances of his lands will hardly lie in this box; and must the inheritor himself have no more, ha?

HORATIO

Not a jot more, my lord.

HAMLET

Is not parchment made of sheepskins?

HORATIO

Ay, my lord, and of calf-skins too.

HAMLET

They are sheep and calves which seek out assurance in that. I will speak to this fellow. Whose grave's this, sirrah?

FIRST CLOWN

Mine, sir.

Sings

O, a pit of clay for to be made
For such a guest is meet.

HAMLET

I think it be thine, indeed; for thou liest in't.

FIRST CLOWN

You lie out on't, sir, and therefore it is not yours: for my part, I do not lie in't, and yet it is mine.

HAMLET

Thou dost lie in't, to be in't and say it is thine: 'tis for the dead, not for the quick; therefore thou liest.

FIRST CLOWN

'Tis a quick lie, sir; 'twill away gain, from me to you.

HAMLET

What man dost thou dig it for?

FIRST CLOWN

    For no man, sir.

HAMLET

    What woman, then?

FIRST CLOWN

    For none, neither.

HAMLET

    Who is to be buried in't?

FIRST CLOWN

    One that was a woman, sir; but, rest her soul, she's dead.

HAMLET

    How absolute the knave is! we must speak by the card, or
    equivocation will undo us. By the Lord, Horatio, these three
    years I have taken a note of it; the age is grown so picked that
    the toe of the peasant comes so near the heel of the courtier, he
    gaffs his kibe. How long hast thou been a grave-maker?

FIRST CLOWN

    Of all the days i' the year, I came to't that day that our last king
    Hamlet overcame Fortinbras.

HAMLET

    How long is that since?

FIRST CLOWN

    Cannot you tell that? every fool can tell that: it was the very
    day that young Hamlet was born; he that is mad, and sent into
    England.

HAMLET

    Ay, marry, why was he sent into England?

FIRST CLOWN

    Why, because he was mad: he shall recover his wits there; or, if
    he do not, it's no great matter there.

HAMLET

    Why?

FIRST CLOWN

    'Twill, a not be seen in him there; there the men are as mad as
    he.

HAMLET

    How came he mad?

FIRST CLOWN

Very strangely, they say.

HAMLET

How strangely?

FIRST CLOWN

Faith, e'en with losing his wits.

HAMLET

Upon what ground?

FIRST CLOWN

Why, here in Denmark: I have been sexton here, man and boy, thirty years.

HAMLET

How long will a man lie i' the earth ere he rot?

FIRST CLOWN

I' faith, if he be not rotten before he die—as we have many pocky corses now-a-days, that will scarce hold the laying in—he will last you some eight year or nine year: a tanner will last you nine year.

HAMLET

Why he more than another?

FIRST CLOWN

Why, sir, his hide is so tanned with his trade, that he will keep out water a great while; and your water is a sore decayer of your whoreson dead body. Here's a skull now; this skull has lain in the earth three and twenty years.

HAMLET

Whose was it?

FIRST CLOWN

A whoreson mad fellow's it was: whose do you think it was?

HAMLET

Nay, I know not.

FIRST CLOWN

A pestilence on him for a mad rogue! a' poured a flagon of Rhenish on my head once. This same skull, sir, was Yorick's skull, the king's jester.

HAMLET

This?

FIRST CLOWN

E'en that.

HAMLET

Let me see.

Takes the skull

Alas, poor Yorick! I knew him, Horatio: a fellow of infinite jest, of most excellent fancy: he hath borne me on his back a thousand times; and now, how abhorred in my imagination it is! my gorge rims at it. Here hung those lips that I have kissed I know not how oft. Where be your gibes now? your gambols? your songs? your flashes of merriment, that were wont to set the table on a roar? Not one now, to mock your own grinning? quite chap-fallen? Now get you to my lady's chamber, and tell her, let her paint an inch thick, to this favour she must come; make her laugh at that. Prithee, Horatio, tell me one thing.

HORATIO

What's that, my lord?

HAMLET

Dost thou think Alexander looked o' this fashion i' the earth?

HORATIO

E'en so.

HAMLET

And smelt so? pah!

Puts down the skull

HORATIO

E'en so, my lord.

HAMLET

To what base uses we may return, Horatio! Why may not imagination trace the noble dust of Alexander, till he find it stopping a bung-hole?

HORATIO

'Twere to consider too curiously, to consider so.

HAMLET

No, faith, not a jot; but to follow him thither with modesty enough, and likelihood to lead it: as thus: Alexander died, Alexander was buried, Alexander returneth into dust; the dust is earth; of earth we make loam; and why of that loam, whereto he was converted, might they not stop a beer-barrel? Imperious Caesar, dead and turn'd to clay, Might stop a hole to keep the wind away: O, that that earth, which kept the world in awe, Should patch a wall to expel the winter flaw! But soft! but soft! aside: here comes the king.

Enter Priest, & c. in procession;
the Corpse of OPHELIA, LAERTES *and*
Mourners following; KING CLAUDIUS,
QUEEN GERTRUDE, *their trains, & c*

The queen, the courtiers: who is this they follow?
And with such maimed rites? This doth betoken
The corse they follow did with desperate hand
Fordo its own life: 'twas of some estate.
Couch we awhile, and mark.

Retiring with HORATIO

LAERTES

What ceremony else?

HAMLET

That is Laertes,
A very noble youth: mark.

LAERTES

What ceremony else?

FIRST PRIEST

Her obsequies have been as far enlarged
As we have warrantise: her death was doubtful;
And, but that great command o'ersways the order,
She should in ground unsanctified have lodged
Till the last trumpet: for charitable prayers,
Shards, flints and pebbles should be thrown on her;
Yet here she is allow'd her virgin crants,
Her maiden strewments and the bringing home
Of bell and burial.

LAERTES

Must there no more be done?

FIRST PRIEST

No more be done:
We should profane the service of the dead

To sing a requiem and such rest to her
As to peace-parted souls.
LAERTES
Lay her i' the earth:
And from her fair and unpolluted flesh
May violets spring! I tell thee, churlish priest,
A ministering angel shall my sister be,
When thou liest howling.
HAMLET
What, the fair Ophelia!
QUEEN GERTRUDE
Sweets to the sweet: farewell!
Scattering flowers
I hoped thou shouldst have been my Hamlet's wife;
I thought thy bride-bed to have deck'd, sweet maid,
And not have strew'd thy grave.
LAERTES
O, treble woe
Fall ten times treble on that cursed head,
Whose wicked deed thy most ingenious sense
Deprived thee of! Hold off the earth awhile,
Till I have caught her once more in mine arms:
Leaps into the grave
Now pile your dust upon the quick and dead,
Till of this flat a mountain you have made,
To o'ertop old Pelion, or the skyish head
Of blue Olympus.
HAMLET
[*Advancing*] What is he whose grief
Bears such an emphasis? whose phrase of sorrow
Conjures the wandering stars, and makes them stand
Like wonder-wounded hearers? This is I,
Hamlet the Dane.
Leaps into the grave
LAERTES
The devil take thy soul!
Grappling with him

HAMLET
Thou pray'st not well.
I prithee, take thy fingers from my throat;
For, though I am not splenitive and rash,
Yet have I something in me dangerous,
Which let thy wiseness fear: hold off thy hand.
KING CLAUDIUS
Pluck them asunder.
QUEEN GERTRUDE
Hamlet, Hamlet!
ALL
Gentlemen—
HORATIO
Good my lord, be quiet.
The Attendants part them, and they come out of the grave
HAMLET
Why I will fight with him upon this theme
Until my eyelids will no longer wag.
QUEEN GERTRUDE
O my son, what theme?
HAMLET
I loved Ophelia: forty thousand brothers
Could not, with all their quantity of love,
Make up my sum. What wilt thou do for her?
KING CLAUDIUS
O, he is mad, Laertes.
QUEEN GERTRUDE
For love of God, forbear him.
HAMLET
'Swounds, show me what thou'lt do:
Woo't weep? woo't fight? woo't fast? woo't tear thyself?
Woo't drink up eisel? eat a crocodile?
I'll do't. Dost thou come here to whine?
To outface me with leaping in her grave?
Be buried quick with her, and so will I:
And, if thou prate of mountains, let them throw
Millions of acres on us, till our ground,

Singeing his pate against the burning zone,
Make Ossa like a wart! Nay, an thou'lt mouth,
I'll rant as well as thou.

QUEEN GERTRUDE

This is mere madness:
And thus awhile the fit will work on him;
Anon, as patient as the female dove,
When that her golden couplets are disclosed,
His silence will sit drooping.

HAMLET

Hear you, sir;
What is the reason that you use me thus?
I loved you ever: but it is no matter;
Let Hercules himself do what he may,
The cat will mew and dog will have his day.

Exit

KING CLAUDIUS

I pray you, good Horatio, wait upon him.

Exit HORATIO

To LAERTES

Strengthen your patience in our last night's speech;
We'll put the matter to the present push.
Good Gertrude, set some watch over your son.
This grave shall have a living monument:
An hour of quiet shortly shall we see;
Till then, in patience our proceeding be.

Exeunt

SCENE II.
A HALL IN THE CASTLE.

Enter HAMLET *and* HORATIO

HAMLET

So much for this, sir: now shall you see the other;
You do remember all the circumstance?

HORATIO

Remember it, my lord?

HAMLET
>Sir, in my heart there was a kind of fighting,
>That would not let me sleep: methought I lay
>Worse than the mutines in the bilboes. Rashly,
>And praised be rashness for it, let us know,
>Our indiscretion sometimes serves us well,
>When our deep plots do pall: and that should teach us
>There's a divinity that shapes our ends,
>Rough-hew them how we will—

HORATIO
>That is most certain.

HAMLET
>Up from my cabin,
>My sea-gown scarf'd about me, in the dark
>Groped I to find out them; had my desire.
>Finger'd their packet, and in fine withdrew
>To mine own room again; making so bold,
>My fears forgetting manners, to unseal
>Their grand commission; where I found, Horatio—
>O royal knavery!—an exact command,
>Larded with many several sorts of reasons
>Importing Denmark's health and England's too,
>With, ho! such bugs and goblins in my life,
>That, on the supervise, no leisure bated,
>No, not to stay the grinding of the axe,
>My head should be struck off.

HORATIO
>Is't possible?

HAMLET
>Here's the commission: read it at more leisure.
>But wilt thou hear me how I did proceed?

HORATIO
>I beseech you.

HAMLET
>Being thus be-netted round with villanies—
>Ere I could make a prologue to my brains,
>They had begun the play—I sat me down,

Devised a new commission, wrote it fair:
I once did hold it, as our statists do,
A baseness to write fair and labour'd much
How to forget that learning, but, sir, now
It did me yeoman's service: wilt thou know
The effect of what I wrote?

HORATIO

Ay, good my lord.

HAMLET

An earnest conjuration from the king,
As England was his faithful tributary,
As love between them like the palm might flourish,
As peace should stiff her wheaten garland wear
And stand a comma 'tween their amities,
And many such-like 'As'es of great charge,
That, on the view and knowing of these contents,
Without debatement further, more or less,
He should the bearers put to sudden death,
Not shriving-time allow'd.

HORATIO

How was this seal'd?

HAMLET

Why, even in that was heaven ordinant.
I had my father's signet in my purse,
Which was the model of that Danish seal;
Folded the writ up in form of the other,
Subscribed it, gave't the impression, placed it safely,
The changeling never known. Now, the next day
Was our sea-fight; and what to this was sequent
Thou know'st already.

HORATIO

So Guildenstern and Rosencrantz go to't.

HAMLET

Why, man, they did make love to this employment;
They are not near my conscience; their defeat
Does by their own insinuation grow:
'Tis dangerous when the baser nature comes

Between the pass and fell incensed points
Of mighty opposites.

HORATIO

Why, what a king is this!

HAMLET

Does it not, think'st thee, stand me now upon—
He that hath kill'd my king and whored my mother,
Popp'd in between the election and my hopes,
Thrown out his angle for my proper life,
And with such cozenage—is't not perfect conscience,
To quit him with this arm? and is't not to be damn'd,
To let this canker of our nature come
In further evil?

HORATIO

It must be shortly known to him from England
What is the issue of the business there.

HAMLET

It will be short: the interim is mine;
And a man's life's no more than to say 'One.'
But I am very sorry, good Horatio,
That to Laertes I forgot myself;
For, by the image of my cause, I see
The portraiture of his: I'll court his favours.
But, sure, the bravery of his grief did put me
Into a towering passion.

HORATIO

Peace! who comes here?

Enter OSRIC

OSRIC

Your lordship is right welcome back to Denmark.

HAMLET

I humbly thank you, sir. Dost know this water-fly?

HORATIO

No, my good lord.

HAMLET

Thy state is the more gracious; for 'tis a vice to know him. He
hath much land, and fertile: let a beast be lord of beasts, and his

crib shall stand at the king's mess: 'tis a chough; but, as I say, spacious in the possession of dirt.

OSRIC

Sweet lord, if your lordship were at leisure, I should impart a thing to you from his majesty.

HAMLET

I will receive it, sir, with all diligence of spirit. Put your bonnet to his right use; 'tis for the head.

OSRIC

I thank your lordship, it is very hot.

HAMLET

No, believe me, 'tis very cold; the wind is northerly.

OSRIC

It is indifferent cold, my lord, indeed.

HAMLET

But yet methinks it is very sultry and hot for my complexion.

OSRIC

Exceedingly, my lord; it is very sultry—as 'twere—I cannot tell how. But, my lord, his majesty bade me signify to you that he has laid a great wager on your head: sir, this is the matter—

HAMLET

I beseech you, remember—

HAMLET *moves him to put on his hat*

OSRIC

Nay, good my lord; for mine ease, in good faith. Sir, here is newly come to court Laertes; believe me, an absolute gentleman, full of most excellent differences, of very soft society and great showing: indeed, to speak feelingly of him, he is the card or calendar of gentry, for you shall find in him the continent of what part a gentleman would see.

HAMLET

Sir, his definement suffers no perdition in you; though, I know, to divide him inventorially would dizzy the arithmetic of memory, and yet but yaw neither, in respect of his quick sail. But, in the verity of extolment, I take him to be a soul of great article; and his infusion of such dearth and rareness, as, to make true diction of him, his semblable is his mirror; and who else would trace him, his umbrage, nothing more.

OSRIC

Your lordship speaks most infallibly of him.

HAMLET

The concernancy, sir? why do we wrap the gentleman in our more rawer breath?

OSRIC

Sir?

HORATIO

Is't not possible to understand in another tongue?
You will do't, sir, really.

HAMLET

What imports the nomination of this gentleman?

OSRIC

Of Laertes?

HORATIO

His purse is empty already; all's golden words are spent.

HAMLET

Of him, sir.

OSRIC

I know you are not ignorant—

HAMLET

I would you did, sir; yet, in faith, if you did, it would not much approve me. Well, sir?

OSRIC

You are not ignorant of what excellence Laertes is—

HAMLET

I dare not confess that, lest I should compare with him in excellence; but, to know a man well, were to know himself.

OSRIC

I mean, sir, for his weapon; but in the imputation laid on him by them, in his meed he's unfellowed.

HAMLET

What's his weapon?

OSRIC

Rapier and dagger.

HAMLET

That's two of his weapons: but, well.

OSRIC

The king, sir, hath wagered with him six Barbary horses: against the which he has imponed, as I take it, six French rapiers and poniards, with their assigns, as girdle, hangers, and so: three of the carriages, in faith, are very dear to fancy, very responsive to the hilts, most delicate carriages, and of very liberal conceit.

HAMLET

What call you the carriages?

HORATIO

I knew you must be edified by the margent ere you had done.

OSRIC

The carriages, sir, are the hangers.

HAMLET

The phrase would be more german to the matter, if we could carry cannon by our sides: I would it might be hangers till then. But, on: six Barbary horses against six French swords, their assigns, and three liberal-conceited carriages; that's the French bet against the Danish. Why is this 'imponed,' as you call it?

OSRIC

The king, sir, hath laid, that in a dozen passes between yourself and him, he shall not exceed you three hits: he hath laid on twelve for nine; and it would come to immediate trial, if your lordship would vouchsafe the answer.

HAMLET

How if I answer 'no'?

OSRIC

I mean, my lord, the opposition of your person in trial.

HAMLET

Sir, I will walk here in the hall: if it please his majesty, 'tis the breathing time of day with me; let the foils be brought, the gentleman willing, and the king hold his purpose, I will win for him an I can; if not, I will gain nothing but my shame and the odd hits.

OSRIC

Shall I re-deliver you e'en so?

HAMLET

To this effect, sir; after what flourish your nature will.

OSRIC

I commend my duty to your lordship.

HAMLET

Yours, yours.

Exit OSRIC

He does well to commend it himself; there are no tongues else for's turn.

HORATIO

This lapwing runs away with the shell on his head.

HAMLET

He did comply with his dug, before he sucked it. Thus has he— and many more of the same bevy that I know the dressy age dotes on—only got the tune of the time and outward habit of encounter; a kind of yesty collection, which carries them through and through the most fond and winnowed opinions; and do but blow them to their trial, the bubbles are out.

Enter a Lord

LORD

My lord, his majesty commended him to you by young Osric, who brings back to him that you attend him in the hall: he sends to know if your pleasure hold to play with Laertes, or that you will take longer time.

HAMLET

I am constant to my purpose; they follow the king's pleasure: if his fitness speaks, mine is ready; now or whensoever, provided I be so able as now.

LORD

The king and queen and all are coming down.

HAMLET

In happy time.

LORD

The queen desires you to use some gentle entertainment to Laertes before you fall to play.

HAMLET

She well instructs me.

HORATIO

You will lose this wager, my lord.

HAMLET

I do not think so: since he went into France, I have been in continual practise: I shall win at the odds. But thou wouldst not think how ill all's here about my heart: but it is no matter.

HORATIO

Nay, good my lord—

HAMLET

It is but foolery; but it is such a kind of gain-giving, as would perhaps trouble a woman.

HORATIO

If your mind dislike any thing, obey it: I will forestall their repair hither, and say you are not fit.

HAMLET

Not a whit, we defy augury: there's a special providence in the fall of a sparrow. If it be now, 'tis not to come; if it be not to come, it will be now; if it be not now, yet it will come: the readiness is all: since no man has aught of what he leaves, what is't to leave betimes?

Enter KING CLAUDIUS,
QUEEN GERTRUDE, LAERTES, *Lords,*
OSRIC, *and Attendants with foils, & c*

KING CLAUDIUS

Come, Hamlet, come, and take this hand from me.

KING CLAUDIUS *puts* LAERTES' *hand into* HAMLET'S

HAMLET

Give me your pardon, sir: I've done you wrong;
But pardon't, as you are a gentleman.
This presence knows,
And you must needs have heard, how I am punish'd
With sore distraction. What I have done,
That might your nature, honour and exception
Roughly awake, I here proclaim was madness.
Was't Hamlet wrong'd Laertes? Never Hamlet:
If Hamlet from himself be ta'en away,

And when he's not himself does wrong Laertes,
Then Hamlet does it not, Hamlet denies it.
Who does it, then? His madness: if't be so,
Hamlet is of the faction that is wrong'd;
His madness is poor Hamlet's enemy.
Sir, in this audience,
Let my disclaiming from a purposed evil
Free me so far in your most generous thoughts,
That I have shot mine arrow o'er the house,
And hurt my brother.

LAERTES

I am satisfied in nature,
Whose motive, in this case, should stir me most
To my revenge: but in my terms of honour
I stand aloof; and will no reconcilement,
Till by some elder masters, of known honour,
I have a voice and precedent of peace,
To keep my name ungored. But till that time,
I do receive your offer'd love like love,
And will not wrong it.

HAMLET

I embrace it freely;
And will this brother's wager frankly play.
Give us the foils. Come on.

LAERTES

Come, one for me.

HAMLET

I'll be your foil, Laertes: in mine ignorance
Your skill shall, like a star i' the darkest night,
Stick fiery off indeed.

LAERTES

You mock me, sir.

HAMLET

No, by this hand.

KING CLAUDIUS

Give them the foils, young Osric. Cousin Hamlet,
You know the wager?

HAMLET

Very well, my lord

Your grace hath laid the odds o' the weaker side.

KING CLAUDIUS

I do not fear it; I have seen you both:

But since he is better'd, we have therefore odds.

LAERTES

This is too heavy, let me see another.

HAMLET

This likes me well. These foils have all a length?

They prepare to play

OSRIC

Ay, my good lord.

KING CLAUDIUS

Set me the stoops of wine upon that table.

If Hamlet give the first or second hit,

Or quit in answer of the third exchange,

Let all the battlements their ordnance fire:

The king shall drink to Hamlet's better breath;

And in the cup an union shall he throw,

Richer than that which four successive kings

In Denmark's crown have worn. Give me the cups;

And let the kettle to the trumpet speak,

The trumpet to the cannoneer without,

The cannons to the heavens, the heavens to earth,

'Now the king dunks to Hamlet.' Come, begin:

And you, the judges, bear a wary eye.

HAMLET

Come on, sir.

LAERTES

Come, my lord.

They play

HAMLET

One.

LAERTES

No.

HAMLET
    Judgment.
OSRIC
    A hit, a very palpable hit.
LAERTES
    Well; again.
KING CLAUDIUS
    Stay; give me drink. Hamlet, this pearl is thine;
    Here's to thy health.
    Trumpets sound, and cannon shot off within
    Give him the cup.
HAMLET
    I'll play this bout first; set it by awhile. Come.
    They play
    Another hit; what say you?
LAERTES
    A touch, a touch, I do confess.
KING CLAUDIUS
    Our son shall win.
QUEEN GERTRUDE
    He's fat, and scant of breath.
    Here, Hamlet, take my napkin, rub thy brows;
    The queen carouses to thy fortune, Hamlet.
HAMLET
    Good madam!
KING CLAUDIUS
    Gertrude, do not drink.
QUEEN GERTRUDE
    I will, my lord; I pray you, pardon me.
KING CLAUDIUS
    [*Aside*] It is the poison'd cup: it is too late.
HAMLET
    I dare not drink yet, madam; by and by.
QUEEN GERTRUDE
    Come, let me wipe thy face.
LAERTES
    My lord, I'll hit him now.

KING CLAUDIUS

    I do not think't.

LAERTES

    [*Aside*] And yet 'tis almost 'gainst my conscience.

HAMLET

    Come, for the third, Laertes: you but dally;

    I pray you, pass with your best violence;

    I am afeard you make a wanton of me.

LAERTES

    Say you so? come on.

    They play

OSRIC

    Nothing, neither way.

LAERTES

    Have at you now!

    LAERTES *wounds* HAMLET; *then in scuffling, they change rapiers, and*

    HAMLET *wounds* LAERTES

KING CLAUDIUS

    Part them; they are incensed.

HAMLET

    Nay, come, again.

    QUEEN GERTRUDE *falls*

OSRIC

    Look to the queen there, ho!

HORATIO

    They bleed on both sides. How is it, my lord?

OSRIC

    How is't, Laertes?

LAERTES

    Why, as a woodcock to mine own springe, Osric;

    I am justly kill'd with mine own treachery.

HAMLET

    How does the queen?

KING CLAUDIUS

    She swounds to see them bleed.

QUEEN GERTRUDE

    No, no, the drink, the drink—O my dear Hamlet—

The drink, the drink! I am poison'd.

Dies

HAMLET

O villany! Ho! let the door be lock'd:
Treachery! Seek it out.

LAERTES

It is here, Hamlet: Hamlet, thou art slain;
No medicine in the world can do thee good;
In thee there is not half an hour of life;
The treacherous instrument is in thy hand,
Unbated and envenom'd: the foul practise
Hath turn'd itself on me lo, here I lie,
Never to rise again: thy mother's poison'd:
I can no more: the king, the king's to blame.

HAMLET

The point!—envenom'd too!
Then, venom, to thy work.
Stabs KING CLAUDIUS

ALL

Treason! treason!

KING CLAUDIUS

O, yet defend me, friends; I am but hurt.

HAMLET

Here, thou incestuous, murderous, damned Dane,
Drink off this potion. Is thy union here?
Follow my mother.
KING CLAUDIUS *dies*

LAERTES

He is justly served;
It is a poison temper'd by himself.
Exchange forgiveness with me, noble Hamlet:
Mine and my father's death come not upon thee,
Nor thine on me.
Dies

HAMLET

Heaven make thee free of it! I follow thee.
I am dead, Horatio. Wretched queen, adieu!

You that look pale and tremble at this chance,
That are but mutes or audience to this act,
Had I but time—as this fell sergeant, death,
Is strict in his arrest—O, I could tell you—
But let it be. Horatio, I am dead;
Thou livest; report me and my cause aright
To the unsatisfied.

HORATIO

Never believe it:
I am more an antique Roman than a Dane:
Here's yet some liquor left.

HAMLET

As thou'rt a man,
Give me the cup: let go; by heaven, I'll have't.
O good Horatio, what a wounded name,
Things standing thus unknown, shall live behind me!
If thou didst ever hold me in thy heart
Absent thee from felicity awhile,
And in this harsh world draw thy breath in pain,
To tell my story.
March afar off, and shot within
What warlike noise is this?

OSRIC

Young Fortinbras, with conquest come from Poland,
To the ambassadors of England gives
This warlike volley.

HAMLET

O, I die, Horatio;
The potent poison quite o'er-crows my spirit:
I cannot live to hear the news from England;
But I do prophesy the election lights
On Fortinbras: he has my dying voice;
So tell him, with the occurrents, more and less,
Which have solicited. The rest is silence.
Dies

HORATIO

Now cracks a noble heart. Good night sweet prince:

And flights of angels sing thee to thy rest!
Why does the drum come hither?
March within
    Enter FORTINBRAS, *the English Ambassadors, and others*
PRINCE FORTINBRAS
    Where is this sight?
HORATIO
    What is it ye would see?
    If aught of woe or wonder, cease your search.
PRINCE FORTINBRAS
    This quarry cries on havoc. O proud death,
    What feast is toward in thine eternal cell,
    That thou so many princes at a shot
    So bloodily hast struck?
FIRST AMBASSADOR
    The sight is dismal;
    And our affairs from England come too late:
    The ears are senseless that should give us hearing,
    To tell him his commandment is fulfill'd,
    That Rosencrantz and Guildenstern are dead:
    Where should we have our thanks?
HORATIO
    Not from his mouth,
    Had it the ability of life to thank you:
    He never gave commandment for their death.
    But since, so jump upon this bloody question,
    You from the Polack wars, and you from England,
    Are here arrived give order that these bodies
    High on a stage be placed to the view;
    And let me speak to the yet unknowing world
    How these things came about: so shall you hear
    Of carnal, bloody, and unnatural acts,
    Of accidental judgments, casual slaughters,
    Of deaths put on by cunning and forced cause,
    And, in this upshot, purposes mistook
    Fall'n on the inventors' reads: all this can I
    Truly deliver.

PRINCE FORTINBRAS
    Let us haste to hear it,
    And call the noblest to the audience.
    For me, with sorrow I embrace my fortune:
    I have some rights of memory in this kingdom,
    Which now to claim my vantage doth invite me.
HORATIO
    Of that I shall have also cause to speak,
    And from his mouth whose voice will draw on more;
    But let this same be presently perform'd,
    Even while men's minds are wild; lest more mischance
    On plots and errors, happen.
PRINCE FORTINBRAS
    Let four captains
    Bear Hamlet, like a soldier, to the stage;
    For he was likely, had he been put on,
    To have proved most royally: and, for his passage,
    The soldiers' music and the rites of war
    Speak loudly for him.
    Take up the bodies: such a sight as this
    Becomes the field, but here shows much amiss.
    Go, bid the soldiers shoot.
    A dead march. Exeunt, bearing off the dead bodies;
    after which a peal of ordnance is shot off

Julius Caesar

"The fault, dear Brutus, is not in our stars,
But in ourselves, that we are underlings."

Characters in the Play

JULIUS CAESAR, Roman statesman and general

OCTAVIUS, Triumvir after Caesar's death, later Augustus Caesar, first emperor of Rome

MARK ANTONY, general and friend of Caesar, a Triumvir after his death

LEPIDUS, third member of the Triumvirate

MARCUS BRUTUS, leader of the conspiracy against Caesar

CASSIUS, instigator of the conspiracy

CASCA

TREBONIUS

LIGARIUS } conspirators against Caesar

DECIUS BRUTUS

METELLUS CIMBER

CINNA

CALPURNIA, wife of Caesar

PORTIA, wife of Brutus

CICERO

POPILIUS } senators

PUBLIUS

FLAVIUS and MARULLUS, tribunes

CATO

LUCILIUS

TITINIUS } supportors of Brutus

MESSALA

VOLUMNIUS

ARTEMIDORUS, a teacher of rhetoric

CINNA THE POET

Varro
Clitus
Claudius
Strato } servants to Brutus
Lucius
Dardanius
Pindarus, servant to Cassius
The Ghost of Caesar
A Soothsayer
A Poet
Senators, Citizens, Soldiers, Commoners, Messengers, and Servants

SCENE:
Rome, the conspirators' camp near
Sardis, and the plains of Philippi.

ACT

I

SCENE I.
ROME. A STREET.

Enter Flavius, Marullus,
and certain Commoners

FLAVIUS

    Hence! home, you idle creatures get you home.
    Is this a holiday? What! know you not,
    Being mechanical, you ought not walk
    Upon a labouring day without the sign
    Of your profession? Speak, what trade art thou?

FIRST COMMONER

    Why, sir, a carpenter.

MARULLUS

    Where is thy leather apron and thy rule?
    What dost thou with thy best apparel on?
    You, sir, what trade are you?

SECOND COMMONER

    Truly, sir, in respect of a fine workman, I am but, as you
    would say, a cobbler.

MARULLUS

    But what trade art thou? Answer me directly.

SECOND COMMONER

A trade, sir, that, I hope, I may use with a safe conscience; which is, indeed, sir, a mender of bad soles.

MARULLUS

What trade, thou knave? Thou naughty knave, what trade?

SECOND COMMONER

Nay, I beseech you, sir, be not out with me; yet, if you be out, sir, I can mend you.

MARULLUS

What meanest thou by that? Mend me, thou saucy fellow!

SECOND COMMONER

Why, sir, cobble you.

FLAVIUS

Thou art a cobbler, art thou?

SECOND COMMONER

Truly, sir, all that I live by is with the awl: I meddle with no tradesman's matters, nor women's matters, but with awl. I am, indeed, sir, a surgeon to old shoes; when they are in great danger, I recover them. As proper men as ever trod upon neat's leather have gone upon my handiwork.

FLAVIUS

But wherefore art not in thy shop to-day?
Why dost thou lead these men about the streets?

SECOND COMMONER

Truly, sir, to wear out their shoes, to get myself into more work. But, indeed, sir, we make holiday, to see Caesar and to rejoice in his triumph.

MARULLUS

Wherefore rejoice? What conquest brings he home?
What tributaries follow him to Rome,
To grace in captive bonds his chariot-wheels?
You blocks, you stones, you worse than senseless things!
O you hard hearts, you cruel men of Rome,
Knew you not Pompey? Many a time and oft
Have you climb'd up to walls and battlements,
To towers and windows, yea, to chimney-tops,

Your infants in your arms, and there have sat
The livelong day, with patient expectation,
To see great Pompey pass the streets of Rome:
And when you saw his chariot but appear,
Have you not made an universal shout,
That Tiber trembled underneath her banks,
To hear the replication of your sounds
Made in her concave shores?
And do you now put on your best attire?
And do you now cull out a holiday?
And do you now strew flowers in his way
That comes in triumph over Pompey's blood? Be gone!
Run to your houses, fall upon your knees,
Pray to the gods to intermit the plague
That needs must light on this ingratitude.

FLAVIUS

Go, go, good countrymen, and, for this fault,
Assemble all the poor men of your sort;
Draw them to Tiber banks, and weep your tears
Into the channel, till the lowest stream
Do kiss the most exalted shores of all.

Exeunt all the Commoners

See whether their basest metal be not moved;
They vanish tongue-tied in their guiltiness.
Go you down that way towards the Capitol;
This way will I. Disrobe the images,
If you do find them deck'd with ceremonies.

MARULLUS

May we do so?
You know it is the feast of Lupercal.

FLAVIUS

It is no matter; let no images
Be hung with Caesar's trophies. I'll about,
And drive away the vulgar from the streets:
So do you too, where you perceive them thick.
These growing feathers pluck'd from Caesar's wing

Will make him fly an ordinary pitch,
Who else would soar above the view of men
And keep us all in servile fearfulness.

Exeunt

SCENE II.
A PUBLIC PLACE.

Flourish. Enter CAESAR; ANTONY, *for the course;*
CALPURNIA, PORTIA, DECIUS BRUTUS, CICERO,
BRUTUS, CASSIUS, *and* CASCA; *a great crowd following,*
among them a Soothsayer

CAESAR
    Calpurnia!
CASCA
    Peace, ho! Caesar speaks.
CAESAR
    Calpurnia!
CALPURNIA
    Here, my lord.
CAESAR
    Stand you directly in Antonius' way,
    When he doth run his course. Antonius!
ANTONY
    Caesar, my lord?
CAESAR
    Forget not, in your speed, Antonius,
    To touch Calpurnia; for our elders say,
    The barren, touched in this holy chase,
    Shake off their sterile curse.
ANTONY
    I shall remember:
    When Caesar says 'do this,' it is perform'd.
CAESAR
    Set on; and leave no ceremony out.

Flourish

SOOTHSAYER
     Caesar!
CAESAR
     Ha! Who calls?
CASCA
     Bid every noise be still: peace yet again!
CAESAR
     Who is it in the press that calls on me?
     I hear a tongue, shriller than all the music,
     Cry 'Caesar!' Speak; Caesar is turn'd to hear.
SOOTHSAYER
     Beware the ides of March.
CAESAR
     What man is that?
BRUTUS
     A soothsayer bids you beware the ides of March.
CAESAR
     Set him before me; let me see his face.
CASSIUS
     Fellow, come from the throng; look upon Caesar.
CAESAR
     What say'st thou to me now? Speak once again.
SOOTHSAYER
     Beware the ides of March.
CAESAR
     He is a dreamer; let us leave him: pass.

                              Sennet. Exeunt all except
                              BRUTUS *and* CASSIUS

CASSIUS
     Will you go see the order of the course?
BRUTUS
     Not I.
CASSIUS
     I pray you, do.
BRUTUS
     I am not gamesome: I do lack some part
     Of that quick spirit that is in Antony.

Let me not hinder, Cassius, your desires;
I'll leave you.

CASSIUS
Brutus, I do observe you now of late:
I have not from your eyes that gentleness
And show of love as I was wont to have:
You bear too stubborn and too strange a hand
Over your friend that loves you.

BRUTUS
Cassius,
Be not deceived: if I have veil'd my look,
I turn the trouble of my countenance
Merely upon myself. Vexed I am
Of late with passions of some difference,
Conceptions only proper to myself,
Which give some soil perhaps to my behaviors;
But let not therefore my good friends be grieved—
Among which number, Cassius, be you one—
Nor construe any further my neglect,
Than that poor Brutus, with himself at war,
Forgets the shows of love to other men.

CASSIUS
Then, Brutus, I have much mistook your passion;
By means whereof this breast of mine hath buried
Thoughts of great value, worthy cogitations.
Tell me, good Brutus, can you see your face?

BRUTUS
No, Cassius; for the eye sees not itself,
But by reflection, by some other things.

CASSIUS
'Tis just;
And it is very much lamented, Brutus,
That you have no such mirrors as will turn
Your hidden worthiness into your eye,
That you might see your shadow. I have heard,
Where many of the best respect in Rome,
Except immortal Caesar, speaking of Brutus

And groaning underneath this age's yoke,
Have wish'd that noble Brutus had his eyes.

BRUTUS

Into what dangers would you lead me, Cassius,
That you would have me seek into myself
For that which is not in me?

CASSIUS

Therefore, good Brutus, be prepared to hear;
And since you know you cannot see yourself
So well as by reflection, I, your glass,
Will modestly discover to yourself
That of yourself which you yet know not of.
And be not jealous on me, gentle Brutus:
Were I a common laugher, or did use
To stale with ordinary oaths my love
To every new protester; if you know
That I do fawn on men and hug them hard
And after scandal them, or if you know
That I profess myself in banqueting
To all the rout, then hold me dangerous.

Flourish, and shout

BRUTUS

What means this shouting? I do fear, the people
Choose Caesar for their king.

CASSIUS

Ay, do you fear it?
Then must I think you would not have it so.

BRUTUS

I would not, Cassius; yet I love him well.
But wherefore do you hold me here so long?
What is it that you would impart to me?
If it be aught toward the general good,
Set honour in one eye and death i' the other,
And I will look on both indifferently;
For let the gods so speed me as I love
The name of honour more than I fear death.

CASSIUS

    I know that virtue to be in you, Brutus,
    As well as I do know your outward favour.
    Well, honour is the subject of my story.
    I cannot tell what you and other men
    Think of this life; but, for my single self,
    I had as lief not be as live to be
    In awe of such a thing as I myself.
    I was born free as Caesar; so were you.
    We both have fed as well, and we can both
    Endure the winter's cold as well as he.
    For once, upon a raw and gusty day,
    The troubled Tiber chafing with her shores,
    Caesar said to me 'Darest thou, Cassius, now
    Leap in with me into this angry flood,
    And swim to yonder point?' Upon the word,
    Accoutred as I was, I plunged in
    And bade him follow; so indeed he did.
    The torrent roar'd, and we did buffet it
    With lusty sinews, throwing it aside
    And stemming it with hearts of controversy;
    But ere we could arrive the point proposed,
    Caesar cried 'Help me, Cassius, or I sink!'
    I, as Aeneas, our great ancestor,
    Did from the flames of Troy upon his shoulder
    The old Anchises bear, so from the waves of Tiber
    Did I the tired Caesar. And this man
    Is now become a god, and Cassius is
    A wretched creature and must bend his body,
    If Caesar carelessly but nod on him.
    He had a fever when he was in Spain,
    And when the fit was on him, I did mark
    How he did shake. 'Tis true, this god did shake.
    His coward lips did from their colour fly,
    And that same eye whose bend doth awe the world
    Did lose his lustre. I did hear him groan.
    Ay, and that tongue of his that bade the Romans

Mark him and write his speeches in their books,
Alas, it cried 'Give me some drink, Titinius,'
As a sick girl. Ye gods, it doth amaze me
A man of such a feeble temper should
So get the start of the majestic world
And bear the palm alone.

Shout. Flourish

BRUTUS

Another general shout!
I do believe that these applauses are
For some new honours that are heap'd on Caesar.

CASSIUS

Why, man, he doth bestride the narrow world
Like a Colossus, and we petty men
Walk under his huge legs and peep about
To find ourselves dishonourable graves.
Men at some time are masters of their fates:
The fault, dear Brutus, is not in our stars,
But in ourselves, that we are underlings.
Brutus and Caesar: what should be in that 'Caesar'?
Why should that name be sounded more than yours?
Write them together, yours is as fair a name.
Sound them, it doth become the mouth as well;
Weigh them, it is as heavy; conjure with 'em,
Brutus will start a spirit as soon as Caesar.
Now, in the names of all the gods at once,
Upon what meat doth this our Caesar feed,
That he is grown so great? Age, thou art shamed!
Rome, thou hast lost the breed of noble bloods!
When went there by an age, since the great flood,
But it was famed with more than with one man?
When could they say till now, that talk'd of Rome,
That her wide walls encompass'd but one man?
Now is it Rome indeed and room enough,
When there is in it but one only man.
O, you and I have heard our fathers say,
There was a Brutus once that would have brook'd

The eternal devil to keep his state in Rome
As easily as a king.

BRUTUS

That you do love me, I am nothing jealous;
What you would work me to, I have some aim;
How I have thought of this and of these times,
I shall recount hereafter; for this present,
I would not, so with love I might entreat you,
Be any further moved. What you have said
I will consider; what you have to say
I will with patience hear, and find a time
Both meet to hear and answer such high things.
Till then, my noble friend, chew upon this:
Brutus had rather be a villager
Than to repute himself a son of Rome
Under these hard conditions as this time
Is like to lay upon us.

CASSIUS

I am glad that my weak words
Have struck but thus much show of fire from Brutus.

BRUTUS

The games are done and Caesar is returning.

CASSIUS

As they pass by, pluck Casca by the sleeve;
And he will, after his sour fashion, tell you
What hath proceeded worthy note to-day.

Re-enter CAESAR *and his Train*

BRUTUS

I will do so. But, look you, Cassius,
The angry spot doth glow on Caesar's brow,
And all the rest look like a chidden train;
Calpurnia's cheek is pale; and Cicero
Looks with such ferret and such fiery eyes
As we have seen him in the Capitol,
Being cross'd in conference by some senators.

CASSIUS

Casca will tell us what the matter is.

CAESAR
  Antonius!
ANTONY
  Caesar?
CAESAR
  Let me have men about me that are fat;
  Sleek-headed men and such as sleep o' nights.
  Yond Cassius has a lean and hungry look;
  He thinks too much: such men are dangerous.
ANTONY
  Fear him not, Caesar; he's not dangerous;
  He is a noble Roman and well given.
CAESAR
  Would he were fatter! But I fear him not.
  Yet if my name were liable to fear,
  I do not know the man I should avoid
  So soon as that spare Cassius. He reads much;
  He is a great observer and he looks
  Quite through the deeds of men: he loves no plays,
  As thou dost, Antony; he hears no music.
  Seldom he smiles, and smiles in such a sort
  As if he mock'd himself and scorn'd his spirit
  That could be moved to smile at anything.
  Such men as he be never at heart's ease
  Whiles they behold a greater than themselves,
  And therefore are they very dangerous.
  I rather tell thee what is to be fear'd
  Than what I fear; for always I am Caesar.
  Come on my right hand, for this ear is deaf,
  And tell me truly what thou think'st of him.
                        Sennet. Exeunt CAESAR *and*
                          all his Train, but CASCA

CASCA
  You pull'd me by the cloak; would you speak with me?
BRUTUS
  Ay, Casca; tell us what hath chanced to-day,
  That Caesar looks so sad?

CASCA

Why, you were with him, were you not?

BRUTUS

I should not then ask Casca what had chanced.

CASCA

Why, there was a crown offered him: and being offered him, he put it by with the back of his hand, thus; and then the people fell a-shouting.

BRUTUS

What was the second noise for?

CASCA

Why, for that too.

CASSIUS

They shouted thrice: what was the last cry for?

CASCA

Why, for that too.

BRUTUS

Was the crown offered him thrice?

CASCA

Ay, marry, was't, and he put it by thrice, every time gentler than other, and at every putting-by mine honest neighbours shouted.

CASSIUS

Who offered him the crown?

CASCA

Why, Antony.

BRUTUS

Tell us the manner of it, gentle Casca.

CASCA

I can as well be hanged as tell the manner of it: it was mere foolery; I did not mark it. I saw Mark Antony offer him a crown—yet 'twas not a crown neither, 'twas one of these coronets—and, as I told you, he put it by once; but, for all that, to my thinking, he ain have had it. Then he offered it to him again; then he ʼ again; but, to my thinking, he was very loath to lay his off it. And then he offered it the third time; he put it the ne by; and still as he refused it, the rabblement hooted pped their chapped hands and threw up their sweaty night-caps and uttered such a deal of stinking breath because Caesar refused the crown that it had almost choked Caesar; for he swooned and fell down at it. And for mine own part, I durst not laugh, for fear of opening my lips and receiving the bad air.

CASSIUS

But, soft, I pray you: what, did Caesar swoon?

CASCA

He fell down in the market-place, and foamed at mouth, and was speechless.

BRUTUS

'Tis very like: he hath the failing sickness.

CASSIUS

No, Caesar hath it not; but you and I,
And honest Casca, we have the falling sickness.

CASCA

I know not what you mean by that; but, I am sure, Caesar fell down. If the tag-rag people did not clap him and hiss him, according as he pleased and displeased them, as they use to do the players in the theatre, I am no true man.

BRUTUS

What said he when he came unto himself?

CASCA

Marry, before he fell down, when he perceived the common herd was glad he refused the crown, he plucked me ope his doublet and offered them his throat to cut. An I had been a man of any occupation, if I would not have taken him at a word, I would I might go to hell among the rogues. And so he fell. When he came to himself again, he said, If he had done or said anything amiss, he desired their worships to think it was his infirmity. Three or four wenches, where I stood, cried 'Alas, good soul!' and forgave him with all their hearts. But there's no heed to be taken of them; if Caesar had stabbed their mothers, they would have done no less.

BRUTUS

And after that, he came, thus sad, away?

CASCA

Ay.

CASSIUS

    Did Cicero say anything?

CASCA

    Ay, he spoke Greek.

CASSIUS

    To what effect?

CASCA

    Nay, an I tell you that, I'll ne'er look you i' the face again. But those that understood him smiled at one another and shook their heads; but, for mine own part, it was Greek to me. I could tell you more news too: Marullus and Flavius, for pulling scarfs off Caesar's images, are put to silence. Fare you well. There was more foolery yet, if I could remember it.

CASSIUS

    Will you sup with me to-night, Casca?

CASCA

    No, I am promised forth.

CASSIUS

    Will you dine with me to-morrow?

CASCA

    Ay, if I be alive and your mind hold and your dinner worth the eating.

CASSIUS

    Good: I will expect you.

CASCA

    Do so. Farewell, both.

Exit

BRUTUS

    What a blunt fellow is this grown to be!
    He was quick mettle when he went to school.

CASSIUS

    So is he now in execution
    Of any bold or noble enterprise,
    However he puts on this tardy form.
    This rudeness is a sauce to his good wit,
    Which gives men stomach to digest his words
    With better appetite.

BRUTUS

    And so it is. For this time I will leave you:
    To-morrow, if you please to speak with me,
    I will come home to you; or, if you will,
    Come home to me, and I will wait for you.

CASSIUS

    I will do so: till then, think of the world.

Exit BRUTUS

    Well, Brutus, thou art noble; yet, I see,
    Thy honourable metal may be wrought
    From that it is disposed. Therefore it is meet
    That noble minds keep ever with their likes;
    For who so firm that cannot be seduced?
    Caesar doth bear me hard; but he loves Brutus.
    If I were Brutus now and he were Cassius,
    He should not humour me. I will this night,
    In several hands, in at his windows throw,
    As if they came from several citizens,
    Writings all tending to the great opinion
    That Rome holds of his name; wherein obscurely
    Caesar's ambition shall be glanced at.
    And after this let Caesar seat him sure;
    For we will shake him, or worse days endure.

Exit

SCENE III.
THE SAME. A STREET.

Thunder and lightning. Enter from opposite sides,
CASCA, with his sword drawn, and CICERO

CICERO

    Good even, Casca: brought you Caesar home?
    Why are you breathless? and why stare you so?

CASCA

    Are not you moved, when all the sway of earth
    Shakes like a thing unfirm? O Cicero,
    I have seen tempests, when the scolding winds

Have rived the knotty oaks, and I have seen
The ambitious ocean swell and rage and foam,
To be exalted with the threatening clouds;
But never till to-night, never till now,
Did I go through a tempest dropping fire.
Either there is a civil strife in heaven,
Or else the world, too saucy with the gods,
Incenses them to send destruction.

CICERO
Why, saw you anything more wonderful?

CASCA
A common slave—you know him well by sight—
Held up his left hand, which did flame and burn
Like twenty torches join'd, and yet his hand,
Not sensible of fire, remain'd unscorch'd.
Besides—I ha' not since put up my sword—
Against the Capitol I met a lion,
Who glared upon me, and went surly by,
Without annoying me: and there were drawn
Upon a heap a hundred ghastly women,
Transformed with their fear; who swore they saw
Men all in fire walk up and down the streets.
And yesterday the bird of night did sit
Even at noon-day upon the market-place,
Hooting and shrieking. When these prodigies
Do so conjointly meet, let not men say
'These are their reasons—they are natural,'
For, I believe, they are portentous things
Unto the climate that they point upon.

CICERO
Indeed, it is a strange-disposed time;
But men may construe things after their fashion,
Clean from the purpose of the things themselves.
Come Caesar to the Capitol to-morrow?

CASCA
He doth; for he did bid Antonius
Send word to you he would be there to-morrow.

CICERO

Good night then, Casca: this disturbed sky
Is not to walk in.

CASCA

Farewell, Cicero.

Exit CICERO

Enter CASSIUS

CASSIUS

Who's there?

CASCA

A Roman.

CASSIUS

Casca, by your voice.

CASCA

Your ear is good. Cassius, what night is this!

CASSIUS

A very pleasing night to honest men.

CASCA

Who ever knew the heavens menace so?

CASSIUS

Those that have known the earth so full of faults.
For my part, I have walk'd about the streets,
Submitting me unto the perilous night,
And, thus unbraced, Casca, as you see,
Have bared my bosom to the thunder-stone;
And when the cross blue lightning seem'd to open
The breast of heaven, I did present myself
Even in the aim and very flash of it.

CASCA

But wherefore did you so much tempt the heavens?
It is the part of men to fear and tremble,
When the most mighty gods by tokens send
Such dreadful heralds to astonish us.

CASSIUS

You are dull, Casca, and those sparks of life
That should be in a Roman you do want,
Or else you use not. You look pale and gaze

And put on fear and cast yourself in wonder,
To see the strange impatience of the heavens:
But if you would consider the true cause
Why all these fires, why all these gliding ghosts,
Why birds and beasts from quality and kind,
Why old men fool and children calculate,
Why all these things change from their ordinance
Their natures and preformed faculties
To monstrous quality—why, you shall find
That heaven hath infused them with these spirits,
To make them instruments of fear and warning
Unto some monstrous state.
Now could I, Casca, name to thee a man
Most like this dreadful night,
That thunders, lightens, opens graves, and roars
As doth the lion in the Capitol;
A man no mightier than thyself or me
In personal action, yet prodigious grown,
And fearful, as these strange eruptions are.

CASCA

'Tis Caesar that you mean; is it not, Cassius?

CASSIUS

Let it be who it is: for Romans now
Have thews and limbs like to their ancestors.
But, woe the while! our fathers' minds are dead,
And we are govern'd with our mothers' spirits;
Our yoke and sufferance show us womanish.

CASCA

Indeed, they say the senators to-morrow
Mean to establish Caesar as a king;
And he shall wear his crown by sea and land,
In every place, save here in Italy.

CASSIUS

I know where I will wear this dagger then;
Cassius from bondage will deliver Cassius.
Therein, ye gods, you make the weak most strong;
Therein, ye gods, you tyrants do defeat.

Nor stony tower, nor walls of beaten brass,
Nor airless dungeon, nor strong links of iron,
Can be retentive to the strength of spirit;
But life, being weary of these worldly bars,
Never lacks power to dismiss itself.
If I know this, know all the world besides,
That part of tyranny that I do bear
I can shake off at pleasure.

Thunder still

CASCA
So can I;
So every bondman in his own hand bears
The power to cancel his captivity.

CASSIUS
And why should Caesar be a tyrant then?
Poor man! I know he would not be a wolf,
But that he sees the Romans are but sheep;
He were no lion, were not Romans hinds.
Those that with haste will make a mighty fire
Begin it with weak straws: what trash is Rome,
What rubbish and what offal, when it serves
For the base matter to illuminate
So vile a thing as Caesar! But, O grief,
Where hast thou led me? I perhaps speak this
Before a willing bondman; then I know
My answer must be made. But I am arm'd,
And dangers are to me indifferent.

CASCA
You speak to Casca, and to such a man
That is no fleering tell-tale. Hold, my hand:
Be factious for redress of all these griefs,
And I will set this foot of mine as far
As who goes farthest.

CASSIUS
There's a bargain made.
Now know you, Casca, I have moved already
Some certain of the noblest-minded Romans

To undergo with me an enterprise
Of honourable-dangerous consequence;
And I do know, by this, they stay for me
In Pompey's porch: for now, this fearful night,
There is no stir or walking in the streets;
And the complexion of the element
In favour's like the work we have in hand,
Most bloody, fiery, and most terrible.

CASCA
Stand close awhile, for here comes one in haste.

CASSIUS
'Tis Cinna; I do know him by his gait;
He is a friend.

Enter CINNA

Cinna, where haste you so?

CINNA
To find out you. Who's that? Metellus Cimber?

CASSIUS
No, it is Casca; one incorporate
To our attempts. Am I not stay'd for, Cinna?

CINNA
I am glad on't. What a fearful night is this!
There's two or three of us have seen strange sights.

CASSIUS
Am I not stay'd for? Tell me.

CINNA
Yes, you are. O Cassius, if you could
But win the noble Brutus to our party—

CASSIUS
Be you content: good Cinna, take this paper,
And look you lay it in the praetor's chair,
Where Brutus may but find it; and throw this
In at his window; set this up with wax
Upon old Brutus' statue: all this done,
Repair to Pompey's porch, where you shall find us.
Is Decius Brutus and Trebonius there?

CINNA

    All but Metellus Cimber; and he's gone
    To seek you at your house. Well, I will hie,
    And so bestow these papers as you bade me.

CASSIUS

    That done, repair to Pompey's theatre.

                                   Exit CINNA

    Come, Casca, you and I will yet ere day
    See Brutus at his house: three parts of him
    Is ours already, and the man entire
    Upon the next encounter yields him ours.

CASCA

    O, he sits high in all the people's hearts;
    And that which would appear offence in us,
    His countenance, like richest alchemy,
    Will change to virtue and to worthiness.

CASSIUS

    Him and his worth and our great need of him
    You have right well conceited. Let us go,
    For it is after midnight; and ere day
    We will awake him and be sure of him.

                                   Exeunt

ACT

II

SCENE I.
ROME. BRUTUS'S ORCHARD.

Enter BRUTUS

BRUTUS
What, Lucius, ho!
I cannot, by the progress of the stars,
Give guess how near to day. Lucius, I say!
I would it were my fault to sleep so soundly.
When, Lucius, when? awake, I say! what, Lucius!
Enter LUCIUS

LUCIUS
Call'd you, my lord?
BRUTUS
Get me a taper in my study, Lucius;
When it is lighted, come and call me here.
LUCIUS
I will, my lord.

Exit

BRUTUS
It must be by his death; and for my part,
I know no personal cause to spurn at him,

But for the general. He would be crown'd:
How that might change his nature, there's the question.
It is the bright day that brings forth the adder,
And that craves wary walking. Crown him—that!
And then, I grant, we put a sting in him
That at his will he may do danger with.
The abuse of greatness is, when it disjoins
Remorse from power: and, to speak truth of Caesar,
I have not known when his affections sway'd
More than his reason. But 'tis a common proof,
That lowliness is young ambition's ladder,
Whereto the climber-upward turns his face;
But when he once attains the upmost round.
He then unto the ladder turns his back,
Looks in the clouds, scorning the base degrees
By which he did ascend. So Caesar may.
Then, lest he may, prevent. And, since the quarrel
Will bear no colour for the thing he is,
Fashion it thus—that what he is, augmented,
Would run to these and these extremities;
And therefore think him as a serpent's egg
Which, hatch'd, would, as his kind, grow mischievous,
And kill him in the shell.

Re-enter LUCIUS

LUCIUS

The taper burneth in your closet, sir.
Searching the window for a flint, I found
This paper, thus seal'd up; and, I am sure,
It did not lie there when I went to bed.

Gives him the letter

BRUTUS

Get you to bed again; it is not day.
Is not to-morrow, boy, the ides of March?

LUCIUS

I know not, sir.

BRUTUS

Look in the calendar, and bring me word.

LUCIUS

    I will, sir.

Exit

BRUTUS

    The exhalations whizzing in the air
    Give so much light that I may read by them.

Opens the letter and reads

    'Brutus, thou sleep'st. Awake, and see thyself.
    Shall Rome, &c. Speak, strike, redress!
    Brutus, thou sleep'st; awake!'
    Such instigations have been often dropp'd
    Where I have took them up.
    'Shall Rome, &c.' Thus must I piece it out:
    Shall Rome stand under one man's awe? What, Rome?
    My ancestors did from the streets of Rome
    The Tarquin drive, when he was call'd a king.
    'Speak, strike, redress!' Am I entreated
    To speak and strike? O Rome, I make thee promise,
    If the redress will follow, thou receivest
    Thy full petition at the hand of Brutus!

Re-enter LUCIUS

LUCIUS

    Sir, March is wasted fourteen days.

Knocking within

BRUTUS

    'Tis good. Go to the gate; somebody knocks.

Exit LUCIUS

    Since Cassius first did whet me against Caesar,
    I have not slept.
    Between the acting of a dreadful thing
    And the first motion, all the interim is
    Like a phantasma, or a hideous dream.
    The Genius and the mortal instruments
    Are then in council; and the state of man,
    Like to a little kingdom, suffers then
    The nature of an insurrection.

Re-enter LUCIUS

LUCIUS

Sir, 'tis your brother Cassius at the door,
Who doth desire to see you.

BRUTUS

Is he alone?

LUCIUS

No, sir, there are more with him.

BRUTUS

Do you know them?

LUCIUS

No, sir; their hats are pluck'd about their ears,
And half their faces buried in their cloaks,
That by no means I may discover them
By any mark of favour.

BRUTUS

Let 'em enter.

Exit LUCIUS

They are the faction. O conspiracy,
Shamest thou to show thy dangerous brow by night,
When evils are most free? O, then by day
Where wilt thou find a cavern dark enough
To mask thy monstrous visage? Seek none, conspiracy;
Hide it in smiles and affability!
For if thou path, thy native semblance on,
Not Erebus itself were dim enough
To hide thee from prevention.

Enter the conspirators,
CASSIUS, CASCA, DECIUS BRUTUS,
CINNA, METELLUS CIMBER, *and* TREBONIUS

CASSIUS

I think we are too bold upon your rest.
Good morrow, Brutus; do we trouble you?

BRUTUS

I have been up this hour, awake all night.
Know I these men that come along with you?

CASSIUS

Yes, every man of them, and no man here

But honours you; and every one doth wish
You had but that opinion of yourself
Which every noble Roman bears of you.
This is Trebonius.

BRUTUS

He is welcome hither.

CASSIUS

This, Decius Brutus.

BRUTUS

He is welcome too.

CASSIUS

This, Casca; this, Cinna; and this, Metellus Cimber.

BRUTUS

They are all welcome.
What watchful cares do interpose themselves
Betwixt your eyes and night?

CASSIUS

Shall I entreat a word?

BRUTUS and CASSIUS whisper

DECIUS BRUTUS

Here lies the east. Doth not the day break here?

CASCA

No.

CINNA

O, pardon, sir, it doth; and yon grey lines
That fret the clouds are messengers of day.

CASCA

You shall confess that you are both deceived.
Here, as I point my sword, the sun arises,
Which is a great way growing on the south,
Weighing the youthful season of the year.
Some two months hence up higher toward the north
He first presents his fire; and the high east
Stands, as the Capitol, directly here.

BRUTUS

Give me your hands all over, one by one.

CASSIUS

    And let us swear our resolution.

BRUTUS

    No, not an oath: if not the face of men,
    The sufferance of our souls, the time's abuse,
    If these be motives weak, break off betimes,
    And every man hence to his idle bed;
    So let high-sighted tyranny range on,
    Till each man drop by lottery. But if these,
    As I am sure they do, bear fire enough
    To kindle cowards and to steel with valour
    The melting spirits of women, then, countrymen,
    What need we any spur but our own cause,
    To prick us to redress? what other bond
    Than secret Romans, that have spoke the word,
    And will not palter? and what other oath
    Than honesty to honesty engaged,
    That this shall be, or we will fall for it?
    Swear priests and cowards and men cautelous,
    Old feeble carrions and such suffering souls
    That welcome wrongs; unto bad causes swear
    Such creatures as men doubt; but do not stain
    The even virtue of our enterprise,
    Nor the insuppressive mettle of our spirits,
    To think that or our cause or our performance
    Did need an oath; when every drop of blood
    That every Roman bears, and nobly bears,
    Is guilty of a several bastardy,
    If he do break the smallest particle
    Of any promise that hath pass'd from him.

CASSIUS

    But what of Cicero? Shall we sound him?
    I think he will stand very strong with us.

CASCA

    Let us not leave him out.

CINNA

    No, by no means.

METELLUS CIMBER

    O, let us have him, for his silver hairs
    Will purchase us a good opinion
    And buy men's voices to commend our deeds.
    It shall be said, his judgment ruled our hands;
    Our youths and wildness shall no whit appear,
    But all be buried in his gravity.

BRUTUS

    O, name him not! Let us not break with him;
    For he will never follow anything
    That other men begin.

CASSIUS

    Then leave him out.

CASCA

    Indeed he is not fit.

DECIUS BRUTUS

    Shall no man else be touch'd but only Caesar?

CASSIUS

    Decius, well urged: I think it is not meet,
    Mark Antony, so well beloved of Caesar,
    Should outlive Caesar: we shall find of him
    A shrewd contriver; and, you know, his means,
    If he improve them, may well stretch so far
    As to annoy us all: which to prevent,
    Let Antony and Caesar fall together.

BRUTUS

    Our course will seem too bloody, Caius Cassius,
    To cut the head off and then hack the limbs,
    Like wrath in death and envy afterwards;
    For Antony is but a limb of Caesar.
    Let us be sacrificers, but not butchers, Caius.
    We all stand up against the spirit of Caesar;
    And in the spirit of men there is no blood.
    O, that we then could come by Caesar's spirit,
    And not dismember Caesar! But, alas,
    Caesar must bleed for it! And, gentle friends,
    Let's kill him boldly, but not wrathfully;

Let's carve him as a dish fit for the gods,
Not hew him as a carcass fit for hounds:
And let our hearts, as subtle masters do,
Stir up their servants to an act of rage,
And after seem to chide 'em. This shall make
Our purpose necessary and not envious:
Which so appearing to the common eyes,
We shall be call'd purgers, not murderers.
And for Mark Antony, think not of him;
For he can do no more than Caesar's arm
When Caesar's head is off.

CASSIUS

Yet I fear him;
For in the engrafted love he bears to Caesar—

BRUTUS

Alas, good Cassius, do not think of him!
If he love Caesar, all that he can do
Is to himself, take thought and die for Caesar;
And that were much he should; for he is given
To sports, to wildness and much company.

TREBONIUS

There is no fear in him; let him not die;
For he will live, and laugh at this hereafter.

Clock strikes

BRUTUS

Peace! Count the clock.

CASSIUS

The clock hath stricken three.

TREBONIUS

'Tis time to part.

CASSIUS

But it is doubtful yet,
Whether Caesar will come forth to-day, or no;
For he is superstitious grown of late,
Quite from the main opinion he held once
Of fantasy, of dreams and ceremonies:
It may be, these apparent prodigies,

The unaccustom'd terror of this night,
And the persuasion of his augurers,
May hold him from the Capitol to-day.

DECIUS BRUTUS

Never fear that: if he be so resolved,
I can o'ersway him; for he loves to hear
That unicorns may be betray'd with trees,
And bears with glasses, elephants with holes,
Lions with toils and men with flatterers;
But when I tell him he hates flatterers,
He says he does, being then most flattered.
Let me work;
For I can give his humour the true bent,
And I will bring him to the Capitol.

CASSIUS

Nay, we will all of us be there to fetch him.

BRUTUS

By the eighth hour: is that the uttermost?

CINNA

Be that the uttermost, and fail not then.

METELLUS CIMBER

Caius Ligarius doth bear Caesar hard,
Who rated him for speaking well of Pompey.
I wonder none of you have thought of him.

BRUTUS

Now, good Metellus, go along by him.
He loves me well, and I have given him reasons;
Send him but hither, and I'll fashion him.

CASSIUS

The morning comes upon's. We'll leave you, Brutus.
And, friends, disperse yourselves; but all remember
What you have said, and show yourselves true Romans.

BRUTUS

Good gentlemen, look fresh and merrily;
Let not our looks put on our purposes,
But bear it as our Roman actors do,
With untired spirits and formal constancy.

And so good morrow to you every one.

Exeunt all but BRUTUS

Boy! Lucius! Fast asleep? It is no matter;
Enjoy the honey-heavy dew of slumber:
Thou hast no figures nor no fantasies,
Which busy care draws in the brains of men;
Therefore thou sleep'st so sound.

Enter PORTIA

PORTIA
Brutus, my lord!
BRUTUS
Portia, what mean you? Wherefore rise you now?
It is not for your health thus to commit
Your weak condition to the raw cold morning.
PORTIA
Nor for yours neither. You've ungently, Brutus,
Stole from my bed: and yesternight, at supper,
You suddenly arose, and walk'd about,
Musing and sighing, with your arms across,
And when I ask'd you what the matter was,
You stared upon me with ungentle looks;
I urged you further; then you scratch'd your head,
And too impatiently stamp'd with your foot.
Yet I insisted, yet you answer'd not,
But, with an angry wafture of your hand,
Gave sign for me to leave you: so I did;
Fearing to strengthen that impatience
Which seem'd too much enkindled, and withal
Hoping it was but an effect of humour,
Which sometime hath his hour with every man.
It will not let you eat, nor talk, nor sleep;
And could it work so much upon your shape
As it hath much prevail'd on your condition,
I should not know you, Brutus. Dear my lord,
Make me acquainted with your cause of grief.
BRUTUS
I am not well in health, and that is all.

PORTIA

    Brutus is wise, and, were he not in health,
    He would embrace the means to come by it.

BRUTUS

    Why, so I do. Good Portia, go to bed.

PORTIA

    Is Brutus sick, and is it physical
    To walk unbraced and suck up the humours
    Of the dank morning? What, is Brutus sick,
    And will he steal out of his wholesome bed,
    To dare the vile contagion of the night
    And tempt the rheumy and unpurged air
    To add unto his sickness? No, my Brutus;
    You have some sick offence within your mind,
    Which, by the right and virtue of my place,
    I ought to know of: and, upon my knees,
    I charm you, by my once-commended beauty,
    By all your vows of love and that great vow
    Which did incorporate and make us one,
    That you unfold to me, yourself, your half,
    Why you are heavy, and what men to-night
    Have had to resort to you; for here have been
    Some six or seven, who did hide their faces
    Even from darkness.

BRUTUS

    Kneel not, gentle Portia.

PORTIA

    I should not need, if you were gentle Brutus.
    Within the bond of marriage, tell me, Brutus,
    Is it excepted I should know no secrets
    That appertain to you? Am I yourself
    But, as it were, in sort or limitation?
    To keep with you at meals, comfort your bed,
    And talk to you sometimes? Dwell I but in the suburbs
    Of your good pleasure? If it be no more,
    Portia is Brutus' harlot, not his wife.

BRUTUS

    You are my true and honourable wife,
    As dear to me as are the ruddy drops
    That visit my sad heart.

PORTIA

    If this were true, then should I know this secret.
    I grant I am a woman; but withal
    A woman that Lord Brutus took to wife.
    I grant I am a woman; but withal
    A woman well-reputed, Cato's daughter.
    Think you I am no stronger than my sex,
    Being so father'd and so husbanded?
    Tell me your counsels, I will not disclose 'em.
    I have made strong proof of my constancy,
    Giving myself a voluntary wound
    Here, in the thigh: can I bear that with patience.
    And not my husband's secrets?

BRUTUS

    O ye gods,
    Render me worthy of this noble wife!

                      Knocking within

    Hark, hark! one knocks. Portia, go in awhile;
    And by and by thy bosom shall partake
    The secrets of my heart.
    All my engagements I will construe to thee,
    All the charactery of my sad brows.
    Leave me with haste.

                                    Exit PORTIA

    Lucius, who's that knocks?

                Re-enter LUCIUS *with* LIGARIUS

LUCIUS

    He is a sick man that would speak with you.

BRUTUS

    Caius Ligarius, that Metellus spake of.
    Boy, stand aside. Caius Ligarius, how?

LIGARIUS

    Vouchsafe good morrow from a feeble tongue.

BRUTUS

    O, what a time have you chose out, brave Caius,

    To wear a kerchief! Would you were not sick!

LIGARIUS

    I am not sick, if Brutus have in hand

    Any exploit worthy the name of honour.

BRUTUS

    Such an exploit have I in hand, Ligarius,

    Had you a healthful ear to hear of it.

LIGARIUS

    By all the gods that Romans bow before,

    I here discard my sickness. [*Pulls off his kerchief*] Soul of Rome!

    Brave son, derived from honourable loins!

    Thou, like an exorcist, hast conjured up

    My mortified spirit. Now bid me run,

    And I will strive with things impossible;

    Yea, get the better of them. What's to do?

BRUTUS

    A piece of work that will make sick men whole.

LIGARIUS

    But are not some whole that we must make sick?

BRUTUS

    That must we also. What it is, my Caius,

    I shall unfold to thee, as we are going

    To whom it must be done.

LIGARIUS

    Set on your foot,

    And with a heart new-fired I follow you,

    To do I know not what; but it sufficeth

    That Brutus leads me on. [*Thunder.*]

BRUTUS

    Follow me, then.

                                       Exeunt

SCENE II.
CAESAR'S HOUSE.

Thunder and lightning. Enter CAESAR, *in his night-gown*

CAESAR

    Nor heaven nor earth have been at peace to-night:
    Thrice hath Calpurnia in her sleep cried out,
    'Help, ho! They murder Caesar!' Who's within?

Enter a Servant

SERVANT

    My lord?

CAESAR

    Go bid the priests do present sacrifice
    And bring me their opinions of success.

SERVANT

    I will, my lord.

Exit

Enter CALPURNIA

CALPURNIA

    What mean you, Caesar? Think you to walk forth?
    You shall not stir out of your house to-day.

CAESAR

    Caesar shall forth: the things that threaten'd me
    Ne'er look'd but on my back. When they shall see
    The face of Caesar, they are vanished.

CALPURNIA

    Caesar, I never stood on ceremonies,
    Yet now they fright me. There is one within,
    Besides the things that we have heard and seen,
    Recounts most horrid sights seen by the watch.
    A lioness hath whelped in the streets;
    And graves have yawn'd, and yielded up their dead;
    Fierce fiery warriors fought upon the clouds,
    In ranks and squadrons and right form of war,
    Which drizzled blood upon the Capitol;
    The noise of battle hurtled in the air,
    Horses did neigh, and dying men did groan,

And ghosts did shriek and squeal about the streets.
O Caesar! these things are beyond all use,
And I do fear them.

CAESAR

What can be avoided
Whose end is purposed by the mighty gods?
Yet Caesar shall go forth; for these predictions
Are to the world in general as to Caesar.

CALPURNIA

When beggars die, there are no comets seen;
The heavens themselves blaze forth the death of princes.

CAESAR

Cowards die many times before their deaths;
The valiant never taste of death but once.
Of all the wonders that I yet have heard.
It seems to me most strange that men should fear;
Seeing that death, a necessary end,
Will come when it will come.

Re-enter Servant

What say the augurers?

SERVANT

They would not have you to stir forth to-day.
Plucking the entrails of an offering forth,
They could not find a heart within the beast.

CAESAR

The gods do this in shame of cowardice.
Caesar should be a beast without a heart,
If he should stay at home to-day for fear.
No, Caesar shall not: danger knows full well
That Caesar is more dangerous than he:
We are two lions litter'd in one day,
And I the elder and more terrible;
And Caesar shall go forth.

CALPURNIA

Alas, my lord,
Your wisdom is consumed in confidence.
Do not go forth to-day: call it my fear

That keeps you in the house, and not your own.
We'll send Mark Antony to the Senate House,
And he shall say you are not well to-day.
Let me, upon my knee, prevail in this.

CAESAR

Mark Antony shall say I am not well,
And, for thy humour, I will stay at home.

Enter DECIUS BRUTUS

Here's Decius Brutus, he shall tell them so.

DECIUS BRUTUS

Caesar, all hail! Good morrow, worthy Caesar.
I come to fetch you to the Senate House.

CAESAR

And you are come in very happy time,
To bear my greeting to the senators
And tell them that I will not come to-day.
Cannot, is false, and that I dare not, falser;
I will not come to-day: tell them so, Decius.

CALPURNIA

Say he is sick.

CAESAR

Shall Caesar send a lie?
Have I in conquest stretch'd mine arm so far,
To be afraid to tell greybeards the truth?
Decius, go tell them Caesar will not come.

DECIUS BRUTUS

Most mighty Caesar, let me know some cause,
Lest I be laugh'd at when I tell them so.

CAESAR

The cause is in my will: I will not come;
That is enough to satisfy the senate.
But for your private satisfaction,
Because I love you, I will let you know:
Calpurnia here, my wife, stays me at home.
She dreamt to-night she saw my statua,
Which, like a fountain with an hundred spouts,
Did run pure blood: and many lusty Romans

Came smiling, and did bathe their hands in it.
And these does she apply for warnings, and portents,
And evils imminent; and on her knee
Hath begg'd that I will stay at home to-day.

DECIUS BRUTUS

This dream is all amiss interpreted;
It was a vision fair and fortunate.
Your statue spouting blood in many pipes,
In which so many smiling Romans bathed,
Signifies that from you great Rome shall suck
Reviving blood, and that great men shall press
For tinctures, stains, relics and cognizance.
This by Calpurnia's dream is signified.

CAESAR

And this way have you well expounded it.

DECIUS BRUTUS

I have, when you have heard what I can say—
And know it now: the senate have concluded
To give this day a crown to mighty Caesar.
If you shall send them word you will not come,
Their minds may change. Besides, it were a mock
Apt to be render'd, for some one to say
'Break up the senate till another time,
When Caesar's wife shall meet with better dreams.'
If Caesar hide himself, shall they not whisper
'Lo, Caesar is afraid'?
Pardon me, Caesar; for my dear dear love
To our proceeding bids me tell you this;
And reason to my love is liable.

CAESAR

How foolish do your fears seem now, Calpurnia!
I am ashamed I did yield to them.
Give me my robe, for I will go.

Enter PUBLIUS, BRUTUS, LIGARIUS, METELLUS,
CASCA, TREBONIUS, *and* CINNA

And look where Publius is come to fetch me.

PUBLIUS
Good morrow, Caesar.
CAESAR
Welcome, Publius.
What, Brutus, are you stirr'd so early too?
Good morrow, Casca. Caius Ligarius,
Caesar was ne'er so much your enemy
As that same ague which hath made you lean.
What is't o'clock?
BRUTUS
Caesar, 'tis strucken eight.
CAESAR
I thank you for your pains and courtesy.

Enter ANTONY

See! Antony, that revels long o' nights,
Is notwithstanding up. Good morrow, Antony.
ANTONY
So to most noble Caesar.
CAESAR
Bid them prepare within.
I am to blame to be thus waited for.
Now, Cinna. Now, Metellus. What, Trebonius!
I have an hour's talk in store for you.
Remember that you call on me to-day;
Be near me, that I may remember you.
TREBONIUS
Caesar, I will.
[*Aside*]
And so near will I be,
That your best friends shall wish I had been further.
CAESAR
Good friends, go in, and taste some wine with me;
And we, like friends, will straightway go together.
BRUTUS
[*Aside*] That every like is not the same, O Caesar,
The heart of Brutus yearns to think upon!

Exeunt

SCENE III.
A STREET NEAR THE CAPITOL.

Enter ARTEMIDORUS, *reading a paper*

ARTEMIDORUS

'Caesar, beware of Brutus; take heed of Cassius; come not
near Casca; have an eye to Cinna; trust not Trebonius; mark
well Metellus Cimber; Decius Brutus loves thee not; thou hast
wronged Caius Ligarius. There is but one mind in all these men,
and it is bent against Caesar. If thou beest not immortal, look
about you. Security gives way to conspiracy. The mighty gods
defend thee!

Thy lover,

ARTEMIDORUS.'

Here will I stand till Caesar pass along,
And as a suitor will I give him this.
My heart laments that virtue cannot live
Out of the teeth of emulation.
If thou read this, O Caesar, thou mayst live;
If not, the Fates with traitors do contrive.

Exit

SCENE IV.
ANOTHER PART OF THE SAME STREET,
BEFORE THE HOUSE OF BRUTUS.

Enter PORTIA *and* LUCIUS

PORTIA

I prithee, boy, run to the Senate House;
Stay not to answer me, but get thee gone.
Why dost thou stay?

LUCIUS

To know my errand, madam.

PORTIA

I would have had thee there, and here again,
Ere I can tell thee what thou shouldst do there.
O constancy, be strong upon my side!

Set a huge mountain 'tween my heart and tongue!
I have a man's mind, but a woman's might.
How hard it is for women to keep counsel!
Art thou here yet?

LUCIUS

Madam, what should I do?
Run to the Capitol, and nothing else?
And so return to you, and nothing else?

PORTIA

Yes, bring me word, boy, if thy lord look well,
For he went sickly forth: and take good note
What Caesar doth, what suitors press to him.
Hark, boy! what noise is that?

LUCIUS

I hear none, madam.

PORTIA

Prithee, listen well.
I heard a bustling rumour, like a fray,
And the wind brings it from the Capitol.

LUCIUS

Sooth, madam, I hear nothing.

Enter the Soothsayer

PORTIA

Come hither, fellow. Which way hast thou been?

SOOTHSAYER

At mine own house, good lady.

PORTIA

What is't o'clock?

SOOTHSAYER

About the ninth hour, lady.

PORTIA

Is Caesar yet gone to the Capitol?

SOOTHSAYER

Madam, not yet: I go to take my stand,
To see him pass on to the Capitol.

PORTIA

Thou hast some suit to Caesar, hast thou not?

SOOTHSAYER

    That I have, lady. If it will please Caesar
    To be so good to Caesar as to hear me,
    I shall beseech him to befriend himself.

PORTIA

    Why, know'st thou any harm's intended towards him?

SOOTHSAYER

    None that I know will be, much that I fear may chance.
    Good morrow to you. Here the street is narrow;
    The throng that follows Caesar at the heels,
    Of senators, of praetors, common suitors,
    Will crowd a feeble man almost to death.
    I'll get me to a place more void, and there
    Speak to great Caesar as he comes along.

Exit

PORTIA

    I must go in. Ay me, how weak a thing
    The heart of woman is! O Brutus,
    The heavens speed thee in thine enterprise!
    Sure, the boy heard me: Brutus hath a suit
    That Caesar will not grant. O, I grow faint.
    Run, Lucius, and commend me to my lord;
    Say I am merry: come to me again,
    And bring me word what he doth say to thee.

Exeunt severally

ACT

SCENE I.
ROME. BEFORE THE CAPITOL;
THE SENATE SITTING ABOVE.

A crowd of people; among them ARTEMIDORUS *and
the Soothsayer. Flourish. Enter* CAESAR, BRUTUS,
CASSIUS, CASCA, DECIUS BRUTUS, METELLUS CIMBER,
TREBONIUS, CINNA, ANTONY, LEPIDUS, POPILIUS,
PUBLIUS, *and others*

CAESAR
    [*To the Soothsayer*] The ides of March are come.
SOOTHSAYER
    Ay, Caesar; but not gone.
ARTEMIDORUS
    Hail, Caesar! Read this schedule.
DECIUS BRUTUS
    Trebonius doth desire you to o'erread,
    At your best leisure, this his humble suit.
ARTEMIDORUS
    O Caesar, read mine first; for mine's a suit
    That touches Caesar nearer. Read it, great Caesar.

CAESAR

What touches us ourself shall be last served.

ARTEMIDORUS

Delay not, Caesar; read it instantly.

CAESAR

What, is the fellow mad?

PUBLIUS

Sirrah, give place.

CASSIUS

What, urge you your petitions in the street?
Come to the Capitol.

*CAESAR goes up to the Senate House,
the rest following*

POPILIUS

I wish your enterprise to-day may thrive.

CASSIUS

What enterprise, Popilius?

POPILIUS

Fare you well.

Advances to CAESAR

BRUTUS

What said Popilius Lena?

CASSIUS

He wish'd to-day our enterprise might thrive.
I fear our purpose is discovered.

BRUTUS

Look, how he makes to Caesar; mark him.

CASSIUS

Casca, be sudden, for we fear prevention.
Brutus, what shall be done? If this be known,
Cassius or Caesar never shall turn back,
For I will slay myself.

BRUTUS

Cassius, be constant.
Popilius Lena speaks not of our purposes;
For, look, he smiles, and Caesar doth not change.

CASSIUS
>Trebonius knows his time; for, look you, Brutus.
>He draws Mark Antony out of the way.

>*Exeunt* ANTONY *and*
>TREBONIUS

DECIUS BRUTUS
>Where is Metellus Cimber? Let him go,
>And presently prefer his suit to Caesar.

BRUTUS
>He is address'd; press near and second him.

CINNA
>Casca, you are the first that rears your hand.

CAESAR
>Are we all ready? What is now amiss
>That Caesar and his senate must redress?

METELLUS CIMBER
>Most high, most mighty, and most puissant Caesar,
>Metellus Cimber throws before thy seat
>An humble heart.

>*Kneeling*

CAESAR
>I must prevent thee, Cimber.
>These couchings and these lowly courtesies
>Might fire the blood of ordinary men,
>And turn pre-ordinance and first decree
>Into the law of children. Be not fond,
>To think that Caesar bears such rebel blood
>That will be thaw'd from the true quality
>With that which melteth fools; I mean, sweet words,
>Low-crooked court'sies and base spaniel-fawning.
>Thy brother by decree is banished:
>If thou dost bend and pray and fawn for him,
>I spurn thee like a cur out of my way.
>Know, Caesar doth not wrong, nor without cause
>Will he be satisfied.

METELLUS CIMBER
>Is there no voice more worthy than my own

To sound more sweetly in great Caesar's ear
For the repealing of my banish'd brother?
BRUTUS
I kiss thy hand, but not in flattery, Caesar;
Desiring thee that Publius Cimber may
Have an immediate freedom of repeal.
CAESAR
What, Brutus!
CASSIUS
Pardon, Caesar! Caesar, pardon!
As low as to thy foot doth Cassius fall,
To beg enfranchisement for Publius Cimber.
CASSIUS
I could be well moved, if I were as you;
If I could pray to move, prayers would move me;
But I am constant as the northern star,
Of whose true-fix'd and resting quality
There is no fellow in the firmament.
The skies are painted with unnumber'd sparks,
They are all fire and every one doth shine,
But there's but one in all doth hold his place.
So in the world; 'tis furnish'd well with men,
And men are flesh and blood, and apprehensive;
Yet in the number I do know but one
That unassailable holds on his rank,
Unshaked of motion: and that I am he,
Let me a little show it, even in this;
That I was constant Cimber should be banish'd,
And constant do remain to keep him so.
CINNA
O Caesar!
CAESAR
Hence! Wilt thou lift up Olympus?
DECIUS BRUTUS
Great Caesar!
CAESAR
Doth not Brutus bootless kneel?

CASCA

Speak, hands for me!

CASCA first, then the other
Conspirators and BRUTUS stab CAESAR

CAESAR

Et tu, Brute! Then fall, Caesar.

Dies

CINNA

Liberty! Freedom! Tyranny is dead!
Run hence, proclaim, cry it about the streets.

CASSIUS

Some to the common pulpits, and cry out
'Liberty, freedom, and enfranchisement!'

BRUTUS

People and senators, be not affrighted.
Fly not; stand stiff. Ambition's debt is paid.

CASCA

Go to the pulpit, Brutus.

DECIUS BRUTUS

And Cassius too.

BRUTUS

Where's Publius?

CINNA

Here, quite confounded with this mutiny.

METELLUS CIMBER

Stand fast together, lest some friend of Caesar's
Should chance—

BRUTUS

Talk not of standing. Publius, good cheer!
There is no harm intended to your person,
Nor to no Roman else: so tell them, Publius.

CASSIUS

And leave us, Publius; lest that the people,
Rushing on us, should do your age some mischief.

BRUTUS

Do so: and let no man abide this deed,
But we the doers.

CASSIUS

    Where is Antony?

TREBONIUS

    Fled to his house amazed.

    Men, wives and children stare, cry out and run

    As it were doomsday.

BRUTUS

    Fates, we will know your pleasures.

    That we shall die, we know; 'tis but the time

    And drawing days out, that men stand upon.

CASSIUS

    Why, he that cuts off twenty years of life

    Cuts off so many years of fearing death.

BRUTUS

    Grant that, and then is death a benefit.

    So are we Caesar's friends, that have abridged

    His time of fearing death. Stoop, Romans, stoop,

    And let us bathe our hands in Caesar's blood

    Up to the elbows, and besmear our swords.

    Then walk we forth, even to the market-place,

    And, waving our red weapons o'er our heads,

    Let's all cry 'Peace, freedom and liberty!'

CASSIUS

    Stoop, then, and wash. How many ages hence

    Shall this our lofty scene be acted over

    In states unborn and accents yet unknown!

BRUTUS

    How many times shall Caesar bleed in sport,

    That now on Pompey's basis lies along

    No worthier than the dust!

CASSIUS

    So oft as that shall be,

    So often shall the knot of us be call'd

    The men that gave their country liberty.

DECIUS BRUTUS

    What, shall we forth?

CASSIUS
    Ay, every man away.
    Brutus shall lead; and we will grace his heels
    With the most boldest and best hearts of Rome.
Enter a Servant

BRUTUS
    Soft! who comes here? A friend of Antony's.

SERVANT
    Thus, Brutus, did my master bid me kneel;
    Thus did Mark Antony bid me fall down;
    And, being prostrate, thus he bade me say:
    Brutus is noble, wise, valiant, and honest;
    Caesar was mighty, bold, royal, and loving.
    Say I love Brutus, and I honour him;
    Say I fear'd Caesar, honour'd him and loved him.
    If Brutus will vouchsafe that Antony
    May safely come to him, and be resolved
    How Caesar hath deserved to lie in death,
    Mark Antony shall not love Caesar dead
    So well as Brutus living; but will follow
    The fortunes and affairs of noble Brutus
    Thorough the hazards of this untrod state
    With all true faith. So says my master Antony.

BRUTUS
    Thy master is a wise and valiant Roman;
    I never thought him worse.
    Tell him, so please him come unto this place,
    He shall be satisfied; and, by my honour,
    Depart untouch'd.

SERVANT
    I'll fetch him presently.

Exit

BRUTUS
    I know that we shall have him well to friend.

CASSIUS
    I wish we may: but yet have I a mind

That fears him much; and my misgiving still
Falls shrewdly to the purpose.
BRUTUS
But here comes Antony.

Re-enter ANTONY

Welcome, Mark Antony.
ANTONY
O mighty Caesar! dost thou lie so low?
Are all thy conquests, glories, triumphs, spoils,
Shrunk to this little measure? Fare thee well.
I know not, gentlemen, what you intend,
Who else must be let blood, who else is rank:
If I myself, there is no hour so fit
As Caesar's death hour, nor no instrument
Of half that worth as those your swords, made rich
With the most noble blood of all this world.
I do beseech ye, if you bear me hard,
Now, whilst your purpled hands do reek and smoke,
Fulfil your pleasure. Live a thousand years,
I shall not find myself so apt to die.
No place will please me so, no mean of death,
As here by Caesar, and by you cut off,
The choice and master spirits of this age.
BRUTUS
O Antony! beg not your death of us.
Though now we must appear bloody and cruel,
As, by our hands and this our present act,
You see we do, yet see you but our hands
And this the bleeding business they have done:
Our hearts you see not; they are pitiful;
And pity to the general wrong of Rome—
As fire drives out fire, so pity pity—
Hath done this deed on Caesar. For your part,
To you our swords have leaden points, Mark Antony:
Our arms, in strength of malice, and our hearts
Of brothers' temper, do receive you in
With all kind love, good thoughts, and reverence.

CASSIUS
>Your voice shall be as strong as any man's
>In the disposing of new dignities.

BRUTUS
>Only be patient till we have appeased
>The multitude, beside themselves with fear,
>And then we will deliver you the cause,
>Why I, that did love Caesar when I struck him,
>Have thus proceeded.

ANTONY
>I doubt not of your wisdom.
>Let each man render me his bloody hand:
>First, Marcus Brutus, will I shake with you;
>Next, Caius Cassius, do I take your hand;
>Now, Decius Brutus, yours: now yours, Metellus;
>Yours, Cinna; and, my valiant Casca, yours.
>Though last, not last in love, yours, good Trebonius.
>Gentlemen all—alas, what shall I say?
>My credit now stands on such slippery ground,
>That one of two bad ways you must conceit me,
>Either a coward or a flatterer.
>That I did love thee, Caesar, O, 'tis true!
>If then thy spirit look upon us now,
>Shall it not grieve thee dearer than thy death,
>To see thy thy Anthony making his peace,
>Shaking the bloody fingers of thy foes,
>Most noble! in the presence of thy corse?
>Had I as many eyes as thou hast wounds,
>Weeping as fast as they stream forth thy blood,
>It would become me better than to close
>In terms of friendship with thine enemies.
>Pardon me, Julius! Here wast thou bay'd, brave hart;
>Here didst thou fall; and here thy hunters stand,
>Sign'd in thy spoil, and crimson'd in thy lethe.
>O world, thou wast the forest to this hart;
>And this, indeed, O world, the heart of thee!

How like a deer, strucken by many princes,
Dost thou here lie!

CASSIUS

Mark Antony—

ANTONY

Pardon me, Caius Cassius.
The enemies of Caesar shall say this;
Then, in a friend, it is cold modesty.

CASSIUS

I blame you not for praising Caesar so;
But what compact mean you to have with us?
Will you be prick'd in number of our friends,
Or shall we on, and not depend on you?

ANTONY

Therefore I took your hands, but was, indeed,
Sway'd from the point, by looking down on Caesar.
Friends am I with you all and love you all,
Upon this hope, that you shall give me reasons
Why and wherein Caesar was dangerous.

BRUTUS

Or else were this a savage spectacle.
Our reasons are so full of good regard
That were you, Antony, the son of Caesar,
You should be satisfied.

ANTONY

That's all I seek;
And am moreover suitor that I may
Produce his body to the market-place;
And in the pulpit, as becomes a friend,
Speak in the order of his funeral.

BRUTUS

You shall, Mark Antony.

CASSIUS

Brutus, a word with you.

Aside to BRUTUS

You know not what you do. Do not consent
That Antony speak in his funeral.

Know you how much the people may be moved
By that which he will utter?

BRUTUS

By your pardon;
I will myself into the pulpit first,
And show the reason of our Caesar's death.
What Antony shall speak, I will protest
He speaks by leave and by permission,
And that we are contented Caesar shall
Have all true rites and lawful ceremonies.
It shall advantage more than do us wrong.

CASSIUS

I know not what may fall; I like it not.

BRUTUS

Mark Antony, here, take you Caesar's body.
You shall not in your funeral speech blame us,
But speak all good you can devise of Caesar,
And say you do't by our permission;
Else shall you not have any hand at all
About his funeral: and you shall speak
In the same pulpit whereto I am going,
After my speech is ended.

ANTONY

Be it so.
I do desire no more.

BRUTUS

Prepare the body then, and follow us.

Exeunt all but ANTONY

ANTONY

O, pardon me, thou bleeding piece of earth,
That I am meek and gentle with these butchers!
Thou art the ruins of the noblest man
That ever lived in the tide of times.
Woe to the hand that shed this costly blood!
Over thy wounds now do I prophesy—
Which, like dumb mouths, do ope their ruby lips,
To beg the voice and utterance of my tongue—

A curse shall light upon the limbs of men;
Domestic fury and fierce civil strife
Shall cumber all the parts of Italy;
Blood and destruction shall be so in use
And dreadful objects so familiar
That mothers shall but smile when they behold
Their infants quarter'd with the hands of war;
All pity choked with custom of fell deeds;
And Caesar's spirit, ranging for revenge,
With Ate by his side come hot from hell,
Shall in these confines with a monarch's voice
Cry 'Havoc,' and let slip the dogs of war;
That this foul deed shall smell above the earth
With carrion men, groaning for burial.

Enter a Servant

You serve Octavius Caesar, do you not?

SERVANT

I do, Mark Antony.

ANTONY

Caesar did write for him to come to Rome.

SERVANT

He did receive his letters, and is coming;
And bid me say to you by word of mouth—
O Caesar!

Seeing the body

ANTONY

Thy heart is big, get thee apart and weep.
Passion, I see, is catching; for mine eyes,
Seeing those beads of sorrow stand in thine,
Began to water. Is thy master coming?

SERVANT

He lies to-night within seven leagues of Rome.

ANTONY

Post back with speed, and tell him what hath chanced:
Here is a mourning Rome, a dangerous Rome,
No Rome of safety for Octavius yet;
Hie hence, and tell him so. Yet, stay awhile;

Thou shalt not back till I have borne this corse
Into the market-place: there shall I try
In my oration, how the people take
The cruel issue of these bloody men;
According to the which, thou shalt discourse
To young Octavius of the state of things.
Lend me your hand.

Exeunt with Caesar's *body*

SCENE II.
THE FORUM.

Enter Brutus *and* Cassius, *and a throng of Citizens*

CITIZENS

We will be satisfied! Let us be satisfied!

BRUTUS

Then follow me, and give me audience, friends.
Cassius, go you into the other street,
And part the numbers.
Those that will hear me speak, let 'em stay here;
Those that will follow Cassius, go with him;
And public reasons shall be rendered
Of Caesar's death.

FIRST CITIZEN

I will hear Brutus speak.

SECOND CITIZEN

I will hear Cassius; and compare their reasons,
When severally we hear them rendered.

Exit Cassius, *with some of the Citizens.*
Brutus *goes into the pulpit*

THIRD CITIZEN

The noble Brutus is ascended. Silence!

BRUTUS

Be patient till the last.
Romans, countrymen, and lovers! hear me for my cause, and
be silent, that you may hear. Believe me for mine honour, and
have respect to mine honour, that you may believe. Censure me

in your wisdom, and awake your senses, that you may the better judge. If there be any in this assembly, any dear friend of Caesar's, to him I say, that Brutus' love to Caesar was no less than his. If then that friend demand why Brutus rose against Caesar, this is my answer: Not that I loved Caesar less, but that I loved Rome more. Had you rather Caesar were living and die all slaves, than that Caesar were dead, to live all free men? As Caesar loved me, I weep for him; as he was fortunate, I rejoice at it; as he was valiant, I honour him; but, as he was ambitious, I slew him. There is tears for his love; joy for his fortune; honour for his valour; and death for his ambition. Who is here so base that would be a bondman? If any, speak; for him have I offended. Who is here so rude that would not be a Roman? If any, speak; for him have I offended. Who is here so vile that will not love his country? If any, speak; for him have I offended. I pause for a reply.

ALL

None, Brutus, none.

BRUTUS

Then none have I offended. I have done no more to Caesar than you shall do to Brutus. The question of his death is enrolled in the Capitol; his glory not extenuated, wherein he was worthy, nor his offences enforced, for which he suffered death.

Enter ANTONY *and others, with* CAESAR'S *body*

Here comes his body, mourned by Mark Antony: who, though he had no hand in his death, shall receive the benefit of his dying, a place in the commonwealth; as which of you shall not? With this I depart—that, as I slew my best lover for the good of Rome, I have the same dagger for myself, when it shall please my country to need my death.

ALL

Live, Brutus! live, live!

FIRST CITIZEN

Bring him with triumph home unto his house.

SECOND CITIZEN

Give him a statue with his ancestors.

THIRD CITIZEN

Let him be Caesar.

FOURTH CITIZEN
    Caesar's better parts
    Shall be crown'd in Brutus.
FIRST CITIZEN
    We'll bring him to his house with shouts and clamours.
BRUTUS
    My countrymen—
SECOND CITIZEN
    Peace, silence! Brutus speaks.
FIRST CITIZEN
    Peace, ho!
BRUTUS
    Good countrymen, let me depart alone,
    And, for my sake, stay here with Antony.
    Do grace to Caesar's corpse, and grace his speech
    Tending to Caesar's glories; which Mark Antony,
    By our permission, is allow'd to make.
    I do entreat you, not a man depart,
    Save I alone, till Antony have spoke.

Exit

FIRST CITIZEN
    Stay, ho! and let us hear Mark Antony.
THIRD CITIZEN
    Let him go up into the public chair;
    We'll hear him. Noble Antony, go up.
ANTONY
    For Brutus' sake, I am beholding to you.
Goes into the pulpit
FOURTH CITIZEN
    What does he say of Brutus?
THIRD CITIZEN
    He says, for Brutus' sake,
    He finds himself beholding to us all.
FOURTH CITIZEN
    'Twere best he speak no harm of Brutus here.
FIRST CITIZEN
    This Caesar was a tyrant.

THIRD CITIZEN

Nay, that's certain.

We are blest that Rome is rid of him.

SECOND CITIZEN

Peace! let us hear what Antony can say.

ANTONY

You gentle Romans—

CITIZENS

Peace, ho! let us hear him.

ANTONY

Friends, Romans, countrymen, lend me your ears;
I come to bury Caesar, not to praise him.
The evil that men do lives after them;
The good is oft interred with their bones;
So let it be with Caesar. The noble Brutus
Hath told you Caesar was ambitious.
If it were so, it was a grievous fault,
And grievously hath Caesar answer'd it.
Here, under leave of Brutus and the rest—
For Brutus is an honourable man;
So are they all, all honourable men—
Come I to speak in Caesar's funeral.
He was my friend, faithful and just to me;
But Brutus says he was ambitious;
And Brutus is an honourable man.
He hath brought many captives home to Rome
Whose ransoms did the general coffers fill;
Did this in Caesar seem ambitious?
When that the poor have cried, Caesar hath wept;
Ambition should be made of sterner stuff.
Yet Brutus says he was ambitious;
And Brutus is an honourable man.
You all did see that on the Lupercal
I thrice presented him a kingly crown,
Which he did thrice refuse: was this ambition?
Yet Brutus says he was ambitious;
And, sure, he is an honourable man.

I speak not to disprove what Brutus spoke,
But here I am to speak what I do know.
You all did love him once, not without cause;
What cause withholds you then, to mourn for him?
O judgment! thou art fled to brutish beasts,
And men have lost their reason. Bear with me;
My heart is in the coffin there with Caesar,
And I must pause till it come back to me.

FIRST CITIZEN

Methinks there is much reason in his sayings.

SECOND CITIZEN

If thou consider rightly of the matter,
Caesar has had great wrong.

THIRD CITIZEN

Has he, masters?
I fear there will a worse come in his place.

FOURTH CITIZEN

Mark'd ye his words? He would not take the crown;
Therefore 'tis certain he was not ambitious.

FIRST CITIZEN

If it be found so, some will dear abide it.

SECOND CITIZEN

Poor soul! his eyes are red as fire with weeping.

THIRD CITIZEN

There's not a nobler man in Rome than Antony.

FOURTH CITIZEN

Now mark him, he begins again to speak.

ANTONY

But yesterday the word of Caesar might
Have stood against the world; now lies he there.
And none so poor to do him reverence.
O masters, if I were disposed to stir
Your hearts and minds to mutiny and rage,
I should do Brutus wrong, and Cassius wrong,
Who, you all know, are honourable men.
I will not do them wrong; I rather choose
To wrong the dead, to wrong myself and you,

Than I will wrong such honourable men.
But here's a parchment with the seal of Caesar;
I found it in his closet, 'tis his will.
Let but the commons hear this testament—
Which, pardon me, I do not mean to read—
And they would go and kiss dead Caesar's wounds
And dip their napkins in his sacred blood,
Yea, beg a hair of him for memory,
And, dying, mention it within their wills,
Bequeathing it as a rich legacy
Unto their issue.

FOURTH CITIZEN
We'll hear the will: read it, Mark Antony.

ALL
The will, the will! We will hear Caesar's will.

ANTONY
Have patience, gentle friends, I must not read it;
It is not meet you know how Caesar loved you.
You are not wood, you are not stones, but men;
And, being men, bearing the will of Caesar,
It will inflame you, it will make you mad:
'Tis good you know not that you are his heirs;
For, if you should, O, what would come of it!

FOURTH CITIZEN
Read the will; we'll hear it, Antony;
You shall read us the will, Caesar's will.

ANTONY
Will you be patient? Will you stay awhile?
I have o'ershot myself to tell you of it:
I fear I wrong the honourable men
Whose daggers have stabb'd Caesar; I do fear it.

FOURTH CITIZEN
They were traitors: honourable men!

ALL
The will! the testament!

SECOND CITIZEN
They were villains, murderers: the will! Read the will.

ANTONY
You will compel me, then, to read the will?
Then make a ring about the corpse of Caesar,
And let me show you him that made the will.
Shall I descend? and will you give me leave?
SEVERAL CITIZENS
Come down.
SECOND CITIZEN
Descend.
THIRD CITIZEN
You shall have leave.

ANTONY comes down

FOURTH CITIZEN
A ring! Stand round.
FIRST CITIZEN
Stand from the hearse, stand from the body.
SECOND CITIZEN
Room for Antony, most noble Antony.
ANTONY
Nay, press not so upon me; stand far off.
SEVERAL CITIZENS
Stand back. Room! bear back.
ANTONY
If you have tears, prepare to shed them now.
You all do know this mantle: I remember
The first time ever Caesar put it on;
'Twas on a summer's evening, in his tent,
That day he overcame the Nervii.
Look, in this place ran Cassius' dagger through;
See what a rent the envious Casca made;
Through this the well-beloved Brutus stabb'd;
And as he pluck'd his cursed steel away,
Mark how the blood of Caesar follow'd it,
As rushing out of doors, to be resolved
If Brutus so unkindly knock'd, or no;
For Brutus, as you know, was Caesar's angel:
Judge, O you gods, how dearly Caesar loved him!

This was the most unkindest cut of all;
For when the noble Caesar saw him stab,
Ingratitude, more strong than traitors' arms,
Quite vanquish'd him: then burst his mighty heart;
And, in his mantle muffling up his face,
Even at the base of Pompey's statua,
Which all the while ran blood, great Caesar fell.
O, what a fall was there, my countrymen!
Then I, and you, and all of us fell down,
Whilst bloody treason flourish'd over us.
O, now you weep; and, I perceive, you feel
The dint of pity. These are gracious drops.
Kind souls, what, weep you when you but behold
Our Caesar's vesture wounded? Look you here,
Here is himself, marr'd, as you see, with traitors.

FIRST CITIZEN
O piteous spectacle!

SECOND CITIZEN
O noble Caesar!

THIRD CITIZEN
O woeful day!

FOURTH CITIZEN
O traitors, villains!

FIRST CITIZEN
O most bloody sight!

SECOND CITIZEN
We will be revenged.

ALL
Revenge! About! Seek! Burn! Fire! Kill! Slay!
Let not a traitor live!

ANTONY
Stay, countrymen.

FIRST CITIZEN
Peace there! Hear the noble Antony.

SECOND CITIZEN
We'll hear him, we'll follow him, we'll die with him.

ANTONY
>Good friends, sweet friends, let me not stir you up
>To such a sudden flood of mutiny.
>They that have done this deed are honourable:
>What private griefs they have, alas, I know not,
>That made them do it: they are wise and honourable,
>And will, no doubt, with reasons answer you.
>I come not, friends, to steal away your hearts:
>I am no orator, as Brutus is;
>But, as you know me all, a plain blunt man,
>That love my friend; and that they know full well
>That gave me public leave to speak of him:
>For I have neither wit, nor words, nor worth,
>Action, nor utterance, nor the power of speech,
>To stir men's blood: I only speak right on;
>I tell you that which you yourselves do know;
>Show you sweet Caesar's wounds, poor poor dumb mouths,
>And bid them speak for me: but were I Brutus,
>And Brutus Antony, there were an Antony
>Would ruffle up your spirits and put a tongue
>In every wound of Caesar that should move
>The stones of Rome to rise and mutiny.

ALL
>We'll mutiny.

FIRST CITIZEN
>We'll burn the house of Brutus.

THIRD CITIZEN
>Away, then! Come, seek the conspirators.

ANTONY
>Yet hear me, countrymen; yet hear me speak.

ALL
>Peace, ho! Hear Antony. Most noble Antony!

ANTONY
>Why, friends, you go to do you know not what:
>Wherein hath Caesar thus deserved your loves?
>Alas, you know not: I must tell you then:
>You have forgot the will I told you of.

ALL

Most true. The will! Let's stay and hear the will.

ANTONY

Here is the will, and under Caesar's seal.
To every Roman citizen he gives,
To every several man, seventy-five drachmas.

SECOND CITIZEN

Most noble Caesar! We'll revenge his death.

THIRD CITIZEN

O royal Caesar!

ANTONY

Hear me with patience.

ALL

Peace, ho!

ANTONY

Moreover, he hath left you all his walks,
His private arbours and new-planted orchards,
On this side Tiber; he hath left them you,
And to your heirs for ever, common pleasures,
To walk abroad, and recreate yourselves.
Here was a Caesar! When comes such another?

FIRST CITIZEN

Never, never! Come, away, away!
We'll burn his body in the holy place,
And with the brands fire the traitors' houses.
Take up the body.

SECOND CITIZEN

Go fetch fire.

THIRD CITIZEN

Pluck down benches.

FOURTH CITIZEN

Pluck down forms, windows, anything.

Exeunt Citizens
with the body

ANTONY

Now let it work. Mischief, thou art afoot,
Take thou what course thou wilt!

Enter a Servant

How now, fellow!

SERVANT

Sir, Octavius is already come to Rome.

ANTONY

Where is he?

SERVANT

He and Lepidus are at Caesar's house.

ANTONY

And thither will I straight to visit him.
He comes upon a wish. Fortune is merry,
And in this mood will give us anything.

SERVANT

I heard him say, Brutus and Cassius
Are rid like madmen through the gates of Rome.

ANTONY

Belike they had some notice of the people,
How I had moved them. Bring me to Octavius.

Exeunt

SCENE III.
A STREET.

Enter CINNA *the Poet*

CINNA THE POET

I dreamt to-night that I did feast with Caesar,
And things unlucky charge my fantasy.
I have no will to wander forth of doors,
Yet something leads me forth.

Enter Citizens

FIRST CITIZEN

What is your name?

SECOND CITIZEN

Whither are you going?

THIRD CITIZEN

Where do you dwell?

FOURTH CITIZEN

Are you a married man or a bachelor?

SECOND CITIZEN

Answer every man directly.

FIRST CITIZEN

Ay, and briefly.

FOURTH CITIZEN

Ay, and wisely.

THIRD CITIZEN

Ay, and truly, you were best.

CINNA THE POET

What is my name? Whither am I going? Where do I dwell? Am I a married man or a bachelor? Then, to answer every man directly and briefly, wisely and truly: wisely I say, I am a bachelor.

SECOND CITIZEN

That's as much as to say, they are fools that marry: you'll bear me a bang for that, I fear. Proceed; directly.

CINNA THE POET

Directly, I am going to Caesar's funeral.

FIRST CITIZEN

As a friend or an enemy?

CINNA THE POET

As a friend.

SECOND CITIZEN

That matter is answered directly.

FOURTH CITIZEN

For your dwelling—briefly.

CINNA THE POET

Briefly, I dwell by the Capitol.

THIRD CITIZEN

Your name, sir, truly.

CINNA THE POET

Truly, my name is Cinna.

FIRST CITIZEN

Tear him to pieces; he's a conspirator!

CINNA THE POET

I am Cinna the poet, I am Cinna the poet.

FOURTH CITIZEN
Tear him for his bad verses, tear him for his bad verses.
CINNA THE POET
I am not Cinna the conspirator.
FOURTH CITIZEN
It is no matter, his name's Cinna; pluck but his name out of his heart, and turn him going.
THIRD CITIZEN
Tear him, tear him! Come, brands ho! fire-brands! To Brutus', to Cassius'! Burn all! some to Decius' house, and some to Casca's; some to Ligarius'. Away, go!

Exeunt

ACT

IV

SCENE I.
A HOUSE IN ROME.

ANTONY, OCTAVIUS, *and*
LEPIDUS, *seated at a table*

ANTONY

These many, then, shall die; their names are prick'd.

OCTAVIUS

Your brother too must die. Consent you, Lepidus?

LEPIDUS

I do consent.

OCTAVIUS

Prick him down, Antony.

LEPIDUS

Upon condition Publius shall not live,
Who is your sister's son, Mark Antony.

ANTONY

He shall not live; look, with a spot I damn him.
But, Lepidus, go you to Caesar's house;
Fetch the will hither, and we shall determine
How to cut off some charge in legacies.

Julius Caesar

LEPIDUS
    What, shall I find you here?
OCTAVIUS
    Or here, or at the Capitol.

Exit LEPIDUS

ANTONY
    This is a slight unmeritable man,
    Meet to be sent on errands. Is it fit,
    The three-fold world divided, he should stand
    One of the three to share it?
OCTAVIUS
    So you thought him;
    And took his voice who should be prick'd to die,
    In our black sentence and proscription.
ANTONY
    Octavius, I have seen more days than you;
    And though we lay these honours on this man,
    To ease ourselves of divers slanderous loads,
    He shall but bear them as the ass bears gold,
    To groan and sweat under the business,
    Either led or driven, as we point the way;
    And having brought our treasure where we will,
    Then take we down his load, and turn him off,
    Like to the empty ass, to shake his ears,
    And graze in commons.
OCTAVIUS
    You may do your will;
    But he's a tried and valiant soldier.
ANTONY
    So is my horse, Octavius; and for that
    I do appoint him store of provender:
    It is a creature that I teach to fight,
    To wind, to stop, to run directly on,
    His corporal motion govern'd by my spirit.
    And, in some taste, is Lepidus but so:
    He must be taught and train'd and bid go forth;

A barren-spirited fellow; one that feeds
On abjects, orts and imitations,
Which, out of use and staled by other men,
Begin his fashion: do not talk of him,
But as a property. And now, Octavius,
Listen great things: Brutus and Cassius
Are levying powers: we must straight make head;
Therefore let our alliance be combined,
Our best friends made, our means stretch'd
And let us presently go sit in council,
How covert matters may be best disclosed,
And open perils surest answered.

OCTAVIUS

Let us do so; for we are at the stake,
And bay'd about with many enemies;
And some that smile have in their hearts, I fear,
Millions of mischiefs.

Exeunt

SCENE II.
CAMP NEAR SARDIS.
BEFORE BRUTUS'S TENT.

Drum. Enter BRUTUS, LUCILIUS, LUCIUS,
and Soldiers; TITINIUS *and* PINDARUS *meeting them*

BRUTUS

Stand, ho!

LUCILIUS

Give the word, ho! and stand.

BRUTUS

What now, Lucilius? Is Cassius near?

LUCILIUS

He is at hand; and Pindarus is come
To do you salutation from his master.

BRUTUS

He greets me well. Your master, Pindarus,
In his own change, or by ill officers,

Hath given me some worthy cause to wish
Things done, undone: but, if he be at hand,
I shall be satisfied.

PINDARUS

I do not doubt
But that my noble master will appear
Such as he is, full of regard and honour.

BRUTUS

He is not doubted. A word, Lucilius;
How he received you, let me be resolved.

LUCILIUS

With courtesy and with respect enough;
But not with such familiar instances,
Nor with such free and friendly conference,
As he hath used of old.

BRUTUS

Thou hast described
A hot friend cooling: ever note, Lucilius,
When love begins to sicken and decay,
It useth an enforced ceremony.
There are no tricks in plain and simple faith;
But hollow men, like horses hot at hand,
Make gallant show and promise of their mettle;
But when they should endure the bloody spur,
They fall their crests, and, like deceitful jades,
Sink in the trial. Comes his army on?

LUCILIUS

They mean this night in Sardis to be quarter'd;
The greater part, the horse in general,
Are come with Cassius.

BRUTUS

Hark! he is arrived.
                    Low march within
March gently on to meet him.
                    Enter CASSIUS *and his powers*

CASSIUS

Stand, ho!

BRUTUS
    Stand, ho! Speak the word along.
FIRST SOLDIER
    Stand!
SECOND SOLDIER
    Stand!
THIRD SOLDIER
    Stand!
CASSIUS
    Most noble brother, you have done me wrong.
BRUTUS
    Judge me, you gods! wrong I mine enemies?
    And, if not so, how should I wrong a brother?
CASSIUS
    Brutus, this sober form of yours hides wrongs;
    And when you do them—
BRUTUS
    Cassius, be content;
    Speak your griefs softly; I do know you well.
    Before the eyes of both our armies here,
    Which should perceive nothing but love from us,
    Let us not wrangle. Bid them move away;
    Then in my tent, Cassius, enlarge your griefs,
    And I will give you audience.
CASSIUS
    Pindarus,
    Bid our commanders lead their charges off
    A little from this ground.
BRUTUS
    Lucilius, do you the like; and let no man
    Come to our tent till we have done our conference.
    Let Lucius and Titinius guard our door.

                                        Exeunt

SCENE III.
BRUTUS'S TENT.

Enter BRUTUS *and* CASSIUS

CASSIUS

    That you have wrong'd me doth appear in this:
    You have condemn'd and noted Lucius Pella
    For taking bribes here of the Sardians;
    Wherein my letters, praying on his side,
    Because I knew the man, were slighted off.

BRUTUS

    You wronged yourself to write in such a case.

CASSIUS

    In such a time as this it is not meet
    That every nice offence should bear his comment.

BRUTUS

    Let me tell you, Cassius, you yourself
    Are much condemn'd to have an itching palm;
    To sell and mart your offices for gold
    To undeservers.

CASSIUS

    I an itching palm!
    You know that you are Brutus that speak this,
    Or, by the gods, this speech were else your last.

BRUTUS

    The name of Cassius honours this corruption,
    And chastisement doth therefore hide his head.

CASSIUS

    Chastisement!

BRUTUS

    Remember March, the ides of March remember:
    Did not great Julius bleed for justice' sake?
    What villain touch'd his body, that did stab,
    And not for justice? What, shall one of us
    That struck the foremost man of all this world
    But for supporting robbers, shall we now
    Contaminate our fingers with base bribes,

And sell the mighty space of our large honours
For so much trash as may be grasped thus?
I had rather be a dog, and bay the moon,
Than such a Roman.

CASSIUS

    Brutus, bay not me;
I'll not endure it: you forget yourself,
To hedge me in; I am a soldier, I,
Older in practise, abler than yourself
To make conditions.

BRUTUS

    Go to; you are not, Cassius.

CASSIUS

    I am.

BRUTUS

    I say you are not.

CASSIUS

    Urge me no more, I shall forget myself;
Have mind upon your health, tempt me no further.

BRUTUS

    Away, slight man!

CASSIUS

    Is't possible?

BRUTUS

    Hear me, for I will speak.
Must I give way and room to your rash choler?
Shall I be frighted when a madman stares?

CASSIUS

    O ye gods, ye gods! must I endure all this?

BRUTUS

    All this! Ay, more! Fret till your proud heart break.
Go show your slaves how choleric you are,
And make your bondmen tremble. Must I budge?
Must I observe you? Must I stand and crouch
Under your testy humour? By the gods
You shall digest the venom of your spleen,
Though it do split you; for, from this day forth,

I'll use you for my mirth, yea, for my laughter,
When you are waspish.

CASSIUS

Is it come to this?

BRUTUS

You say you are a better soldier:
Let it appear so; make your vaunting true,
And it shall please me well: for mine own part,
I shall be glad to learn of noble men.

CASSIUS

You wrong me every way; you wrong me, Brutus;
I said, an elder soldier, not a better.
Did I say 'better'?

BRUTUS

If you did, I care not.

CASSIUS

When Caesar lived, he durst not thus have moved me.

BRUTUS

Peace, peace! You durst not so have tempted him.

CASSIUS

I durst not!

BRUTUS

No.

CASSIUS

What, durst not tempt him!

BRUTUS

For your life you durst not!

CASSIUS

Do not presume too much upon my love;
I may do that I shall be sorry for.

BRUTUS

You have done that you should be sorry for.
There is no terror, Cassius, in your threats,
For I am arm'd so strong in honesty
That they pass by me as the idle wind,
Which I respect not. I did send to you

For certain sums of gold, which you denied me;
For I can raise no money by vile means.
By heaven, I had rather coin my heart,
And drop my blood for drachmas, than to wring
From the hard hands of peasants their vile trash
By any indirection: I did send
To you for gold to pay my legions,
Which you denied me: was that done like Cassius?
Should I have answer'd Caius Cassius so?
When Marcus Brutus grows so covetous,
To lock such rascal counters from his friends,
Be ready, gods, with all your thunderbolts;
Dash him to pieces!

CASSIUS

I denied you not.

BRUTUS

You did.

CASSIUS

I did not. He was but a fool
That brought my answer back.
Brutus hath rived my heart.
A friend should bear his friend's infirmities,
But Brutus makes mine greater than they are.

BRUTUS

I do not, till you practise them on me.

CASSIUS

You love me not.

BRUTUS

I do not like your faults.

CASSIUS

A friendly eye could never see such faults.

BRUTUS

A flatterer's would not, though they do appear
As huge as high Olympus.

CASSIUS

Come, Antony, and young Octavius, come,

Revenge yourselves alone on Cassius,
For Cassius is aweary of the world;
Hated by one he loves; braved by his brother;
Check'd like a bondman; all his faults observed,
Set in a notebook, learn'd, and conn'd by rote,
To cast into my teeth. O, I could weep
My spirit from mine eyes! There is my dagger,
And here my naked breast; within, a heart
Dearer than Plutus' mine, richer than gold:
If that thou be'st a Roman, take it forth;
I, that denied thee gold, will give my heart:
Strike, as thou didst at Caesar; for, I know,
When thou didst hate him worst, thou lovedst him better
Than ever thou lovedst Cassius.

BRUTUS

Sheathe your dagger:
Be angry when you will, it shall have scope;
Do what you will, dishonour shall be humour.
O Cassius, you are yoked with a lamb
That carries anger as the flint bears fire;
Who, much enforced, shows a hasty spark,
And straight is cold again.

CASSIUS

Hath Cassius lived
To be but mirth and laughter to his Brutus,
When grief, and blood ill-temper'd, vexeth him?

BRUTUS

When I spoke that, I was ill-temper'd too.

CASSIUS

Do you confess so much? Give me your hand.

BRUTUS

And my heart too.

CASSIUS

O Brutus!

BRUTUS

What's the matter?

CASSIUS

    Have not you love enough to bear with me,
    When that rash humour which my mother gave me
    Makes me forgetful?

BRUTUS

    Yes, Cassius; and, from henceforth,
    When you are over-earnest with your Brutus,
    He'll think your mother chides, and leave you so.

POET

    [*Within*] Let me go in to see the generals;
    There is some grudge between 'em, 'tis not meet
    They be alone.

LUCILIUS

    [*Within*] You shall not come to them.

POET

    [*Within*] Nothing but death shall stay me.

                 Enter Poet, followed by LUCILIUS,
                      TITINIUS, *and* LUCIUS

CASSIUS

    How now! What's the matter?

POET

    For shame, you generals! What do you mean?
    Love, and be friends, as two such men should be;
    For I have seen more years, I'm sure, than ye.

CASSIUS

    Ha, ha! How vilely doth this cynic rhyme!

BRUTUS

    Get you hence, sirrah; saucy fellow, hence!

CASSIUS

    Bear with him, Brutus; 'tis his fashion.

BRUTUS

    I'll know his humour, when he knows his time:
    What should the wars do with these jigging fools?
    Companion, hence!

CASSIUS

    Away, away, be gone!

                                Exit Poet

BRUTUS

    Lucilius and Titinius, bid the commanders

    Prepare to lodge their companies to-night.

CASSIUS

    And come yourselves, and bring Messala with you

    Immediately to us.

Exeunt LUCILIUS *and* TITINIUS

BRUTUS

    Lucius, a bowl of wine!

Exit LUCIUS

CASSIUS

    I did not think you could have been so angry.

BRUTUS

    O Cassius, I am sick of many griefs!

CASSIUS

    Of your philosophy you make no use,

    If you give place to accidental evils.

BRUTUS

    No man bears sorrow better. Portia is dead.

CASSIUS

    Ha! Portia?

BRUTUS

    She is dead.

CASSIUS

    How 'scaped I killing when I cross'd you so?

    O insupportable and touching loss!

    Upon what sickness?

BRUTUS

    Impatient of my absence,

    And grief that young Octavius with Mark Antony

    Have made themselves so strong; for with her death

    That tidings came—with this she fell distract,

    And, her attendants absent, swallow'd fire.

CASSIUS

    And died so?

BRUTUS

    Even so.

CASSIUS

    O ye immortal gods!

                Re-enter LUCIUS, *with wine and taper*

BRUTUS

    Speak no more of her. Give me a bowl of wine.

    In this I bury all unkindness, Cassius.

CASSIUS

    My heart is thirsty for that noble pledge.

    Fill, Lucius, till the wine o'erswell the cup;

    I cannot drink too much of Brutus' love.

BRUTUS

    Come in, Titinius!

                                  Exit LUCIUS

              Re-enter TITINIUS, *with* MESSALA

    Welcome, good Messala!

    Now sit we close about this taper here,

    And call in question our necessities.

CASSIUS

    Portia, art thou gone?

BRUTUS

    No more, I pray you.

    Messala, I have here received letters,

    That young Octavius and Mark Antony

    Come down upon us with a mighty power,

    Bending their expedition toward Philippi.

MESSALA

    Myself have letters of the selfsame tenor.

BRUTUS

    With what addition?

MESSALA

    That by proscription and bills of outlawry,

    Octavius, Antony, and Lepidus,

    Have put to death an hundred senators.

BRUTUS

    Therein our letters do not well agree;

    Mine speak of seventy senators that died

    By their proscriptions, Cicero being one.

CASSIUS
> Cicero one!

MESSALA
> Cicero is dead,
> And by that order of proscription.
> Had you your letters from your wife, my lord?

BRUTUS
> No, Messala.

MESSALA
> Nor nothing in your letters writ of her?

BRUTUS
> Nothing, Messala.

MESSALA
> That, methinks, is strange.

BRUTUS
> Why ask you? Hear you aught of her in yours?

MESSALA
> No, my lord.

BRUTUS
> Now, as you are a Roman, tell me true.

MESSALA
> Then like a Roman bear the truth I tell:
> For certain she is dead, and by strange manner.

BRUTUS
> Why, farewell, Portia. We must die, Messala.
> With meditating that she must die once,
> I have the patience to endure it now.

MESSALA
> Even so great men great losses should endure.

CASSIUS
> I have as much of this in art as you,
> But yet my nature could not bear it so.

BRUTUS
> Well, to our work alive. What do you think
> Of marching to Philippi presently?

CASSIUS
> I do not think it good.

BRUTUS

Your reason?

CASSIUS

This it is:

'Tis better that the enemy seek us;

So shall he waste his means, weary his soldiers,

Doing himself offence; whilst we, lying still,

Are full of rest, defense, and nimbleness.

BRUTUS

Good reasons must, of force, give place to better.

The people 'twixt Philippi and this ground

Do stand but in a forced affection;

For they have grudged us contribution:

The enemy, marching along by them,

By them shall make a fuller number up,

Come on refresh'd, new-added, and encouraged;

From which advantage shall we cut him off,

If at Philippi we do face him there,

These people at our back.

CASSIUS

Hear me, good brother.

BRUTUS

Under your pardon. You must note beside,

That we have tried the utmost of our friends,

Our legions are brim-full, our cause is ripe:

The enemy increaseth every day;

We, at the height, are ready to decline.

There is a tide in the affairs of men,

Which, taken at the flood, leads on to fortune;

Omitted, all the voyage of their life

Is bound in shallows and in miseries.

On such a full sea are we now afloat;

And we must take the current when it serves,

Or lose our ventures.

CASSIUS

Then, with your will, go on;

We'll along ourselves, and meet them at Philippi.

BRUTUS

    The deep of night is crept upon our talk,
    And nature must obey necessity;
    Which we will niggard with a little rest.
    There is no more to say?

CASSIUS

    No more. Good night:
    Early to-morrow will we rise, and hence.

BRUTUS

    Lucius!

Enter LUCIUS

    My gown.

Exit LUCIUS

    Farewell, good Messala.
    Good night, Titinius. Noble, noble Cassius,
    Good night, and good repose!

CASSIUS

    O my dear brother,
    This was an ill beginning of the night!
    Never come such division 'tween our souls!
    Let it not, Brutus.

BRUTUS

    Everything is well.

CASSIUS

    Good night, my lord.

BRUTUS

    Good night, good brother.

TITINIUS MESSALA

    Good night, Lord Brutus.

BRUTUS

    Farewell, every one.

Exeunt all but BRUTUS
Re-enter LUCIUS, with the gown

    Give me the gown. Where is thy instrument?

LUCIUS

    Here in the tent.

BRUTUS

What, thou speak'st drowsily?
Poor knave, I blame thee not; thou art o'erwatch'd.
Call Claudius and some other of my men:
I'll have them sleep on cushions in my tent.

LUCIUS

Varro and Claudius!

Enter VARRO *and* CLAUDIUS

VARRO

Calls my lord?

BRUTUS

I pray you, sirs, lie in my tent and sleep;
It may be I shall raise you by and by
On business to my brother Cassius.

VARRO

So please you, we will stand and watch your pleasure.

BRUTUS

I will not have it so. Lie down, good sirs;
It may be I shall otherwise bethink me.
Look, Lucius, here's the book I sought for so;
I put it in the pocket of my gown.

VARRO *and* CLAUDIUS *lie down*

LUCIUS

I was sure your lordship did not give it me.

BRUTUS

Bear with me, good boy, I am much forgetful.
Canst thou hold up thy heavy eyes awhile,
And touch thy instrument a strain or two?

LUCIUS

Ay, my lord, an't please you.

BRUTUS

It does, my boy.
I trouble thee too much, but thou art willing.

LUCIUS

It is my duty, sir.

BRUTUS

    I should not urge thy duty past thy might;

    I know young bloods look for a time of rest.

LUCIUS

    I have slept, my lord, already.

BRUTUS

    It was well done; and thou shalt sleep again;

    I will not hold thee long: if I do live,

    I will be good to thee.

               Music, and a song

    This is a sleepy tune. O murderous slumber!

    Lay'st thou thy leaden mace upon my boy,

    That plays thee music? Gentle knave, good night;

    I will not do thee so much wrong to wake thee:

    If thou dost nod, thou break'st thy instrument;

    I'll take it from thee; and, good boy, good night.

    Let me see, let me see; is not the leaf turn'd down

    Where I left reading? Here it is, I think.

           Enter the Ghost of CAESAR

    How ill this taper burns! Ha! who comes here?

    I think it is the weakness of mine eyes

    That shapes this monstrous apparition.

    It comes upon me. Art thou anything?

    Art thou some god, some angel, or some devil,

    That makest my blood cold and my hair to stare?

    Speak to me what thou art.

GHOST

    Thy evil spirit, Brutus.

BRUTUS

    Why comest thou?

GHOST

    To tell thee thou shalt see me at Philippi.

BRUTUS

    Well; then I shall see thee again?

GHOST

    Ay, at Philippi.

BRUTUS

Why, I will see thee at Philippi, then.

Exit Ghost

Now I have taken heart thou vanishest:
Ill spirit, I would hold more talk with thee.
Boy, Lucius! Varro! Claudius! Sirs, awake! Claudius!

LUCIUS

The strings, my lord, are false.

BRUTUS

He thinks he still is at his instrument.
Lucius, awake!

LUCIUS

My lord!

BRUTUS

Didst thou dream, Lucius, that thou so criedst out?

LUCIUS

My lord, I do not know that I did cry.

BRUTUS

Yes, that thou didst. Didst thou see anything?

LUCIUS

Nothing, my lord.

BRUTUS

Sleep again, Lucius. Sirrah Claudius!
                                        To VARRO

Fellow thou, awake!

VARRO

My lord?

CLAUDIUS

My lord?

BRUTUS

Why did you so cry out, sirs, in your sleep?

VARRO CLAUDIUS

Did we, my lord?

BRUTUS

Ay: saw you anything?

VARRO

No, my lord, I saw nothing.

CLAUDIUS
>Nor I, my lord.

BRUTUS
>Go and commend me to my brother Cassius;
>Bid him set on his powers betimes before,
>And we will follow.

VARRO CLAUDIUS
>It shall be done, my lord.

Exeunt

ACT

V

SCENE I.
THE PLAINS OF PHILIPPI.

Enter OCTAVIUS, ANTONY, *and their army*

OCTAVIUS

    Now, Antony, our hopes are answered:
    You said the enemy would not come down,
    But keep the hills and upper regions;
    It proves not so: their battles are at hand;
    They mean to warn us at Philippi here,
    Answering before we do demand of them.

ANTONY

    Tut, I am in their bosoms, and I know
    Wherefore they do it: they could be content
    To visit other places; and come down
    With fearful bravery, thinking by this face
    To fasten in our thoughts that they have courage;
    But 'tis not so.

                Enter a Messenger

MESSENGER

    Prepare you, generals:
    The enemy comes on in gallant show;

Their bloody sign of battle is hung out,
And something to be done immediately.

ANTONY

Octavius, lead your battle softly on,
Upon the left hand of the even field.

OCTAVIUS

Upon the right hand I; keep thou the left.

ANTONY

Why do you cross me in this exigent?

OCTAVIUS

I do not cross you; but I will do so.

March

Drum. Enter BRUTUS, CASSIUS, *and
their Army;* LUCILIUS, TITINIUS,
MESSALA, *and others*

BRUTUS

They stand, and would have parley.

CASSIUS

Stand fast, Titinius: we must out and talk.

OCTAVIUS

Mark Antony, shall we give sign of battle?

ANTONY

No, Caesar, we will answer on their charge.
Make forth; the generals would have some words.

OCTAVIUS

Stir not until the signal.

BRUTUS

Words before blows. Is it so, countrymen?

OCTAVIUS

Not that we love words better, as you do.

BRUTUS

Good words are better than bad strokes, Octavius.

ANTONY

In your bad strokes, Brutus, you give good words:
Witness the hole you made in Caesar's heart,
Crying 'Long live! Hail, Caesar!'

CASSIUS
    Antony,
    The posture of your blows are yet unknown;
    But for your words, they rob the Hybla bees,
    And leave them honeyless.
ANTONY
    Not stingless too.
BRUTUS
    O, yes, and soundless too;
    For you have stol'n their buzzing, Antony,
    And very wisely threat before you sting.
ANTONY
    Villains, you did not so, when your vile daggers
    Hack'd one another in the sides of Caesar:
    You show'd your teeth like apes, and fawn'd like hounds,
    And bow'd like bondmen, kissing Caesar's feet;
    Whilst damned Casca, like a cur, behind
    Struck Caesar on the neck. O you flatterers!
CASSIUS
    Flatterers! Now, Brutus, thank yourself:
    This tongue had not offended so to-day,
    If Cassius might have ruled.
OCTAVIUS
    Come, come, the cause: if arguing make us sweat,
    The proof of it will turn to redder drops. Look;
    I draw a sword against conspirators;
    When think you that the sword goes up again?
    Never, till Caesar's three and thirty wounds
    Be well avenged; or till another Caesar
    Have added slaughter to the sword of traitors.
BRUTUS
    Caesar, thou canst not die by traitors' hands,
    Unless thou bring'st them with thee.
OCTAVIUS
    So I hope;
    I was not born to die on Brutus' sword.

BRUTUS

O, if thou wert the noblest of thy strain,
Young man, thou couldst not die more honourable.

CASSIUS

A peevish schoolboy, worthless of such honour,
Join'd with a masker and a reveller!

ANTONY

Old Cassius still!

OCTAVIUS

Come, Antony, away!
Defiance, traitors, hurl we in your teeth:
If you dare fight to-day, come to the field;
If not, when you have stomachs.

Exeunt OCTAVIUS, ANTONY,
and their army

CASSIUS

Why, now, blow wind, swell billow and swim bark!
The storm is up, and all is on the hazard.

BRUTUS

Ho, Lucilius! hark, a word with you.

LUCILIUS

[*Standing forth*] My lord?

BRUTUS *and* LUCILIUS *converse apart*

CASSIUS

Messala!

MESSALA

[*Standing forth*] What says my general?

CASSIUS

Messala,
This is my birth-day; as this very day
Was Cassius born. Give me thy hand, Messala.
Be thou my witness that against my will,
As Pompey was, am I compell'd to set
Upon one battle all our liberties.
You know that I held Epicurus strong
And his opinion: now I change my mind,
And partly credit things that do presage.

Coming from Sardis, on our former ensign
Two mighty eagles fell, and there they perch'd,
Gorging and feeding from our soldiers' hands;
Who to Philippi here consorted us:
This morning are they fled away and gone;
And in their steads do ravens, crows and kites,
Fly o'er our heads and downward look on us,
As we were sickly prey: their shadows seem
A canopy most fatal, under which
Our army lies, ready to give up the ghost.

MESSALA
Believe not so.

CASSIUS
I but believe it partly;
For I am fresh of spirit and resolved
To meet all perils very constantly.

BRUTUS
Even so, Lucilius.

CASSIUS
Now, most noble Brutus,
The gods to-day stand friendly, that we may,
Lovers in peace, lead on our days to age!
But since the affairs of men rest still incertain,
Let's reason with the worst that may befall.
If we do lose this battle, then is this
The very last time we shall speak together.
What are you then determined to do?

BRUTUS
Even by the rule of that philosophy
By which I did blame Cato for the death
Which he did give himself, I know not how,
But I do find it cowardly and vile,
For fear of what might fall, so to prevent
The time of life—arming myself with patience
To stay the providence of some high powers
That govern us below.

CASSIUS

    Then, if we lose this battle,
    You are contented to be led in triumph
    Thorough the streets of Rome?

BRUTUS

    No, Cassius, no: think not, thou noble Roman,
    That ever Brutus will go bound to Rome;
    He bears too great a mind. But this same day
    Must end that work the ides of March begun;
    And whether we shall meet again I know not.
    Therefore our everlasting farewell take:
    For ever, and for ever, farewell, Cassius!
    If we do meet again, why, we shall smile;
    If not, why then, this parting was well made.

CASSIUS

    For ever, and for ever, farewell, Brutus!
    If we do meet again, we'll smile indeed;
    If not, 'tis true this parting was well made.

BRUTUS

    Why, then, lead on. O, that a man might know
    The end of this day's business ere it come!
    But it sufficeth that the day will end,
    And then the end is known. Come, ho! away!

                        Exeunt

SCENE II.
THE SAME. THE FIELD OF BATTLE.

Alarum. Enter BRUTUS *and* MESSALA

BRUTUS

    Ride, ride, Messala, ride, and give these bills
    Unto the legions on the other side.

                  Loud alarum

    Let them set on at once; for I perceive
    But cold demeanor in Octavius' wing,
    And sudden push gives them the overthrow.

Ride, ride, Messala: let them all come down.

Exeunt

SCENE III.
ANOTHER PART OF THE FIELD.

Alarums. Enter CASSIUS *and* TITINIUS

CASSIUS
O, look, Titinius, look, the villains fly!
Myself have to mine own turn'd enemy.
This ensign here of mine was turning back;
I slew the coward, and did take it from him.

TITINIUS
O Cassius, Brutus gave the word too early;
Who, having some advantage on Octavius,
Took it too eagerly: his soldiers fell to spoil,
Whilst we by Antony are all enclosed.

Enter PINDARUS

PINDARUS
Fly further off, my lord, fly further off;
Mark Antony is in your tents, my lord
Fly, therefore, noble Cassius, fly far off.

CASSIUS
This hill is far enough. Look, look, Titinius;
Are those my tents where I perceive the fire?

TITINIUS
They are, my lord.

CASSIUS
Titinius, if thou lovest me,
Mount thou my horse, and hide thy spurs in him,
Till he have brought thee up to yonder troops,
And here again; that I may rest assured
Whether yond troops are friend or enemy.

TITINIUS
I will be here again, even with a thought.

Exit

CASSIUS

    Go, Pindarus, get higher on that hill;

    My sight was ever thick; regard Titinius,

    And tell me what thou notest about the field.

               PINDARUS *ascends the hill*

    This day I breathed first: time is come round,

    And where I did begin, there shall I end;

    My life is run his compass. Sirrah, what news?

PINDARUS

    [*Above*] O my lord!

CASSIUS

    What news?

PINDARUS

    [*Above*] Titinius is enclosed round about

    With horsemen, that make to him on the spur;

    Yet he spurs on. Now they are almost on him.

    Now, Titinius! Now some light. O, he lights too.

    He's ta'en.

                   Shout

    And, hark! They shout for joy.

CASSIUS

    Come down; behold no more.

    O, coward that I am, to live so long,

    To see my best friend ta'en before my face!

               PINDARUS *descends*

    Come hither, sirrah:

    In Parthia did I take thee prisoner;

    And then I swore thee, saving of thy life,

    That whatsoever I did bid thee do,

    Thou shouldst attempt it. Come now, keep thine oath;

    Now be a freeman: and with this good sword,

    That ran through Caesar's bowels, search this bosom.

    Stand not to answer: here, take thou the hilts;

    And, when my face is cover'd, as 'tis now,

    Guide thou the sword.

               PINDARUS *stabs him*

Caesar, thou art revenged,
Even with the sword that kill'd thee.

Dies

PINDARUS
    So, I am free; yet would not so have been,
    Durst I have done my will. O Cassius,
    Far from this country Pindarus shall run,
    Where never Roman shall take note of him.

Exit

Re-enter TITINIUS *with* MESSALA

MESSALA
    It is but change, Titinius; for Octavius
    Is overthrown by noble Brutus' power,
    As Cassius' legions are by Antony.
TITINIUS
    These tidings will well comfort Cassius.
MESSALA
    Where did you leave him?
TITINIUS
    All disconsolate,
    With Pindarus his bondman, on this hill.
MESSALA
    Is not that he t hat lies upon the ground?
TITINIUS
    He lies not like the living. O my heart!
MESSALA
    Is not that he?
TITINIUS
    No, this was he, Messala,
    But Cassius is no more. O setting sun,
    As in thy red rays thou dost sink to-night,
    So in his red blood Cassius' day is set;
    The sun of Rome is set! Our day is gone;
    Clouds, dews, and dangers come; our deeds are done!
    Mistrust of my success hath done this deed.

MESSALA

    Mistrust of good success hath done this deed.

    O hateful error, melancholy's child,

    Why dost thou show to the apt thoughts of men

    The things that are not? O error, soon conceived,

    Thou never comest unto a happy birth,

    But kill'st the mother that engender'd thee!

TITINIUS

    What, Pindarus! Where art thou, Pindarus?

MESSALA

    Seek him, Titinius, whilst I go to meet

    The noble Brutus, thrusting this report

    Into his ears; I may say, thrusting it;

    For piercing steel and darts envenomed

    Shall be as welcome to the ears of Brutus

    As tidings of this sight.

TITINIUS

    Hie you, Messala,

    And I will seek for Pindarus the while.

Exit MESSALA

    Why didst thou send me forth, brave Cassius?

    Did I not meet thy friends? and did not they

    Put on my brows this wreath of victory,

    And bid me give it thee? Didst thou not hear their shouts?

    Alas, thou hast misconstrued every thing!

    But, hold thee, take this garland on thy brow;

    Thy Brutus bid me give it thee, and I

    Will do his bidding. Brutus, come apace,

    And see how I regarded Caius Cassius.

    By your leave, gods—this is a Roman's part

    Come, Cassius' sword, and find Titinius' heart.

Kills himself

Alarum. Re-enter MESSALA,

with BRUTUS, CATO,

STRATO, VOLUMNIUS, *and* LUCILIUS

BRUTUS

    Where, where, Messala, doth his body lie?

MESSALA
  Lo, yonder, and Titinius mourning it.
BRUTUS
  Titinius' face is upward.
CATO
  He is slain.
BRUTUS
  O Julius Caesar, thou art mighty yet!
  Thy spirit walks abroad and turns our swords
  In our own proper entrails.

Low alarums

CATO
  Brave Titinius!
  Look, whether he have not crown'd dead Cassius!
BRUTUS
  Are yet two Romans living such as these?
  The last of all the Romans, fare thee well!
  It is impossible that ever Rome
  Should breed thy fellow. Friends, I owe more tears
  To this dead man than you shall see me pay.
  I shall find time, Cassius, I shall find time.
  Come, therefore, and to Thasos send his body:
  His funerals shall not be in our camp,
  Lest it discomfort us. Lucilius, come;
  And come, young Cato; let us to the field.
  Labeo and Flavius, set our battles on:
  'Tis three o'clock; and, Romans, yet ere night
  We shall try fortune in a second fight.

Exeunt

SCENE IV.
ANOTHER PART OF THE FIELD.

Alarum. Enter fighting, Soldiers of both armies;
then BRUTUS, CATO, LUCILIUS, *and others*

BRUTUS
  Yet, countrymen, O, yet hold up your heads!

CATO
>What bastard doth not? Who will go with me?
>I will proclaim my name about the field:
>I am the son of Marcus Cato, ho!
>A foe to tyrants, and my country's friend;
>I am the son of Marcus Cato, ho!

BRUTUS
>And I am Brutus, Marcus Brutus, I;
>Brutus, my country's friend; know me for Brutus!

>>*Exit*

LUCILIUS
>O young and noble Cato, art thou down?
>Why, now thou diest as bravely as Titinius;
>And mayst be honour'd, being Cato's son.

FIRST SOLDIER
>Yield, or thou diest.

LUCILIUS
>Only I yield to die.
>There is so much that thou wilt kill me straight.

>>*Offering money*

>Kill Brutus, and be honour'd in his death.

FIRST SOLDIER
>We must not. A noble prisoner!

SECOND SOLDIER
>Room, ho! Tell Antony, Brutus is ta'en.

FIRST SOLDIER
>I'll tell the news. Here comes the general.

>>*Enter* ANTONY

>Brutus is ta'en, Brutus is ta'en, my lord.

ANTONY
>Where is he?

LUCILIUS
>Safe, Antony; Brutus is safe enough.
>I dare assure thee that no enemy
>Shall ever take alive the noble Brutus.
>The gods defend him from so great a shame!

When you do find him, or alive or dead,
He will be found like Brutus, like himself.

ANTONY

This is not Brutus, friend; but, I assure you,
A prize no less in worth: keep this man safe;
Give him all kindness: I had rather have
Such men my friends than enemies. Go on,
And see whether Brutus be alive or dead;
And bring us word unto Octavius' tent
How every thing is chanced.

Exeunt

SCENE V.
ANOTHER PART OF THE FIELD.

Enter BRUTUS, DARDANIUS,
CLITUS, STRATO, *and* VOLUMNIUS

BRUTUS

Come, poor remains of friends, rest on this rock.

CLITUS

Statilius show'd the torchlight, but, my lord,
He came not back: he is or ta'en or slain.

BRUTUS

Sit thee down, Clitus: slaying is the word;
It is a deed in fashion. Hark thee, Clitus.

Whispers

CLITUS

What, I, my lord? No, not for all the world.

BRUTUS

Peace then! no words.

CLITUS

I'll rather kill myself.

BRUTUS

Hark thee, Dardanius!

Whispers

DARDANIUS

Shall I do such a deed?

CLITUS
> O Dardanius!

DARDANIUS
> O Clitus!

CLITUS
> What ill request did Brutus make to thee?

DARDANIUS
> To kill him, Clitus. Look, he meditates.

CLITUS
> Now is that noble vessel full of grief,
> That it runs over even at his eyes.

BRUTUS
> Come hither, good Volumnius; list a word.

VOLUMNIUS
> What says my lord?

BRUTUS
> Why, this, Volumnius:
> The ghost of Caesar hath appear'd to me
> Two several times by night; at Sardis once,
> And, this last night, here in Philippi fields:
> I know my hour is come.

VOLUMNIUS
> Not so, my lord.

BRUTUS
> Nay, I am sure it is, Volumnius.
> Thou seest the world, Volumnius, how it goes;
> Our enemies have beat us to the pit:
> > *Low alarums*
> It is more worthy to leap in ourselves,
> Than tarry till they push us. Good Volumnius,
> Thou know'st that we two went to school together:
> Even for that our love of old, I prithee,
> Hold thou my sword-hilts, whilst I run on it.

VOLUMNIUS
> That's not an office for a friend, my lord.
> > *Alarum still*

CLITUS

Fly, fly, my lord; there is no tarrying here.

BRUTUS

Farewell to you; and you; and you, Volumnius.
Strato, thou hast been all this while asleep;
Farewell to thee too, Strato. Countrymen,
My heart doth joy that yet in all my life
I found no man but he was true to me.
I shall have glory by this losing day
More than Octavius and Mark Antony
By this vile conquest shall attain unto.
So fare you well at once; for Brutus' tongue
Hath almost ended his life's history:
Night hangs upon mine eyes; my bones would rest,
That have but labour'd to attain this hour.

Alarum. Cry within, 'Fly, fly, fly!'

CLITUS

Fly, my lord, fly.

BRUTUS

Hence! I will follow.

Exeunt CLITUS, DARDANIUS,
and VOLUMNIUS

I prithee, Strato, stay thou by thy lord:
Thou art a fellow of a good respect;
Thy life hath had some smatch of honour in it.
Hold then my sword, and turn away thy face,
While I do run upon it. Wilt thou, Strato?

STRATO

Give me your hand first. Fare you well, my lord.

BRUTUS

Farewell, good Strato.

Runs on his sword

Caesar, now be still:
I kill'd not thee with half so good a will.

Dies

Alarum. Retreat. Enter OCTAVIUS, ANTONY,
MESSALA, LUCILIUS, *and the army*

OCTAVIUS

    What man is that?

MESSALA

    My master's man. Strato, where is thy master?

STRATO

    Free from the bondage you are in, Messala:
    The conquerors can but make a fire of him;
    For Brutus only overcame himself,
    And no man else hath honour by his death.

LUCILIUS

    So Brutus should be found. I thank thee, Brutus,
    That thou hast proved Lucilius' saying true.

OCTAVIUS

    All that served Brutus, I will entertain them.
    Fellow, wilt thou bestow thy time with me?

STRATO

    Ay, if Messala will prefer me to you.

OCTAVIUS

    Do so, good Messala.

MESSALA

    How died my master, Strato?

STRATO

    I held the sword, and he did run on it.

MESSALA

    Octavius, then take him to follow thee,
    That did the latest service to my master.

ANTONY

    This was the noblest Roman of them all.
    All the conspirators save only he
    Did that they did in envy of great Caesar;
    He only, in a general honest thought
    And common good to all, made one of them.
    His life was gentle, and the elements
    So mix'd in him that Nature might stand up
    And say to all the world 'This was a man!'

OCTAVIUS

    According to his virtue let us use him,

With all respect and rites of burial.
Within my tent his bones to-night shall lie,
Most like a soldier, order'd honourably.
So call the field to rest; and let's away,
To part the glories of this happy day.

Exeunt

Macbeth

"The weird sisters, hand in hand,
Posters of the sea and land,
Thus do go about, about:"

Characters in the Play

DUNCAN, King of Scotland
MACBETH, Thane of Glamis and Cawdor, a general in the King's army
LADY MACBETH, his wife
MACDUFF, Thane of Fife, a nobleman of Scotland
LADY MACDUFF, his wife
MALCOLM, elder son of Duncan
DONALBAIN, younger son of Duncan
BANQUO, Thane of Lochaber, a general in the King's army
FLEANCE, his son
LENNOX, ROSS, MENTEITH, ANGUS, CAITHNESS, noblemen of Scotland
SIWARD, Earl of Northumberland, general of the English forces
YOUNG SIWARD, his son
SEYTON, attendant to Macbeth
HECATE, Queen of the Witches
Witches
Boy, Son of Macduff
Gentlewoman attending on Lady Macbeth
An English Doctor
A Scottish Doctor
A Sergeant
A Porter
An Old Man
The Ghost of Banquo and other Apparitions
Lords, Gentlemen, Officers, Soldiers, Murtherers, Attendants, and Messengers

SCENE:
Scotland and England.

ACT

I

SCENE I.
A DESERT PLACE.

Thunder and lightning. Enter three Witches

FIRST WITCH

    When shall we three meet again
    In thunder, lightning, or in rain?

SECOND WITCH

    When the hurlyburly's done,
    When the battle's lost and won.

THIRD WITCH

    That will be ere the set of sun.

FIRST WITCH

    Where the place?

SECOND WITCH

    Upon the heath.

THIRD WITCH

    There to meet with Macbeth.

FIRST WITCH

    I come, Graymalkin!

SECOND WITCH

    Paddock calls.

THIRD WITCH
    Anon.
ALL
    Fair is foul, and foul is fair:
    Hover through the fog and filthy air.

Exeunt

SCENE II.
A CAMP NEAR FORRES.

Alarum within.
Enter DUNCAN, MALCOLM, DONALBAIN, LENNOX,
with Attendants, meeting a bleeding Sergeant

DUNCAN
    What bloody man is that? He can report,
    As seemeth by his plight, of the revolt
    The newest state.
MALCOLM
    This is the sergeant
    Who like a good and hardy soldier fought
    'Gainst my captivity. Hail, brave friend!
    Say to the king the knowledge of the broil
    As thou didst leave it.
SERGEANT
    Doubtful it stood;
    As two spent swimmers, that do cling together
    And choke their art. The merciless Macdonwald—
    Worthy to be a rebel, for to that
    The multiplying villanies of nature
    Do swarm upon him—from the western isles
    Of kerns and gallowglasses is supplied;
    And fortune, on his damned quarrel smiling,
    Show'd like a rebel's whore: but all's too weak:
    For brave Macbeth—well he deserves that name—
    Disdaining fortune, with his brandish'd steel,
    Which smoked with bloody execution,
    Like valour's minion carved out his passage

Till he faced the slave;
Which ne'er shook hands, nor bade farewell to him,
Till he unseam'd him from the nave to the chaps,
And fix'd his head upon our battlements.

DUNCAN
O valiant cousin! worthy gentleman!

SERGEANT
As whence the sun 'gins his reflection
Shipwrecking storms and direful thunders break,
So from that spring whence comfort seem'd to come
Discomfort swells. Mark, king of Scotland, mark:
No sooner justice had with valour arm'd
Compell'd these skipping kerns to trust their heels,
But the Norweyan lord surveying vantage,
With furbish'd arms and new supplies of men
Began a fresh assault.

DUNCAN
Dismay'd not this
Our captains, Macbeth and Banquo?

SERGEANT
Yes;
As sparrows eagles, or the hare the lion.
If I say sooth, I must report they were
As cannons overcharged with double cracks, so they
Doubly redoubled strokes upon the foe:
Except they meant to bathe in reeking wounds,
Or memorise another Golgotha,
I cannot tell.
But I am faint, my gashes cry for help.

DUNCAN
So well thy words become thee as thy wounds;
They smack of honour both. Go get him surgeons.

Exit Sergeant, attended

Who comes here?

Enter ROSS

MALCOLM
The worthy thane of Ross.

LENNOX

What a haste looks through his eyes! So should he look
That seems to speak things strange.

ROSS

God save the king!

DUNCAN

Whence camest thou, worthy thane?

ROSS

From Fife, great king;
Where the Norweyan banners flout the sky
And fan our people cold. Norway himself,
With terrible numbers,
Assisted by that most disloyal traitor
The thane of Cawdor, began a dismal conflict;
Till that Bellona's bridegroom, lapp'd in proof,
Confronted him with self-comparisons,
Point against point rebellious, arm 'gainst arm.
Curbing his lavish spirit: and, to conclude,
The victory fell on us.

DUNCAN

Great happiness!

ROSS

That now
Sweno, the Norways' king, craves composition:
Nor would we deign him burial of his men
Till he disbursed at Saint Colme's inch
Ten thousand dollars to our general use.

DUNCAN

No more that thane of Cawdor shall deceive
Our bosom interest: go pronounce his present death,
And with his former title greet Macbeth.

ROSS

I'll see it done.

DUNCAN

What he hath lost noble Macbeth hath won.

Exeunt

SCENE III.
A HEATH NEAR FORRES.

Thunder. Enter the three Witches

FIRST WITCH
Where hast thou been, sister?

SECOND WITCH
Killing swine.

THIRD WITCH
Sister, where thou?

FIRST WITCH
A sailor's wife had chestnuts in her lap,
And munch'd, and munch'd, and munch'd:—
'Give me,' quoth I:
'Aroint thee, witch!' the rump-fed ronyon cries.
Her husband's to Aleppo gone, master o'the *Tiger*:
But in a sieve I'll thither sail,
And, like a rat without a tail,
I'll do, I'll do, and I'll do.

SECOND WITCH
I'll give thee a wind.

FIRST WITCH
Thou'rt kind.

THIRD WITCH
And I another.

FIRST WITCH
I myself have all the other,
And the very ports they blow,
All the quarters that they know
I'the shipman's card.
I will drain him dry as hay:
Sleep shall neither night nor day
Hang upon his pent-house lid;
He shall live a man forbid:
Weary se'nnights nine times nine
Shall he dwindle, peak and pine:
Though his bark cannot be lost,

Yet it shall be tempest-tost.
Look what I have.
SECOND WITCH
Show me, show me.
FIRST WITCH
Here I have a pilot's thumb,
Wreck'd as homeward he did come.

Drum within

THIRD WITCH
A drum, a drum!
Macbeth doth come.
ALL
The weird sisters, hand in hand,
Posters of the sea and land,
Thus do go about, about:
Thrice to thine and thrice to mine
And thrice again, to make up nine.
Peace! the charm's wound up.

Enter MACBETH *and* BANQUO

MACBETH
So foul and fair a day I have not seen.
BANQUO
How far is't call'd to Forres? What are these
So wither'd and so wild in their attire,
That look not like the inhabitants o'the earth,
And yet are on't? Live you? or are you aught
That man may question? You seem to understand me,
By each at once her chappy finger laying
Upon her skinny lips: you should be women,
And yet your beards forbid me to interpret
That you are so.
MACBETH
Speak, if you can: what are you?
FIRST WITCH
All hail, Macbeth! hail to thee, thane of Glamis!
SECOND WITCH
All hail, Macbeth, hail to thee, thane of Cawdor!

THIRD WITCH
    All hail, Macbeth, thou shalt be king hereafter!
BANQUO
    Good sir, why do you start; and seem to fear
    Things that do sound so fair? I'the name of truth,
    Are ye fantastical, or that indeed
    Which outwardly ye show? My noble partner
    You greet with present grace and great prediction
    Of noble having and of royal hope,
    That he seems rapt withal: to me you speak not.
    If you can look into the seeds of time,
    And say which grain will grow and which will not,
    Speak then to me, who neither beg nor fear
    Your favours nor your hate.
FIRST WITCH
    Hail!
SECOND WITCH
    Hail!
THIRD WITCH
    Hail!
FIRST WITCH
    Lesser than Macbeth, and greater.
SECOND WITCH
    Not so happy, yet much happier.
THIRD WITCH
    Thou shalt get kings, though thou be none:
    So all hail, Macbeth and Banquo!
FIRST WITCH
    Banquo and Macbeth, all hail!
MACBETH
    Stay, you imperfect speakers, tell me more:
    By Sinel's death I know I am thane of Glamis;
    But how of Cawdor? the thane of Cawdor lives,
    A prosperous gentleman; and to be king
    Stands not within the prospect of belief,
    No more than to be Cawdor. Say from whence
    You owe this strange intelligence? or why

Upon this blasted heath you stop our way
With such prophetic greeting? Speak, I charge you.

Witches vanish

BANQUO

The earth hath bubbles, as the water has,
And these are of them. Whither are they vanish'd?

MACBETH

Into the air; and what seem'd corporal melted
As breath into the wind. Would they had stay'd!

BANQUO

Were such things here as we do speak about?
Or have we eaten on the insane root
That takes the reason prisoner?

MACBETH

Your children shall be kings.

BANQUO

You shall be king.

MACBETH

And thane of Cawdor too: went it not so?

BANQUO

To the selfsame tune and words. Who's here?

Enter ROSS *and* ANGUS

ROSS

The king hath happily received, Macbeth,
The news of thy success; and when he reads
Thy personal venture in the rebels' fight,
His wonders and his praises do contend
Which should be thine or his: silenced with that,
In viewing o'er the rest o'the selfsame day,
He finds thee in the stout Norweyan ranks,
Nothing afeard of what thyself didst make,
Strange images of death. As thick as hail
Came post with post; and every one did bear
Thy praises in his kingdom's great defence,
And pour'd them down before him.

ANGUS

We are sent

To give thee from our royal master thanks;
Only to herald thee into his sight,
Not pay thee.

ROSS

And, for an earnest of a greater honour,
He bade me, from him, call thee thane of Cawdor:
In which addition, hail, most worthy thane!
For it is thine.

BANQUO

What, can the devil speak true?

MACBETH

The thane of Cawdor lives: why do you dress me
In borrow'd robes?

ANGUS

Who was the thane lives yet;
But under heavy judgment bears that life
Which he deserves to lose. Whether he was combined
With those of Norway, or did line the rebel
With hidden help and vantage, or that with both
He labour'd in his country's wreck, I know not;
But treasons capital, confess'd and proved,
Have overthrown him.

MACBETH

[*Aside*] Glamis, and thane of Cawdor!
The greatest is behind.

To ROSS *and* ANGUS

Thanks for your pains.

To BANQUO

Do you not hope your children shall be kings,
When those that gave the thane of Cawdor to me
Promised no less to them?

BANQUO

That trusted home
Might yet enkindle you unto the crown,
Besides the thane of Cawdor. But 'tis strange:
And oftentimes, to win us to our harm,
The instruments of darkness tell us truths,

Win us with honest trifles, to betray's
In deepest consequence.
Cousins, a word, I pray you.

MACBETH

[*Aside*] Two truths are told,
As happy prologues to the swelling act
Of the imperial theme.—I thank you, gentlemen.
[*Aside*] This supernatural soliciting
Cannot be ill, cannot be good: if ill,
Why hath it given me earnest of success,
Commencing in a truth? I am thane of Cawdor:
If good, why do I yield to that suggestion
Whose horrid image doth unfix my hair
And make my seated heart knock at my ribs,
Against the use of nature? Present fears
Are less than horrible imaginings:
My thought, whose murder yet is but fantastical,
Shakes so my single state of man that function
Is smother'd in surmise, and nothing is
But what is not.

BANQUO

Look, how our partner's rapt.

MACBETH

[*Aside*] If chance will have me king, why, chance may crown me,
Without my stir.

BANQUO

New horrors come upon him,
Like our strange garments, cleave not to their mould
But with the aid of use.

MACBETH

[*Aside*] Come what come may,
Time and the hour runs through the roughest day.

BANQUO

Worthy Macbeth, we stay upon your leisure.

MACBETH

Give me your favour: my dull brain was wrought
With things forgotten. Kind gentlemen, your pains

Are register'd where every day I turn
The leaf to read them. Let us toward the king.
Think upon what hath chanced, and, at more time,
The interim having weigh'd it, let us speak
Our free hearts each to other.

BANQUO
Very gladly.

MACBETH
Till then, enough. Come, friends.

Exeunt

SCENE IV.
FORRES. THE PALACE.

Flourish. Enter DUNCAN, MALCOLM, DONALBAIN,
LENNOX, *and Attendants*

DUNCAN
Is execution done on Cawdor? Are not
Those in commission yet return'd?

MALCOLM
My liege,
They are not yet come back. But I have spoke
With one that saw him die: who did report
That very frankly he confess'd his treasons,
Implored your highness' pardon and set forth
A deep repentance: nothing in his life
Became him like the leaving it; he died
As one that had been studied in his death
To throw away the dearest thing he owed,
As 'twere a careless trifle.

DUNCAN
There's no art
To find the mind's construction in the face:
He was a gentleman on whom I built
An absolute trust.

Enter MACBETH, BANQUO, ROSS, *and* ANGUS
O worthiest cousin!

The sin of my ingratitude even now
Was heavy on me: thou art so far before
That swiftest wing of recompense is slow
To overtake thee. Would thou hadst less deserved,
That the proportion both of thanks and payment
Might have been mine! only I have left to say,
More is thy due than more than all can pay.

MACBETH

The service and the loyalty I owe,
In doing it, pays itself. Your highness' part
Is to receive our duties; and our duties
Are to your throne and state children and servants,
Which do but what they should, by doing every thing
Safe toward your love and honour.

DUNCAN

Welcome hither:
I have begun to plant thee, and will labour
To make thee full of growing. Noble Banquo,
That hast no less deserved, nor must be known
No less to have done so, let me enfold thee
And hold thee to my heart.

BANQUO

There if I grow,
The harvest is your own.

DUNCAN

My plenteous joys,
Wanton in fulness, seek to hide themselves
In drops of sorrow. Sons, kinsmen, thanes,
And you whose places are the nearest, know
We will establish our estate upon
Our eldest, Malcolm, whom we name hereafter
The Prince of Cumberland; which honour must
Not unaccompanied invest him only,
But signs of nobleness, like stars, shall shine
On all deservers. From hence to Inverness,
And bind us further to you.

MACBETH

The rest is labour, which is not used for you:
I'll be myself the harbinger and make joyful
The hearing of my wife with your approach;
So humbly take my leave.

DUNCAN

My worthy Cawdor!

MACBETH

[*Aside*] The Prince of Cumberland! that is a step
On which I must fall down, or else o'erleap,
For in my way it lies. Stars, hide your fires;
Let not light see my black and deep desires:
The eye wink at the hand; yet let that be,
Which the eye fears, when it is done, to see.

Exit

DUNCAN

True, worthy Banquo; he is full so valiant,
And in his commendations I am fed;
It is a banquet to me. Let's after him,
Whose care is gone before to bid us welcome:
It is a peerless kinsman.

Flourish. Exeunt

SCENE V.
INVERNESS. MACBETH'S CASTLE.

Enter LADY MACBETH, *reading a letter*

LADY MACBETH

'They met me in the day of success: and I have learned by the perfectest report,
they have more in them than mortal knowledge. When I burned in desire to
question them further, they made themselves air, into which they vanished.
Whiles I stood rapt in the wonder of it, came missives from the king, who
all-hailed me "Thane of Cawdor;" by which title, before, these weird sisters
saluted me, and referred me to the coming on of time, with "Hail, king that
shalt be!" This have I thought good to deliver thee, my dearest partner of
greatness, that thou mightst not lose the dues of rejoicing, by being ignorant of
what greatness is promised thee. Lay it to thy heart, and farewell.'

Glamis thou art, and Cawdor; and shalt be
What thou art promised: yet do I fear thy nature;
It is too full o'the milk of human kindness
To catch the nearest way: thou wouldst be great;
Art not without ambition, but without
The illness should attend it: what thou wouldst highly,
That wouldst thou holily; wouldst not play false,
And yet wouldst wrongly win: thou'ldst have, great Glamis,
That which cries 'Thus thou must do, if thou have it;
And that which rather thou dost fear to do
Than wishest should be undone.' Hie thee hither,
That I may pour my spirits in thine ear;
And chastise with the valour of my tongue
All that impedes thee from the golden round,
Which fate and metaphysical aid doth seem
To have thee crown'd withal.

Enter a Messenger

What is your tidings?

MESSENGER

The king comes here to-night.

LADY MACBETH

Thou'rt mad to say it:
Is not thy master with him? who, were't so,
Would have inform'd for preparation.

MESSENGER

So please you, it is true: our thane is coming:
One of my fellows had the speed of him,
Who, almost dead for breath, had scarcely more
Than would make up his message.

LADY MACBETH

Give him tending;
He brings great news.

Exit Messenger

The raven himself is hoarse
That croaks the fatal entrance of Duncan
Under my battlements. Come, you spirits
That tend on mortal thoughts, unsex me here,

And fill me from the crown to the toe top-full
Of direst cruelty! make thick my blood;
Stop up the access and passage to remorse,
That no compunctious visitings of nature
Shake my fell purpose, nor keep peace between
The effect and it! Come to my woman's breasts,
And take my milk for gall, you murdering ministers,
Wherever in your sightless substances
You wait on nature's mischief! Come, thick night,
And pall thee in the dunnest smoke of hell,
That my keen knife see not the wound it makes,
Nor heaven peep through the blanket of the dark,
To cry 'Hold, hold!'

Enter MACBETH

Great Glamis! worthy Cawdor!
Greater than both, by the all-hail hereafter!
Thy letters have transported me beyond
This ignorant present, and I feel now
The future in the instant.

MACBETH

My dearest love,
Duncan comes here to-night.

LADY MACBETH

And when goes hence?

MACBETH

To-morrow, as he purposes.

LADY MACBETH

O, never
Shall sun that morrow see!
Your face, my thane, is as a book where men
May read strange matters. To beguile the time,
Look like the time; bear welcome in your eye,
Your hand, your tongue: look like the innocent flower,
But be the serpent under't. He that's coming
Must be provided for: and you shall put
This night's great business into my dispatch;
Which shall to all our nights and days to come

Give solely sovereign sway and masterdom.

MACBETH

    We will speak further.

LADY MACBETH

    Only look up clear;
    To alter favour ever is to fear:
    Leave all the rest to me.

Exeunt

SCENE VI.
BEFORE MACBETH'S CASTLE.

Hautboys and torches. Enter DUNCAN,
MALCOLM, DONALBAIN, BANQUO, LENNOX, MACDUFF,
ROSS, ANGUS, *and Attendants*

DUNCAN

    This castle hath a pleasant seat; the air
    Nimbly and sweetly recommends itself
    Unto our gentle senses.

BANQUO

    This guest of summer,
    The temple-haunting martlet, does approve,
    By his loved mansionry, that the heaven's breath
    Smells wooingly here: no jutty, frieze,
    Buttress, nor coign of vantage, but this bird
    Hath made his pendent bed and procreant cradle:
    Where they most breed and haunt, I have observed,
    The air is delicate.

Enter LADY MACBETH

DUNCAN

    See, see, our honour'd hostess!
    The love that follows us sometime is our trouble,
    Which still we thank as love. Herein I teach you
    How you shall bid God 'ild us for your pains,
    And thank us for your trouble.

LADY MACBETH

    All our service

In every point twice done and then done double
Were poor and single business to contend
Against those honours deep and broad wherewith
Your majesty loads our house: for those of old,
And the late dignities heap'd up to them,
We rest your hermits.

DUNCAN

Where's the thane of Cawdor?
We coursed him at the heels, and had a purpose
To be his purveyor: but he rides well;
And his great love, sharp as his spur, hath holp him
To his home before us. Fair and noble hostess,
We are your guest to-night.

LADY MACBETH

Your servants ever
Have theirs, themselves and what is theirs, in compt,
To make their audit at your highness' pleasure,
Still to return your own.

DUNCAN

Give me your hand;
Conduct me to mine host: we love him highly,
And shall continue our graces towards him.
By your leave, hostess.

Exeunt

SCENE VII.
MACBETH'S CASTLE.

Hautboys and torches. Enter a Sewer, and divers
Servants with dishes and service, and pass over the stage.
Then enter MACBETH

MACBETH

If it were done when 'tis done, then 'twere well
It were done quickly: if the assassination
Could trammel up the consequence, and catch
With his surcease success; that but this blow
Might be the be-all and the end-all here,

But here, upon this bank and shoal of time,
We'ld jump the life to come. But in these cases
We still have judgment here; that we but teach
Bloody instructions, which, being taught, return
To plague the inventor: this even-handed justice
Commends the ingredients of our poison'd chalice
To our own lips. He's here in double trust;
First, as I am his kinsman and his subject,
Strong both against the deed; then, as his host,
Who should against his murderer shut the door,
Not bear the knife myself. Besides, this Duncan
Hath borne his faculties so meek, hath been
So clear in his great office, that his virtues
Will plead like angels, trumpet-tongued, against
The deep damnation of his taking-off;
And pity, like a naked new-born babe,
Striding the blast, or heaven's cherubim, horsed
Upon the sightless couriers of the air,
Shall blow the horrid deed in every eye,
That tears shall drown the wind. I have no spur
To prick the sides of my intent, but only
Vaulting ambition, which o'erleaps itself
And falls on the other.

Enter LADY MACBETH

How now! what news?

LADY MACBETH

He has almost supp'd: why have you left the chamber?

MACBETH

Hath he ask'd for me?

LADY MACBETH

Know you not he has?

MACBETH

We will proceed no further in this business:
He hath honour'd me of late; and I have bought
Golden opinions from all sorts of people,
Which would be worn now in their newest gloss,
Not cast aside so soon.

LADY MACBETH
Was the hope drunk
Wherein you dress'd yourself? hath it slept since?
And wakes it now, to look so green and pale
At what it did so freely? From this time
Such I account thy love. Art thou afeard
To be the same in thine own act and valour
As thou art in desire? Wouldst thou have that
Which thou esteem'st the ornament of life,
And live a coward in thine own esteem,
Letting 'I dare not' wait upon 'I would,'
Like the poor cat i'the adage?

MACBETH
Prithee, peace:
I dare do all that may become a man;
Who dares do more is none.

LADY MACBETH
What beast was't, then,
That made you break this enterprise to me?
When you durst do it, then you were a man;
And, to be more than what you were, you would
Be so much more the man. Nor time nor place
Did then adhere, and yet you would make both:
They have made themselves, and that their fitness now
Does unmake you. I have given suck, and know
How tender 'tis to love the babe that milks me:
I would, while it was smiling in my face,
Have pluck'd my nipple from his boneless gums,
And dash'd the brains out, had I so sworn as you
Have done to this.

MACBETH
If we should fail?

LADY MACBETH
We fail!
But screw your courage to the sticking-place,
And we'll not fail. When Duncan is asleep—
Whereto the rather shall his day's hard journey

Soundly invite him—his two chamberlains
Will I with wine and wassail so convince
That memory, the warder of the brain,
Shall be a fume, and the receipt of reason
A limbeck only: when in swinish sleep
Their drenched natures lie as in a death,
What cannot you and I perform upon
The unguarded Duncan? what not put upon
His spongy officers, who shall bear the guilt
Of our great quell?

MACBETH

Bring forth men-children only;
For thy undaunted mettle should compose
Nothing but males. Will it not be received,
When we have mark'd with blood those sleepy two
Of his own chamber and used their very daggers,
That they have done't?

LADY MACBETH

Who dares receive it other,
As we shall make our griefs and clamour roar
Upon his death?

MACBETH

I am settled, and bend up
Each corporal agent to this terrible feat.
Away, and mock the time with fairest show:
False face must hide what the false heart doth know.

Exeunt

ACT

II

SCENE I.
COURT OF MACBETH'S CASTLE.

Enter BANQUO, *and* FLEANCE *bearing a torch before him*
BANQUO
How goes the night, boy?
FLEANCE
The moon is down; I have not heard the clock.
BANQUO
And she goes down at twelve.
FLEANCE
I take't, 'tis later, sir.
BANQUO
Hold, take my sword. There's husbandry in heaven;
Their candles are all out. Take thee that too.
A heavy summons lies like lead upon me,
And yet I would not sleep: merciful powers,
Restrain in me the cursed thoughts that nature
Gives way to in repose!
   Enter MACBETH, *and a Servant with a torch*
Give me my sword.
Who's there?

MACBETH
    A friend.
BANQUO
    What, sir, not yet at rest? The king's a-bed:
    He hath been in unusual pleasure, and
    Sent forth great largess to your offices.
    This diamond he greets your wife withal,
    By the name of most kind hostess; and shut up
    In measureless content.
MACBETH
    Being unprepared,
    Our will became the servant to defect;
    Which else should free have wrought.
BANQUO
    All's well.
    I dreamt last night of the three weird sisters:
    To you they have show'd some truth.
MACBETH
    I think not of them:
    Yet, when we can entreat an hour to serve,
    We would spend it in some words upon that business,
    If you would grant the time.
BANQUO
    At your kind'st leisure.
MACBETH
    If you shall cleave to my consent, when 'tis,
    It shall make honour for you.
BANQUO
    So I lose none
    In seeking to augment it, but still keep
    My bosom franchised and allegiance clear,
    I shall be counsell'd.
MACBETH
    Good repose the while!
BANQUO
    Thanks, sir: the like to you!

Exeunt BANQUO and FLEANCE

MACBETH

    Go bid thy mistress, when my drink is ready,
    She strike upon the bell. Get thee to bed.

Exit Servant

    Is this a dagger which I see before me,
    The handle toward my hand? Come, let me clutch thee.
    I have thee not, and yet I see thee still.
    Art thou not, fatal vision, sensible
    To feeling as to sight? or art thou but
    A dagger of the mind, a false creation,
    Proceeding from the heat-oppressed brain?
    I see thee yet, in form as palpable
    As this which now I draw.
    Thou marshall'st me the way that I was going;
    And such an instrument I was to use.
    Mine eyes are made the fools o'the other senses,
    Or else worth all the rest; I see thee still,
    And on thy blade and dudgeon gouts of blood,
    Which was not so before. There's no such thing:
    It is the bloody business which informs
    Thus to mine eyes. Now o'er the one halfworld
    Nature seems dead, and wicked dreams abuse
    The curtain'd sleep; witchcraft celebrates
    Pale Hecate's offerings, and wither'd murder,
    Alarum'd by his sentinel, the wolf,
    Whose howl's his watch, thus with his stealthy pace.
    With Tarquin's ravishing strides, towards his design
    Moves like a ghost. Thou sure and firm-set earth,
    Hear not my steps, which way they walk, for fear
    Thy very stones prate of my whereabout,
    And take the present horror from the time,
    Which now suits with it. Whiles I threat, he lives:
    Words to the heat of deeds too cold breath gives.

A bell rings

    I go, and it is done; the bell invites me.

Hear it not, Duncan; for it is a knell
That summons thee to heaven or to hell.

Exit

SCENE II.
THE SAME.

Enter LADY MACBETH

LADY MACBETH

That which hath made them drunk hath made me bold;
What hath quench'd them hath given me fire.
Hark! Peace!
It was the owl that shriek'd, the fatal bellman,
Which gives the stern'st good-night. He is about it:
The doors are open; and the surfeited grooms
Do mock their charge with snores: I have drugg'd
their possets,
That death and nature do contend about them,
Whether they live or die.

MACBETH

[*Within*] Who's there? what, ho!

LADY MACBETH

Alack, I am afraid they have awaked,
And 'tis not done. The attempt and not the deed
Confounds us. Hark! I laid their daggers ready;
He could not miss 'em. Had he not resembled
My father as he slept, I had done't.

Enter MACBETH

My husband!

MACBETH

I have done the deed. Didst thou not hear a noise?

LADY MACBETH

I heard the owl scream and the crickets cry.
Did not you speak?

MACBETH

When?

LADY MACBETH
Now.
MACBETH
As I descended?
LADY MACBETH
Ay.
MACBETH
Hark!
Who lies i'the second chamber?
LADY MACBETH
Donalbain.
MACBETH
This is a sorry sight.
Looking on his hands
LADY MACBETH
A foolish thought, to say a sorry sight.
MACBETH
There's one did laugh in's sleep, and one cried 'Murder!'
That they did wake each other: I stood and heard them:
But they did say their prayers, and address'd them
Again to sleep.
LADY MACBETH
There are two lodged together.
MACBETH
One cried 'God bless us!' and 'Amen' the other;
As they had seen me with these hangman's hands.
Listening their fear, I could not say 'Amen,'
When they did say 'God bless us!'
LADY MACBETH
Consider it not so deeply.
MACBETH
But wherefore could not I pronounce 'Amen'?
I had most need of blessing, and 'Amen'
Stuck in my throat.
LADY MACBETH
These deeds must not be thought
After these ways; so, it will make us mad.

MACBETH

Methought I heard a voice cry 'sleep no more!
Macbeth does murder sleep', the innocent sleep,
Sleep that knits up the ravell'd sleeve of care,
The death of each day's life, sore labour's bath,
Balm of hurt minds, great nature's second course,
Chief nourisher in life's feast'

LADY MACBETH

What do you mean?

MACBETH

Still it cried 'sleep no more!' to all the house:
'Glamis hath murder'd sleep, and therefore Cawdor
Shall sleep no more; Macbeth shall sleep no more.'

LADY MACBETH

Who was it that thus cried? Why, worthy thane,
You do unbend your noble strength, to think
So brainsickly of things. Go get some water,
And wash this filthy witness from your hand.
Why did you bring these daggers from the place?
They must lie there: go carry them; and smear
The sleepy grooms with blood.

MACBETH

I'll go no more:
I am afraid to think what I have done;
Look on't again I dare not.

LADY MACBETH

Infirm of purpose!
Give me the daggers: the sleeping and the dead
Are but as pictures: 'tis the eye of childhood
That fears a painted devil. If he do bleed,
I'll gild the faces of the grooms withal;
For it must seem their guilt.

Exit. Knocking within

MACBETH

Whence is that knocking?
How is't with me, when every noise appals me?
What hands are here? ha! they pluck out mine eyes.

Will all great Neptune's ocean wash this blood
Clean from my hand? No, this my hand will rather
The multitudinous seas in incarnadine,
Making the green one red.

Re-enter LADY MACBETH

LADY MACBETH
My hands are of your colour; but I shame
To wear a heart so white.

Knocking within

I hear a knocking
At the south entry: retire we to our chamber;
A little water clears us of this deed:
How easy is it, then! Your constancy
Hath left you unattended.

Knocking within

Hark! more knocking.
Get on your nightgown, lest occasion call us,
And show us to be watchers. Be not lost
So poorly in your thoughts.

MACBETH
To know my deed, 'twere best not know myself.

Knocking within

Wake Duncan with thy knocking! I would thou couldst!

Exeunt

SCENE III.
THE SAME.

Knocking within. Enter a Porter

PORTER
Here's a knocking indeed! If a man were porter of hell-gate, he
should have old turning the key.

Knocking within

Knock, knock, knock! Who's there, i'the name of Beelzebub?
Here's a farmer, that hanged himself on the expectation of
plenty: come in time; have napkins enow about you; here you'll
sweat for't.

Knocking within

Knock, knock! Who's there, in the other devil's name? Faith, here's an equivocator, that could swear in both the scales against either scale; who committed treason enough for God's sake, yet could not equivocate to heaven: O, come in, equivocator.

Knocking within

Knock, knock, knock! Who's there? Faith, here's an English tailor come hither, for stealing out of a French hose: come in, tailor; here you may roast your goose.

Knocking within

Knock, knock; never at quiet! What are you? But this place is too cold for hell. I'll devil-porter it no further: I had thought to have let in some of all professions that go the primrose way to the everlasting bonfire.

Knocking within

Anon, anon! I pray you, remember the porter.

Opens the gate.

Enter MACDUFF *and* LENNOX

MACDUFF

Was it so late, friend, ere you went to bed,
That you do lie so late?

PORTER

'Faith sir, we were carousing till the second cock: and drink, sir, is a great provoker of three things.

MACDUFF

What three things does drink especially provoke?

PORTER

Marry, sir, nose-painting, sleep, and urine. Lechery, sir, it provokes, and unprovokes; it provokes the desire, but it takes away the performance: therefore, much drink may be said to be an equivocator with lechery: it makes him, and it mars him; it sets him on, and it takes him off; it persuades him, and disheartens him; makes him stand to, and not stand to; in conclusion, equivocates him in a sleep, and, giving him the lie, leaves him.

MACDUFF

I believe drink gave thee the lie last night.

PORTER

That it did, sir, i'the very throat on me: but I requited him for his
lie; and, I think, being too strong for him, though he took up my
legs sometime, yet I made a shift to cast him.

MACDUFF

Is thy master stirring?

Enter MACBETH

Our knocking has awaked him; here he comes.

LENNOX

Good morrow, noble sir.

MACBETH

Good morrow, both.

MACDUFF

Is the king stirring, worthy thane?

MACBETH

Not yet.

MACDUFF

He did command me to call timely on him:
I have almost slipp'd the hour.

MACBETH

I'll bring you to him.

MACDUFF

I know this is a joyful trouble to you;
But yet 'tis one.

MACBETH

The labour we delight in physics pain.
This is the door.

MACDUFF

I'll make so bold to call,
For 'tis my limited service.

Exit

LENNOX

Goes the king hence to-day?

MACBETH

He does: he did appoint so.

LENNOX

The night has been unruly: where we lay,

Our chimneys were blown down; and, as they say,
Lamentings heard i'the air; strange screams of death,
And prophesying with accents terrible
Of dire combustion and confused events
New hatch'd to the woeful time: the obscure bird
Clamour'd the livelong night: some say, the earth
Was feverous and did shake.

MACBETH

'Twas a rough night.

LENNOX

My young remembrance cannot parallel
A fellow to it.

Re-enter MACDUFF

MACDUFF

O horror, horror, horror! Tongue nor heart
Cannot conceive nor name thee!

MACBETH, LENNOX

What's the matter.

MACDUFF

Confusion now hath made his masterpiece!
Most sacrilegious murder hath broke ope
The Lord's anointed temple, and stole thence
The life o'the building!

MACBETH

What is't you say? the life?

LENNOX

Mean you his majesty?

MACDUFF

Approach the chamber, and destroy your sight
With a new Gorgon: do not bid me speak;
See, and then speak yourselves.

Exeunt MACBETH *and* LENNOX

Awake, awake!
Ring the alarum-bell. Murder and treason!
Banquo and Donalbain! Malcolm! awake!
Shake off this downy sleep, death's counterfeit,
And look on death itself! up, up, and see

The great doom's image! Malcolm! Banquo!
As from your graves rise up, and walk like sprites,
To countenance this horror! Ring the bell.

Bell rings
Enter LADY MACBETH

LADY MACBETH

What's the business,
That such a hideous trumpet calls to parley
The sleepers of the house? speak, speak!

MACDUFF

O gentle lady,
'Tis not for you to hear what I can speak:
The repetition, in a woman's ear,
Would murder as it fell.

Enter BANQUO

O Banquo, Banquo,
Our royal master's murder'd!

LADY MACBETH

Woe, alas!
What, in our house?

BANQUO

Too cruel any where.
Dear Duff, I prithee, contradict thyself,
And say it is not so.

Re-enter MACBETH *and* LENNOX, *with* ROSS

MACBETH

Had I but died an hour before this chance,
I had lived a blessed time; for, from this instant,
There's nothing serious in mortality:
All is but toys: renown and grace is dead;
The wine of life is drawn, and the mere lees
Is left this vault to brag of.

Enter MALCOLM *and* DONALBAIN

DONALBAIN

What is amiss?

MACBETH

You are, and do not know't:

The spring, the head, the fountain of your blood
Is stopp'd; the very source of it is stopp'd.
MACDUFF

Your royal father's murder'd.
MALCOLM

O, by whom?
LENNOX

Those of his chamber, as it seem'd, had done 't:
Their hands and faces were an badged with blood;
So were their daggers, which unwiped we found
Upon their pillows:
They stared, and were distracted; no man's life
Was to be trusted with them.
MACBETH

O, yet I do repent me of my fury,
That I did kill them.
MACDUFF

Wherefore did you so?
MACBETH

Who can be wise, amazed, temperate and furious,
Loyal and neutral, in a moment? No man:
The expedition my violent love
Outrun the pauser, reason. Here lay Duncan,
His silver skin laced with his golden blood;
And his gash'd stabs look'd like a breach in nature
For ruin's wasteful entrance: there, the murderers,
Steep'd in the colours of their trade, their daggers
Unmannerly breech'd with gore: who could refrain,
That had a heart to love, and in that heart
Courage to make's love known?
LADY MACBETH

Help me hence, ho!
MACDUFF

Look to the lady.
MALCOLM

[*Aside to* DONALBAIN] Why do we hold our tongues,
That most may claim this argument for ours?

DONALBAIN

[*Aside to* MALCOLM] What should be spoken here, where our fate,
Hid in an auger-hole, may rush, and seize us?
Let's away;
Our tears are not yet brew'd.

MALCOLM

[*Aside to* DONALBAIN] Nor our strong sorrow
Upon the foot of motion.

BANQUO

Look to the lady:

LADY MACBETH *is carried out*

And when we have our naked frailties hid,
That suffer in exposure, let us meet,
And question this most bloody piece of work,
To know it further. Fears and scruples shake us:
In the great hand of God I stand; and thence
Against the undivulged pretence I fight
Of treasonous malice.

MACDUFF

And so do I.

ALL

So all.

MACBETH

Let's briefly put on manly readiness,
And meet i'the hall together.

ALL

Well contented.

Exeunt all but MALCOLM *and* DONALBAIN

MALCOLM

What will you do? Let's not consort with them:
To show an unfelt sorrow is an office
Which the false man does easy. I'll to England.

DONALBAIN

To Ireland, I; our separated fortune
Shall keep us both the safer: where we are,
There's daggers in men's smiles: the near in blood,
The nearer bloody.

MALCOLM

    This murderous shaft that's shot
    Hath not yet lighted, and our safest way
    Is to avoid the aim. Therefore, to horse;
    And let us not be dainty of leave-taking,
    But shift away: there's warrant in that theft
    Which steals itself, when there's no mercy left.

Exeunt

SCENE IV.
OUTSIDE MACBETH'S CASTLE.

Enter ROSS *and an old Man*

OLD MAN

    Threescore and ten I can remember well:
    Within the volume of which time I have seen
    Hours dreadful and things strange; but this sore night
    Hath trifled former knowings.

ROSS

    Ah, good father,
    Thou seest, the heavens, as troubled with man's act,
    Threaten his bloody stage: by the clock, 'tis day,
    And yet dark night strangles the travelling lamp:
    Is't night's predominance, or the day's shame,
    That darkness does the face of earth entomb,
    When living light should kiss it?

OLD MAN

    'Tis unnatural,
    Even like the deed that's done. On Tuesday last,
    A falcon, towering in her pride of place,
    Was by a mousing owl hawk'd at and kill'd.

ROSS

    And Duncan's horses—a thing most strange and certain—
    Beauteous and swift, the minions of their race,
    Turn'd wild in nature, broke their stalls, flung out,
    Contending 'gainst obedience, as they would make
    War with mankind.

OLD MAN
    'Tis said they eat each other.
ROSS
    They did so, to the amazement of mine eyes
    That look'd upon't. Here comes the good Macduff.
                    Enter MACDUFF
    How goes the world, sir, now?
MACDUFF
    Why, see you not?
ROSS
    Is't known who did this more than bloody deed?
MACDUFF
    Those that Macbeth hath slain.
ROSS
    Alas, the day!
    What good could they pretend?
MACDUFF
    They were suborn'd:
    Malcolm and Donalbain, the king's two sons,
    Are stol'n away and fled; which puts upon them
    Suspicion of the deed.
ROSS
    'Gainst nature still!
    Thriftless ambition, that wilt ravin up
    Thine own life's means! Then 'tis most like
    The sovereignty will fall upon Macbeth.
MACDUFF
    He is already named, and gone to Scone
    To be invested.
ROSS
    Where is Duncan's body?
MACDUFF
    Carried to Colmekill,
    The sacred storehouse of his predecessors,
    And guardian of their bones.
ROSS
    Will you to Scone?

MACDUFF
    No, cousin, I'll to Fife.
ROSS
    Well, I will thither.
MACDUFF
    Well, may you see things well done there: Adieu!
    Lest our old robes sit easier than our new!
ROSS
    Farewell, father.
OLD MAN
    God's benison go with you; and with those
    That would make good of bad, and friends of foes!

Exeunt

ACT

III

SCENE I.
FORRES. THE PALACE.

Enter BANQUO

BANQUO

 Thou hast it now: king, Cawdor, Glamis, all,
 As the weird women promised, and, I fear,
 Thou play'dst most foully for't: yet it was said
 It should not stand in thy posterity,
 But that myself should be the root and father
 Of many kings. If there come truth from them—
 As upon thee, Macbeth, their speeches shine—
 Why, by the verities on thee made good,
 May they not be my oracles as well,
 And set me up in hope? But hush! no more.
    Sennet sounded. Enter MACBETH,
   as king, LADY MACBETH, *as queen,* LENNOX,
    ROSS, *Lords, Ladies, and Attendants*

MACBETH

 Here's our chief guest.

LADY MACBETH

 If he had been forgotten,

It had been as a gap in our great feast,
And all-thing unbecoming.

MACBETH
To-night we hold a solemn supper sir,
And I'll request your presence.

BANQUO
Let your highness
Command upon me; to the which my duties
Are with a most indissoluble tie
For ever knit.

MACBETH
Ride you this afternoon?

BANQUO
Ay, my good lord.

MACBETH
We should have else desired your good advice,
Which still hath been both grave and prosperous,
In this day's council; but we'll take to-morrow.
Is't far you ride?

Banquo
As far, my lord, as will fill up the time
'Twixt this and supper: go not my horse the better,
I must become a borrower of the night
For a dark hour or twain.

MACBETH
Fail not our feast.

BANQUO
My lord, I will not.

MACBETH
We hear, our bloody cousins are bestow'd
In England and in Ireland, not confessing
Their cruel parricide, filling their hearers
With strange invention: but of that to-morrow,
When therewithal we shall have cause of state
Craving us jointly. Hie you to horse: Adieu,
Till you return at night. Goes Fleance with you?

BANQUO

Ay, my good lord: our time does call upon's.

MACBETH

I wish your horses swift and sure of foot;
And so I do commend you to their backs. Farewell.

Exit BANQUO

Let every man be master of his time
Till seven at night: to make society
The sweeter welcome, we will keep ourself
Till supper-time alone: while then, God be with you!

Exeunt all but MACBETH, *and an attendant*

Sirrah, a word with you: attend those men
Our pleasure?

ATTENDANT

They are, my lord, without the palace gate.

MACBETH

Bring them before us.

Exit Attendant

To be thus is nothing;
But to be safely thus.—Our fears in Banquo
Stick deep; and in his royalty of nature
Reigns that which would be fear'd: 'tis much he dares;
And, to that dauntless temper of his mind,
He hath a wisdom that doth guide his valour
To act in safety. There is none but he
Whose being I do fear: and, under him,
My Genius is rebuked; as, it is said,
Mark Antony's was by Caesar. He chid the sisters
When first they put the name of king upon me,
And bade them speak to him: then prophet-like
They hail'd him father to a line of kings:
Upon my head they placed a fruitless crown,
And put a barren sceptre in my gripe,
Thence to be wrench'd with an unlineal hand,
No son of mine succeeding. If 't be so,
For Banquo's issue have I filed my mind;

For them the gracious Duncan have I murder'd;
Put rancours in the vessel of my peace
Only for them; and mine eternal jewel
Given to the common enemy of man,
To make them kings, the seed of Banquo kings!
Rather than so, come fate into the list.
And champion me to the utterance! Who's there!

Re-enter Attendant, with two Murderers

Now go to the door, and stay there till we call.

Exit Attendant

Was it not yesterday we spoke together?

FIRST MURDERER

It was, so please your highness.

MACBETH

Well then, now
Have you consider'd of my speeches? Know
That it was he in the times past which held you
So under fortune, which you thought had been
Our innocent self: This I made good to you
In our last conference, pass'd in probation with you,
How you were borne in hand, how cross'd, the instruments,
Who wrought with them, and all things else that might
To half a soul and to a notion crazed
Say 'Thus did Banquo.'

FIRST MURDERER

You made it known to us.

MACBETH

I did so, and went further, which is now
Our point of second meeting. Do you find
Your patience so predominant in your nature
That you can let this go? Are you so gospell'd
To pray for this good man and for his issue,
Whose heavy hand hath bow'd you to the grave
And beggar'd yours for ever?

FIRST MURDERER

We are men, my liege.

MACBETH
　　Ay, in the catalogue ye go for men;
　　As hounds and greyhounds, mongrels, spaniels, curs,
　　Shoughs, water-rugs and demi-wolves, are clept
　　All by the name of dogs: the valued file
　　Distinguishes the swift, the slow, the subtle,
　　The housekeeper, the hunter, every one
　　According to the gift which bounteous nature
　　Hath in him closed; whereby he does receive
　　Particular addition. from the bill
　　That writes them all alike: and so of men.
　　Now, if you have a station in the file,
　　Not i'the worst rank of manhood, say't;
　　And I will put that business in your bosoms,
　　Whose execution takes your enemy off,
　　Grapples you to the heart and love of us,
　　Who wear our health but sickly in his life,
　　Which in his death were perfect.
SECOND MURDERER
　　I am one, my liege,
　　Whom the vile blows and buffets of the world
　　Have so incensed that I am reckless what
　　I do to spite the world.
FIRST MURDERER
　　And I another
　　So weary with disasters, tugg'd with fortune,
　　That I would set my lie on any chance,
　　To mend it, or be rid on't.
MACBETH
　　Both of you
　　Know Banquo was your enemy.
BOTH MURDERERS
　　True, my lord.
MACBETH
　　So is he mine; and in such bloody distance,
　　That every minute of his being thrusts

Against my near'st of life: and though I could
With barefaced power sweep him from my sight
And bid my will avouch it, yet I must not,
For certain friends that are both his and mine,
Whose loves I may not drop, but wail his fall
Who I myself struck down; and thence it is,
That I to your assistance do make love,
Masking the business from the common eye
For sundry weighty reasons.

SECOND MURDERER

We shall, my lord,
Perform what you command us.

FIRST MURDERER

Though our lives—

MACBETH

Your spirits shine through you. Within this hour at most
I will advise you where to plant yourselves;
Acquaint you with the perfect spy o'the time,
The moment on't; for't must be done to-night,
And something from the palace; always thought
That I require a clearness: and with him—
To leave no rubs nor botches in the work—
Fleance his son, that keeps him company,
Whose absence is no less material to me
Than is his father's, must embrace the fate
Of that dark hour. Resolve yourselves apart:
I'll come to you anon.

BOTH MURDERERS

We are resolved, my lord.

MACBETH

I'll call upon you straight: abide within.

Exeunt Murderers

It is concluded. Banquo, thy soul's flight,
If it find heaven, must find it out to-night.

Exit

SCENE II.
THE PALACE.

Enter LADY MACBETH *and a Servant*

LADY MACBETH

    Is Banquo gone from court?

SERVANT

    Ay, madam, but returns again to-night.

LADY MACBETH

    Say to the king, I would attend his leisure
    For a few words.

SERVANT

    Madam, I will.

Exit

LADY MACBETH

    Nought's had, all's spent,
    Where our desire is got without content:
    'Tis safer to be that which we destroy
    Than by destruction dwell in doubtful joy.

Enter MACBETH

    How now, my lord! why do you keep alone,
    Of sorriest fancies your companions making,
    Using those thoughts which should indeed have died
    With them they think on? Things without all remedy
    Should be without regard: what's done is done.

MACBETH

    We have scotch'd the snake, not kill'd it:
    She'll close and be herself, whilst our poor malice
    Remains in danger of her former tooth.
    But let the frame of things disjoint, both the worlds suffer,
    Ere we will eat our meal in fear and sleep
    In the affliction of these terrible dreams
    That shake us nightly: better be with the dead,
    Whom we, to gain our peace, have sent to peace,
    Than on the torture of the mind to lie
    In restless ecstasy. Duncan is in his grave;
    After life's fitful fever he sleeps well;

Treason has done his worst: nor steel, nor poison,
Malice domestic, foreign levy, nothing,
Can touch him further.

LADY MACBETH
Come on;
Gentle my lord, sleek o'er your rugged looks;
Be bright and jovial among your guests to-night.

MACBETH
So shall I, love; and so, I pray, be you:
Let your remembrance apply to Banquo;
Present him eminence, both with eye and tongue:
Unsafe the while, that we
Must lave our honours in these flattering streams,
And make our faces vizards to our hearts,
Disguising what they are.

LADY MACBETH
You must leave this.

MACBETH
O, full of scorpions is my mind, dear wife!
Thou know'st that Banquo, and his Fleance, lives.

LADY MACBETH
But in them nature's copy's not eterne.

MACBETH
There's comfort yet; they are assailable;
Then be thou jocund: ere the bat hath flown
His cloister'd flight, ere to black Hecate's summons
The shard-borne beetle with his drowsy hums
Hath rung night's yawning peal, there shall be done
A deed of dreadful note.

LADY MACBETH
What's to be done?

MACBETH
Be innocent of the knowledge, dearest chuck,
Till thou applaud the deed. Come, seeling night,
Scarf up the tender eye of pitiful day;
And with thy bloody and invisible hand

Cancel and tear to pieces that great bond
Which keeps me pale! Light thickens; and the crow
Makes wing to the rooky wood:
Good things of day begin to droop and drowse;
While night's black agents to their preys do rouse.
Thou marvell'st at my words: but hold thee still;
Things bad begun make strong themselves by ill.
So, prithee, go with me.

Exeunt

SCENE III.
A PARK NEAR THE PALACE.

Enter three Murderers

FIRST MURDERER
    But who did bid thee join with us?
THIRD MURDERER
    Macbeth.
SECOND MURDERER
    He needs not our mistrust, since he delivers
    Our offices and what we have to do
    To the direction just.
FIRST MURDERER
    Then stand with us.
    The west yet glimmers with some streaks of day:
    Now spurs the lated traveller apace
    To gain the timely inn; and near approaches
    The subject of our watch.
THIRD MURDERER
    Hark! I hear horses.
BANQUO
    [*Within*] Give us a light there, ho!
SECOND MURDERER
    Then 'tis he: the rest
    That are within the note of expectation
    Already are i'the court.

FIRST MURDERER
His horses go about.
THIRD MURDERER
Almost a mile: but he does usually,
So all men do, from hence to the palace gate
Make it their walk.
SECOND MURDERER
A light, a light!

Enter BANQUO, *and* FLEANCE *with a torch*

THIRD MURDERER
'Tis he.
FIRST MURDERER
Stand to't.
BANQUO
It will be rain to-night.
FIRST MURDERER
Let it come down.

They set upon BANQUO

BANQUO
O, treachery! Fly, good Fleance, fly, fly, fly!
Thou mayst revenge. O slave!

Dies. FLEANCE *escapes*

THIRD MURDERER
Who did strike out the light?
FIRST MURDERER
Wast not the way?
THIRD MURDERER
There's but one down; the son is fled.
SECOND MURDERER
We have lost
Best half of our affair.
FIRST MURDERER
Well, let's away, and say how much is done.

Exeunt

SCENE IV.
THE SAME. HALL IN THE PALACE.

A banquet prepared. Enter MACBETH, LADY MACBETH,
ROSS, LENNOX, *Lords, and Attendants*

MACBETH
You know your own degrees; sit down: At first
And last the hearty welcome.

LORDS
Thanks to your majesty.

MACBETH
Ourself will mingle with society,
And play the humble host.
Our hostess keeps her state, but in best time
We will require her welcome.

LADY MACBETH
Pronounce it for me, sir, to all our friends;
For my heart speaks they are welcome.
First Murderer appears at the door

MACBETH
See, they encounter thee with their hearts' thanks.
Both sides are even: here I'll sit i'the midst:
Be large in mirth; anon we'll drink a measure
The table round.
Approaching the door
There's blood on thy face.

FIRST MURDERER
'Tis Banquo's then.

MACBETH
'Tis better thee without than he within.
Is he dispatch'd?

FIRST MURDERER
My lord, his throat is cut; that I did for him.

MACBETH
Thou art the best o'the cut-throats: yet he's good
That did the like for Fleance: if thou didst it,
Thou art the nonpareil.

FIRST MURDERER

 Most royal sir,

 Fleance is 'scaped.

MACBETH

 Then comes my fit again: I had else been perfect,

 Whole as the marble, founded as the rock,

 As broad and general as the casing air:

 But now I am cabin'd, cribb'd, confined, bound in

 To saucy doubts and fears. But Banquo's safe?

FIRST MURDERER

 Ay, my good lord: safe in a ditch he bides,

 With twenty trenched gashes on his head;

 The least a death to nature.

MACBETH

 Thanks for that:

 There the grown serpent lies; the worm that's fled

 Hath nature that in time will venom breed,

 No teeth for the present. Get thee gone: to-morrow

 We'll hear, ourselves, again.

             Exit Murderer

LADY MACBETH

 My royal lord,

 You do not give the cheer: the feast is sold

 That is not often vouch'd, while 'tis a-making,

 'Tis given with welcome: to feed were best at home;

 From thence the sauce to meat is ceremony;

 Meeting were bare without it.

MACBETH

 Sweet remembrancer!

 Now, good digestion wait on appetite,

 And health on both!

LENNOX

 May't please your highness sit.

   The Ghost of Banquo enters, and sits in MACBETH'S *place*

MACBETH

 Here had we now our country's honour roof'd,

 Were the graced person of our Banquo present;

Who may I rather challenge for unkindness
Than pity for mischance!

ROSS

His absence, sir,
Lays blame upon his promise. Please't your highness
To grace us with your royal company.

MACBETH

The table's full.

LENNOX

Here is a place reserved, sir.

MACBETH

Where?

LENNOX

Here, my good lord. What is't that moves your highness?

MACBETH

Which of you have done this?

LORDS

What, my good lord?

MACBETH

Thou canst not say I did it: never shake
Thy gory locks at me.

ROSS

Gentlemen, rise: his highness is not well.

LADY MACBETH

Sit, worthy friends: my lord is often thus,
And hath been from his youth: pray you, keep seat;
The fit is momentary; upon a thought
He will again be well: if much you note him,
You shall offend him and extend his passion:
Feed, and regard him not. Are you a man?

MACBETH

Ay, and a bold one, that dare look on that
Which might appal the devil.

LADY MACBETH

O proper stuff!
This is the very painting of your fear:
This is the air-drawn dagger which, you said,

Led you to Duncan. O, these flaws and starts,
Impostors to true fear, would well become
A woman's story at a winter's fire,
Authorized by her grandam. Shame itself!
Why do you make such faces? When all's done,
You look but on a stool.

MACBETH

Prithee, see there! behold! look! lo! how say you?
Why, what care I? If thou canst nod, speak too.
If charnel-houses and our graves must send
Those that we bury back, our monuments
Shall be the maws of kites.

Ghost of Banquo vanishes

LADY MACBETH

What, quite unmann'd in folly?

MACBETH

If I stand here, I saw him.

LADY MACBETH

Fie, for shame!

MACBETH

Blood hath been shed ere now, i'the olden time,
Ere human statute purged the gentle weal;
Ay, and since too, murders have been perform'd
Too terrible for the ear: the times have been,
That, when the brains were out, the man would die,
And there an end; but now they rise again,
With twenty mortal murders on their crowns,
And push us from our stools: this is more strange
Than such a murder is.

LADY MACBETH

My worthy lord,
Your noble friends do lack you.

MACBETH

I do forget.
Do not muse at me, my most worthy friends,
I have a strange infirmity, which is nothing
To those that know me. Come, love and health to all;

Then I'll sit down. Give me some wine; fill full.
I drink to the general joy o'the whole table,
And to our dear friend Banquo, whom we miss;
Would he were here! to all, and him, we thirst,
And all to all.

LORDS

Our duties, and the pledge.

Re-enter Ghost of Banquo

MACBETH

Avaunt! and quit my sight! let the earth hide thee!
Thy bones are marrowless, thy blood is cold;
Thou hast no speculation in those eyes
Which thou dost glare with!

LADY MACBETH

Think of this, good peers,
But as a thing of custom: 'tis no other;
Only it spoils the pleasure of the time.

MACBETH

What man dare, I dare:
Approach thou like the rugged Russian bear,
The arm'd rhinoceros, or the Hyrcan tiger;
Take any shape but that, and my firm nerves
Shall never tremble: or be alive again,
And dare me to the desert with thy sword;
If trembling I inhabit then, protest me
The baby of a girl. Hence, horrible shadow!
Unreal mockery, hence!

Ghost of Banquo vanishes

Why, so: being gone,
I am a man again. Pray you, sit still.

LADY MACBETH

You have displaced the mirth, broke the good meeting,
With most admired disorder.

MACBETH

Can such things be,
And overcome us like a summer's cloud,
Without our special wonder? You make me strange

Even to the disposition that I owe,
When now I think you can behold such sights,
And keep the natural ruby of your cheeks,
When mine is blanched with fear.

ROSS

What sights, my lord?

LADY MACBETH

I pray you, speak not; he grows worse and worse;
Question enrages him. At once, good night:
Stand not upon the order of your going,
But go at once.

LENNOX

Good night; and better health
Attend his majesty!

LADY MACBETH

A kind good night to all!

Exeunt all but MACBETH *and* LADY MACBETH

MACBETH

It will have blood; they say, blood will have blood:
Stones have been known to move and trees to speak;
Augurs and understood relations have
By magot-pies and choughs and rooks brought forth
The secret'st man of blood. What is the night?

LADY MACBETH

Almost at odds with morning, which is which.

MACBETH

How say'st thou, that Macduff denies his person
At our great bidding?

LADY MACBETH

Did you send to him, sir?

MACBETH

I hear it by the way; but I will send:
There's not a one of them but in his house
I keep a servant fee'd. I will to-morrow,
And betimes I will, to the weird sisters:
More shall they speak; for now I am bent to know,
By the worst means, the worst. For mine own good,

All causes shall give way: I am in blood
Stepp'd in so far that, should I wade no more,
Returning were as tedious as go o'er:
Strange things I have in head, that will to hand;
Which must be acted ere they may be scann'd.

LADY MACBETH

You lack the season of all natures, sleep.

MACBETH

Come, we'll to sleep. My strange and self-abuse
Is the initiate fear that wants hard use:
We are yet but young in deed.

Exeunt

SCENE V.
A HEATH.

Thunder. Enter the three Witches meeting HECATE

FIRST WITCH

Why, how now, Hecate! you look angerly.

HECATE

Have I not reason, beldams as you are,
Saucy and overbold? How did you dare
To trade and traffic with Macbeth
In riddles and affairs of death;
And I, the mistress of your charms,
The close contriver of all harms,
Was never call'd to bear my part,
Or show the glory of our art?
And, which is worse, all you have done
Hath been but for a wayward son,
Spiteful and wrathful, who, as others do,
Loves for his own ends, not for you.
But make amends now: get you gone,
And at the pit of Acheron
Meet me i'the morning: thither he
Will come to know his destiny:
Your vessels and your spells provide,

Your charms and every thing beside.
I am for the air; this night I'll spend
Unto a dismal and a fatal end:
Great business must be wrought ere noon:
Upon the corner of the moon
There hangs a vaporous drop profound;
I'll catch it ere it come to ground:
And that distill'd by magic sleights
Shall raise such artificial sprites
As by the strength of their illusion
Shall draw him on to his confusion:
He shall spurn fate, scorn death, and bear
He hopes 'bove wisdom, grace and fear:
And you all know, security
Is mortals' chiefest enemy.

   Music and a song within: 'Come away, come away,' etc.

Hark! I am call'd; my little spirit, see,
Sits in a foggy cloud, and stays for me.

              Exit

FIRST WITCH
 Come, let's make haste; she'll soon be back again.

             Exeunt

SCENE VI.
FORRES. THE PALACE.

Enter LENNOX *and another Lord*

LENNOX
 My former speeches have but hit your thoughts,
 Which can interpret further: only, I say,
 Things have been strangely borne. The gracious Duncan
 Was pitied of Macbeth: marry, he was dead:
 And the right-valiant Banquo walk'd too late;
 Whom, you may say, if't please you, Fleance kill'd,
 For Fleance fled: men must not walk too late.
 Who cannot want the thought how monstrous
 It was for Malcolm and for Donalbain

To kill their gracious father? damned fact!
How it did grieve Macbeth! did he not straight
In pious rage the two delinquents tear,
That were the slaves of drink and thralls of sleep?
Was not that nobly done? Ay, and wisely too;
For 'twould have anger'd any heart alive
To hear the men deny't. So that, I say,
He has borne all things well: and I do think
That had he Duncan's sons under his key—
As, an't please heaven, he shall not—they should find
What 'twere to kill a father; so should Fleance.
But, peace! for from broad words and 'cause he fail'd
His presence at the tyrant's feast, I hear
Macduff lives in disgrace: sir, can you tell
Where he bestows himself?

LORD

The son of Duncan,
From whom this tyrant holds the due of birth
Lives in the English court, and is received
Of the most pious Edward with such grace
That the malevolence of fortune nothing
Takes from his high respect: thither Macduff
Is gone to pray the holy king, upon his aid
To wake Northumberland and warlike Siward:
That, by the help of these—with Him above
To ratify the work—we may again
Give to our tables meat, sleep to our nights,
Free from our feasts and banquets bloody knives,
Do faithful homage and receive free honours:
All which we pine for now: and this report
Hath so exasperate the king that he
Prepares for some attempt of war.

LENNOX

Sent he to Macduff?

LORD

He did: and with an absolute 'Sir, not I,'
The cloudy messenger turns me his back,

And hums, as who should say 'You'll rue the time
That clogs me with this answer.'

LENNOX

And that well might
Advise him to a caution, to hold what distance
His wisdom can provide. Some holy angel
Fly to the court of England and unfold
His message ere he come, that a swift blessing
May soon return to this our suffering country
Under a hand accursed!

LORD

I'll send my prayers with him.

Exeunt

ACT

IV

SCENE I.
A CAVERN. IN THE MIDDLE,
A BOILING CAULDRON.

Thunder. Enter the three Witches

FIRST WITCH
    Thrice the brinded cat hath mew'd.
SECOND WITCH
    Thrice and once the hedge-pig whined.
THIRD WITCH
    Harpier cries 'Tis time, 'tis time.
FIRST WITCH
    Round about the cauldron go;
    In the poison'd entrails throw.
    Toad, that under cold stone
    Days and nights has thirty-one
    Swelter'd venom sleeping got,
    Boil thou first i'the charmed pot.
ALL
    Double, double toil and trouble;
    Fire burn, and cauldron bubble.

SECOND WITCH

> Fillet of a fenny snake,
> In the cauldron boil and bake;
> Eye of newt and toe of frog,
> Wool of bat and tongue of dog,
> Adder's fork and blind-worm's sting,
> Lizard's leg and owlet's wing,
> For a charm of powerful trouble,
> Like a hell-broth boil and bubble.

ALL

> Double, double toil and trouble;
> Fire burn and cauldron bubble.

THIRD WITCH

> Scale of dragon, tooth of wolf,
> Witches' mummy, maw and gulf
> Of the ravin'd salt-sea shark,
> Root of hemlock digg'd i'the dark,
> Liver of blaspheming Jew,
> Gall of goat, and slips of yew
> Silver'd in the moon's eclipse,
> Nose of Turk and Tartar's lips,
> Finger of birth-strangled babe
> Ditch-deliver'd by a drab,
> Make the gruel thick and slab:
> Add thereto a tiger's chaudron,
> For the ingredients of our cauldron.

ALL

> Double, double toil and trouble;
> Fire burn and cauldron bubble.

SECOND WITCH

> Cool it with a baboon's blood,
> Then the charm is firm and good.

Enter HECATE *to the other three Witches*

HECATE

> O well done! I commend your pains;
> And every one shall share i'the gains;
> And now about the cauldron sing,

Live elves and fairies in a ring,
Enchanting all that you put in.
    Music and a song: 'Black spirits,' etc
    HECATE *retires*
SECOND WITCH
By the pricking of my thumbs,
Something wicked this way comes.
Open, locks,
Whoever knocks!
                    Enter MACBETH
MACBETH
How now, you secret, black, and midnight hags!
What is't you do?
ALL
A deed without a name.
MACBETH
I conjure you, by that which you profess,
Howe'er you come to know it, answer me:
Though you untie the winds and let them fight
Against the churches; though the yesty waves
Confound and swallow navigation up;
Though bladed corn be lodged and trees blown down;
Though castles topple on their warders' heads;
Though palaces and pyramids do slope
Their heads to their foundations; though the treasure
Of nature's germens tumble all together,
Even till destruction sicken; answer me
To what I ask you.
FIRST WITCH
Speak.
SECOND WITCH
Demand.
THIRD WITCH
We'll answer.
FIRST WITCH
Say, if thou'dst rather hear it from our mouths,
Or from our masters?

MACBETH

    Call 'em; let me see 'em.

FIRST WITCH

    Pour in sow's blood, that hath eaten
    Her nine farrow; grease that's sweaten
    From the murderer's gibbet throw
    Into the flame.

ALL

    Come, high or low;
    Thyself and office deftly show!

          Thunder. First Apparition: an armed Head

MACBETH

    Tell me, thou unknown power—

FIRST WITCH

    He knows thy thought:
    Hear his speech, but say thou nought.

FIRST APPARITION

    Macbeth! Macbeth! Macbeth! beware Macduff;
    Beware the thane of Fife. Dismiss me. Enough.

          Descends

MACBETH

    Whate'er thou art, for thy good caution, thanks;
    Thou hast harp'd my fear aright: but one word more—

FIRST WITCH

    He will not be commanded: here's another,
    More potent than the first.

          Thunder. Second Apparition: A bloody Child

SECOND APPARITION

    Macbeth! Macbeth! Macbeth!

MACBETH

    Had I three ears, I'ld hear thee.

SECOND APPARITION

    Be bloody, bold, and resolute; laugh to scorn
    The power of man, for none of woman born
    Shall harm Macbeth.

          Descends

MACBETH

    Then live, Macduff: what need I fear of thee?
    But yet I'll make assurance double sure,
    And take a bond of fate: thou shalt not live;
    That I may tell pale-hearted fear it lies,
    And sleep in spite of thunder.
                Thunder. Third Apparition:
             a Child crowned, with a tree in his hand
    What is this
    That rises like the issue of a king,
    And wears upon his baby-brow the round
    And top of sovereignty?

ALL

    Listen, but speak not to't.

THIRD APPARITION

    Be lion-mettled, proud; and take no care
    Who chafes, who frets, or where conspirers are:
    Macbeth shall never vanquish'd be until
    Great Birnam wood to high Dunsinane hill
    Shall come against him.
                Descends

MACBETH

    That will never be
    Who can impress the forest, bid the tree
    Unfix his earth-bound root? Sweet bodements! good!
    Rebellion's head, rise never till the wood
    Of Birnam rise, and our high-placed Macbeth
    Shall live the lease of nature, pay his breath
    To time and mortal custom. Yet my heart
    Throbs to know one thing: tell me, if your art
    Can tell so much: shall Banquo's issue ever
    Reign in this kingdom?

ALL

    Seek to know no more.

MACBETH

    I will be satisfied: deny me this,

And an eternal curse fall on you! Let me know.
Why sinks that cauldron? and what noise is this?

Hautboys

FIRST WITCH

Show!

SECOND WITCH

Show!

THIRD WITCH

Show!

ALL

Show his eyes, and grieve his heart;
Come like shadows, so depart!

A show of Eight Kings, the last with a glass in his hand; Ghost of Banquo following

MACBETH

Thou art too like the spirit of Banquo: down!
Thy crown does sear mine eye-balls. And thy hair,
Thou other gold-bound brow, is like the first.
A third is like the former. Filthy hags!
Why do you show me this? A fourth! Start, eyes!
What, will the line stretch out to the crack of doom?
Another yet! A seventh! I'll see no more:
And yet the eighth appears, who bears a glass
Which shows me many more; and some I see
That two-fold balls and treble scepters carry:
Horrible sight! Now, I see, 'tis true;
For the blood-bolter'd Banquo smiles upon me,
And points at them for his.

Apparitions vanish

What, is this so?

FIRST WITCH

Ay, sir, all this is so: but why
Stands Macbeth thus amazedly?
Come, sisters, cheer we up his sprites,
And show the best of our delights:
I'll charm the air to give a sound,
While you perform your antic round:

That this great king may kindly say,
Our duties did his welcome pay.

Music. The witches dance and then vanish, with HECATE

MACBETH

Where are they? Gone? Let this pernicious hour
Stand aye accursed in the calendar!
Come in, without there!

Enter LENNOX

LENNOX

What's your grace's will?

MACBETH

Saw you the weird sisters?

LENNOX

No, my lord.

MACBETH

Came they not by you?

LENNOX

No, indeed, my lord.

MACBETH

Infected be the air whereon they ride;
And damn'd all those that trust them! I did hear
The galloping of horse: who was't came by?

LENNOX

'Tis two or three, my lord, that bring you word
Macduff is fled to England.

MACBETH

Fled to England!

LENNOX

Ay, my good lord.

MACBETH

Time, thou anticipatest my dread exploits:
The flighty purpose never is o'ertook
Unless the deed go with it; from this moment
The very firstlings of my heart shall be
The firstlings of my hand. And even now,
To crown my thoughts with acts, be it thought and done:

The castle of Macduff I will surprise;
Seize upon Fife; give to the edge o'the sword
His wife, his babes, and all unfortunate souls
That trace him in his line. No boasting like a fool;
This deed I'll do before this purpose cool.
But no more sights!—Where are these gentlemen?
Come, bring me where they are.

Exeunt

SCENE II.
FIFE. MACDUFF'S CASTLE.

Enter LADY MACDUFF, *her Son, and* ROSS

LADY MACDUFF

What had he done, to make him fly the land?

ROSS

You must have patience, madam.

LADY MACDUFF

He had none:
His flight was madness: when our actions do not,
Our fears do make us traitors.

ROSS

You know not
Whether it was his wisdom or his fear.

LADY MACDUFF

Wisdom! to leave his wife, to leave his babes,
His mansion and his titles in a place
From whence himself does fly? He loves us not;
He wants the natural touch: for the poor wren,
The most diminutive of birds, will fight,
Her young ones in her nest, against the owl.
All is the fear and nothing is the love;
As little is the wisdom, where the flight
So runs against all reason.

ROSS

My dearest coz,
I pray you, school yourself: but for your husband,

He is noble, wise, judicious, and best knows
The fits o'the season. I dare not speak much further;
But cruel are the times, when we are traitors
And do not know ourselves, when we hold rumour
From what we fear, yet know not what we fear,
But float upon a wild and violent sea
Each way and move. I take my leave of you:
Shall not be long but I'll be here again:
Things at the worst will cease, or else climb upward
To what they were before. My pretty cousin,
Blessing upon you!

LADY MACDUFF
Father'd he is, and yet he's fatherless.

ROSS
I am so much a fool, should I stay longer,
It would be my disgrace and your discomfort:
I take my leave at once.

Exit

LADY MACDUFF
Sirrah, your father's dead;
And what will you do now? How will you live?

SON
As birds do, mother.

LADY MACDUFF
What, with worms and flies?

SON
With what I get, I mean; and so do they.

LADY MACDUFF
Poor bird! thou'ldst never fear the net nor lime,
The pitfall nor the gin.

SON
Why should I, mother? Poor birds they are not set for.
My father is not dead, for all your saying.

LADY MACDUFF
Yes, he is dead; how wilt thou do for a father?

SON
Nay, how will you do for a husband?

LADY MACDUFF

Why, I can buy me twenty at any market.

SON

Then you'll buy 'em to sell again.

LADY MACDUFF

Thou speak'st with all thy wit: and yet, i'faith,
With wit enough for thee.

SON

Was my father a traitor, mother?

LADY MACDUFF

Ay, that he was.

SON

What is a traitor?

LADY MACDUFF

Why, one that swears and lies.

SON

And be all traitors that do so?

LADY MACDUFF

Every one that does so is a traitor, and must be hanged.

SON

And must they all be hanged that swear and lie?

LADY MACDUFF

Every one.

SON

Who must hang them?

LADY MACDUFF

Why, the honest men.

SON

Then the liars and swearers are fools, for there are liars and
swearers enow to beat the honest men and hang up them.

LADY MACDUFF

Now, God help thee, poor monkey!
But how wilt thou do for a father?

SON

If he were dead, you'ld weep for him: if you would not, it were a
good sign that I should quickly have a new father.

LADY MACDUFF
Poor prattler, how thou talk'st!

Enter a Messenger

MESSENGER
Bless you, fair dame! I am not to you known,
Though in your state of honour I am perfect.
I doubt some danger does approach you nearly:
If you will take a homely man's advice,
Be not found here; hence, with your little ones.
To fright you thus, methinks, I am too savage;
To do worse to you were fell cruelty,
Which is too nigh your person. Heaven preserve you!
I dare abide no longer.

Exit

LADY MACDUFF
Whither should I fly?
I have done no harm. But I remember now
I am in this earthly world; where to do harm
Is often laudable, to do good sometime
Accounted dangerous folly: why then, alas,
Do I put up that womanly defence,
To say I have done no harm?

Enter Murderers

What are these faces?

FIRST MURDERER
Where is your husband?

LADY MACDUFF
I hope, in no place so unsanctified
Where such as thou mayst find him.

FIRST MURDERER
He's a traitor.

SON
Thou liest, thou shag-hair'd villain!

FIRST MURDERER
What, you egg!

Stabbing him

Young fry of treachery!

SON

    He has kill'd me, mother:
    Run away, I pray you!

Dies

Exit LADY MACDUFF, *crying 'Murder!'*
Exeunt Murderers, following her

SCENE III.
ENGLAND.
BEFORE THE KING'S PALACE.

Enter MALCOLM *and* MACDUFF

MALCOLM

    Let us seek out some desolate shade, and there
    Weep our sad bosoms empty.

MACDUFF

    Let us rather
    Hold fast the mortal sword, and like good men
    Bestride our down-fall'n birthdom: each new morn
    New widows howl, new orphans cry, new sorrows
    Strike heaven on the face, that it resounds
    As if it felt with Scotland and yell'd out
    Like syllable of dolour.

MALCOLM

    What I believe I'll wail,
    What know believe, and what I can redress,
    As I shall find the time to friend, I will.
    What you have spoke, it may be so perchance.
    This tyrant, whose sole name blisters our tongues,
    Was once thought honest: you have loved him well.
    He hath not touch'd you yet. I am young; but something
    You may deserve of him through me, and wisdom
    To offer up a weak poor innocent lamb
    To appease an angry god.

MACDUFF

    I am not treacherous.

• 484 •

MALCOLM
    But Macbeth is.
    A good and virtuous nature may recoil
    In an imperial charge. But I shall crave your pardon;
    That which you are my thoughts cannot transpose:
    Angels are bright still, though the brightest fell;
    Though all things foul would wear the brows of grace,
    Yet grace must still look so.
MACDUFF
    I have lost my hopes.
MALCOLM
    Perchance even there where I did find my doubts.
    Why in that rawness left you wife and child,
    Those precious motives, those strong knots of love,
    Without leave-taking? I pray you,
    Let not my jealousies be your dishonours,
    But mine own safeties. You may be rightly just,
    Whatever I shall think.
MACDUFF
    Bleed, bleed, poor country!
    Great tyranny! lay thou thy basis sure,
    For goodness dare not cheque thee: wear thou thy wrongs;
    The title is affeer'd! Fare thee well, lord:
    I would not be the villain that thou think'st
    For the whole space that's in the tyrant's grasp,
    And the rich East to boot.
MALCOLM
    Be not offended:
    I speak not as in absolute fear of you.
    I think our country sinks beneath the yoke;
    It weeps, it bleeds; and each new day a gash
    Is added to her wounds: I think withal
    There would be hands uplifted in my right;
    And here from gracious England have I offer
    Of goodly thousands: but, for all this,
    When I shall tread upon the tyrant's head,
    Or wear it on my sword, yet my poor country

Shall have more vices than it had before,
More suffer and more sundry ways than ever,
By him that shall succeed.

MACDUFF

What should he be?

MALCOLM

It is myself I mean: in whom I know
All the particulars of vice so grafted
That, when they shall be open'd, black Macbeth
Will seem as pure as snow, and the poor state
Esteem him as a lamb, being compared
With my confineless harms.

MACDUFF

Not in the legions
Of horrid hell can come a devil more damn'd
In evils to top Macbeth.

MALCOLM

I grant him bloody,
Luxurious, avaricious, false, deceitful,
Sudden, malicious, smacking of every sin
That has a name: but there's no bottom, none,
In my voluptuousness: your wives, your daughters,
Your matrons and your maids, could not fill up
The cistern of my lust, and my desire
All continent impediments would o'erbear
That did oppose my will: better Macbeth
Than such an one to reign.

MACDUFF

Boundless intemperance
In nature is a tyranny; it hath been
The untimely emptying of the happy throne
And fall of many kings. But fear not yet
To take upon you what is yours: you may
Convey your pleasures in a spacious plenty,
And yet seem cold, the time you may so hoodwink.
We have willing dames enough: there cannot be
That vulture in you, to devour so many

As will to greatness dedicate themselves,
Finding it so inclined.

MALCOLM

With this there grows
In my most ill-composed affection such
A stanchless avarice that, were I king,
I should cut off the nobles for their lands,
Desire his jewels and this other's house:
And my more-having would be as a sauce
To make me hunger more; that I should forge
Quarrels unjust against the good and loyal,
Destroying them for wealth.

MACDUFF

This avarice
Sticks deeper, grows with more pernicious root
Than summer-seeming lust, and it hath been
The sword of our slain kings: yet do not fear;
Scotland hath foisons to fill up your will.
Of your mere own: all these are portable,
With other graces weigh'd.

MALCOLM

But I have none: the king-becoming graces,
As justice, verity, temperance, stableness,
Bounty, perseverance, mercy, lowliness,
Devotion, patience, courage, fortitude,
I have no relish of them, but abound
In the division of each several crime,
Acting it many ways. Nay, had I power, I should
Pour the sweet milk of concord into hell,
Uproar the universal peace, confound
All unity on earth.

MACDUFF

O Scotland, Scotland!

MALCOLM

If such a one be fit to govern, speak:
I am as I have spoken.

MACDUFF

    Fit to govern!
No, not to live. O nation miserable,
With an untitled tyrant bloody-scepter'd,
When shalt thou see thy wholesome days again,
Since that the truest issue of thy throne
By his own interdiction stands accursed,
And does blaspheme his breed? Thy royal father
Was a most sainted king: the queen that bore thee,
Oftener upon her knees than on her feet,
Died every day she lived. Fare thee well!
These evils thou repeat'st upon thyself
Have banish'd me from Scotland. O my breast,
Thy hope ends here!

MALCOLM

    Macduff, this noble passion,
Child of integrity, hath from my soul
Wiped the black scruples, reconciled my thoughts
To thy good truth and honour. Devilish Macbeth
By many of these trains hath sought to win me
Into his power, and modest wisdom plucks me
From over-credulous haste: but God above
Deal between thee and me! for even now
I put myself to thy direction, and
Unspeak mine own detraction, here abjure
The taints and blames I laid upon myself,
For strangers to my nature. I am yet
Unknown to woman, never was forsworn,
Scarcely have coveted what was mine own,
At no time broke my faith, would not betray
The devil to his fellow and delight
No less in truth than life: my first false speaking
Was this upon myself: what I am truly,
Is thine and my poor country's to command:
Whither indeed, before thy here-approach,
Old Siward, with ten thousand warlike men,
Already at a point, was setting forth.

Now we'll together; and the chance of goodness
Be like our warranted quarrel! Why are you silent?
MACDUFF
Such welcome and unwelcome things at once
'Tis hard to reconcile.

Enter a Doctor

MALCOLM
Well; more anon.—Comes the king forth, I pray you?
DOCTOR
Ay, sir; there are a crew of wretched souls
That stay his cure: their malady convinces
The great assay of art; but at his touch—
Such sanctity hath heaven given his hand—
They presently amend.
MALCOLM
I thank you, doctor.

Exit Doctor

MACDUFF
What's the disease he means?
MALCOLM
'Tis call'd the evil:
A most miraculous work in this good king;
Which often, since my here-remain in England,
I have seen him do. How he solicits heaven,
Himself best knows: but strangely-visited people,
All swoln and ulcerous, pitiful to the eye,
The mere despair of surgery, he cures,
Hanging a golden stamp about their necks,
Put on with holy prayers: and 'tis spoken,
To the succeeding royalty he leaves
The healing benediction. With this strange virtue,
He hath a heavenly gift of prophecy,
And sundry blessings hang about his throne,
That speak him full of grace.

Enter ROSS

MACDUFF
See, who comes here?

MALCOLM
My countryman; but yet I know him not.

MACDUFF
My ever-gentle cousin, welcome hither.

MALCOLM
I know him now. Good God, betimes remove
The means that makes us strangers!

ROSS
Sir, amen.

MACDUFF
Stands Scotland where it did?

ROSS
Alas, poor country!
Almost afraid to know itself. It cannot
Be call'd our mother, but our grave; where nothing,
But who knows nothing, is once seen to smile;
Where sighs and groans and shrieks that rend the air
Are made, not mark'd; where violent sorrow seems
A modern ecstasy; the dead man's knell
Is there scarce ask'd for who; and good men's lives
Expire before the flowers in their caps,
Dying or ere they sicken.

MACDUFF
O, relation
Too nice, and yet too true!

MALCOLM
What's the newest grief?

ROSS
That of an hour's age doth hiss the speaker:
Each minute teems a new one.

MACDUFF
How does my wife?

ROSS
Why, well.

MACDUFF
And all my children?

ROSS

Well too.

MACDUFF

The tyrant has not batter'd at their peace?

ROSS

No; they were well at peace when I did leave 'em.

MACDUFF

But not a niggard of your speech: how goes't?

ROSS

When I came hither to transport the tidings,
Which I have heavily borne, there ran a rumour
Of many worthy fellows that were out;
Which was to my belief witness'd the rather,
For that I saw the tyrant's power a-foot:
Now is the time of help; your eye in Scotland
Would create soldiers, make our women fight,
To doff their dire distresses.

MALCOLM

Be't their comfort
We are coming thither: gracious England hath
Lent us good Siward and ten thousand men;
An older and a better soldier none
That Christendom gives out.

ROSS

Would I could answer
This comfort with the like! But I have words
That would be howl'd out in the desert air,
Where hearing should not latch them.

MACDUFF

What concern they?
The general cause? or is it a fee-grief
Due to some single breast?

ROSS

No mind that's honest
But in it shares some woe; though the main part
Pertains to you alone.

MACDUFF
  If it be mine,
  Keep it not from me, quickly let me have it.
ROSS
  Let not your ears despise my tongue for ever,
  Which shall possess them with the heaviest sound
  That ever yet they heard.
MACDUFF
  Hum! I guess at it.
ROSS
  Your castle is surprised; your wife and babes
  Savagely slaughter'd: to relate the manner,
  Were, on the quarry of these murder'd deer,
  To add the death of you.
MALCOLM
  Merciful heaven!
  What, man! Ne'er pull your hat upon your brows;
  Give sorrow words: the grief that does not speak
  Whispers the o'er-fraught heart and bids it break.
MACDUFF
  My children too?
ROSS
  Wife, children, servants, all
  That could be found.
MACDUFF
  And I must be from thence!
  My wife kill'd too?
ROSS
  I have said.
MALCOLM
  Be comforted:
  Let's make us medicines of our great revenge,
  To cure this deadly grief.
MACDUFF
  He has no children. All my pretty ones?
  Did you say all? O hell-kite! All?

What, all my pretty chickens and their dam
At one fell swoop?

MALCOLM

Dispute it like a man.

MACDUFF

I shall do so;
But I must also feel it as a man:
I cannot but remember such things were,
That were most precious to me. Did heaven look on,
And would not take their part? Sinful Macduff,
They were all struck for thee! naught that I am,
Not for their own demerits, but for mine,
Fell slaughter on their souls. Heaven rest them now!

MALCOLM

Be this the whetstone of your sword: let grief
Convert to anger; blunt not the heart, enrage it.

MACDUFF

O, I could play the woman with mine eyes
And braggart with my tongue! But, gentle heavens,
Cut short all intermission; front to front
Bring thou this fiend of Scotland and myself;
Within my sword's length set him; if he 'scape,
Heaven forgive him too!

MALCOLM

This tune goes manly.
Come, go we to the king; our power is ready;
Our lack is nothing but our leave; Macbeth
Is ripe for shaking, and the powers above
Put on their instruments. Receive what cheer you may:
The night is long that never finds the day.

Exeunt

ACT

V

SCENE I.
DUNSINANE. ANTE-ROOM IN THE CASTLE.

Enter a Doctor of Physic and a Waiting-Gentlewoman

DOCTOR

I have two nights watched with you, but can perceive no truth in your report. When was it she last walked?

GENTLEWOMAN

Since his majesty went into the field, I have seen her rise from her bed, throw her night-gown upon her, unlock her closet, take forth paper, fold it, write upon't, read it, afterwards seal it, and again return to bed; yet all this while in a most fast sleep.

DOCTOR

A great perturbation in nature, to receive at once the benefit of sleep, and do the effects of watching! In this slumbery agitation, besides her walking and other actual performances, what, at any time, have you heard her say?

GENTLEWOMAN

That, sir, which I will not report after her.

DOCTOR

You may to me: and 'tis most meet you should.

GENTLEWOMAN

Neither to you nor any one; having no witness to confirm my speech.

Enter LADY MACBETH, *with a taper*

Lo you, here she comes! This is her very guise; and, upon my life, fast asleep. Observe her; stand close.

DOCTOR

How came she by that light?

GENTLEWOMAN

Why, it stood by her: she has light by her continually; 'tis her command.

DOCTOR

You see, her eyes are open.

GENTLEWOMAN

Ay, but their sense is shut.

DOCTOR

What is it she does now? Look, how she rubs her hands.

GENTLEWOMAN

It is an accustomed action with her, to seem thus washing her hands: I have known her continue in this a quarter of an hour.

LADY MACBETH

Yet here's a spot.

DOCTOR

Hark! she speaks: I will set down what comes from her, to satisfy my remembrance the more strongly.

LADY MACBETH

Out, damned spot! out, I say!—One: two: why, then, 'tis time to do't.—Hell is murky!—Fie, my lord, fie! a soldier, and afeard? What need we fear who knows it, when none can call our power to account?—Yet who would have thought the old man to have had so much blood in him.

DOCTOR

Do you mark that?

LADY MACBETH

The thane of Fife had a wife: where is she now?—What, will these hands ne'er be clean?—No more o' that, my lord, no more o'that: you mar all with this starting.

DOCTOR

Go to, go to; you have known what you should not.

GENTLEWOMAN

She has spoke what she should not, I am sure of that: heaven knows what she has known.

LADY MACBETH

Here's the smell of the blood still: all the perfumes of Arabia will not sweeten this little hand. Oh, oh, oh!

DOCTOR

What a sigh is there! The heart is sorely charged.

GENTLEWOMAN

I would not have such a heart in my bosom for the dignity of the whole body.

DOCTOR

Well, well, well—

GENTLEWOMAN

Pray God it be, sir.

DOCTOR

This disease is beyond my practise: yet I have known those which have walked in their sleep who have died holily in their beds.

LADY MACBETH

Wash your hands, put on your nightgown; look not so pale.—I tell you yet again, Banquo's buried; he cannot come out on's grave.

DOCTOR

Even so?

LADY MACBETH

To bed, to bed! there's knocking at the gate: come, come, come, come, give me your hand. What's done cannot be undone.—To bed, to bed, to bed!

Exit

DOCTOR

Will she go now to bed?

GENTLEWOMAN

Directly.

DOCTOR

Foul whisperings are abroad: unnatural deeds

Do breed unnatural troubles: infected minds
To their deaf pillows will discharge their secrets:
More needs she the divine than the physician.
God, God forgive us all! Look after her;
Remove from her the means of all annoyance,
And still keep eyes upon her. So, good night:
My mind she has mated, and amazed my sight.
I think, but dare not speak.

GENTLEWOMAN

Good night, good doctor.

Exeunt

SCENE II.
THE COUNTRY NEAR DUNSINANE.

Drum and colours. Enter MENTEITH, CAITHNESS, ANGUS,
LENNOX, *and Soldiers*

MENTEITH

The English power is near, led on by Malcolm,
His uncle Siward and the good Macduff:
Revenges burn in them; for their dear causes
Would to the bleeding and the grim alarm
Excite the mortified man.

ANGUS

Near Birnam wood
Shall we well meet them; that way are they coming.

CAITHNESS

Who knows if Donalbain be with his brother?

LENNOX

For certain, sir, he is not: I have a file
Of all the gentry: there is Siward's son,
And many unrough youths that even now
Protest their first of manhood.

MENTEITH

What does the tyrant?

CAITHNESS

Great Dunsinane he strongly fortifies:

Some say he's mad; others that lesser hate him
Do call it valiant fury: but, for certain,
He cannot buckle his distemper'd cause
Within the belt of rule.

ANGUS

Now does he feel
His secret murders sticking on his hands;
Now minutely revolts upbraid his faith-breach;
Those he commands move only in command,
Nothing in love: now does he feel his title
Hang loose about him, like a giant's robe
Upon a dwarfish thief.

MENTEITH

Who then shall blame
His pester'd senses to recoil and start,
When all that is within him does condemn
Itself for being there?

CAITHNESS

Well, march we on,
To give obedience where 'tis truly owed:
Meet we the medicine of the sickly weal,
And with him pour we in our country's purge
Each drop of us.

LENNOX

Or so much as it needs,
To dew the sovereign flower and drown the weeds.
Make we our march towards Birnam.

Exeunt, marching

SCENE III.
DUNSINANE. A ROOM IN THE CASTLE.

Enter MACBETH, *Doctor, and Attendants*

MACBETH

Bring me no more reports; let them fly all:
Till Birnam wood remove to Dunsinane,
I cannot taint with fear. What's the boy Malcolm?

Was he not born of woman? The spirits that know
All mortal consequences have pronounced me thus:
'Fear not, Macbeth; no man that's born of woman
Shall e'er have power upon thee.' Then fly, false thanes,
And mingle with the English epicures:
The mind I sway by and the heart I bear
Shall never sag with doubt nor shake with fear.

Enter a Servant

The devil damn thee black, thou cream-faced loon!
Where got'st thou that goose look?

SERVANT

There is ten thousand—

MACBETH

Geese, villain!

SERVANT

Soldiers, sir.

MACBETH

Go prick thy face, and over-red thy fear,
Thou lily-liver'd boy. What soldiers, patch?
Death of thy soul! those linen cheeks of thine
Are counsellors to fear. What soldiers, whey-face?

SERVANT

The English force, so please you.

MACBETH

Take thy face hence.

Exit Servant

Seyton!—I am sick at heart,
When I behold—Seyton, I say!—This push
Will cheer me ever, or disseat me now.
I have lived long enough: my way of life
Is fall'n into the sear, the yellow leaf;
And that which should accompany old age,
As honour, love, obedience, troops of friends,
I must not look to have; but, in their stead,
Curses, not loud but deep, mouth-honour, breath,
Which the poor heart would fain deny, and dare not. Seyton!

Enter SEYTON

SEYTON

What is your gracious pleasure?

MACBETH

What news more?

SEYTON

All is confirm'd, my lord, which was reported.

MACBETH

I'll fight till from my bones my flesh be hack'd.
Give me my armour.

SEYTON

'Tis not needed yet.

MACBETH

I'll put it on.
Send out more horses; skirr the country round;
Hang those that talk of fear. Give me mine armour.
How does your patient, doctor?

DOCTOR

Not so sick, my lord,
As she is troubled with thick coming fancies,
That keep her from her rest.

MACBETH

Cure her of that.
Canst thou not minister to a mind diseased,
Pluck from the memory a rooted sorrow,
Raze out the written troubles of the brain
And with some sweet oblivious antidote
Cleanse the stuff'd bosom of that perilous stuff
Which weighs upon the heart?

DOCTOR

Therein the patient
Must minister to himself.

MACBETH

Throw physic to the dogs; I'll none of it.
Come, put mine armour on; give me my staff.
Seyton, send out. Doctor, the thanes fly from me.
Come, sir, dispatch. If thou couldst, doctor, cast
The water of my land, find her disease,

And purge it to a sound and pristine health,
I would applaud thee to the very echo,
That should applaud again.—Pull't off, I say.—
What rhubarb, cyme, or what purgative drug,
Would scour these English hence? Hear'st thou of them?

DOCTOR
Ay, my good lord; your royal preparation
Makes us hear something.

MACBETH
Bring it after me.
I will not be afraid of death and bane,
Till Birnam forest come to Dunsinane.

DOCTOR
[*Aside*] Were I from Dunsinane away and clear,
Profit again should hardly draw me here.

Exeunt

SCENE IV.
COUNTRY NEAR BIRNAM WOOD.

Drum and colours. Enter MALCOLM, SIWARD *and*
YOUNG SIWARD, MACDUFF, MENTEITH, CAITHNESS, ANGUS,
LENNOX, ROSS, *and Soldiers, marching*

MALCOLM
Cousins, I hope the days are near at hand
That chambers will be safe.

MENTEITH
We doubt it nothing.

SIWARD
What wood is this before us?

MENTEITH
The wood of Birnam.

MALCOLM
Let every soldier hew him down a bough
And bear't before him: thereby shall we shadow
The numbers of our host and make discovery
Err in report of us.

SOLDIERS

    It shall be done.

SIWARD

    We learn no other but the confident tyrant
    Keeps still in Dunsinane, and will endure
    Our setting down before't.

MALCOLM

    'Tis his main hope:
    For where there is advantage to be given,
    Both more and less have given him the revolt,
    And none serve with him but constrained things
    Whose hearts are absent too.

MACDUFF

    Let our just censures
    Attend the true event, and put we on
    Industrious soldiership.

SIWARD

    The time approaches
    That will with due decision make us know
    What we shall say we have and what we owe.
    Thoughts speculative their unsure hopes relate,
    But certain issue strokes must arbitrate:
    Towards which advance the war.

Exeunt, marching

SCENE V.
DUNSINANE. WITHIN THE CASTLE.

Enter MACBETH, SEYTON, *and*
Soldiers, with drum and colours

MACBETH

    Hang out our banners on the outward walls;
    The cry is still 'They come:' our castle's strength
    Will laugh a siege to scorn: here let them lie
    Till famine and the ague eat them up:
    Were they not forced with those that should be ours,
    We might have met them dareful, beard to beard,

And beat them backward home.

A cry of women within

What is that noise?

SEYTON

It is the cry of women, my good lord.

Exit

MACBETH

I have almost forgot the taste of fears;
The time has been, my senses would have cool'd
To hear a night-shriek; and my fell of hair
Would at a dismal treatise rouse and stir
As life were in't: I have supp'd full with horrors;
Direness, familiar to my slaughterous thoughts
Cannot once start me.

Re-enter SEYTON

Wherefore was that cry?

SEYTON

The queen, my lord, is dead.

MACBETH

She should have died hereafter;
There would have been a time for such a word.
To-morrow, and to-morrow, and to-morrow,
Creeps in this petty pace from day to day
To the last syllable of recorded time,
And all our yesterdays have lighted fools
The way to dusty death. Out, out, brief candle!
Life's but a walking shadow, a poor player
That struts and frets his hour upon the stage
And then is heard no more: it is a tale
Told by an idiot, full of sound and fury,
Signifying nothing.

Enter a Messenger

Thou comest to use thy tongue; thy story quickly.

MESSENGER

Gracious my lord,
I should report that which I say I saw,
But know not how to do it.

MACBETH

    Well, say, sir.

MESSENGER

    As I did stand my watch upon the hill,
    I look'd toward Birnam, and anon, methought,
    The wood began to move.

MACBETH

    Liar and slave!

MESSENGER

    Let me endure your wrath, if't be not so:
    Within this three mile may you see it coming;
    I say, a moving grove.

MACBETH

    If thou speak'st false,
    Upon the next tree shalt thou hang alive,
    Till famine cling thee: if thy speech be sooth,
    I care not if thou dost for me as much.
    I pull in resolution, and begin
    To doubt the equivocation of the fiend
    That lies like truth: 'Fear not, till Birnam wood
    Do come to Dunsinane:' and now a wood
    Comes toward Dunsinane. Arm, arm, and out!
    If this which he avouches does appear,
    There is nor flying hence nor tarrying here.
    I gin to be aweary of the sun,
    And wish the estate o'the world were now undone.
    Ring the alarum-bell! Blow, wind! come, wrack!
    At least we'll die with harness on our back.

Exeunt

SCENE VI.
DUNSINANE. BEFORE THE CASTLE.

Drum and colours. Enter MALCOLM, SIWARD,
MACDUFF, *and their Army, with boughs*

MALCOLM

    Now near enough: your leafy screens throw down.

And show like those you are. You, worthy uncle,
Shall, with my cousin, your right-noble son,
Lead our first battle: worthy Macduff and we
Shall take upon's what else remains to do,
According to our order.

SIWARD

Fare you well.
Do we but find the tyrant's power to-night,
Let us be beaten, if we cannot fight.

MACDUFF

Make all our trumpets speak; give them all breath,
Those clamorous harbingers of blood and death.

Exeunt

SCENE VII.
ANOTHER PART OF THE FIELD.

Alarums. Enter MACBETH

MACBETH

They have tied me to a stake; I cannot fly,
But, bear-like, I must fight the course. What's he
That was not born of woman? Such a one
Am I to fear, or none.

Enter YOUNG SIWARD

YOUNG SIWARD

What is thy name?

MACBETH

Thou'lt be afraid to hear it.

YOUNG SIWARD

No; though thou call'st thyself a hotter name
Than any is in hell.

MACBETH

My name's Macbeth.

YOUNG SIWARD

The devil himself could not pronounce a title
More hateful to mine ear.

MACBETH

    No, nor more fearful.

YOUNG SIWARD

    Thou liest, abhorred tyrant; with my sword
    I'll prove the lie thou speak'st.

             They fight and YOUNG SIWARD *is slain*

MACBETH

    Thou wast born of woman
    But swords I smile at, weapons laugh to scorn,
    Brandish'd by man that's of a woman born.

                                                    Exit

                Alarums. Enter MACDUFF

MACDUFF

    That way the noise is. Tyrant, show thy face!
    If thou be'st slain and with no stroke of mine,
    My wife and children's ghosts will haunt me still.
    I cannot strike at wretched kerns, whose arms
    Are hired to bear their staves: either thou, Macbeth,
    Or else my sword with an unbatter'd edge
    I sheathe again undeeded. There thou shouldst be;
    By this great clatter, one of greatest note
    Seems bruited. Let me find him, fortune!
    And more I beg not.

                                                  Exit.

        Alarums. Enter MALCOLM *and* SIWARD

SIWARD

    This way, my lord; the castle's gently render'd:
    The tyrant's people on both sides do fight;
    The noble thanes do bravely in the war;
    The day almost itself professes yours,
    And little is to do.

MALCOLM

    We have met with foes
    That strike beside us.

SIWARD

    Enter, sir, the castle.

                                  Exeunt. Alarums

SCENE VIII.
ANOTHER PART OF THE FIELD.

Enter MACBETH

MACBETH

Why should I play the Roman fool, and die
On mine own sword? whiles I see lives, the gashes
Do better upon them.

Enter MACDUFF

MACDUFF

Turn, hell-hound, turn!

MACBETH

Of all men else I have avoided thee:
But get thee back; my soul is too much charged
With blood of thine already.

MACDUFF

I have no words:
My voice is in my sword: thou bloodier villain
Than terms can give thee out!

They fight

MACBETH

Thou losest labour:
As easy mayst thou the intrenchant air
With thy keen sword impress as make me bleed:
Let fall thy blade on vulnerable crests;
I bear a charmed life, which must not yield,
To one of woman born.

MACDUFF

Despair thy charm;
And let the angel whom thou still hast served
Tell thee, Macduff was from his mother's womb
Untimely ripp'd.

MACBETH

Accursed be that tongue that tells me so,
For it hath cow'd my better part of man!
And be these juggling fiends no more believed,
That palter with us in a double sense;

That keep the word of promise to our ear,
And break it to our hope. I'll not fight with thee.

MACDUFF

Then yield thee, coward,
And live to be the show and gaze o'the time:
We'll have thee, as our rarer monsters are,
Painted on a pole, and underwrit,
'Here may you see the tyrant.'

MACBETH

I will not yield,
To kiss the ground before young Malcolm's feet,
And to be baited with the rabble's curse.
Though Birnam wood be come to Dunsinane,
And thou opposed, being of no woman born,
Yet I will try the last. Before my body
I throw my warlike shield. Lay on, Macduff,
And damn'd be him that first cries, 'Hold, enough!'

Exeunt, fighting. Alarums

*Retreat. Flourish. Enter, with drum and
colours,* MALCOLM, SIWARD, ROSS,
the other Thanes, and Soldiers

MALCOLM

I would the friends we miss were safe arrived.

SIWARD

Some must go off: and yet, by these I see,
So great a day as this is cheaply bought.

MALCOLM

Macduff is missing, and your noble son.

ROSS

Your son, my lord, has paid a soldier's debt:
He only lived but till he was a man;
The which no sooner had his prowess confirm'd
In the unshrinking station where he fought,
But like a man he died.

SIWARD

Then he is dead?

ROSS

Ay, and brought off the field: your cause of sorrow
Must not be measured by his worth, for then
It hath no end.

SIWARD

Had he his hurts before?

ROSS

Ay, on the front.

SIWARD

Why then, God's soldier be he!
Had I as many sons as I have hairs,
I would not wish them to a fairer death:
And so, his knell is knoll'd.

MALCOLM

He's worth more sorrow,
And that I'll spend for him.

SIWARD

He's worth no more
They say he parted well, and paid his score:
And so, God be with him! Here comes newer comfort.

Re-enter MACDUFF, *with* MACBETH'S *head*

MACDUFF

Hail, king! for so thou art: behold, where stands
The usurper's cursed head: the time is free:
I see thee compass'd with thy kingdom's pearl,
That speak my salutation in their minds;
Whose voices I desire aloud with mine:
Hail, King of Scotland!

ALL

Hail, King of Scotland!

Flourish

MALCOLM

We shall not spend a large expense of time
Before we reckon with your several loves,
And make us even with you. My thanes and kinsmen,
Henceforth be earls, the first that ever Scotland
In such an honour named. What's more to do,

Which would be planted newly with the time,
As calling home our exiled friends abroad
That fled the snares of watchful tyranny;
Producing forth the cruel ministers
Of this dead butcher and his fiend-like queen,
Who, as 'tis thought, by self and violent hands
Took off her life; this, and what needful else
That calls upon us, by the grace of Grace,
We will perform in measure, time and place:
So, thanks to all at once and to each one,
Whom we invite to see us crown'd at Scone.

Flourish. Exeunt

Othello

"O, beware, my lord, of jealousy;
It is the green-eyed monster which doth mock
The meat it feeds on;"

Characters in the Play

OTHELLO, the Moor, general of the Venetian forces
DESDEMONA, his wife
IAGO, ensign to Othello
EMILIA, his wife, lady-in-waiting to Desdemona
CASSIO, lieutenant to Othello
The DUKE OF VENICE
BRABANTIO, Venetian Senator, father of Desdemona
GRATIANO, nobleman of Venice, brother of Brabantio
LODOVICO, nobleman of Venice, kinsman of Brabantio
RODERIGO, rejected suitor of Desdemona
BIANCA, mistress of Cassio
MONTANO, a Cypriot official
A Clown in service to Othello
Senators, Sailors, Messengers, Officers, Gentlemen, Musicians, and Attendants

SCENE:
Venice and Cyprus.

ACT

I

SCENE I.
VENICE. A STREET.

Enter RODERIGO *and* IAGO

RODERIGO

    Tush! never tell me; I take it much unkindly
    That thou, Iago, who hast had my purse
    As if the strings were thine, shouldst know of this.

IAGO

    'Sblood, but you will not hear me:
    If ever I did dream of such a matter, Abhor me.

RODERIGO

    Thou told'st me thou didst hold him in thy hate.

IAGO

    Despise me, if I do not. Three great ones of the city,
    In personal suit to make me his lieutenant,
    Off-capp'd to him: and, by the faith of man,
    I know my price, I am worth no worse a place:
    But he; as loving his own pride and purposes,
    Evades them, with a bombast circumstance
    Horribly stuff'd with epithets of war;
    And, in conclusion,

Nonsuits my mediators; for, 'Certes,' says he,
'I have already chose my officer.'
And what was he?
Forsooth, a great arithmetician,
One Michael Cassio, a Florentine,
A fellow almost damn'd in a fair wife;
That never set a squadron in the field,
Nor the division of a battle knows
More than a spinster; unless the bookish theoric,
Wherein the toged consuls can propose
As masterly as he: mere prattle, without practise,
Is all his soldiership. But he, sir, had the election:
And I, of whom his eyes had seen the proof
At Rhodes, at Cyprus and on other grounds
Christian and heathen, must be be-lee'd and calm'd
By debitor and creditor: this counter-caster,
He, in good time, must his lieutenant be,
And I—God bless the mark!—his Moorship's ancient.

RODERIGO

By heaven, I rather would have been his hangman.

IAGO

Why, there's no remedy; 'tis the curse of service,
Preferment goes by letter and affection,
And not by old gradation, where each second
Stood heir to the first. Now, sir, be judge yourself,
Whether I in any just term am affined
To love the Moor.

RODERIGO

I would not follow him then.

IAGO

O, sir, content you;
I follow him to serve my turn upon him:
We cannot all be masters, nor all masters
Cannot be truly follow'd. You shall mark
Many a duteous and knee-crooking knave,
That, doting on his own obsequious bondage,
Wears out his time, much like his master's ass,

For nought but provender, and when he's old, cashier'd:
Whip me such honest knaves. Others there are
Who, trimm'd in forms and visages of duty,
Keep yet their hearts attending on themselves,
And, throwing but shows of service on their lords,
Do well thrive by them and when they have lined their coats
Do themselves homage: these fellows have some soul;
And such a one do I profess myself. For, sir,
It is as sure as you are Roderigo,
Were I the Moor, I would not be Iago:
In following him, I follow but myself;
Heaven is my judge, not I for love and duty,
But seeming so, for my peculiar end:
For when my outward action doth demonstrate
The native act and figure of my heart
In compliment extern, 'tis not long after
But I will wear my heart upon my sleeve
For daws to peck at: I am not what I am.

RODERIGO

What a full fortune does the thick-lips owe
If he can carry't thus!

IAGO

Call up her father,
Rouse him: make after him, poison his delight,
Proclaim him in the streets; incense her kinsmen,
And, though he in a fertile climate dwell,
Plague him with flies: though that his joy be joy,
Yet throw such changes of vexation on't,
As it may lose some colour.

RODERIGO

Here is her father's house; I'll call aloud.

IAGO

Do, with like timorous accent and dire yell
As when, by night and negligence, the fire
Is spied in populous cities.

RODERIGO

What, ho, Brabantio! Signior Brabantio, ho!

IAGO

Awake! what, ho, Brabantio! thieves! thieves! thieves!
Look to your house, your daughter and your bags!
Thieves! thieves!

BRABANTIO *appears above, at a window*

BRABANTIO

What is the reason of this terrible summons?
What is the matter there?

RODERIGO

Signior, is all your family within?

IAGO

Are your doors lock'd?

BRABANTIO

Why, wherefore ask you this?

IAGO

Zounds, sir, you're robb'd; for shame, put on your gown;
Your heart is burst, you have lost half your soul;
Even now, now, very now, an old black ram
Is tupping your white ewe. Arise, arise;
Awake the snorting citizens with the bell,
Or else the devil will make a grandsire of you:
Arise, I say.

BRABANTIO

What, have you lost your wits?

RODERIGO

Most reverend signior, do you know my voice?

BRABANTIO

Not I what are you?

RODERIGO

My name is Roderigo.

BRABANTIO

The worser welcome:
I have charged thee not to haunt about my doors:
In honest plainness thou hast heard me say
My daughter is not for thee; and now, in madness,
Being full of supper and distempering draughts,

Upon malicious bravery, dost thou come
To start my quiet.

RODERIGO

Sir, sir, sir—

BRABANTIO

But thou must needs be sure
My spirit and my place have in them power
To make this bitter to thee.

RODERIGO

Patience, good sir.

BRABANTIO

What tell'st thou me of robbing? This is Venice;
My house is not a grange.

RODERIGO

Most grave Brabantio,
In simple and pure soul I come to you.

IAGO

Zounds, sir, you are one of those that will not serve God, if the devil bid you. Because we come to do you service and you think we are ruffians, you'll have your daughter covered with a Barbary horse; you'll have your nephews neigh to you; you'll have coursers for cousins and gennets for germans.

BRABANTIO

What profane wretch art thou?

IAGO

I am one, sir, that comes to tell you your daughter and the Moor are now making the beast with two backs.

BRABANTIO

Thou art a villain.

IAGO

You are—a senator.

BRABANTIO

This thou shalt answer; I know thee, Roderigo.

RODERIGO

Sir, I will answer any thing. But, I beseech you,
If't be your pleasure and most wise consent,

As partly I find it is, that your fair daughter,
At this odd-even and dull watch o' the night,
Transported, with no worse nor better guard
But with a knave of common hire, a gondolier,
To the gross clasps of a lascivious Moor—
If this be known to you and your allowance,
We then have done you bold and saucy wrongs;
But if you know not this, my manners tell me
We have your wrong rebuke. Do not believe
That, from the sense of all civility,
I thus would play and trifle with your reverence:
Your daughter, if you have not given her leave,
I say again, hath made a gross revolt;
Tying her duty, beauty, wit and fortunes
In an extravagant and wheeling stranger
Of here and every where. Straight satisfy yourself:
If she be in her chamber or your house,
Let loose on me the justice of the state
For thus deluding you.

BRABANTIO

Strike on the tinder, ho!
Give me a taper! call up all my people!
This accident is not unlike my dream:
Belief of it oppresses me already.
Light, I say! light!

Exit above

IAGO

Farewell; for I must leave you:
It seems not meet, nor wholesome to my place,
To be produced—as, if I stay, I shall—
Against the Moor: for, I do know, the state,
However this may gall him with some check,
Cannot with safety cast him, for he's embark'd
With such loud reason to the Cyprus wars,
Which even now stand in act, that, for their souls,
Another of his fathom they have none,
To lead their business: in which regard,

Though I do hate him as I do hell-pains.
Yet, for necessity of present life,
I must show out a flag and sign of love,
Which is indeed but sign. That you shall surely find him,
Lead to the Sagittary the raised search;
And there will I be with him. So, farewell.

Exit

Enter, below, BRABANTIO, *and
Servants with torches*

BRABANTIO
It is too true an evil: gone she is;
And what's to come of my despised time
Is nought but bitterness. Now, Roderigo,
Where didst thou see her? O unhappy girl!
With the Moor, say'st thou? Who would be a father!
How didst thou know 'twas she? O she deceives me
Past thought! What said she to you? Get more tapers:
Raise all my kindred. Are they married, think you?

RODERIGO
Truly, I think they are.

BRABANTIO
O heaven! How got she out? O treason of the blood!
Fathers, from hence trust not your daughters' minds
By what you see them act. Is there not charms
By which the property of youth and maidhood
May be abused? Have you not read, Roderigo,
Of some such thing?

RODERIGO
Yes, sir, I have indeed.

BRABANTIO
Call up my brother. O, would you had had her!
Some one way, some another. Do you know
Where we may apprehend her and the Moor?

RODERIGO
I think I can discover him, if you please,
To get good guard and go along with me.

BRABANTIO

    Pray you, lead on. At every house I'll call;
    I may command at most. Get weapons, ho!
    And raise some special officers of night.
    On, good Roderigo: I'll deserve your pains.

Exeunt

SCENE II.
ANOTHER STREET.

Enter OTHELLO, IAGO, *and*
Attendants with torches

IAGO

    Though in the trade of war I have slain men,
    Yet do I hold it very stuff o' the conscience
    To do no contrived murder: I lack iniquity
    Sometimes to do me service: nine or ten times
    I had thought to have yerk'd him here under the ribs.

OTHELLO

    'Tis better as it is.

IAGO

    Nay, but he prated,
    And spoke such scurvy and provoking terms
    Against your honour
    That, with the little godliness I have,
    I did full hard forbear him. But, I pray you, sir,
    Are you fast married? Be assured of this,
    That the magnifico is much beloved,
    And hath in his effect a voice potential
    As double as the Duke's: he will divorce you;
    Or put upon you what restraint and grievance
    The law, with all his might to enforce it on,
    Will give him cable.

OTHELLO

    Let him do his spite:
    My services which I have done the signiory
    Shall out-tongue his complaints. 'Tis yet to know—

Which, when I know that boasting is an honour,
I shall promulgate—I fetch my life and being
From men of royal siege, and my demerits
May speak unbonneted to as proud a fortune
As this that I have reach'd: for know, Iago,
But that I love the gentle Desdemona,
I would not my unhoused free condition
Put into circumscription and confine
For the sea's worth. But, look! what lights come yond?

IAGO

Those are the raised father and his friends:
You were best go in.

OTHELLO

Not I I must be found:
My parts, my title and my perfect soul
Shall manifest me rightly. Is it they?

IAGO

By Janus, I think no.

Enter CASSIO, *and certain Officers with torches*

OTHELLO

The servants of the Duke, and my lieutenant.
The goodness of the night upon you, friends!
What is the news?

CASSIO

The Duke does greet you, general,
And he requires your haste-post-haste appearance,
Even on the instant.

OTHELLO

What is the matter, think you?

CASSIO

Something from Cyprus as I may divine:
It is a business of some heat: the galleys
Have sent a dozen sequent messengers
This very night at one another's heels,
And many of the consuls, raised and met,
Are at the Duke's already: you have been hotly call'd for;
When, being not at your lodging to be found,

The Senate hath sent about three several quests
To search you out.

OTHELLO

'Tis well I am found by you.
I will but spend a word here in the house,
And go with you.

Exit

CASSIO

Ancient, what makes he here?

IAGO

Faith, he to-night hath boarded a land carrack:
If it prove lawful prize, he's made for ever.

CASSIO

I do not understand.

IAGO

He's married.

CASSIO

To who?

Re-enter OTHELLO

IAGO

Marry, to—Come, captain, will you go?

OTHELLO

Have with you.

CASSIO

Here comes another troop to seek for you.

IAGO

It is Brabantio. General, be advised;
He comes to bad intent.

Enter BRABANTIO, RODERIGO, *and*
Officers with torches and weapons

OTHELLO

Holla! stand there!

RODERIGO

Signior, it is the Moor.

BRABANTIO

Down with him, thief!

They draw on both sides

IAGO

You, Roderigo! come, sir, I am for you.

OTHELLO

Keep up your bright swords, for the dew will rust them.
Good signior, you shall more command with years
Than with your weapons.

BRABANTIO

O thou foul thief, where hast thou stow'd my daughter?
Damn'd as thou art, thou hast enchanted her;
For I'll refer me to all things of sense,
If she in chains of magic were not bound,
Whether a maid so tender, fair and happy,
So opposite to marriage that she shunned
The wealthy curled darlings of our nation,
Would ever have, to incur a general mock,
Run from her guardage to the sooty bosom
Of such a thing as thou, to fear, not to delight.
Judge me the world, if 'tis not gross in sense
That thou hast practised on her with foul charms,
Abused her delicate youth with drugs or minerals
That weaken motion: I'll have't disputed on;
'Tis probable and palpable to thinking.
I therefore apprehend and do attach thee
For an abuser of the world, a practiser
Of arts inhibited and out of warrant.
Lay hold upon him: if he do resist,
Subdue him at his peril.

OTHELLO

Hold your hands,
Both you of my inclining, and the rest:
Were it my cue to fight, I should have known it
Without a prompter. Where will you that I go
To answer this your charge?

BRABANTIO

To prison, till fit time
Of law and course of direct session
Call thee to answer.

OTHELLO

    What if I do obey?
    How may the Duke be therewith satisfied,
    Whose messengers are here about my side,
    Upon some present business of the state
    To bring me to him?

FIRST OFFICER

    'Tis true, most worthy signior;
    The Duke's in council and your noble self,
    I am sure, is sent for.

BRABANTIO

    How! The Duke in council!
    In this time of the night! Bring him away:
    Mine's not an idle cause: the Duke himself,
    Or any of my brothers of the state,
    Cannot but feel this wrong as 'twere their own;
    For if such actions may have passage free,
    Bond-slaves and pagans shall our statesmen be.

Exeunt

SCENE III.
A COUNCIL CHAMBER.

*The DUKE and Senators sitting
at a table; Officers attending*

DUKE OF VENICE

    There is no composition in these news
    That gives them credit.

FIRST SENATOR

    Indeed, they are disproportion'd;
    My letters say a hundred and seven galleys.

DUKE OF VENICE

    And mine, a hundred and forty.

SECOND SENATOR

    And mine, two hundred:
    But though they jump not on a just account—
    As in these cases, where the aim reports,

'Tis oft with difference—yet do they all confirm
A Turkish fleet, and bearing up to Cyprus.

DUKE OF VENICE

Nay, it is possible enough to judgment:
I do not so secure me in the error,
But the main article I do approve
In fearful sense.

SAILOR

[*Within*] What, ho! what, ho! what, ho!

FIRST OFFICER

A messenger from the galleys.

Enter a Sailor

DUKE OF VENICE

Now, what's the business?

SAILOR

The Turkish preparation makes for Rhodes;
So was I bid report here to the state
By Signior Angelo.

DUKE OF VENICE

How say you by this change?

FIRST SENATOR

This cannot be,
By no assay of reason: 'tis a pageant,
To keep us in false gaze. When we consider
The importancy of Cyprus to the Turk,
And let ourselves again but understand,
That as it more concerns the Turk than Rhodes,
So may he with more facile question bear it,
For that it stands not in such warlike brace,
But altogether lacks the abilities
That Rhodes is dress'd in: if we make thought of this,
We must not think the Turk is so unskilful
To leave that latest which concerns him first,
Neglecting an attempt of ease and gain,
To wake and wage a danger profitless.

DUKE OF VENICE

Nay, in all confidence, he's not for Rhodes.

FIRST OFFICER
    Here is more news.
                            Enter a Messenger
MESSENGER
    The Ottomites, reverend and gracious,
    Steering with due course towards the isle of Rhodes,
    Have there injointed them with an after fleet.
FIRST SENATOR
    Ay, so I thought. How many, as you guess?
MESSENGER
    Of thirty sail: and now they do restem
    Their backward course, bearing with frank appearance
    Their purposes toward Cyprus. Signior Montano,
    Your trusty and most valiant servitor,
    With his free duty recommends you thus,
    And prays you to believe him.
DUKE OF VENICE
    'Tis certain, then, for Cyprus.
    Marcus Luccicos, is not he in town?
FIRST SENATOR
    He's now in Florence.
DUKE OF VENICE
    Write from us to him; post-post-haste dispatch.
FIRST SENATOR
    Here comes Brabantio and the valiant Moor.
                    Enter BRABANTIO, OTHELLO,
                    IAGO, RODERIGO, *and Officers*
DUKE OF VENICE
    Valiant Othello, we must straight employ you
    Against the general enemy Ottoman.
                            To BRABANTIO
    I did not see you; welcome, gentle signior;
    We lack'd your counsel and your help tonight.
BRABANTIO
    So did I yours. Good your grace, pardon me;
    Neither my place nor aught I heard of business
    Hath raised me from my bed, nor doth the general care

Take hold on me, for my particular grief
Is of so flood-gate and o'erbearing nature
That it engluts and swallows other sorrows
And it is still itself.
DUKE OF VENICE
Why, what's the matter?
BRABANTIO
My daughter! O, my daughter!
DUKE OF VENICE AND SENATOR
Dead?
BRABANTIO
Ay, to me;
She is abused, stol'n from me, and corrupted
By spells and medicines bought of mountebanks;
For nature so preposterously to err,
Being not deficient, blind, or lame of sense,
Sans witchcraft could not.
DUKE OF VENICE
Whoe'er he be that in this foul proceeding
Hath thus beguiled your daughter of herself
And you of her, the bloody book of law
You shall yourself read in the bitter letter
After your own sense, yea, though our proper son
Stood in your action.
BRABANTIO
Humbly I thank your grace.
Here is the man, this Moor, whom now, it seems,
Your special mandate for the state-affairs
Hath hither brought.
DUKE OF VENICE AND SENATOR
We are very sorry for't.
DUKE OF VENICE
[To OTHELLO] What, in your own part, can you say to this?
BRABANTIO
Nothing, but this is so.
OTHELLO
Most potent, grave, and reverend signiors,

My very noble and approved good masters,
That I have ta'en away this old man's daughter,
It is most true; true, I have married her:
The very head and front of my offending
Hath this extent, no more. Rude am I in my speech,
And little bless'd with the soft phrase of peace:
For since these arms of mine had seven years' pith,
Till now some nine moons wasted, they have used
Their dearest action in the tented field,
And little of this great world can I speak,
More than pertains to feats of broil and battle,
And therefore little shall I grace my cause
In speaking for myself. Yet, by your gracious patience,
I will a round unvarnish'd tale deliver
Of my whole course of love; what drugs, what charms,
What conjuration and what mighty magic,
For such proceeding I am charged withal,
I won his daughter.

BRABANTIO

A maiden never bold;
Of spirit so still and quiet, that her motion
Blush'd at herself; and she, in spite of nature,
Of years, of country, credit, every thing,
To fall in love with what she fear'd to look on!
It is a judgment maim'd and most imperfect
That will confess perfection so could err
Against all rules of nature, and must be driven
To find out practises of cunning hell,
Why this should be. I therefore vouch again
That with some mixtures powerful o'er the blood,
Or with some dram conjured to this effect,
He wrought upon her.

DUKE OF VENICE

To vouch this, is no proof,
Without more wider and more overt test
Than these thin habits and poor likelihoods
Of modern seeming do prefer against him.

FIRST SENATOR
But, Othello, speak:
Did you by indirect and forced courses
Subdue and poison this young maid's affections?
Or came it by request and such fair question
As soul to soul affordeth?
OTHELLO
I do beseech you,
Send for the lady to the Sagittary,
And let her speak of me before her father:
If you do find me foul in her report,
The trust, the office I do hold of you,
Not only take away, but let your sentence
Even fall upon my life.
DUKE OF VENICE
Fetch Desdemona hither.
OTHELLO
Ancient, conduct them: you best know the place.

Exeunt IAGO *and Attendants*

And, till she come, as truly as to heaven
I do confess the vices of my blood,
So justly to your grave ears I'll present
How I did thrive in this fair lady's love,
And she in mine.
DUKE OF VENICE
Say it, Othello.
OTHELLO
Her father loved me; oft invited me;
Still question'd me the story of my life,
From year to year, the battles, sieges, fortunes,
That I have passed.
I ran it through, even from my boyish days,
To the very moment that he bade me tell it;
Wherein I spake of most disastrous chances,
Of moving accidents by flood and field
Of hair-breadth scapes i' the imminent deadly breach,
Of being taken by the insolent foe

And sold to slavery, of my redemption thence
And portance in my travels' history:
Wherein of antres vast and deserts idle,
Rough quarries, rocks and hills whose heads touch heaven
It was my hint to speak—such was the process;
And of the Cannibals that each other eat,
The Anthropophagi and men whose heads
Do grow beneath their shoulders. This to hear
Would Desdemona seriously incline:
But still the house-affairs would draw her thence:
Which ever as she could with haste dispatch,
She'ld come again, and with a greedy ear
Devour up my discourse: which I observing,
Took once a pliant hour, and found good means
To draw from her a prayer of earnest heart
That I would all my pilgrimage dilate,
Whereof by parcels she had something heard,
But not intentively: I did consent,
And often did beguile her of her tears,
When I did speak of some distressful stroke
That my youth suffer'd. My story being done,
She gave me for my pains a world of sighs:
She swore, in faith, 'twas strange, 'twas passing strange,
'Twas pitiful, 'twas wondrous pitiful:
She wish'd she had not heard it, yet she wish'd
That heaven had made her such a man: she thank'd me,
And bade me, if I had a friend that loved her,
I should but teach him how to tell my story.
And that would woo her. Upon this hint I spake:
She loved me for the dangers I had pass'd,
And I loved her that she did pity them.
This only is the witchcraft I have used:
Here comes the lady; let her witness it.

   Enter DESDEMONA, IAGO, *and Attendants*

DUKE OF VENICE
 I think this tale would win my daughter too.
 Good Brabantio,

Take up this mangled matter at the best:
Men do their broken weapons rather use
Than their bare hands.

BRABANTIO

I pray you, hear her speak:
If she confess that she was half the wooer,
Destruction on my head, if my bad blame
Light on the man! Come hither, gentle mistress:
Do you perceive in all this noble company
Where most you owe obedience?

DESDEMONA

My noble father,
I do perceive here a divided duty:
To you I am bound for life and education;
My life and education both do learn me
How to respect you; you are the lord of duty;
I am hitherto your daughter: but here's my husband,
And so much duty as my mother show'd
To you, preferring you before her father,
So much I challenge that I may profess
Due to the Moor my lord.

BRABANTIO

God be wi' you! I have done.
Please it your grace, on to the state-affairs:
I had rather to adopt a child than get it.
Come hither, Moor:
I here do give thee that with all my heart
Which, but thou hast already, with all my heart
I would keep from thee. For your sake, jewel,
I am glad at soul I have no other child:
For thy escape would teach me tyranny,
To hang clogs on them. I have done, my lord.

DUKE OF VENICE

Let me speak like yourself, and lay a sentence,
Which, as a grise or step, may help these lovers
Into your favour.
When remedies are past, the griefs are ended

By seeing the worst, which late on hopes depended.
To mourn a mischief that is past and gone
Is the next way to draw new mischief on.
What cannot be preserved when fortune takes
Patience her injury a mockery makes.
The robb'd that smiles steals something from the thief;
He robs himself that spends a bootless grief.

BRABANTIO

So let the Turk of Cyprus us beguile;
We lose it not, so long as we can smile.
He bears the sentence well that nothing bears
But the free comfort which from thence he hears,
But he bears both the sentence and the sorrow
That, to pay grief, must of poor patience borrow.
These sentences, to sugar, or to gall,
Being strong on both sides, are equivocal:
But words are words; I never yet did hear
That the bruised heart was pierced through the ear.
I humbly beseech you, proceed to the affairs of state.

DUKE OF VENICE

The Turk with a most mighty preparation makes for Cyprus.
Othello, the fortitude of the place is best known to you; and
though we have there a substitute of most allowed sufficiency,
yet opinion, a sovereign mistress of effects, throws a more safer
voice on you: you must therefore be content to slubber the gloss
of your new fortunes with this more stubborn and boisterous
expedition.

OTHELLO

The tyrant custom, most grave senators,
Hath made the flinty and steel couch of war
My thrice-driven bed of down: I do agnise
A natural and prompt alacrity
I find in hardness, and do undertake
These present wars against the Ottomites.
Most humbly therefore bending to your state,
I crave fit disposition for my wife.
Due reference of place and exhibition,

With such accommodation and besort
As levels with her breeding.

DUKE OF VENICE

If you please,
Be't at her father's.

BRABANTIO

I'll not have it so.

OTHELLO

Nor I.

DESDEMONA

Nor I; I would not there reside,
To put my father in impatient thoughts
By being in his eye. Most gracious Duke,
To my unfolding lend your prosperous ear;
And let me find a charter in your voice,
To assist my simpleness.

DUKE OF VENICE

What would you, Desdemona?

DESDEMONA

That I did love the Moor to live with him,
My downright violence and storm of fortunes
May trumpet to the world: my heart's subdued
Even to the very quality of my lord:
I saw Othello's visage in his mind,
And to his honour and his valiant parts
Did I my soul and fortunes consecrate.
So that, dear lords, if I be left behind,
A moth of peace, and he go to the war,
The rites for which I love him are bereft me,
And I a heavy interim shall support
By his dear absence. Let me go with him.

OTHELLO

Let her have your voices.
Vouch with me, heaven, I therefore beg it not,
To please the palate of my appetite,
Nor to comply with heat—the young affects
In me defunct—and proper satisfaction.

But to be free and bounteous to her mind:
And heaven defend your good souls, that you think
I will your serious and great business scant
For she is with me: no, when light-wing'd toys
Of feather'd Cupid seal with wanton dullness
My speculative and officed instruments,
That my disports corrupt and taint my business,
Let housewives make a skillet of my helm,
And all indign and base adversities
Make head against my estimation!

DUKE OF VENICE

Be it as you shall privately determine,
Either for her stay or going: the affair cries haste,
And speed must answer it.

FIRST SENATOR

You must away to-night.

DESDEMONA

To-night, my lord!

DUKE OF VENICE

This night.

OTHELLO

With all my heart.

DUKE OF VENICE

At nine i' the morning here we'll meet again.
Othello, leave some officer behind,
And he shall our commission bring to you;
With such things else of quality and respect
As doth import you.

OTHELLO

So please your grace, my ancient;
A man he is of honest and trust:
To his conveyance I assign my wife,
With what else needful your good grace shall think
To be sent after me.

DUKE OF VENICE

Let it be so.
Good night to every one.

To Brabantio

And, noble signior,
If virtue no delighted beauty lack,
Your son-in-law is far more fair than black.

FIRST SENATOR

Adieu, brave Moor, use Desdemona well.

BRABANTIO

Look to her, Moor, if thou hast eyes to see:
She has deceived her father, and may thee.

Exeunt DUKE OF VENICE,
Senators, Officers, & c

OTHELLO

My life upon her faith! Honest Iago,
My Desdemona must I leave to thee:
I prithee, let thy wife attend on her:
And bring them after in the best advantage.
Come, Desdemona: I have but an hour
Of love, of worldly matters and direction,
To spend with thee: we must obey the time.

Exeunt OTHELLO *and* DESDEMONA

RODERIGO

Iago—

IAGO

What say'st thou, noble heart?

RODERIGO

What will I do, thinkest thou?

IAGO

Why, go to bed, and sleep.

RODERIGO

I will incontinently drown myself.

IAGO

If thou dost, I shall never love thee after. Why, thou silly
gentleman!

RODERIGO

It is silliness to live when to live is torment; and then have we a
prescription to die when death is our physician.

IAGO

O villainous! I have looked upon the world for four times seven years; and since I could distinguish betwixt a benefit and an injury, I never found man that knew how to love himself. Ere I would say, I would drown myself for the love of a guinea-hen, I would change my humanity with a baboon.

RODERIGO

What should I do? I confess it is my shame to be so fond; but it is not in my virtue to amend it.

IAGO

Virtue! a fig! 'tis in ourselves that we are thus or thus. Our bodies are our gardens, to the which our wills are gardeners: so that if we will plant nettles, or sow lettuce, set hyssop and weed up thyme, supply it with one gender of herbs, or distract it with many, either to have it sterile with idleness, or manured with industry, why, the power and corrigible authority of this lies in our wills. If the balance of our lives had not one scale of reason to poise another of sensuality, the blood and baseness of our natures would conduct us to most preposterous conclusions: but we have reason to cool our raging motions, our carnal stings, our unbitted lusts, whereof I take this that you call love to be a sect or scion.

RODERIGO

It cannot be.

IAGO

It is merely a lust of the blood and a permission of the will. Come, be a man. Drown thyself! drown cats and blind puppies. I have professed me thy friend and I confess me knit to thy deserving with cables of perdurable toughness; I could never better stead thee than now. Put money in thy purse; follow thou the wars; defeat thy favour with an usurped beard; I say, put money in thy purse. It cannot be that Desdemona should long continue her love to the Moor—put money in thy purse—nor he his to her: it was a violent commencement, and thou shalt see an answerable sequestration:—put but money in thy purse. These Moors are changeable in their wills: fill thy purse with money:—the food that to him now is as luscious as locusts, shall be to him shortly as bitter as coloquintida. She must change for youth: when she is sated with his body, she will find the error of her choice: she must have change, she must: therefore put money in thy purse. If thou wilt needs damn thyself, do it a more delicate way than drowning. Make all the money thou canst: if sanctimony and a frail vow betwixt an erring barbarian and a super-subtle Venetian not too hard for my wits and all the tribe of hell, thou shalt enjoy her; therefore make money. A pox of drowning thyself! it is clean out of the way: seek thou rather to be hanged in compassing thy joy than to be drowned and go without her.

RODERIGO

Wilt thou be fast to my hopes, if I depend on the issue?

IAGO

Thou art sure of me:—go, make money:—I have told thee often, and I re-tell thee again and again, I hate the Moor: my cause is hearted; thine hath no less reason. Let us be conjunctive in our revenge against him: if thou canst cuckold him, thou dost thyself a pleasure, me a sport. There are many events in the womb of time which will be delivered. Traverse! go, provide thy money. We will have more of this to-morrow. Adieu.

RODERIGO

Where shall we meet i' the morning?

IAGO

At my lodging.

RODERIGO

I'll be with thee betimes.

IAGO

Go to; farewell. Do you hear, Roderigo?

RODERIGO

What say you?

IAGO

No more of drowning, do you hear?

RODERIGO

I am changed.

IAGO

Go to; farewell. Put money enough in your purse.

RODERIGO
I'll go sell all my land.

Exit RODERIGO

IAGO
Thus do I ever make my fool my purse:
For I mine own gain'd knowledge should profane,
If I would time expend with such a snipe.
But for my sport and profit. I hate the Moor:
And it is thought abroad, that 'twixt my sheets
He has done my office: I know not if't be true;
But I, for mere suspicion in that kind,
Will do as if for surety. He holds me well;
The better shall my purpose work on him.
Cassio's a proper man: let me see now:
To get his place and to plume up my will
In double knavery—How, how? Let's see:—
After some time, to abuse Othello's ear
That he is too familiar with his wife.
He hath a person and a smooth dispose
To be suspected, framed to make women false.
The Moor is of a free and open nature,
That thinks men honest that but seem to be so,
And will as tenderly be led by the nose
As asses are.
I have't. It is engender'd. Hell and night
Must bring this monstrous birth to the world's light.

Exit

ACT

II

SCENE I.
A SEA-PORT IN CYPRUS.
AN OPEN PLACE NEAR THE QUAY.

Enter MONTANO *and two Gentlemen*

MONTANO
  What from the cape can you discern at sea?
FIRST GENTLEMAN
  Nothing at all: it is a high-wrought flood;
  I cannot, 'twixt the heaven and the main,
  Descry a sail.
MONTANO
  Methinks the wind hath spoke aloud at land;
  A fuller blast ne'er shook our battlements:
  If it hath ruffian'd so upon the sea,
  What ribs of oak, when mountains melt on them,
  Can hold the mortise? What shall we hear of this?
SECOND GENTLEMAN
  A segregation of the Turkish fleet:
  For do but stand upon the foaming shore,
  The chidden billow seems to pelt the clouds;

The wind-shaked surge, with high and monstrous mane,
Seems to cast water on the burning bear,
And quench the guards of the ever-fixed pole:
I never did like molestation view
On the enchafed flood.

MONTANO
If that the Turkish fleet
Be not enshelter'd and embay'd, they are drown'd:
It is impossible they bear it out.

Enter a third Gentleman

THIRD GENTLEMAN
News, lads! our wars are done.
The desperate tempest hath so bang'd the Turks,
That their designment halts: a noble ship of Venice
Hath seen a grievous wreck and sufferance
On most part of their fleet.

MONTANO
How! Is this true?

THIRD GENTLEMAN
The ship is here put in,
A Veronesa; Michael Cassio,
Lieutenant to the warlike Moor Othello,
Is come on shore: the Moor himself at sea,
And is in full commission here for Cyprus.

MONTANO
I am glad on't; 'tis a worthy governor.

THIRD GENTLEMAN
But this same Cassio, though he speak of comfort
Touching the Turkish loss, yet he looks sadly,
And prays the Moor be safe; for they were parted
With foul and violent tempest.

MONTANO
Pray heavens he be;
For I have served him, and the man commands
Like a full soldier. Let's to the seaside, ho!
As well to see the vessel that's come in
As to throw out our eyes for brave Othello,

Even till we make the main and the aerial blue
An indistinct regard.

THIRD GENTLEMAN

Come, let's do so:
For every minute is expectancy
Of more arrivance.

Enter CASSIO

CASSIO

Thanks, you the valiant of this warlike isle,
That so approve the Moor! O, let the heavens
Give him defence against the elements,
For I have lost us him on a dangerous sea.

MONTANO

Is he well shipp'd?

CASSIO

His bark is stoutly timber'd, his pilot
Of very expert and approved allowance;
Therefore my hopes, not surfeited to death, Stand in bold cure.

A cry within 'A sail, a sail, a sail!'
Enter a Messenger

CASSIO

What noise?

MESSENGER

The town is empty; on the brow o' the sea
Stand ranks of people, and they cry 'A sail!'

CASSIO

My hopes do shape him for the governor.

Guns heard

SECOND GENTLEMAN

They do discharge their shot of courtesy:
Our friends at least.

CASSIO

I pray you, sir, go forth,
And give us truth who 'tis that is arrived.

SECOND GENTLEMAN

I shall.

Exit

MONTANO
    But, good lieutenant, is your general wived?
CASSIO
    Most fortunately: he hath achieved a maid
    That paragons description and wild fame;
    One that excels the quirks of blazoning pens,
    And in the essential vesture of creation
    Does tire the ingener.
Re-enter second Gentleman
    How now! Who has put in?
SECOND GENTLEMAN
    'Tis one Iago, ancient to the general.
CASSIO
    'Has had most favourable and happy speed:
    Tempests themselves, high seas, and howling winds,
    The gutter'd rocks and congregated sands—
    Traitors ensteep'd to clog the guiltless keel,
    As having sense of beauty, do omit
    Their mortal natures, letting go safely by
    The divine Desdemona.
MONTANO
    What is she?
CASSIO
    She that I spake of, our great captain's captain,
    Left in the conduct of the bold Iago,
    Whose footing here anticipates our thoughts
    A se'nnight's speed. Great Jove, Othello guard,
    And swell his sail with thine own powerful breath,
    That he may bless this bay with his tall ship,
    Make love's quick pants in Desdemona's arms,
    Give renew'd fire to our extinct spirits
    And bring all Cyprus comfort!
Enter DESDEMONA, EMILIA,
IAGO, RODERIGO, *and Attendants*
    O, behold,
    The riches of the ship is come on shore!
    Ye men of Cyprus, let her have your knees.

Hail to thee, lady! and the grace of heaven,
Before, behind thee, and on every hand,
Enwheel thee round!

DESDEMONA

I thank you, valiant Cassio.
What tidings can you tell me of my lord?

CASSIO

He is not yet arrived: nor know I aught
But that he's well and will be shortly here.

DESDEMONA

O, but I fear—How lost you company?

CASSIO

The great contention of the sea and skies
Parted our fellowship—But, hark! a sail.

Within: 'A sail, a sail!' Guns heard

SECOND GENTLEMAN

They give their greeting to the citadel;
This likewise is a friend.

CASSIO

See for the news.

Exit Gentleman

Good ancient, you are welcome.

To EMILIA

Welcome, mistress.
Let it not gall your patience, good Iago,
That I extend my manners; 'tis my breeding
That gives me this bold show of courtesy.

Kissing her

IAGO

Sir, would she give you so much of her lips
As of her tongue she oft bestows on me,
You'll have enough.

DESDEMONA

Alas, she has no speech.

IAGO

In faith, too much;
I find it still, when I have list to sleep:

Marry, before your ladyship, I grant,
She puts her tongue a little in her heart,
And chides with thinking.

EMILIA

You have little cause to say so.

IAGO

Come on, come on; you are pictures out of doors, Bells in your
parlors, wild-cats in your kitchens, Saints m your injuries, devils
being offended, Players in your housewifery, and housewives' in
your beds.

DESDEMONA

O, fie upon thee, slanderer!

IAGO

Nay, it is true, or else I am a Turk:
You rise to play and go to bed to work.

EMILIA

You shall not write my praise.

IAGO

No, let me not.

DESDEMONA

What wouldst thou write of me, if thou shouldst praise me?

IAGO

O gentle lady, do not put me to't;
For I am nothing, if not critical.

DESDEMONA

Come on assay. There's one gone to the harbour?

IAGO

Ay, madam.

DESDEMONA

I am not merry; but I do beguile
The thing I am, by seeming otherwise.
Come, how wouldst thou praise me?

IAGO

I am about it; but indeed my invention
Comes from my pate as birdlime does from frize;
It plucks out brains and all: but my Muse labours,
And thus she is deliver'd.

If she be fair and wise, fairness and wit,
The one's for use, the other useth it.

DESDEMONA

Well praised! How if she be black and witty?

IAGO

If she be black, and thereto have a wit,
She'll find a white that shall her blackness fit.

DESDEMONA

Worse and worse.

EMILIA

How if fair and foolish?

IAGO

She never yet was foolish that was fair;
For even her folly help'd her to an heir.

DESDEMONA

These are old fond paradoxes to make fools laugh i' the alehouse.
What miserable praise hast thou for her that's foul and foolish?

IAGO

There's none so foul and foolish thereunto,
But does foul pranks which fair and wise ones do.

DESDEMONA

O heavy ignorance! thou praisest the worst best. But what praise
couldst thou bestow on a deserving woman indeed, one that, in
the authority of her merit, did justly put on the vouch of very
malice itself?

IAGO

She that was ever fair and never proud,
Had tongue at will and yet was never loud,
Never lack'd gold and yet went never gay,
Fled from her wish and yet said 'Now I may,'
She that being anger'd, her revenge being nigh,
Bade her wrong stay and her displeasure fly,
She that in wisdom never was so frail
To change the cod's head for the salmon's tail;
She that could think and ne'er disclose her mind,
See suitors following and not look behind,
She was a wight, if ever such wight were—

DESDEMONA

To do what?

IAGO

To suckle fools and chronicle small beer.

DESDEMONA

O most lame and impotent conclusion! Do not learn of him, Emilia, though he be thy husband. How say you, Cassio? is he not a most profane and liberal counsellor?

CASSIO

He speaks home, madam: You may relish him more in the soldier than in the scholar.

IAGO

[*Aside*] He takes her by the palm: ay, well said, whisper: with as little a web as this will I ensnare as great a fly as Cassio. Ay, smile upon her, do; I will gyve thee in thine own courtship. You say true; 'tis so, indeed: if such tricks as these strip you out of your lieutenantry, it had been better you had not kissed your three fingers so oft, which now again you are most apt to play the sir in. Very good; well kissed! an excellent courtesy! 'tis so, indeed. Yet again your fingers to your lips? would they were clyster-pipes for your sake!

Trumpet within

The Moor! I know his trumpet.

CASSIO

'Tis truly so.

DESDEMONA

Let's meet him and receive him.

CASSIO

Lo, where he comes!

Enter OTHELLO *and Attendants*

OTHELLO

O my fair warrior!

DESDEMONA

My dear Othello!

OTHELLO

It gives me wonder great as my content
To see you here before me. O my soul's joy!

If after every tempest come such calms,
May the winds blow till they have waken'd death!
And let the labouring bark climb hills of seas
Olympus-high and duck again as low
As hell's from heaven! If it were now to die,
'Twere now to be most happy; for, I fear,
My soul hath her content so absolute
That not another comfort like to this
Succeeds in unknown fate.

DESDEMONA

The heavens forbid
But that our loves and comforts should increase,
Even as our days do grow!

OTHELLO

Amen to that, sweet powers!
I cannot speak enough of this content;
It stops me here; it is too much of joy:
And this, and this, the greatest discords be

Kissing her

That e'er our hearts shall make!

IAGO

[*Aside*] O, you are well tuned now!
But I'll set down the pegs that make this music,
As honest as I am.

OTHELLO

Come, let us to the castle.
News, friends; our wars are done, the Turks are drown'd.
How does my old acquaintance of this isle?
Honey, you shall be well desired in Cyprus;
I have found great love amongst them. O my sweet,
I prattle out of fashion, and I dote
In mine own comforts. I prithee, good Iago,
Go to the bay and disembark my coffers:
Bring thou the master to the citadel;
He is a good one, and his worthiness
Does challenge much respect. Come, Desdemona,
Once more, well met at Cyprus.

Exeunt OTHELLO,
DESDEMONA, *and Attendants*

IAGO

[*To one leaving*] Do thou meet me presently at the harbour. [*To* RODERIGO] Come hither. If thou be'st valiant—as, they say, base men being in love have then a nobility in their natures more than is native to them—list me. The lieutenant tonight watches on the court of guard:—first, I must tell thee this—Desdemona is directly in love with him.

RODERIGO

With him! Why, 'tis not possible.

IAGO

Lay thy finger thus, and let thy soul be instructed. Mark me with what violence she first loved the Moor, but for bragging and telling her fantastical lies: and will she love him still for prating? Let not thy discreet heart think it. Her eye must be fed; and what delight shall she have to look on the devil? When the blood is made dull with the act of sport, there should be, again to inflame it and to give satiety a fresh appetite, loveliness in favour, sympathy in years, manners and beauties; all which the Moor is defective in: now, for want of these required conveniences, her delicate tenderness will find itself abused, begin to heave the gorge, disrelish and abhor the Moor; very nature will instruct her in it and compel her to some second choice. Now, sir, this granted—as it is a most pregnant and unforced position—who stands so eminent in the degree of this fortune as Cassio does? A knave very voluble; no further conscionable than in putting on the mere form of civil and humane seeming, for the better compassing of his salt and most hidden loose affection? Why, none; why, none: a slipper and subtle knave, a finder of occasions, that has an eye can stamp and counterfeit advantages, though true advantage never present itself; a devilish knave. Besides, the knave is handsome, young, and hath all those requisites in him that folly and green minds look after: a pestilent complete knave; and the woman hath found him already.

RODERIGO

    I cannot believe that in her; she's full of most blessed condition.

IAGO

    Blessed fig's-end! the wine she drinks is made of grapes: if she had been blessed, she would never have loved the Moor. Blessed pudding! Didst thou not see her paddle with the palm of his hand? Didst not mark that?

RODERIGO

    Yes, that I did; but that was but courtesy.

IAGO

    Lechery, by this hand; an index and obscure prologue to the history of lust and foul thoughts. They met so near with their lips that their breaths embraced together. Villainous thoughts, Roderigo! when these mutualities so marshal the way, hard at hand comes the master and main exercise, the incorporate conclusion, Pish! But, sir, be you ruled by me: I have brought you from Venice. Watch you to-night; for the command, I'll lay't upon you. Cassio knows you not. I'll not be far from you: do you find some occasion to anger Cassio, either by speaking too loud, or tainting his discipline; or from what other course you please, which the time shall more favourably minister.

RODERIGO

    Well.

IAGO

    Sir, he is rash and very sudden in choler, and haply with his truncheon may strike at you: provoke him, that he may; for even out of that will I cause these of Cyprus to mutiny; whose qualification shall come into no true taste again but by the displanting of Cassio. So shall you have a shorter journey to your desires by the means I shall then have to prefer them; and the impediment most profitably removed, without the which there were no expectation of our prosperity.

RODERIGO

    I will do this, if I can bring it to any opportunity.

IAGO

    I warrant thee. Meet me by and by at the citadel:
    I must fetch his necessaries ashore. Farewell.

RODERIGO

Adieu.

Exit

IAGO

That Cassio loves her, I do well believe it;
That she loves him, 'tis apt and of great credit:
The Moor, howbeit that I endure him not,
Is of a constant, loving, noble nature,
And I dare think he'll prove to Desdemona
A most dear husband. Now, I do love her too;
Not out of absolute lust, though per-adventure
I stand accountant for as great a sin,
But partly led to diet my revenge,
For that I do suspect the lusty Moor
Hath leap'd into my seat; the thought whereof
Doth, like a poisonous mineral, gnaw my inwards;
And nothing can or shall content my soul
Till I am even'd with him, wife for wife,
Or failing so, yet that I put the Moor
At least into a jealousy so strong
That judgment cannot cure. Which thing to do,
If this poor trash of Venice, whom I trash
For his quick hunting, stand the putting on,
I'll have our Michael Cassio on the hip,
Abuse him to the Moor in the rank garb—
For I fear Cassio with my night-cap too—
Make the Moor thank me, love me and reward me.
For making him egregiously an ass
And practising upon his peace and quiet
Even to madness. 'Tis here, but yet confused:
Knavery's plain face is never seen tin used.

Exit

SCENE II.
A STREET.

Enter a Herald with a proclamation; People following

HERALD

It is Othello's pleasure, our noble and valiant general, that, upon certain tidings now arrived, importing the mere perdition of the Turkish fleet, every man put himself into triumph; some to dance, some to make bonfires, each man to what sport and revels his addiction leads him: for, besides these beneficial news, it is the celebration of his nuptial. So much was his pleasure should be proclaimed. All offices are open, and there is full liberty of feasting from this present hour of five till the bell have told eleven. Heaven bless the isle of Cyprus and our noble general Othello!

Exeunt

SCENE III.
A HALL IN THE CASTLE.

Enter OTHELLO, DESDEMONA, CASSIO, *and Attendants*

OTHELLO

Good Michael, look you to the guard to-night:
Let's teach ourselves that honourable stop,
Not to outsport discretion.

CASSIO

Iago hath direction what to do;
But, notwithstanding, with my personal eye
Will I look to't.

OTHELLO

Iago is most honest.
Michael, good night: to-morrow with your earliest
Let me have speech with you.

To DESDEMONA

Come, my dear love,
The purchase made, the fruits are to ensue;

That profit's yet to come 'tween me and you.
Good night.

Exeunt OTHELLO,
DESDEMONA, *and Attendants*

Enter IAGO

CASSIO

Welcome, Iago; we must to the watch.

IAGO

Not this hour, lieutenant; 'tis not yet ten o' the clock. Our general cast us thus early for the love of his Desdemona; who let us not therefore blame: he hath not yet made wanton the night with her; and she is sport for Jove.

CASSIO

She's a most exquisite lady.

IAGO

And, I'll warrant her, fun of game.

CASSIO

Indeed, she's a most fresh and delicate creature.

IAGO

What an eye she has! methinks it sounds a parley of provocation.

CASSIO

An inviting eye; and yet methinks right modest.

IAGO

And when she speaks, is it not an alarm to love?

CASSIO

She is indeed perfection.

IAGO

Well, happiness to their sheets! Come, lieutenant, I have a stoup of wine; and here without are a brace of Cyprus gallants that would fain have a measure to the health of black Othello.

CASSIO

Not to-night, good Iago: I have very poor and unhappy brains for drinking: I could well wish courtesy would invent some other custom of entertainment.

IAGO

O, they are our friends; but one cup: I'll drink for you.

CASSIO

I have drunk but one cup to-night, and that was craftily qualified too, and, behold, what innovation it makes here: I am unfortunate in the infirmity, and dare not task my weakness with any more.

IAGO

What, man! 'tis a night of revels: the gallants desire it.

CASSIO

Where are they?

IAGO

Here at the door; I pray you, call them in.

CASSIO

I'll do't; but it dislikes me.

Exit

IAGO

If I can fasten but one cup upon him,
With that which he hath drunk to-night already,
He'll be as full of quarrel and offence
As my young mistress' dog. Now, my sick fool Roderigo,
Whom love hath turn'd almost the wrong side out,
To Desdemona hath to-night caroused
Potations pottle deep; and he's to watch:
Three lads of Cyprus, noble swelling spirits,
That hold their honours in a wary distance,
The very elements of this warlike isle,
Have I to-night fluster'd with flowing cups,
And they watch too. Now, 'mongst this flock of drunkards,
Am I to put our Cassio in some action
That may offend the isle—but here they come:
If consequence do but approve my dream,
My boat sails freely, both with wind and stream.

Re-enter CASSIO; *with him* MONTANO *and*
Gentlemen; servants following with wine

CASSIO

'Fore God, they have given me a rouse already.

MONTANO

Good faith, a little one; not past a pint, as I am a soldier.

IAGO

Some wine, ho!

Sings

And let me the canakin clink, clink;

And let me the canakin clink

A soldier's a man;

A life's but a span;

Why, then, let a soldier drink.

Some wine, boys!

CASSIO

'Fore God, an excellent song.

IAGO

I learned it in England, where, indeed, they are most potent in potting: your Dane, your German, and your swag-bellied Hollander—Drink, ho!—are nothing to your English.

CASSIO

Is your Englishman so expert in his drinking?

IAGO

Why, he drinks you, with facility, your Dane dead drunk; he sweats not to overthrow your Almain; he gives your Hollander a vomit, ere the next pottle can be filled.

CASSIO

To the health of our general!

MONTANO

I am for it, lieutenant; and I'll do you justice.

IAGO

O sweet England!

Sings

King Stephen was a worthy peer,

His breeches cost him but a crown;

He held them sixpence all too dear,

With that he call'd the tailor lown.

He was a wight of high renown,

And thou art but of low degree:

'Tis pride that pulls the country down;

Then take thine auld cloak about thee.

Some wine, ho!

CASSIO

Why, this is a more exquisite song than the other.

IAGO

Will you hear't again?

CASSIO

No; for I hold him to be unworthy of his place that does those things. Well, God's above all; and there be souls must be saved, and there be souls must not be saved.

IAGO

It's true, good lieutenant.

CASSIO

For mine own part—no offence to the general, nor any man of quality—I hope to be saved.

IAGO

And so do I too, lieutenant.

CASSIO

Ay, but, by your leave, not before me; the lieutenant is to be saved before the ancient. Let's have no more of this; let's to our affairs. Forgive us our sins! Gentlemen, let's look to our business. Do not think, gentlemen. I am drunk: this is my ancient; this is my right hand, and this is my left: I am not drunk now; I can stand well enough, and speak well enough.

ALL

Excellent well.

CASSIO

Why, very well then; you must not think then that I am drunk.

Exit

MONTANO

To the platform, masters; come, let's set the watch.

IAGO

You see this fellow that is gone before;
He is a soldier fit to stand by Caesar
And give direction: and do but see his vice;
'Tis to his virtue a just equinox,
The one as long as the other: 'tis pity of him.
I fear the trust Othello puts him in.

On some odd time of his infirmity,
Will shake this island.

MONTANO

But is he often thus?

IAGO

'Tis evermore the prologue to his sleep:
He'll watch the horologe a double set,
If drink rock not his cradle.

MONTANO

It were well
The general were put in mind of it.
Perhaps he sees it not; or his good nature
Prizes the virtue that appears in Cassio,
And looks not on his evils: is not this true?

Enter RODERIGO

IAGO

[*Aside to him*] How now, Roderigo!
I pray you, after the lieutenant; go.

Exit RODERIGO

MONTANO

And 'tis great pity that the noble Moor
Should hazard such a place as his own second
With one of an ingraft infirmity:
It were an honest action to say
So to the Moor.

IAGO

Not I, for this fair island:
I do love Cassio well; and would do much
To cure him of this evil—But, hark! What noise?

Cry within: 'Help! help!'
Re-enter CASSIO, *driving in* RODERIGO

CASSIO

You rogue! You rascal!

MONTANO

What's the matter, lieutenant?

CASSIO

A knave teach me my duty! I'll beat the knave into a twiggen bottle.

RODERIGO

Beat me!

CASSIO

Dost thou prate, rogue?

Striking RODERIGO

MONTANO

Nay, good lieutenant;

Staying him

I pray you, sir, hold your hand.

CASSIO

Let me go, sir,
Or I'll knock you o'er the mazzard.

MONTANO

Come, come, you're drunk.

CASSIO

Drunk!

They fight

IAGO

[*Aside to* RODERIGO] Away, I say; go out, and cry a mutiny.

Exit RODERIGO

Nay, good lieutenant—alas, gentlemen—
Help, ho!—Lieutenant—sir—Montano—sir;
Help, masters!—Here's a goodly watch indeed!

Bell rings

Who's that which rings the bell? Diablo, ho!
The town will rise: God's will, lieutenant, hold!
You will be shamed for ever.

Re-enter OTHELLO *and Attendants*

OTHELLO

What is the matter here?

MONTANO

Zounds, I bleed still; I am hurt to the death.

Faints

OTHELLO
  Hold, for your lives!
IAGO
  Hold, ho! Lieutenant—sir—Montano—gentlemen—
  Have you forgot all sense of place and duty?
  Hold! the general speaks to you; hold, hold, for shame!
OTHELLO
  Why, how now, ho! from whence ariseth this?
  Are we turn'd Turks, and to ourselves do that
  Which heaven hath forbid the Ottomites?
  For Christian shame, put by this barbarous brawl:
  He that stirs next to carve for his own rage
  Holds his soul light; he dies upon his motion.
  Silence that dreadful bell: it frights the isle
  From her propriety. What is the matter, masters?
  Honest Iago, that look'st dead with grieving,
  Speak, who began this? On thy love, I charge thee.
IAGO
  I do not know: friends all but now, even now,
  In quarter, and in terms like bride and groom
  Divesting them for bed; and then, but now—
  As if some planet had unwitted men—
  Swords out, and tilting one at other's breast,
  In opposition bloody. I cannot speak
  Any beginning to this peevish odds;
  And would in action glorious I had lost
  Those legs that brought me to a part of it!
OTHELLO
  How comes it, Michael, you are thus forgot?
CASSIO
  I pray you, pardon me; I cannot speak.
OTHELLO
  Worthy Montano, you were wont be civil;
  The gravity and stillness of your youth
  The world hath noted, and your name is great
  In mouths of wisest censure: what's the matter,
  That you unlace your reputation thus

And spend your rich opinion for the name
Of a night-brawler? Give me answer to it.

MONTANO

Worthy Othello, I am hurt to danger:
Your officer, Iago, can inform you,
While I spare speech, which something now offends me,
Of all that I do know: nor know I aught
By me that's said or done amiss this night;
Unless self-charity be sometimes a vice,
And to defend ourselves it be a sin
When violence assails us.

OTHELLO

Now, by heaven,
My blood begins my safer guides to rule;
And passion, having my best judgment collied,
Assays to lead the way: if I once stir,
Or do but lift this arm, the best of you
Shall sink in my rebuke. Give me to know
How this foul rout began, who set it on;
And he that is approved in this offence,
Though he had twinn'd with me, both at a birth,
Shall lose me. What! in a town of war,
Yet wild, the people's hearts brimful of fear,
To manage private and domestic quarrel,
In night, and on the court and guard of safety!
'Tis monstrous. Iago, who began't?

MONTANO

If partially affined, or leagued in office,
Thou dost deliver more or less than truth,
Thou art no soldier.

IAGO

Touch me not so near:
I had rather have this tongue cut from my mouth
Than it should do offence to Michael Cassio;
Yet, I persuade myself, to speak the truth
Shall nothing wrong him. Thus it is, general.
Montano and myself being in speech,

There comes a fellow crying out for help:
And Cassio following him with determined sword,
To execute upon him. Sir, this gentleman
Steps in to Cassio, and entreats his pause:
Myself the crying fellow did pursue,
Lest by his clamour—as it so fell out—
The town might fall in fright: he, swift of foot,
Outran my purpose; and I return'd the rather
For that I heard the clink and fall of swords,
And Cassio high in oath; which till to-night
I ne'er might say before. When I came back—
For this was brief—I found them close together,
At blow and thrust; even as again they were
When you yourself did part them.
More of this matter cannot I report:
But men are men; the best sometimes forget:
Though Cassio did some little wrong to him,
As men in rage strike those that wish them best,
Yet surely Cassio, I believe, received
From him that fled some strange indignity,
Which patience could not pass.

OTHELLO

I know, Iago,
Thy honesty and love doth mince this matter,
Making it light to Cassio. Cassio, I love thee
But never more be officer of mine.

Re-enter DESDEMONA, *attended*

Look, if my gentle love be not raised up!
I'll make thee an example.

DESDEMONA

What's the matter?

OTHELLO

All's well now, sweeting; come away to bed.
[*To* MONTANIO]
Sir, for your hurts, myself will be your surgeon:
Lead him off.

MONTANO *is led off*

Iago, look with care about the town,
And silence those whom this vile brawl distracted.
Come, Desdemona: 'tis the soldiers' life
To have their balmy slumbers waked with strife.

Exeunt all but IAGO *and* CASSIO

IAGO

What, are you hurt, lieutenant?

CASSIO

Ay, past all surgery.

IAGO

Marry, heaven forbid!

CASSIO

Reputation, reputation, reputation! O, I have lost my reputation! I have lost the immortal part of myself, and what remains is bestial. My reputation, Iago, my reputation!

IAGO

As I am an honest man, I thought you had received some bodily wound; there is more sense in that than in reputation. Reputation is an idle and most false imposition: oft got without merit, and lost without deserving: you have lost no reputation at all, unless you repute yourself such a loser. What, man! there are ways to recover the general again: you are but now cast in his mood, a punishment more in policy than in malice, even so as one would beat his offenceless dog to affright an imperious lion: sue to him again, and he's yours.

CASSIO

I will rather sue to be despised than to deceive so good a commander with so slight, so drunken, and so indiscreet an officer. Drunk! And speak parrot! And squabble, swagger, swear! And discourse fustian with one's own shadow! O thou invisible spirit of wine, if thou hast no name to be known by, let us call thee devil!

IAGO

What was he that you followed with your sword? What had he done to you?

CASSIO

I know not.

IAGO

Is't possible?

CASSIO

I remember a mass of things, but nothing distinctly; a quarrel, but nothing wherefore. O God, that men should put an enemy in their mouths to steal away their brains! that we should, with joy, pleasance revel and applause, transform ourselves into beasts!

IAGO

Why, but you are now well enough: how came you thus recovered?

CASSIO

It hath pleased the devil drunkenness to give place to the devil wrath; one unperfectness shows me another, to make me frankly despise myself.

IAGO

Come, you are too severe a moraler: as the time, the place, and the condition of this country stands, I could heartily wish this had not befallen; but, since it is as it is, mend it for your own good.

CASSIO

I will ask him for my place again; he shall tell me I am a drunkard! Had I as many mouths as Hydra, such an answer would stop them all. To be now a sensible man, by and by a fool, and presently a beast! O strange! Every inordinate cup is unblessed and the ingredient is a devil.

IAGO

Come, come, good wine is a good familiar creature, if it be well used: exclaim no more against it. And, good lieutenant, I think you think I love you.

CASSIO

I have well approved it, sir. I drunk!

IAGO

You or any man living may be drunk! at a time, man. I'll tell you what you shall do. Our general's wife is now the general: may say so in this respect, for that he hath devoted and given up himself to the contemplation, mark, and denotement of her parts and graces: confess yourself freely to her; importune her help to put you in your place again: she is of so free, so kind, so apt, so blessed a disposition, she holds it a vice in her goodness not to do more than she is requested: this broken joint between you and her husband entreat her to splinter; and, my fortunes against any lay worth naming, this crack of your love shall grow stronger than it was before.

CASSIO

You advise me well.

IAGO

I protest, in the sincerity of love and honest kindness.

CASSIO

I think it freely; and betimes in the morning I will beseech the virtuous Desdemona to undertake for me: I am desperate of my fortunes if they check me here.

IAGO

You are in the right. Good night, lieutenant; I must to the watch.

CASSIO

Good night, honest Iago.

Exit

IAGO

And what's he then that says I play the villain?
When this advice is free I give and honest,
Probal to thinking and indeed the course
To win the Moor again? For 'tis most easy
The inclining Desdemona to subdue
In any honest suit: she's framed as fruitful
As the free elements. And then for her
To win the Moor—were't to renounce his baptism,
All seals and symbols of redeemed sin,
His soul is so enfetter'd to her love,
That she may make, unmake, do what she list,
Even as her appetite shall play the god
With his weak function. How am I then a villain
To counsel Cassio to this parallel course,
Directly to his good? Divinity of hell!
When devils will the blackest sins put on,

They do suggest at first with heavenly shows,
As I do now: for whiles this honest fool
Plies Desdemona to repair his fortunes
And she for him pleads strongly to the Moor,
I'll pour this pestilence into his ear,
That she repeals him for her body's lust;
And by how much she strives to do him good,
She shall undo her credit with the Moor.
So will I turn her virtue into pitch,
And out of her own goodness make the net
That shall enmesh them all.

Re-enter RODERIGO

How now, Roderigo!

RODERIGO

I do follow here in the chase, not like a hound that hunts, but one that fills up the cry. My money is almost spent; I have been to-night exceedingly well cudgelled; and I think the issue will be, I shall have so much experience for my pains, and so, with no money at all and a little more wit, return again to Venice.

IAGO

How poor are they that have not patience!
What wound did ever heal but by degrees?
Thou know'st we work by wit, and not by witchcraft;
And wit depends on dilatory time.
Does't not go well? Cassio hath beaten thee.
And thou, by that small hurt, hast cashier'd Cassio:
Though other things grow fair against the sun,
Yet fruits that blossom first will first be ripe:
Content thyself awhile. By the mass, 'tis morning;
Pleasure and action make the hours seem short.
Retire thee; go where thou art billeted:
Away, I say; thou shalt know more hereafter:
Nay, get thee gone.

Exit RODERIGO

Two things are to be done:
My wife must move for Cassio to her mistress;

I'll set her on;
Myself the while to draw the Moor apart,
And bring him jump when he may Cassio find
Soliciting his wife: ay, that's the way
Dull not device by coldness and delay.

Exit

ACT

III

SCENE I.
BEFORE THE CASTLE.

Enter Cassio *and some Musicians*

CASSIO
    Masters, play here; I will content your pains;
    Something that's brief; and bid 'Good morrow, general.'
    Music

                    Enter Clown

CLOWN
    Why masters, have your instruments been in Naples, that
    they speak i' the nose thus?
FIRST MUSICIAN
    How, sir, how!
CLOWN
    Are these, I pray you, wind-instruments?
FIRST MUSICIAN
    Ay, marry, are they, sir.
CLOWN
    O, thereby hangs a tail.
FIRST MUSICIAN
    Whereby hangs a tale, sir?

CLOWN

    Marry. Sir, by many a wind-instrument that I know. But, masters, here's money for you: and the general so likes your music, that he desires you, for love's sake, to make no more noise with it.

FIRST MUSICIAN

    Well, sir, we will not.

CLOWN

    If you have any music that may not be heard, to't again: but, as they say to hear music the general does not greatly care.

FIRST MUSICIAN

    We have none such, sir.

CLOWN

    Then put up your pipes in your bag, for I'll away: go; vanish into air; away!

Exeunt Musicians

CASSIO

    Dost thou hear, my honest friend?

CLOWN

    No, I hear not your honest friend; I hear you.

CASSIO

    Prithee, keep up thy quillets. There's a poor piece of gold for thee: if the gentlewoman that attends the general's wife be stirring, tell her there's one Cassio entreats her a little favour of speech: wilt thou do this?

CLOWN

    She is stirring, sir: if she will stir hither, I shall seem to notify unto her.

CASSIO

    Do, good my friend.

Exit Clown

Enter IAGO

    In happy time, Iago.

IAGO

    You have not been abed, then?

CASSIO

    Why, no; the day had broke
    Before we parted. I have made bold, Iago,

To send in to your wife: my suit to her
Is, that she will to virtuous Desdemona
Procure me some access.

IAGO

I'll send her to you presently;
And I'll devise a mean to draw the Moor
Out of the way, that your converse and business
May be more free.

CASSIO

I humbly thank you for't.

Exit IAGO

I never knew
A Florentine more kind and honest.

Enter EMILIA

EMILIA

Good morrow, good Lieutenant: I am sorry
For your displeasure; but all will sure be well.
The general and his wife are talking of it;
And she speaks for you stoutly: the Moor replies,
That he you hurt is of great fame in Cyprus,
And great affinity, and that in wholesome wisdom
He might not but refuse you; but he protests he loves you
And needs no other suitor but his likings
To take the safest occasion by the front
To bring you in again.

CASSIO

Yet, I beseech you,
If you think fit, or that it may be done,
Give me advantage of some brief discourse
With Desdemona alone.

EMILIA

Pray you, come in;
I will bestow you where you shall have time
To speak your bosom freely.

CASSIO

I am much bound to you.

Exeunt

SCENE II.
A ROOM IN THE CASTLE.

Enter OTHELLO, IAGO, *and Gentlemen*

OTHELLO

    These letters give, Iago, to the pilot;
    And by him do my duties to the senate:
    That done, I will be walking on the works;
    Repair there to me.

IAGO

    Well, my good lord, I'll do't.

OTHELLO

    This fortification, gentlemen, shall we see't?

GENTLEMAN

    We'll wait upon your lordship.

Exeunt

SCENE III.
THE GARDEN OF THE CASTLE.

Enter DESDEMONA, CASSIO, *and* EMILIA

DESDEMONA

    Be thou assured, good Cassio, I will do
    All my abilities in thy behalf.

EMILIA

    Good madam, do: I warrant it grieves my husband,
    As if the case were his.

DESDEMONA

    O, that's an honest fellow. Do not doubt, Cassio,
    But I will have my lord and you again
    As friendly as you were.

CASSIO

    Bounteous madam,
    Whatever shall become of Michael Cassio,
    He's never any thing but your true servant.

DESDEMONA

    I know't; I thank you. You do love my lord:

You have known him long; and be you well assured
He shall in strangeness stand no further off
Than in a politic distance.

CASSIO
Ay, but, lady,
That policy may either last so long,
Or feed upon such nice and waterish diet,
Or breed itself so out of circumstance,
That, I being absent and my place supplied,
My general will forget my love and service.

DESDEMONA
Do not doubt that; before Emilia here
I give thee warrant of thy place: assure thee,
If I do vow a friendship, I'll perform it
To the last article: my lord shall never rest;
I'll watch him tame and talk him out of patience;
His bed shall seem a school, his board a shrift;
I'll intermingle every thing he does
With Cassio's suit: therefore be merry, Cassio;
For thy solicitor shall rather die
Than give thy cause away.

EMILIA
Madam, here comes my lord.

CASSIO
Madam, I'll take my leave.

DESDEMONA
Why, stay, and hear me speak.

CASSIO
Madam, not now: I am very ill at ease,
Unfit for mine own purposes.

DESDEMONA
Well, do your discretion.

Exit CASSIO

Enter OTHELLO *and* IAGO

IAGO
Ha! I like not that.

OTHELLO
What dost thou say?
IAGO
Nothing, my lord: or if—I know not what.
OTHELLO
Was not that Cassio parted from my wife?
IAGO
Cassio, my lord! No, sure, I cannot think it,
That he would sneak away so guilty-like,
Seeing you coming.
OTHELLO
I do believe 'twas he.
DESDEMONA
How now, my lord!
I have been talking with a suitor here,
A man that languishes in your displeasure.
OTHELLO
Who is't you mean?
DESDEMONA
Why, your lieutenant, Cassio. Good my lord,
If I have any grace or power to move you,
His present reconciliation take;
For if he be not one that truly loves you,
That errs in ignorance and not in cunning,
I have no judgment in an honest face:
I prithee, call him back.
OTHELLO
Went he hence now?
DESDEMONA
Ay, sooth; so humbled
That he hath left part of his grief with me,
To suffer with him. Good love, call him back.
OTHELLO
Not now, sweet Desdemona; some other time.
DESDEMONA
But shall't be shortly?

OTHELLO

    The sooner, sweet, for you.

DESDEMONA

    Shall't be to-night at supper?

OTHELLO

    No, not to-night.

DESDEMONA

    To-morrow dinner, then?

OTHELLO

    I shall not dine at home;
    I meet the captains at the citadel.

DESDEMONA

    Why, then, to-morrow night; or Tuesday morn;
    On Tuesday noon, or night; on Wednesday morn:
    I prithee, name the time, but let it not
    Exceed three days: in faith, he's penitent;
    And yet his trespass, in our common reason—
    Save that, they say, the wars must make examples
    Out of their best—is not almost a fault
    To incur a private check. When shall he come?
    Tell me, Othello: I wonder in my soul,
    What you would ask me, that I should deny,
    Or stand so mammering on. What! Michael Cassio,
    That came a-wooing with you, and so many a time,
    When I have spoke of you dispraisingly,
    Hath ta'en your part; to have so much to do
    To bring him in! Trust me, I could do much—

OTHELLO

    Prithee, no more: let him come when he will;
    I will deny thee nothing.

DESDEMONA

    Why, this is not a boon;
    'Tis as I should entreat you wear your gloves,
    Or feed on nourishing dishes, or keep you warm,
    Or sue to you to do a peculiar profit
    To your own person: nay, when I have a suit
    Wherein I mean to touch your love indeed,

It shall be full of poise and difficult weight
And fearful to be granted.

OTHELLO

I will deny thee nothing:
Whereon, I do beseech thee, grant me this,
To leave me but a little to myself.

DESDEMONA

Shall I deny you? No: farewell, my lord.

OTHELLO

Farewell, my Desdemona: I'll come to thee straight.

DESDEMONA

Emilia, come. Be as your fancies teach you;
Whate'er you be, I am obedient.

Exeunt DESDEMONA *and* EMILIA

OTHELLO

Excellent wretch! Perdition catch my soul,
But I do love thee! and when I love thee not,
Chaos is come again.

IAGO

My noble lord—

OTHELLO

What dost thou say, Iago?

IAGO

Did Michael Cassio, when you woo'd my lady,
Know of your love?

OTHELLO

He did, from first to last: why dost thou ask?

IAGO

But for a satisfaction of my thought;
No further harm.

OTHELLO

Why of thy thought, Iago?

IAGO

I did not think he had been acquainted with her.

OTHELLO

O, yes; and went between us very oft.

IAGO

Indeed!

OTHELLO

Indeed! ay, indeed: discern'st thou aught in that?

Is he not honest?

IAGO

Honest, my lord!

OTHELLO

Honest! ay, honest.

IAGO

My lord, for aught I know.

OTHELLO

What dost thou think?

IAGO

Think, my lord!

OTHELLO

Think, my lord!

By heaven, he echoes me,

As if there were some monster in his thought

Too hideous to be shown. Thou dost mean something:

I heard thee say even now, thou likedst not that,

When Cassio left my wife: what didst not like?

And when I told thee he was of my counsel

In my whole course of wooing, thou criedst 'Indeed!'

And didst contract and purse thy brow together,

As if thou then hadst shut up in thy brain

Some horrible conceit: if thou dost love me,

Show me thy thought.

IAGO

My lord, you know I love you.

OTHELLO

I think thou dost;

And, for I know thou'rt full of love and honesty,

And weigh'st thy words before thou givest them breath,

Therefore these stops of thine fright me the more:

For such things in a false disloyal knave

Are tricks of custom, but in a man that's just

They are close delations, working from the heart
That passion cannot rule.

IAGO

For Michael Cassio,
I dare be sworn I think that he is honest.

OTHELLO

I think so too.

IAGO

Men should be what they seem;
Or those that be not, would they might seem none!

OTHELLO

Certain, men should be what they seem.

IAGO

Why, then, I think Cassio's an honest man.

OTHELLO

Nay, yet there's more in this:
I prithee, speak to me as to thy thinkings,
As thou dost ruminate, and give thy worst of thoughts
The worst of words.

IAGO

Good my lord, pardon me:
Though I am bound to every act of duty,
I am not bound to that all slaves are free to.
Utter my thoughts? Why, say they are vile and false;
As where's that palace whereinto foul things
Sometimes intrude not? Who has a breast so pure,
But some uncleanly apprehensions
Keep leets and law-days and in session sit
With meditations lawful?

OTHELLO

Thou dost conspire against thy friend, Iago,
If thou but think'st him wrong'd and makest his ear
A stranger to thy thoughts.

IAGO

I do beseech you—
Though I perchance am vicious in my guess,
As, I confess, it is my nature's plague

To spy into abuses, and oft my jealousy
Shapes faults that are not—that your wisdom yet,
From one that so imperfectly conceits,
Would take no notice, nor build yourself a trouble
Out of his scattering and unsure observance.
It were not for your quiet nor your good,
Nor for my manhood, honesty, or wisdom,
To let you know my thoughts.

OTHELLO
Zounds! What dost thou mean?

IAGO
Good name in man and woman, dear my lord,
Is the immediate jewel of their souls:
Who steals my purse steals trash; 'tis something, nothing;
'Twas mine, 'tis his, and has been slave to thousands:
But he that filches from me my good name
Robs me of that which not enriches him
And makes me poor indeed.

OTHELLO
By heaven, I'll know thy thoughts.

IAGO
You cannot, if my heart were in your hand;
Nor shall not, whilst 'tis in my custody.

OTHELLO
Ha!

IAGO
O, beware, my lord, of jealousy;
It is the green-eyed monster which doth mock
The meat it feeds on; that cuckold lives in bliss
Who, certain of his fate, loves not his wronger;
But, O, what damned minutes tells he o'er
Who dotes, yet doubts, suspects, yet strongly loves!

OTHELLO
O misery!

IAGO
Poor and content is rich and rich enough,
But riches fineless is as poor as winter

To him that ever fears he shall be poor.
Good heaven, the souls of all my tribe defend
From jealousy!

OTHELLO

Why, why is this?
Think'st thou I'd make a lie of jealousy,
To follow still the changes of the moon
With fresh suspicions? No; to be once in doubt
Is once to be resolved: exchange me for a goat,
When I shall turn the business of my soul
To such exsufflicate and blown surmises,
Matching thy inference. 'Tis not to make me jealous
To say my wife is fair, feeds well, loves company,
Is free of speech, sings, plays and dances well;
Where virtue is, these are more virtuous:
Nor from mine own weak merits will I draw
The smallest fear or doubt of her revolt;
For she had eyes, and chose me. No, Iago;
I'll see before I doubt; when I doubt, prove;
And on the proof, there is no more but this—
Away at once with love or jealousy!

IAGO

I am glad of it; for now I shall have reason
To show the love and duty that I bear you
With franker spirit: therefore, as I am bound,
Receive it from me. I speak not yet of proof.
Look to your wife; observe her well with Cassio;
Wear your eye thus, not jealous nor secure:
I would not have your free and noble nature,
Out of self-bounty, be abused; look to't:
I know our country disposition well;
In Venice they do let heaven see the pranks
They dare not show their husbands; their best conscience
Is not to leave't undone, but keep't unknown.

OTHELLO

Dost thou say so?

IAGO

    She did deceive her father, marrying you;

    And when she seem'd to shake and fear your looks,

    She loved them most.

OTHELLO

    And so she did.

IAGO

    Why, go to then;

    She that, so young, could give out such a seeming,

    To seal her father's eyes up close as oak-

    He thought 'twas witchcraft—but I am much to blame;

    I humbly do beseech you of your pardon

    For too much loving you.

OTHELLO

    I am bound to thee for ever.

IAGO

    I see this hath a little dash'd your spirits.

OTHELLO

    Not a jot, not a jot.

IAGO

    I' faith, I fear it has.

    I hope you will consider what is spoke

    Comes from my love. But I do see you're moved:

    I am to pray you not to strain my speech

    To grosser issues nor to larger reach

    Than to suspicion.

OTHELLO

    I will not.

IAGO

    Should you do so, my lord,

    My speech should fall into such vile success

    As my thoughts aim not at. Cassio's my worthy friend—

    My lord, I see you're moved.

OTHELLO

    No, not much moved:

    I do not think but Desdemona's honest.

IAGO

Long live she so! and long live you to think so!

OTHELLO

And yet, how nature erring from itself—

IAGO

Ay, there's the point: as—to be bold with you—
Not to affect many proposed matches
Of her own clime, complexion, and degree,
Whereto we see in all things nature tends—
Foh! one may smell in such a will most rank,
Foul disproportion thoughts unnatural.
But pardon me; I do not in position
Distinctly speak of her; though I may fear
Her will, recoiling to her better judgment,
May fall to match you with her country forms
And happily repent.

OTHELLO

Farewell, farewell:
If more thou dost perceive, let me know more;
Set on thy wife to observe: leave me, Iago:

IAGO

[*Going*] My lord, I take my leave.

OTHELLO

Why did I marry? This honest creature doubtless
Sees and knows more, much more, than he unfolds.

IAGO

[*Returning*] My lord, I would I might entreat your honour
To scan this thing no further; leave it to time:
Though it be fit that Cassio have his place,
For sure, he fills it up with great ability,
Yet, if you please to hold him off awhile,
You shall by that perceive him and his means:
Note, if your lady strain his entertainment
With any strong or vehement importunity;
Much will be seen in that. In the mean time,
Let me be thought too busy in my fears—

As worthy cause I have to fear I am—
And hold her free, I do beseech your honour.

OTHELLO

Fear not my government.

IAGO

I once more take my leave.

Exit

OTHELLO

This fellow's of exceeding honesty,
And knows all qualities, with a learned spirit,
Of human dealings. If I do prove her haggard,
Though that her jesses were my dear heartstrings,
I'd whistle her off and let her down the wind,
To pray at fortune. Haply, for I am black
And have not those soft parts of conversation
That chamberers have, or for I am declined
Into the vale of years—yet that's not much—
She's gone. I am abused; and my relief
Must be to loathe her. O curse of marriage,
That we can call these delicate creatures ours,
And not their appetites! I had rather be a toad,
And live upon the vapour of a dungeon,
Than keep a corner in the thing I love
For others' uses. Yet, 'tis the plague of great ones;
Prerogatived are they less than the base;
'Tis destiny unshunnable, like death:
Even then this forked plague is fated to us
When we do quicken. Desdemona comes:

Re-enter DESDEMONA *and* EMILIA

If she be false, O, then heaven mocks itself!
I'll not believe it.

DESDEMONA

How now, my dear Othello?
Your dinner, and the generous islanders
By you invited, do attend your presence.

OTHELLO

I am to blame.

DESDEMONA

Why do you speak so faintly?
Are you not well?

OTHELLO

I have a pain upon my forehead here.

DESDEMONA

Faith, that's with watching; 'twill away again:
Let me but bind it hard, within this hour
It will be well.

OTHELLO

Your napkin is too little:

He puts the handkerchief from him; and it drops

Let it alone. Come, I'll go in with you.

DESDEMONA

I am very sorry that you are not well.

Exeunt OTHELLO *and* DESDEMONA

EMILIA

I am glad I have found this napkin:
This was her first remembrance from the Moor:
My wayward husband hath a hundred times
Woo'd me to steal it; but she so loves the token,
For he conjured her she should ever keep it,
That she reserves it evermore about her
To kiss and talk to. I'll have the work ta'en out,
And give't Iago: what he will do with it
Heaven knows, not I;
I nothing but to please his fantasy.

Re-enter IAGO

IAGO

How now! what do you here alone?

EMILIA

Do not you chide; I have a thing for you.

IAGO

A thing for me? It is a common thing—

EMILIA

Ha!

IAGO

    To have a foolish wife.

EMILIA

    O, is that all? What will you give me now

    For the same handkerchief?

IAGO

    What handkerchief?

EMILIA

    What handkerchief?

    Why, that the Moor first gave to Desdemona;

    That which so often you did bid me steal.

IAGO

    Hast stol'n it from her?

EMILIA

    No, 'faith; she let it drop by negligence.

    And, to the advantage, I, being here, took't up.

    Look, here it is.

IAGO

    A good wench; give it me.

EMILIA

    What will you do with't, that you have been so earnest

    To have me filch it?

IAGO

    [*Snatching it*] Why, what's that to you?

EMILIA

    If it be not for some purpose of import,

    Give't me again: poor lady, she'll run mad

    When she shall lack it.

IAGO

    Be not acknown on't; I have use for it.

    Go, leave me.

Exit EMILIA

    I will in Cassio's lodging lose this napkin,

    And let him find it. Trifles light as air

    Are to the jealous confirmations strong

    As proofs of holy writ: this may do something.

    The Moor already changes with my poison:

Dangerous conceits are, in their natures, poisons.
Which at the first are scarce found to distaste,
But with a little act upon the blood.
Burn like the mines of Sulphur. I did say so:
Look, where he comes!

Re-enter OTHELLO

Not poppy, nor mandragora,
Nor all the drowsy syrups of the world,
Shall ever medicine thee to that sweet sleep
Which thou owedst yesterday.

OTHELLO

Ha! ha! false to me, to me?

IAGO

Why, how now, general! no more of that.

OTHELLO

Avaunt! be gone! thou hast set me on the rack:
I swear 'tis better to be much abused
Than but to know't a little.

IAGO

How now, my lord!

OTHELLO

What sense had I of her stol'n hours of lust?
I saw't not, thought it not, it harm'd not me:
I slept the next night well, was free and merry;
I found not Cassio's kisses on her lips:
He that is robb'd, not wanting what is stol'n,
Let him not know't, and he's not robb'd at all.

IAGO

I am sorry to hear this.

OTHELLO

I had been happy, if the general camp,
Pioners and all, had tasted her sweet body,
So I had nothing known. O, now, for ever
Farewell the tranquil mind! farewell content!
Farewell the plumed troop, and the big wars,
That make ambition virtue! O, farewell!
Farewell the neighing steed, and the shrill trump,

The spirit-stirring drum, the ear-piercing fife,
The royal banner, and all quality,
Pride, pomp and circumstance of glorious war!
And, O you mortal engines, whose rude throats
The immortal Jove's dead clamours counterfeit,
Farewell! Othello's occupation's gone!

IAGO

Is't possible, my lord?

OTHELLO

Villain, be sure thou prove my love a whore,

Taking him by the throat

Be sure of it; give me the ocular proof:
Or by the worth of man's eternal soul,
Thou hadst been better have been born a dog
Than answer my waked wrath!

IAGO

Is't come to this?

OTHELLO

Make me to see't; or, at the least, so prove it,
That the probation bear no hinge nor loop
To hang a doubt on; or woe upon thy life!

IAGO

My noble lord—

OTHELLO

If thou dost slander her and torture me,
Never pray more; abandon all remorse;
On horror's head horrors accumulate;
Do deeds to make heaven weep, all earth amazed;
For nothing canst thou to damnation add
Greater than that.

IAGO

O grace! O heaven forgive me!
Are you a man? Have you a soul or sense?
God be wi' you; take mine office. O wretched fool.
That livest to make thine honesty a vice!
O monstrous world! Take note, take note, O world,
To be direct and honest is not safe.

I thank you for this profit; and from hence
I'll love no friend, sith love breeds such offence.

OTHELLO

Nay, stay: thou shouldst be honest.

IAGO

I should be wise, for honesty's a fool
And loses that it works for.

OTHELLO

By the world,
I think my wife be honest and think she is not;
I think that thou art just and think thou art not.
I'll have some proof. Her name, that was as fresh
As Dian's visage, is now begrimed and black
As mine own face. If there be cords, or knives,
Poison, or fire, or suffocating streams,
I'll not endure it. Would I were satisfied!

IAGO

I see, sir, you are eaten up with passion:
I do repent me that I put it to you.
You would be satisfied?

OTHELLO

Would! nay, I will.

IAGO

And may: but, how? How satisfied, my lord?
Would you, the supervisor, grossly gape on—
Behold her topp'd?

OTHELLO

Death and damnation! O!

IAGO

It were a tedious difficulty, I think,
To bring them to that prospect: damn them then,
If ever mortal eyes do see them bolster
More than their own! What then? how then?
What shall I say? Where's satisfaction?
It is impossible you should see this,
Were they as prime as goats, as hot as monkeys,
As salt as wolves in pride, and fools as gross

As ignorance made drunk. But yet, I say,
If imputation and strong circumstances,
Which lead directly to the door of truth,
Will give you satisfaction, you may have't.

OTHELLO
Give me a living reason she's disloyal.

IAGO
I do not like the office:
But, sith I am enter'd in this cause so far,
Prick'd to't by foolish honesty and love,
I will go on. I lay with Cassio lately;
And, being troubled with a raging tooth,
I could not sleep.
There are a kind of men so loose of soul,
That in their sleeps will mutter their affairs:
One of this kind is Cassio:
In sleep I heard him say 'Sweet Desdemona,
Let us be wary, let us hide our loves;'
And then, sir, would he gripe and wring my hand,
Cry 'O sweet creature!' and then kiss me hard,
As if he pluck'd up kisses by the roots
That grew upon my lips: then laid his leg
Over my thigh, and sigh'd, and kiss'd; and then
Cried 'Cursed fate that gave thee to the Moor!'

OTHELLO
O monstrous! monstrous!

IAGO
Nay, this was but his dream.

OTHELLO
But this denoted a foregone conclusion:
'Tis a shrewd doubt, though it be but a dream.

IAGO
And this may help to thicken other proofs
That do demonstrate thinly.

OTHELLO
I'll tear her all to pieces.

IAGO

    Nay, but be wise: yet we see nothing done;
    She may be honest yet. Tell me but this,
    Have you not sometimes seen a handkerchief
    Spotted with strawberries in your wife's hand?

OTHELLO

    I gave her such a one; 'twas my first gift.

IAGO

    I know not that; but such a handkerchief—
    I am sure it was your wife's—did I to-day
    See Cassio wipe his beard with.

OTHELLO

    If it be that—

IAGO

    If it be that, or any that was hers,
    It speaks against her with the other proofs.

OTHELLO

    O, that the slave had forty thousand lives!
    One is too poor, too weak for my revenge.
    Now do I see 'tis true. Look here, Iago;
    All my fond love thus do I blow to heaven.
    'Tis gone.
    Arise, black vengeance, from thy hollow hell!
    Yield up, O love, thy crown and hearted throne
    To tyrannous hate! Swell, bosom, with thy fraught,
    For 'tis of aspics' tongues!

IAGO

    Yet be content.

OTHELLO

    O, blood, blood, blood!

IAGO

    Patience, I say; your mind perhaps may change.

OTHELLO

    Never, Iago: Like to the Pontic sea,
    Whose icy current and compulsive course
    Ne'er feels retiring ebb, but keeps due on

To the Propontic and the Hellespont,
Even so my bloody thoughts, with violent pace,
Shall ne'er look back, ne'er ebb to humble love,
Till that a capable and wide revenge
Swallow them up. Now, by yond marble heaven,

Kneels

In the due reverence of a sacred vow
I here engage my words.

IAGO

Do not rise yet.

Kneels

Witness, you ever-burning lights above,
You elements that clip us round about,
Witness that here Iago doth give up
The execution of his wit, hands, heart,
To wrong'd Othello's service! Let him command,
And to obey shall be in me remorse,
What bloody business ever.

They rise

OTHELLO

I greet thy love,
Not with vain thanks, but with acceptance bounteous,
And will upon the instant put thee to't:
Within these three days let me hear thee say
That Cassio's not alive.

IAGO

My friend is dead; 'tis done at your request:
But let her live.

OTHELLO

Damn her, lewd minx! O, damn her!
Come, go with me apart; I will withdraw,
To furnish me with some swift means of death
For the fair devil. Now art thou my lieutenant.

IAGO

I am your own for ever.

Exeunt

SCENE IV.
BEFORE THE CASTLE.

Enter DESDEMONA, EMILIA, *and Clown*

DESDEMONA

Do you know, sirrah, where Lieutenant Cassio lies?

CLOWN

I dare not say he lies any where.

DESDEMONA

Why, man?

CLOWN

He's a soldier, and for one to say a soldier lies, 'tis stabbing.

DESDEMONA

Go to: where lodges he?

CLOWN

To tell you where he lodges, is to tell you where I lie.

DESDEMONA

Can any thing be made of this?

CLOWN

I know not where he lodges, and for me to devise a lodging and say he lies here or he lies there, were to lie in mine own throat.

DESDEMONA

Can you inquire him out, and be edified by report?

CLOWN

I will catechise the world for him; that is, make questions, and by them answer.

DESDEMONA

Seek him, bid him come hither: tell him I have moved my lord on his behalf, and hope all will be well.

CLOWN

To do this is within the compass of man's wit: and therefore I will attempt the doing it.

Exit

DESDEMONA

Where should I lose that handkerchief, Emilia?

EMILIA

I know not, madam.

DESDEMONA

    Believe me, I had rather have lost my purse
    Full of crusadoes: and, but my noble Moor
    Is true of mind and made of no such baseness
    As jealous creatures are, it were enough
    To put him to ill thinking.

EMILIA

    Is he not jealous?

DESDEMONA

    Who, he? I think the sun where he was born
    Drew all such humours from him.

EMILIA

    Look, where he comes.

DESDEMONA

    I will not leave him now till Cassio
    Be call'd to him.

                      Enter OTHELLO

    How is't with you, my lord?

OTHELLO

    Well, my good lady.

    Aside

    O, hardness to dissemble!—

    How do you, Desdemona?

DESDEMONA

    Well, my good lord.

OTHELLO

    Give me your hand: this hand is moist, my lady.

DESDEMONA

    It yet hath felt no age nor known no sorrow.

OTHELLO

    This argues fruitfulness and liberal heart:
    Hot, hot, and moist: this hand of yours requires
    A sequester from liberty, fasting and prayer,
    Much castigation, exercise devout;
    For here's a young and sweating devil here,
    That commonly rebels. 'Tis a good hand,
    A frank one.

DESDEMONA

    You may, indeed, say so;

    For 'twas that hand that gave away my heart.

OTHELLO

    A liberal hand: the hearts of old gave hands;

    But our new heraldry is hands, not hearts.

DESDEMONA

    I cannot speak of this. Come now, your promise.

OTHELLO

    What promise, chuck?

DESDEMONA

    I have sent to bid Cassio come speak with you.

OTHELLO

    I have a salt and sorry rheum offends me;

    Lend me thy handkerchief.

DESDEMONA

    Here, my lord.

OTHELLO

    That which I gave you.

DESDEMONA

    I have it not about me.

OTHELLO

    Not?

DESDEMONA

    No, indeed, my lord.

OTHELLO

    That is a fault.

    That handkerchief

    Did an Egyptian to my mother give;

    She was a charmer, and could almost read

    The thoughts of people: she told her, while she kept it,

    'Twould make her amiable and subdue my father

    Entirely to her love, but if she lost it

    Or made gift of it, my father's eye

    Should hold her loathed and his spirits should hunt

    After new fancies: she, dying, gave it me;

    And bid me, when my fate would have me wive,

To give it her. I did so: and take heed on't;
Make it a darling like your precious eye;
To lose't or give't away were such perdition
As nothing else could match.

DESDEMONA

Is't possible?

OTHELLO

'Tis true: there's magic in the web of it:
A sibyl, that had number'd in the world
The sun to course two hundred compasses,
In her prophetic fury sew'd the work;
The worms were hallow'd that did breed the silk;
And it was dyed in mummy which the skilful
Conserved of maidens' hearts.

DESDEMONA

Indeed! is't true?

OTHELLO

Most veritable; therefore look to't well.

DESDEMONA

Then would to God that I had never seen't!

OTHELLO

Ha! wherefore?

DESDEMONA

Why do you speak so startingly and rash?

OTHELLO

Is't lost? Is't gone? Speak, is it out o' the way?

DESDEMONA

Heaven bless us!

OTHELLO

Say you?

DESDEMONA

It is not lost; but what an if it were?

OTHELLO

How!

DESDEMONA

I say, it is not lost.

OTHELLO
    Fetch't, let me see't.
DESDEMONA
    Why, so I can, sir, but I will not now.
    This is a trick to put me from my suit:
    Pray you, let Cassio be received again.
OTHELLO
    Fetch me the handkerchief: my mind misgives.
DESDEMONA
    Come, come;
    You'll never meet a more sufficient man.
OTHELLO
    The handkerchief!
DESDEMONA
    I pray, talk me of Cassio.
OTHELLO
    The handkerchief!
DESDEMONA
    A man that all his time
    Hath founded his good fortunes on your love,
    Shared dangers with you—
OTHELLO
    The handkerchief!
DESDEMONA
    I'faith, you are to blame.
OTHELLO
    Away!

                                                                    Exit

EMILIA
    Is not this man jealous?
DESDEMONA
    I ne'er saw this before.
    Sure, there's some wonder in this handkerchief:
    I am most unhappy in the loss of it.
EMILIA
    'Tis not a year or two shows us a man:

They are all but stomachs, and we all but food;
To eat us hungerly, and when they are full,
They belch us. Look you, Cassio and my husband!

Enter CASSIO *and* IAGO

IAGO

There is no other way; 'tis she must do't:
And, lo, the happiness! go, and importune her.

DESDEMONA

How now, good Cassio! what's the news with you?

CASSIO

Madam, my former suit: I do beseech you
That by your virtuous means I may again
Exist, and be a member of his love
Whom I with all the office of my heart
Entirely honour: I would not be delay'd.
If my offence be of such mortal kind
That nor my service past, nor present sorrows,
Nor purposed merit in futurity,
Can ransom me into his love again,
But to know so must be my benefit;
So shall I clothe me in a forced content,
And shut myself up in some other course,
To fortune's alms.

DESDEMONA

Alas, thrice-gentle Cassio!
My advocation is not now in tune;
My lord is not my lord; nor should I know him,
Were he in favour as in humour alter'd.
So help me every spirit sanctified,
As I have spoken for you all my best
And stood within the blank of his displeasure
For my free speech! you must awhile be patient:
What I can do I will; and more I will
Than for myself I dare: let that suffice you.

IAGO

Is my lord angry?

EMILIA

 He went hence but now,

 And certainly in strange unquietness.

IAGO

 Can he be angry? I have seen the cannon,

 When it hath blown his ranks into the air,

 And, like the devil, from his very arm

 Puff'd his own brother:—and can he be angry?

 Something of moment then: I will go meet him:

 There's matter in't indeed, if he be angry.

DESDEMONA

 I prithee, do so.

Exit IAGO

 Something, sure, of state,

 Either from Venice, or some unhatch'd practise

 Made demonstrable here in Cyprus to him,

 Hath puddled his clear spirit: and in such cases

 Men's natures wrangle with inferior things,

 Though great ones are their object. 'Tis even so;

 For let our finger ache, and it endues

 Our other healthful members even to that sense

 Of pain: nay, we must think men are not gods,

 Nor of them look for such observances

 As fit the bridal. Beshrew me much, Emilia,

 I was, unhandsome warrior as I am,

 Arraigning his unkindness with my soul;

 But now I find I had suborn'd the witness,

 And he's indicted falsely.

EMILIA

 Pray heaven it be state-matters, as you think,

 And no conception nor no jealous toy

 Concerning you.

DESDEMONA

 Alas the day! I never gave him cause.

EMILIA

 But jealous souls will not be answer'd so;

 They are not ever jealous for the cause,

But jealous for they are jealous: 'tis a monster
Begot upon itself, born on itself.

DESDEMONA

Heaven keep that monster from Othello's mind!

EMILIA

Lady, amen.

DESDEMONA

I will go seek him. Cassio, walk hereabout:
If I do find him fit, I'll move your suit
And seek to effect it to my uttermost.

CASSIO

I humbly thank your ladyship.

Exeunt DESDEMONA *and* EMILIA

Enter BIANCA

BIANCA

Save you, friend Cassio!

CASSIO

What make you from home?
How is it with you, my most fair Bianca?
I' faith, sweet love, I was coming to your house.

BIANCA

And I was going to your lodging, Cassio.
What, keep a week away? Seven days and nights?
Eight score eight hours? And lovers' absent hours,
More tedious than the dial eight score times?
O weary reckoning!

CASSIO

Pardon me, Bianca:
I have this while with leaden thoughts been press'd:
But I shall, in a more continuate time,
Strike off this score of absence. Sweet Bianca,

Giving her DESDEMONA'S *handkerchief*

Take me this work out.

BIANCA

O Cassio, whence came this?
This is some token from a newer friend:

To the felt absence now I feel a cause:
Is't come to this? Well, well.

CASSIO

Go to, woman!
Throw your vile guesses in the devil's teeth,
From whence you have them. You are jealous now
That this is from some mistress, some remembrance:
No, in good troth, Bianca.

BIANCA

Why, whose is it?

CASSIO

I know not, neither: I found it in my chamber.
I like the work well: ere it be demanded—
As like enough it will—I'ld have it copied:
Take it, and do't; and leave me for this time.

BIANCA

Leave you! wherefore?

CASSIO

I do attend here on the general;
And think it no addition, nor my wish,
To have him see me woman'd.

BIANCA

Why, I pray you?

CASSIO

Not that I love you not.

BIANCA

But that you do not love me.
I pray you, bring me on the way a little,
And say if I shall see you soon at night.

CASSIO

'Tis but a little way that I can bring you;
For I attend here: but I'll see you soon.

BIANCA

'Tis very good; I must be circumstanced.

Exeunt

ACT

IV

SCENE I.
CYPRUS. BEFORE THE CASTLE.

Enter OTHELLO *and* IAGO

IAGO
> Will you think so?

OTHELLO
> Think so, Iago!

IAGO
> What,
> To kiss in private?

OTHELLO
> An unauthorized kiss.

IAGO
> Or to be naked with her friend in bed
> An hour or more, not meaning any harm?

OTHELLO
> Naked in bed, Iago, and not mean harm!
> It is hypocrisy against the devil:
> They that mean virtuously, and yet do so,
> The devil their virtue tempts, and they tempt heaven.

IAGO
So they do nothing, 'tis a venial slip:
But if I give my wife a handkerchief—

OTHELLO
What then?

IAGO
Why, then, 'tis hers, my lord; and, being hers,
She may, I think, bestow't on any man.

OTHELLO
She is protectress of her honour too:
May she give that?

IAGO
Her honour is an essence that's not seen;
They have it very oft that have it not:
But, for the handkerchief—

OTHELLO
By heaven, I would most gladly have forgot it.
Thou said'st, it comes o'er my memory,
As doth the raven o'er the infected house,
Boding to all—he had my handkerchief.

IAGO
Ay, what of that?

OTHELLO
That's not so good now.

IAGO
What,
If I had said I had seen him do you wrong?
Or heard him say—as knaves be such abroad,
Who having, by their own importunate suit,
Or voluntary dotage of some mistress,
Convinced or supplied them, cannot choose
But they must blab—

OTHELLO
Hath he said any thing?

IAGO
He hath, my lord; but be you well assured,
No more than he'll unswear.

OTHELLO

What hath he said?

IAGO

'Faith, that he did—I know not what he did.

OTHELLO

What? what?

IAGO

Lie—

OTHELLO

With her?

IAGO

With her, on her; what you will.

OTHELLO

Lie with her! lie on her! We say lie on her, when they belie her. Lie with her! that's fulsome. Handkerchief—confessions—handkerchief!—To confess, and be hanged for his labour—first, to be hanged, and then to confess. I tremble at it. Nature would not invest herself in such shadowing passion without some instruction. It is not words that shake me thus. Pish! Noses, ears, and lips. Is't possible? Confess—handkerchief!—O devil!—

Falls in a trance

IAGO

Work on,
My medicine, work! Thus credulous fools are caught;
And many worthy and chaste dames even thus,
All guiltless, meet reproach. What, ho! my lord!
My lord, I say! Othello!

Enter CASSIO

How now, Cassio!

CASSIO

What's the matter?

IAGO

My lord is fall'n into an epilepsy:
This is his second fit; he had one yesterday.

CASSIO

Rub him about the temples.

IAGO

No, forbear;
The lethargy must have his quiet course:
If not, he foams at mouth and by and by
Breaks out to savage madness. Look he stirs:
Do you withdraw yourself a little while,
He will recover straight: when he is gone,
I would on great occasion speak with you.

Exit CASSIO

How is it, general? Have you not hurt your head?

OTHELLO

Dost thou mock me?

IAGO

I mock you! no, by heaven.
Would you would bear your fortune like a man!

OTHELLO

A horned man's a monster and a beast.

IAGO

There's many a beast then in a populous city,
And many a civil monster.

OTHELLO

Did he confess it?

IAGO

Good sir, be a man;
Think every bearded fellow that's but yoked
May draw with you: there's millions now alive
That nightly lie in those unproper beds
Which they dare swear peculiar: your case is better.
O, 'tis the spite of hell, the fiend's arch-mock,
To lip a wanton in a secure couch,
And to suppose her chaste! No, let me know;
And knowing what I am, I know what she shall be.

OTHELLO

O, thou art wise; 'tis certain.

IAGO

Stand you awhile apart;
Confine yourself but in a patient list.

Whilst you were here o'erwhelmed with your grief—
A passion most unsuiting such a man—
Cassio came hither: I shifted him away,
And laid good 'scuse upon your ecstasy,
Bade him anon return and here speak with me;
The which he promised. Do but encave yourself,
And mark the fleers, the gibes, and notable scorns,
That dwell in every region of his face;
For I will make him tell the tale anew,
Where, how, how oft, how long ago, and when
He hath, and is again to cope your wife:
I say, but mark his gesture. Marry, patience;
Or I shall say you are all in all in spleen,
And nothing of a man.

OTHELLO

Dost thou hear, Iago?
I will be found most cunning in my patience;
But—dost thou hear?—most bloody.

IAGO

That's not amiss;
But yet keep time in all. Will you withdraw?

                OTHELLO retires

Now will I question Cassio of Bianca,
A housewife that by selling her desires
Buys herself bread and clothes: it is a creature
That dotes on Cassio; as 'tis the strumpet's plague
To beguile many and be beguiled by one:
He, when he hears of her, cannot refrain
From the excess of laughter. Here he comes:

                Re-enter CASSIO

As he shall smile, Othello shall go mad;
And his unbookish jealousy must construe
Poor Cassio's smiles, gestures and light behavior,
Quite in the wrong. How do you now, lieutenant?

CASSIO

The worser that you give me the addition Whose want even
kills me.

IAGO

    Ply Desdemona well, and you are sure on't.

                      Speaking lower

    Now, if this suit lay in Bianco's power,

    How quickly should you speed!

CASSIO

    Alas, poor caitiff!

OTHELLO

    Look, how he laughs already!

IAGO

    I never knew woman love man so.

CASSIO

    Alas, poor rogue! I think, i' faith, she loves me.

OTHELLO

    Now he denies it faintly, and laughs it out.

IAGO

    Do you hear, Cassio?

OTHELLO

    Now he importunes him

    To tell it o'er: go to; well said, well said.

IAGO

    She gives it out that you shall marry hey:

    Do you intend it?

CASSIO

    Ha, ha, ha!

OTHELLO

    Do you triumph, Roman? Do you triumph?

CASSIO

    I marry her! what? a customer! Prithee, bear some charity to my
wit: do not think it so unwholesome. Ha, ha, ha!

OTHELLO

    So, so, so, so: they laugh that win.

IAGO

    'Faith, the cry goes that you shall marry her.

CASSIO

    Prithee, say true.

IAGO

    I am a very villain else.

OTHELLO

    Have you scored me? Well.

CASSIO

    This is the monkey's own giving out: she is persuaded I will marry her, out of her own love and flattery, not out of my promise.

OTHELLO

    Iago beckons me; now he begins the story.

CASSIO

    She was here even now; she haunts me in every place. I was the other day talking on the sea-bank with certain Venetians; and thither comes the bauble, and, by this hand, she falls me thus about my neck—

OTHELLO

    Crying 'O dear Cassio!' as it were: his gesture imports it.

CASSIO

    So hangs, and lolls, and weeps upon me; so hales, and pulls me: ha, ha, ha!

OTHELLO

    Now he tells how she plucked him to my chamber. O, I see that nose of yours, but not that dog I shall throw it to.

CASSIO

    Well, I must leave her company.

IAGO

    Before me! look, where she comes.

CASSIO

    'Tis such another fitchew! marry a perfumed one.

Enter BIANCA

    What do you mean by this haunting of me?

BIANCA

    Let the devil and his dam haunt you! What did you mean by that same handkerchief you gave me even now? I was a fine fool to take it. I must take out the work?—A likely piece of work, that you should find it in your chamber, and not know who left it there! This is some minx's token, and I must take out the work?

There; give it your hobby-horse: wheresoever you had it, I'll take out no work on't.

CASSIO

How now, my sweet Bianca! How now! How now!

OTHELLO

By heaven, that should be my handkerchief!

BIANCA

An you'll come to supper to-night, you may; an you will not, come when you are next prepared for.

Exit

IAGO

After her, after her.

CASSIO

'Faith, I must; she'll rail in the street else.

IAGO

Will you sup there?

CASSIO

'Faith, I intend so.

IAGO

Well, I may chance to see you; for I would very fain speak with you.

CASSIO

Prithee, come; will you?

IAGO

Go to; say no more.

Exit CASSIO

OTHELLO

[*Advancing*] How shall I murder him, Iago?

IAGO

Did you perceive how he laughed at his vice?

OTHELLO

O Iago!

IAGO

And did you see the handkerchief?

OTHELLO

Was that mine?

IAGO

Yours by this hand: and to see how he prizes the foolish woman your wife! she gave it him, and he hath given it his whore.

OTHELLO

I would have him nine years a-killing.

A fine woman! a fair woman! a sweet woman!

IAGO

Nay, you must forget that.

OTHELLO

Ay, let her rot, and perish, and be damned to-night; for she shall not live: no, my heart is turned to stone; I strike it, and it hurts my hand. O, the world hath not a sweeter creature: she might lie by an emperor's side and command him tasks.

IAGO

Nay, that's not your way.

OTHELLO

Hang her! I do but say what she is: so delicate with her needle: an admirable musician: O! she will sing the savageness out of a bear: of so high and plenteous wit and invention:—

IAGO

She's the worse for all this.

OTHELLO

O, a thousand thousand times: and then, of so gentle a condition!

IAGO

Ay, too gentle.

OTHELLO

Nay, that's certain: but yet the pity of it, Iago! O Iago, the pity of it, Iago!

IAGO

If you are so fond over her iniquity, give her patent to offend; for, if it touch not you, it comes near nobody.

OTHELLO

I will chop her into messes: cuckold me!

IAGO

O, 'tis foul in her.

OTHELLO
    With mine officer!

IAGO
    That's fouler.

OTHELLO
    Get me some poison, Iago; this night: I'll not expostulate with her, lest her body and beauty unprovide my mind again: this night, Iago.

IAGO
    Do it not with poison, strangle her in her bed, even the bed she hath contaminated.

OTHELLO
    Good, good: the justice of it pleases: very good.

IAGO
    And for Cassio, let me be his undertaker: you shall hear more by midnight.

OTHELLO
    Excellent good.
                        A trumpet within
    What trumpet is that same?

IAGO
    I warrant, something from Venice, sure. 'Tis Lodovico Come from the Duke: and, see, your wife is with him.
                Enter LODOVICO,
        DESDEMONA, *and Attendants*

LODOVICO
    Save you, worthy general!

OTHELLO
    With all my heart, sir.

LODOVICO
    The Duke and Senators of Venice greet you.
                        Gives him a letter

OTHELLO
    I kiss the instrument of their pleasures.
                    Opens the letter, and reads

DESDEMONA
    And what's the news, good cousin Lodovico?

IAGO

I am very glad to see you, signior
Welcome to Cyprus.

LODOVICO

I thank you. How does Lieutenant Cassio?

IAGO

Lives, sir.

DESDEMONA

Cousin, there's fall'n between him and my lord
An unkind breach: but you shall make all well.

OTHELLO

Are you sure of that?

DESDEMONA

My lord?

OTHELLO

[*Reads*] 'This fail you not to do, as you will—'

LODOVICO

He did not call; he's busy in the paper.
Is there division 'twixt my lord and Cassio?

DESDEMONA

A most unhappy one: I would do much
To atone them, for the love I bear to Cassio.

OTHELLO

Fire and brimstone!

DESDEMONA

My lord?

OTHELLO

Are you wise?

DESDEMONA

What, is he angry?

LODOVICO

May be the letter moved him;
For, as I think, they do command him home,
Deputing Cassio in his government.

DESDEMONA

Trust me, I am glad on't.

OTHELLO
    Indeed!
DESDEMONA
    My lord?
OTHELLO
    I am glad to see you mad.
DESDEMONA
    Why, sweet Othello?
OTHELLO
    [*Striking her*] Devil!
DESDEMONA
    I have not deserved this.
LODOVICO
    My lord, this would not be believed in Venice,
    Though I should swear I saw't: 'tis very much:
    Make her amends; she weeps.
OTHELLO
    O devil, devil!
    If that the earth could teem with woman's tears,
    Each drop she falls would prove a crocodile.
    Out of my sight!
DESDEMONA
    I will not stay to offend you.
    Going
LODOVICO
    Truly, an obedient lady:
    I do beseech your lordship, call her back.
OTHELLO
    Mistress!
DESDEMONA
    My lord?
OTHELLO
    What would you with her, sir?
LODOVICO
    Who, I, my lord?
OTHELLO
    Ay; you did wish that I would make her turn:

Sir, she can turn, and turn, and yet go on,
And turn again; and she can weep, sir, weep;
And she's obedient, as you say, obedient,
Very obedient. Proceed you in your tears.
Concerning this, sir,—O well-painted passion!—
I am commanded home. Get you away;
I'll send for you anon. Sir, I obey the mandate,
And will return to Venice. Hence, avaunt!

Exit DESDEMONA

Cassio shall have my place. And, sir, tonight,
I do entreat that we may sup together:
You are welcome, sir, to Cyprus. Goats and monkeys!

Exit

LODOVICO
Is this the noble Moor whom our full Senate
Call all in all sufficient? Is this the nature
Whom passion could not shake? Whose solid virtue
The shot of accident, nor dart of chance,
Could neither graze nor pierce?

IAGO
He is much changed.

LODOVICO
Are his wits safe? Is he not light of brain?

IAGO
He's that he is: I may not breathe my censure
What he might be: if what he might he is not,
I would to heaven he were!

LODOVICO
What, strike his wife!

IAGO
'Faith, that was not so well; yet would I knew
That stroke would prove the worst!

LODOVICO
Is it his use?
Or did the letters work upon his blood,
And new-create this fault?

IAGO

    Alas, alas!

    It is not honesty in me to speak

    What I have seen and known. You shall observe him,

    And his own courses will denote him so

    That I may save my speech: do but go after,

    And mark how he continues.

LODOVICO

    I am sorry that I am deceived in him.

Exeunt

SCENE II.
A ROOM IN THE CASTLE.

Enter OTHELLO *and* EMILIA

OTHELLO

    You have seen nothing then?

EMILIA

    Nor ever heard, nor ever did suspect.

OTHELLO

    Yes, you have seen Cassio and she together.

EMILIA

    But then I saw no harm, and then I heard

    Each syllable that breath made up between them.

OTHELLO

    What, did they never whisper?

EMILIA

    Never, my lord.

OTHELLO

    Nor send you out o' the way?

EMILIA

    Never.

OTHELLO

    To fetch her fan, her gloves, her mask, nor nothing?

EMILIA

    Never, my lord.

OTHELLO

That's strange.

EMILIA

I durst, my lord, to wager she is honest,
Lay down my soul at stake: if you think other,
Remove your thought; it doth abuse your bosom.
If any wretch have put this in your head,
Let heaven requite it with the serpent's curse!
For, if she be not honest, chaste, and true,
There's no man happy; the purest of their wives
Is foul as slander.

OTHELLO

Bid her come hither: go.

Exit EMILIA

She says enough; yet she's a simple bawd
That cannot say as much. This is a subtle whore,
A closet lock and key of villainous secrets
And yet she'll kneel and pray; I have seen her do't.

Enter DESDEMONA *with* EMILIA

DESDEMONA

My lord, what is your will?

OTHELLO

Pray, chuck, come hither.

DESDEMONA

What is your pleasure?

OTHELLO

Let me see your eyes;
Look in my face.

DESDEMONA

What horrible fancy's this?

OTHELLO

[*To* EMILIA] Some of your function, mistress;
Leave procreants alone and shut the door;
Cough, or cry 'hem,' if any body come:
Your mystery, your mystery: nay, dispatch.

Exit EMILIA

DESDEMONA

    Upon my knees, what doth your speech import?

    I understand a fury in your words.

    But not the words.

OTHELLO

    Why, what art thou?

DESDEMONA

    Your wife, my lord; your true

    And loyal wife.

OTHELLO

    Come, swear it, damn thyself

    Lest, being like one of heaven, the devils themselves

    Should fear to seize thee: therefore be double damn'd:

    Swear thou art honest.

DESDEMONA

    Heaven doth truly know it.

OTHELLO

    Heaven truly knows that thou art false as hell.

DESDEMONA

    To whom, my lord? With whom? How am I false?

OTHELLO

    O Desdemona! away! away! away!

DESDEMONA

    Alas the heavy day! Why do you weep?

    Am I the motive of these tears, my lord?

    If haply you my father do suspect

    An instrument of this your calling back,

    Lay not your blame on me: If you have lost him,

    Why, I have lost him too.

OTHELLO

    Had it pleased heaven

    To try me with affliction; had they rain'd

    All kinds of sores and shames on my bare head.

    Steep'd me in poverty to the very lips,

    Given to captivity me and my utmost hopes,

    I should have found in some place of my soul

    A drop of patience: but, alas, to make me

A fixed figure for the time of scorn
To point his slow unmoving finger at!—O, O!
Yet could I bear that too; well, very well:
But there, where I have garner'd up my heart,
Where either I must live, or bear no life;
The fountain from the which my current runs,
Or else dries up; to be discarded thence!
Or keep it as a cistern for foul toads
To knot and gender in! Turn thy complexion there,
Patience, thou young and rose-lipp'd cherubin—
Ay, there, look grim as hell!

DESDEMONA
I hope my noble lord esteems me honest.

OTHELLO
O, ay; as summer flies are in the shambles,
That quicken even with blowing. O thou weed,
Who art so lovely fair and smell'st so sweet
That the sense aches at thee, would thou hadst ne'er been born!

DESDEMONA
Alas, what ignorant sin have I committed?

OTHELLO
Was this fair paper, this most goodly book,
Made to write 'whore' upon? What committed!
Committed! O thou public commoner!
I should make very forges of my cheeks,
That would to cinders burn up modesty,
Did I but speak thy deeds. What committed!
Heaven stops the nose at it and the moon winks,
The bawdy wind that kisses all it meets
Is hush'd within the hollow mine of earth,
And will not hear it. What committed!
Impudent strumpet!

DESDEMONA
By heaven, you do me wrong.

OTHELLO
Are you not a strumpet?

DESDEMONA
    No, as I am a Christian:
    If to preserve this vessel for my lord
    From any other foul unlawful touch
    Be not to be a strumpet, I am none.

OTHELLO
    What, not a whore?

DESDEMONA
    No, as I shall be saved.

OTHELLO
    Is't possible?

DESDEMONA
    O, heaven forgive us!

OTHELLO
    I cry you mercy, then:
    I took you for that cunning whore of Venice
    That married with Othello.

Raising his voice

    You, mistress,
    That have the office opposite to Saint Peter,
    And keep the gate of hell!

Re-enter EMILIA

    You, you, ay, you!
    We have done our course; there's money for your pains:
    I pray you, turn the key and keep our counsel.

Exit

EMILIA
    Alas, what does this gentleman conceive?
    How do you, madam? How do you, my good lady?

DESDEMONA
    'Faith, half asleep.

EMILIA
    Good madam, what's the matter with my lord?

DESDEMONA
    With who?

EMILIA
    Why, with my lord, madam.

DESDEMONA

    Who is thy lord?

EMILIA

    He that is yours, sweet lady.

DESDEMONA

    I have none: do not talk to me, Emilia;

    I cannot weep; nor answer have I none,

    But what should go by water. Prithee, tonight

    Lay on my bed my wedding sheets: remember;

    And call thy husband hither.

EMILIA

    Here's a change indeed!

Exit

DESDEMONA

    'Tis meet I should be used so, very meet.

    How have I been behaved, that he might stick

    The small'st opinion on my great'st abuse?

               Re-enter EMILIA *with* IAGO

IAGO

    What is your pleasure, madam?

    How is't with you?

DESDEMONA

    I cannot tell. Those that do teach young babes

    Do it with gentle means and easy tasks:

    He might have chid me so; for, in good faith,

    I am a child to chiding.

IAGO

    What's the matter, lady?

EMILIA

    Alas, Iago, my lord hath so bewhored her.

    Thrown such despite and heavy terms upon her,

    As true hearts cannot bear.

DESDEMONA

    Am I that name, Iago?

IAGO

    What name, fair lady?

DESDEMONA

    Such as she says my lord did say I was.

EMILIA

    He call'd her whore: a beggar in his drink

    Could not have laid such terms upon his callat.

IAGO

    Why did he so?

DESDEMONA

    I do not know; I am sure I am none such.

IAGO

    Do not weep, do not weep. Alas the day!

EMILIA

    Hath she forsook so many noble matches,

    Her father and her country and her friends,

    To be call'd whore? Would it not make one weep?

DESDEMONA

    It is my wretched fortune.

IAGO

    Beshrew him for't!

    How comes this trick upon him?

DESDEMONA

    Nay, heaven doth know.

EMILIA

    I will be hang'd, if some eternal villain,

    Some busy and insinuating rogue,

    Some cogging, cozening slave, to get some office,

    Have not devised this slander; I'll be hang'd else.

IAGO

    Fie, there is no such man; it is impossible.

DESDEMONA

    If any such there be, heaven pardon him!

EMILIA

    A halter pardon him! and hell gnaw his bones!

    Why should he call her whore? Who keeps her company?

    What place? What time? What form? What likelihood?

    The Moor's abused by some most villainous knave,

    Some base notorious knave, some scurvy fellow.

O heaven, that such companions thou'ldst unfold,
And put in every honest hand a whip
To lash the rascals naked through the world
Even from the east to the west!

IAGO

Speak within door.

EMILIA

O, fie upon them! Some such squire he was
That turn'd your wit the seamy side without,
And made you to suspect me with the Moor.

IAGO

You are a fool; go to.

DESDEMONA

O good Iago,
What shall I do to win my lord again?
Good friend, go to him; for, by this light of heaven,
I know not how I lost him. Here I kneel:
If e'er my will did trespass 'gainst his love,
Either in discourse of thought or actual deed,
Or that mine eyes, mine ears, or any sense,
Delighted them in any other form;
Or that I do not yet, and ever did.
And ever will—though he do shake me off
To beggarly divorcement—love him dearly,
Comfort forswear me! Unkindness may do much;
And his unkindness may defeat my life,
But never taint my love. I cannot say 'whore:'
It does abhor me now I speak the word;
To do the act that might the addition earn
Not the world's mass of vanity could make me.

IAGO

I pray you, be content; 'tis but his humour:
The business of the state does him offence,
And he does chide with you.

DESDEMONA

If 'twere no other—

IAGO

'Tis but so, I warrant.

Trumpets within

Hark, how these instruments summon you to supper!
The messengers of Venice stay the meat;
Go in, and weep not; all things shall be well.

Exeunt DESDEMONA *and* EMILIA
Enter RODERIGO

How now, Roderigo!

RODERIGO

I do not find that thou dealest justly with me.

IAGO

What in the contrary?

RODERIGO

Every day thou daffest me with some device, Iago; and rather, as it seems to me now, keepest from me all conveniency than suppliest me with the least advantage of hope. I will indeed no longer endure it, nor am I yet persuaded to put up in peace what already I have foolishly suffered.

IAGO

Will you hear me, Roderigo?

RODERIGO

'Faith, I have heard too much, for your words and performances are no kin together.

IAGO

You charge me most unjustly.

RODERIGO

With nought but truth. I have wasted myself out of my means. The jewels you have had from me to deliver to Desdemona would half have corrupted a votarist: you have told me she hath received them and returned me expectations and comforts of sudden respect and acquaintance, but I find none.

IAGO

Well; go to; very well.

RODERIGO

Very well! go to! I cannot go to, man; nor 'tis not very well: by this hand, I say it is scurvy, and begin to find myself fobbed in it.

IAGO

Very well.

RODERIGO

I tell you 'tis not very well. I will make myself known to Desdemona: if she will return me my jewels, I will give over my suit and repent my unlawful solicitation; if not, assure yourself I will seek satisfaction of you.

IAGO

You have said now.

RODERIGO

Ay, and said nothing but what I protest intendment of doing.

IAGO

Why, now I see there's mettle in thee, and even from this instant to build on thee a better opinion than ever before. Give me thy hand, Roderigo: thou hast taken against me a most just exception; but yet, I protest, I have dealt most directly in thy affair.

RODERIGO

It hath not appeared.

IAGO

I grant indeed it hath not appeared, and your suspicion is not without wit and judgment. But, Roderigo, if thou hast that in thee indeed, which I have greater reason to believe now than ever, I mean purpose, courage and valour, this night show it: if thou the next night following enjoy not Desdemona, take me from this world with treachery and devise engines for my life.

RODERIGO

Well, what is it? Is it within reason and compass?

IAGO

Sir, there is especial commission come from Venice to depute Cassio in Othello's place.

RODERIGO

Is that true? Why, then Othello and Desdemona return again to Venice.

IAGO

O, no; he goes into Mauritania and takes away with him the fair Desdemona, unless his abode be lingered here by some accident: wherein none can be so determinate as the removing of Cassio.

RODERIGO

How do you mean, removing of him?

IAGO

Why, by making him uncapable of Othello's place; knocking out his brains.

RODERIGO

And that you would have me to do?

IAGO

Ay, if you dare do yourself a profit and a right. He sups to-night with a harlotry, and thither will I go to him: he knows not yet of his honourable fortune. If you will watch his going thence, which I will fashion to fall out between twelve and one, you may take him at your pleasure: I will be near to second your attempt, and he shall fall between us. Come, stand not amazed at it, but go along with me; I will show you such a necessity in his death that you shall think yourself bound to put it on him. It is now high suppertime, and the night grows to waste: about it.

RODERIGO

I will hear further reason for this.

IAGO

And you shall be satisfied.

Exeunt

SCENE III.
ANOTHER ROOM IN THE CASTLE.

Enter OTHELLO, LODOVICO, DESDEMONA, EMILIA *and Attendants*

LODOVICO

I do beseech you, sir, trouble yourself no further.

OTHELLO

O, pardon me: 'twill do me good to walk.

LODOVICO

Madam, good night; I humbly thank your ladyship.

DESDEMONA

Your honour is most welcome.

OTHELLO

Will you walk, sir? O, Desdemona!

DESDEMONA

My lord?

OTHELLO

Get you to bed on the instant; I will be returned forthwith:
dismiss your attendant there: look it be done.

DESDEMONA

I will, my lord.

Exeunt OTHELLO,
LODOVICO, *and Attendants*

EMILIA

How goes it now? He looks gentler than he did.

DESDEMONA

He says he will return incontinent:
He hath commanded me to go to bed,
And bade me to dismiss you.

EMILIA

Dismiss me!

DESDEMONA

It was his bidding: therefore, good Emilia,
Give me my nightly wearing, and adieu:
We must not now displease him.

EMILIA

I would you had never seen him!

DESDEMONA

So would not I my love doth so approve him,
That even his stubbornness, his checks, his frowns—
Prithee, unpin me—have grace and favour in them.

EMILIA

I have laid those sheets you bade me on the bed.

DESDEMONA

All's one. Good faith, how foolish are our minds!
If I do die before thee prithee, shroud me
In one of those same sheets.

EMILIA

Come, come you talk.

DESDEMONA

    My mother had a maid call'd Barbara:
    She was in love, and he she loved proved mad
    And did forsake her: she had a song of 'willow;'
    An old thing 'twas, but it express'd her fortune,
    And she died singing it: that song to-night
    Will not go from my mind; I have much to do,
    But to go hang my head all at one side,
    And sing it like poor Barbara. Prithee, dispatch.

EMILIA

    Shall I go fetch your night-gown?

DESDEMONA

    No, unpin me here.
    This Lodovico is a proper man.

EMILIA

    A very handsome man.

DESDEMONA

    He speaks well.

EMILIA

    I know a lady in Venice would have walked barefoot to Palestine
    for a touch of his nether lip.

DESDEMONA

    [*Singing*] The poor soul sat sighing by a sycamore tree, Sing all a
    green willow:
    Her hand on her bosom, her head on her knee, Sing willow,
    willow, willow:
    The fresh streams ran by her, and murmur'd her moans; Sing
    willow, willow, willow;
    Her salt tears fell from her, and soften'd the stones;
    Lay by these:—
    Sing willow, willow, willow;
    Prithee, hie thee; he'll come anon:—
    Sing all a green willow must be my garland.
    Let nobody blame him; his scorn I approve—
    Nay, that's not next. Hark! who is't that knocks?

EMILIA

    It's the wind.

DESDEMONA

[*Singing*] I call'd my love false love; but what said he then?
Sing willow, willow, willow:
If I court moe women, you'll couch with moe men!
So, get thee gone; good night Mine eyes do itch;
Doth that bode weeping?

EMILIA

'Tis neither here nor there.

DESDEMONA

I have heard it said so. O, these men, these men!
Dost thou in conscience think—tell me, Emilia—
That there be women do abuse their husbands
In such gross kind?

EMILIA

There be some such, no question.

DESDEMONA

Wouldst thou do such a deed for all the world?

EMILIA

Why, would not you?

DESDEMONA

No, by this heavenly light!

EMILIA

Nor I neither by this heavenly light;
I might do't as well i' the dark.

DESDEMONA

Wouldst thou do such a deed for all the world?

EMILIA

The world's a huge thing: it is a great price.
For a small vice.

DESDEMONA

In troth, I think thou wouldst not.

EMILIA

In troth, I think I should; and undo't when I had done. Marry,
I would not do such a thing for a joint-ring, nor for measures
of lawn, nor for gowns, petticoats, nor caps, nor any petty
exhibition; but for the whole world—why, who would not make

her husband a cuckold to make him a monarch? I should venture
purgatory for't.

DESDEMONA

Beshrew me, if I would do such a wrong For the whole world.

EMILIA

Why the wrong is but a wrong i' the world: and having the world
for your labour, tis a wrong in your own world, and you might
quickly make it right.

DESDEMONA

I do not think there is any such woman.

EMILIA

Yes, a dozen; and as many to the vantage as would store the
world they played for.
But I do think it is their husbands' faults
If wives do fall: say that they slack their duties,
And pour our treasures into foreign laps,
Or else break out in peevish jealousies,
Throwing restraint upon us; or say they strike us,
Or scant our former having in despite;
Why, we have galls, and though we have some grace,
Yet have we some revenge. Let husbands know
Their wives have sense like them: they see and smell
And have their palates both for sweet and sour,
As husbands have. What is it that they do
When they change us for others? Is it sport?
I think it is: and doth affection breed it?
I think it doth: is't frailty that thus errs?
It is so too: and have not we affections,
Desires for sport, and frailty, as men have?
Then let them use us well: else let them know,
The ills we do, their ills instruct us so.

DESDEMONA

Good night, good night: heaven me such uses send,
Not to pick bad from bad, but by bad mend!

Exeunt

ACT

V

SCENE I.
CYPRUS. A STREET.

Enter IAGO *and* RODERIGO

IAGO

    Here, stand behind this bulk; straight will he come:
    Wear thy good rapier bare, and put it home:
    Quick, quick; fear nothing; I'll be at thy elbow:
    It makes us, or it mars us; think on that,
    And fix most firm thy resolution.

RODERIGO

    Be near at hand; I may miscarry in't.

IAGO

    Here, at thy hand: be bold, and take thy stand.
                      Retires

RODERIGO

    I have no great devotion to the deed;
    And yet he hath given me satisfying reasons:
    'Tis but a man gone. Forth, my sword: he dies.

IAGO

    I have rubb'd this young quat almost to the sense,
    And he grows angry. Now, whether he kill Cassio,

Or Cassio him, or each do kill the other,
Every way makes my gain: live Roderigo,
He calls me to a restitution large
Of gold and jewels that I bobb'd from him,
As gifts to Desdemona;
It must not be: if Cassio do remain,
He hath a daily beauty in his life
That makes me ugly; and, besides, the Moor
May unfold me to him; there stand I in much peril:
No, he must die. But so: I hear him coming.
Enter CASSIO

RODERIGO
    I know his gait, 'tis he. Villain, thou diest!
                    Makes a pass at CASSIO
CASSIO
    That thrust had been mine enemy indeed,
    But that my coat is better than thou know'st
    I will make proof of thine.
                Draws, and wounds RODERIGO
RODERIGO
    O, I am slain!

                            IAGO *from behind wounds*
                            CASSIO *in the leg, and exit*
CASSIO
    I am maim'd for ever. Help, ho! murder! murder!
    Falls

                Enter OTHELLO
OTHELLO
    The voice of Cassio: Iago keeps his word.
RODERIGO
    O, villain that I am!
OTHELLO
    It is even so.
CASSIO
    O, help, ho! light! a surgeon!
OTHELLO
    'Tis he:—O brave Iago, honest and just,

That hast such noble sense of thy friend's wrong!
Thou teachest me. Minion, your dear lies dead,
And your unblest fate hies: strumpet, I come.
Forth of my heart those charms, thine eyes, are blotted;
Thy bed, lust-stain'd, shall with lust's blood be spotted.

Exit

Enter LODOVICO *and* GRATIANO

CASSIO

What, ho! no watch? No passage? Murder! murder!

GRATIANO

'Tis some mischance; the cry is very direful.

CASSIO

O, help!

LODOVICO

Hark!

RODERIGO

O wretched villain!

LODOVICO

Two or three groan: it is a heavy night:
These may be counterfeits: let's think't unsafe
To come in to the cry without more help.

RODERIGO

Nobody come? Then shall I bleed to death.

LODOVICO

Hark!

Re-enter IAGO, *with a light*

GRATIANO

Here's one comes in his shirt, with light and weapons.

IAGO

Who's there? Whose noise is this that ones on murder?

LODOVICO

We do not know.

IAGO

Did not you hear a cry?

CASSIO

Here, here! for heaven's sake, help me!

IAGO

    What's the matter?

GRATIANO

    This is Othello's ancient, as I take it.

LODOVICO

    The same indeed; a very valiant fellow.

IAGO

    What are you here that cry so grievously?

CASSIO

    Iago? O, I am spoil'd, undone by villains!

    Give me some help.

IAGO

    O me, lieutenant! what villains have done this?

CASSIO

    I think that one of them is hereabout,

    And cannot make away.

IAGO

    O treacherous villains!

    What are you there? Come in, and give some help.

                To LODOVICO *and* GRATIANO

RODERIGO

    O, help me here!

CASSIO

    That's one of them.

IAGO

    O murderous slave! O villain!

                Stabs RODERIGO

RODERIGO

    O damn'd Iago! O inhuman dog!

IAGO

    Kill men i' the dark! Where be these bloody thieves?

    How silent is this town! Ho! murder! murder!

    What may you be? Are you of good or evil?

LODOVICO

    As you shall prove us, praise us.

IAGO

    Signior Lodovico?

LODOVICO

He, sir.

IAGO

I cry you mercy. Here's Cassio hurt by villains.

GRATIANO

Cassio!

IAGO

How is't, brother!

CASSIO

My leg is cut in two.

IAGO

Marry, heaven forbid!
Light, gentlemen; I'll bind it with my shirt.

Enter BIANCA

BIANCA

What is the matter, ho? Who is't that cried?

IAGO

Who is't that cried!

BIANCA

O my dear Cassio! my sweet Cassio! O Cassio,
Cassio, Cassio!

IAGO

O notable strumpet! Cassio, may you suspect
Who they should be that have thus many led you?

CASSIO

No.

GRATIANO

I am to find you thus: I have been to seek you.

IAGO

Lend me a garter. So. O, for a chair,
To bear him easily hence!

BIANCA

Alas, he faints! O Cassio, Cassio, Cassio!

IAGO

Gentlemen all, I do suspect this trash
To be a party in this injury.

Patience awhile, good Cassio. Come, come;
Lend me a light. Know we this face or no?
Alas my friend and my dear countryman
Roderigo! no:—yes, sure: O heaven! Roderigo.

GRATIANO

What, of Venice?

IAGO

Even he, sir; did you know him?

GRATIANO

Know him! ay.

IAGO

Signior Gratiano? I cry you gentle pardon;
These bloody accidents must excuse my manners,
That so neglected you.

GRATIANO

I am glad to see you.

IAGO

How do you, Cassio? O, a chair, a chair!

GRATIANO

Roderigo!

IAGO

He, he 'tis he.

A chair brought in

O, that's well said; the chair!
Some good man bear him carefully from hence;
I'll fetch the general's surgeon.

To BIANCA

For you, mistress,
Save you your labour. He that lies slain here, Cassio,
Was my dear friend: what malice was between you?

CASSIO

None in the world; nor do I know the man.

IAGO

[*To* BIANCA] What, look you pale? O, bear him out o' the air.

CASSIO *and* RODERIGO *are borne off*

Stay you, good gentlemen. Look you pale, mistress?

Do you perceive the gastness of her eye?
Nay, if you stare, we shall hear more anon.
Behold her well; I pray you, look upon her:
Do you see, gentlemen? Nay, guiltiness will speak,
Though tongues were out of use.

Enter EMILIA

EMILIA
'Las, what's the matter? What's the matter, husband?
IAGO
Cassio hath here been set on in the dark
By Roderigo and fellows that are scaped:
He's almost slain, and Roderigo dead.
EMILIA
Alas, good gentleman! alas, good Cassio!
IAGO
This is the fruit of whoring. Prithee, Emilia,
Go know of Cassio where he supp'd to-night.

To BIANCA

What, do you shake at that?
BIANCA
He supp'd at my house; but I therefore shake not.
IAGO
O, did he so? I charge you, go with me.
EMILIA
Fie, fie upon thee, strumpet!
BIANCA
I am no strumpet; but of life as honest
As you that thus abuse me.
EMILIA
As I! foh! fie upon thee!
IAGO
Kind gentlemen, let's go see poor Cassio dress'd.
Come, mistress, you must tell's another tale.
Emilia run you to the citadel,
And tell my lord and lady what hath happ'd.
Will you go on? I pray.
Aside

This is the night
That either makes me or fordoes me quite.

Exeunt

SCENE II.
A BEDCHAMBER IN THE CASTLE.

DESDEMONA *in bed asleep; a light burning.*
Enter OTHELLO

OTHELLO

It is the cause, it is the cause, my soul—
Let me not name it to you, you chaste stars—
It is the cause. Yet I'll not shed her blood;
Nor scar that whiter skin of hers than snow,
And smooth as monumental alabaster.
Yet she must die, else she'll betray more men.
Put out the light, and then put out the light:
If I quench thee, thou flaming minister,
I can again thy former light restore,
Should I repent me: but once put out thy light,
Thou cunning'st pattern of excelling nature,
I know not where is that Promethean heat
That can thy light relume. When I have pluck'd the rose,
I cannot give it vital growth again.
It must needs wither: I'll smell it on the tree.
Kissing her
Ah balmy breath, that dost almost persuade
Justice to break her sword! One more, one more.
Be thus when thou art dead, and I will kill thee,
And love thee after. One more, and this the last:
So sweet was ne'er so fatal. I must weep,
But they are cruel tears: this sorrow's heavenly;
It strikes where it doth love. She wakes.

DESDEMONA

Who's there? Othello?

OTHELLO

Ay. Desdemona.

DESDEMONA

Will you come to bed, my lord?

OTHELLO

Have you pray'd to-night, Desdemona?

DESDEMONA

Ay, my lord.

OTHELLO

If you bethink yourself of any crime
Unreconciled as yet to heaven and grace,
Solicit for it straight.

DESDEMONA

Alas, my lord, what do you mean by that?

OTHELLO

Well, do it, and be brief; I will walk by:
I would not kill thy unprepared spirit;
No; heaven forfend! I would not kill thy soul.

DESDEMONA

Talk you of killing?

OTHELLO

Ay, I do.

DESDEMONA

Then heaven
Have mercy on me!

OTHELLO

Amen, with all my heart!

DESDEMONA

If you say so, I hope you will not kill me.

OTHELLO

Hum!

DESDEMONA

And yet I fear you; for you are fatal then
When your eyes roll so: why I should fear I know not,
Since guiltiness I know not; but yet I feel I fear.

OTHELLO

Think on thy sins.

DESDEMONA

They are loves I bear to you.

OTHELLO
    Ay, and for that thou diest.
DESDEMONA
    That death's unnatural that kills for loving.
    Alas, why gnaw you so your nether lip?
    Some bloody passion shakes your very frame:
    These are portents; but yet I hope, I hope,
    They do not point on me.
OTHELLO
    Peace, and be still!
DESDEMONA
    I will so. What's the matter?
OTHELLO
    That handkerchief which I so loved and gave thee
    Thou gavest to Cassio.
DESDEMONA
    No, by my life and soul!
    Send for the man, and ask him.
OTHELLO
    Sweet soul, take heed,
    Take heed of perjury; thou art on thy deathbed.
DESDEMONA
    Ay, but not yet to die.
OTHELLO
    Yes, presently:
    Therefore confess thee freely of thy sin;
    For to deny each article with oath
    Cannot remove nor choke the strong conception
    That I do groan withal. Thou art to die.
DESDEMONA
    Then Lord have mercy on me!
OTHELLO
    I say, amen.
DESDEMONA
    And have you mercy too! I never did
    Offend you in my life; never loved Cassio

But with such general warranty of heaven
As I might love: I never gave him token.

OTHELLO

By heaven, I saw my handkerchief in's hand.
O perjured woman! thou dost stone my heart,
And makest me call what I intend to do
A murder, which I thought a sacrifice:
I saw the handkerchief.

DESDEMONA

He found it then;
I never gave it him: send for him hither;
Let him confess a truth.

OTHELLO

He hath confess'd.

DESDEMONA

What, my lord?

OTHELLO

That he hath used thee.

DESDEMONA

How? unlawfully?

OTHELLO

Ay.

DESDEMONA

He will not say so.

OTHELLO

No, his mouth is stopp'd;
Honest Iago hath ta'en order for't.

DESDEMONA

O! my fear interprets: what, is he dead?

OTHELLO

Had all his hairs been lives, my great revenge
Had stomach for them all.

DESDEMONA

Alas! he is betray'd and I undone.

OTHELLO

Out, strumpet! weep'st thou for him to my face?

DESDEMONA

O, banish me, my lord, but kill me not!

OTHELLO

Down, strumpet!

DESDEMONA

Kill me to-morrow: let me live to-night!

OTHELLO

Nay, if you strive—

DESDEMONA

But half an hour!

OTHELLO

Being done, there is no pause.

DESDEMONA

But while I say one prayer!

OTHELLO

It is too late.

He stifles her

DESDEMONA

O lord, Lord, Lord!

EMILIA

[*Within*] My lord , my lord! what, ho! my lord, my lord!

OTHELLO

What noise is this? Not dead? not yet quite dead?

I that am cruel am yet merciful;

I would not have thee linger in thy pain: So, so.

EMILIA

[*Within*] What, ho! my lord, my lord!

OTHELLO

Who's there?

EMILIA

[*Within*] O, good my lord, I would speak a word with you!

OTHELLO

Yes: 'tis Emilia. By and by. She's dead.

'Tis like she comes to speak of Cassio's death—

The noise was here. Ha! no more moving?

Still as the grave. Shall she come in? Were't good?

I think she stirs again:—no. What's best to do?

If she come in, she'll sure speak to my wife:
My wife! my wife! what wife? I have no wife.
O insupportable! O heavy hour!
Methinks it should be now a huge eclipse
Of sun and moon, and that the affrighted globe
Should yawn at alteration.

EMILIA

[*Within*] I do beseech you
That I may speak with you, O, good my lord!

OTHELLO

I had forgot thee: O, come in, Emilia;
Soft; by and by. Let me the curtains draw.
Where art thou?

Unlocks the door
Enter EMILIA

What's the matter with thee now?

EMILIA

O, my good lord, yonder's foul murders done!

OTHELLO

What, now?

EMILIA

But now, my lord.

OTHELLO

It is the very error of the moon;
She comes more nearer earth than she was wont,
And makes men mad.

EMILIA

Cassio, my lord, hath kill'd a young Venetian
Call'd Roderigo.

OTHELLO

Roderigo kill'd!
And Cassio kill'd!

EMILIA

No, Cassio is not kill'd.

OTHELLO

Not Cassio kill'd! then murder's out of tune,
And sweet revenge grows harsh.

DESDEMONA

O, falsely, falsely murder'd!

EMILIA

Alas, what cry is that?

OTHELLO

That! what?

EMILIA

Out, and alas! that was my lady's voice.
Help! help, ho! help! O lady, speak again!
Sweet Desdemona! O sweet mistress, speak!

DESDEMONA

A guiltless death I die.

EMILIA

O, who hath done this deed?

DESDEMONA

Nobody; I myself. Farewell
Commend me to my kind lord: O, farewell!

She dies

OTHELLO

Why, how should she be murder'd?

EMILIA

Alas, who knows?

OTHELLO

You heard her say herself, it was not I.

EMILIA

She said so: I must needs report the truth.

OTHELLO

She's, like a liar, gone to burning hell:
'Twas I that kill'd her.

EMILIA

O, the more angel she,
And you the blacker devil!

OTHELLO

She turn'd to folly, and she was a whore.

EMILIA

Thou dost belie her, and thou art a devil.

OTHELLO
    She was false as water.
EMILIA
    Thou art rash as fire, to say
    That she was false: O, she was heavenly true!
OTHELLO
    Cassio did top her; ask thy husband else.
    O, I were damn'd beneath all depth in hell,
    But that I did proceed upon just grounds
    To this extremity. Thy husband knew it all.
EMILIA
    My husband!
OTHELLO
    Thy husband.
EMILIA
    That she was false to wedlock?
OTHELLO
    Ay, with Cassio. Nay, had she been true,
    If heaven would make me such another world
    Of one entire and Perfect chrysolite,
    I'ld not have sold her for it.
EMILIA
    My husband!
OTHELLO
    Ay, 'twas he that told me first:
    An honest man he is, and hates the slime
    That sticks on filthy deeds.
EMILIA
    My husband!
OTHELLO
    What needs this iteration, woman? I say thy husband.
EMILIA
    O mistress, villainy hath made mocks with love,
    My husband say that she was false!
OTHELLO
    He, woman;

I say thy husband: dost understand the word?
My friend, thy husband, honest, honest Iago.

EMILIA

If he say so, may his pernicious soul
Rot half a grain a day! he lies to the heart:
She was too fond of her most filthy bargain.

OTHELLO

Ha!

EMILIA

Do thy worst:
This deed of thine is no more worthy heaven
Than thou wast worthy her.

OTHELLO

Peace, you were best.

EMILIA

Thou hast not half that power to do me harm
As I have to be hurt. O gull! O dolt!
As ignorant as dirt! thou hast done a deed—
I care not for thy sword; I'll make thee known,
Though I lost twenty lives. Help! help, ho! help!
The Moor hath kill'd my mistress! Murder! murder!

Enter MONTANO, GRATIANO,
IAGO, *and others*

MONTANO

What is the matter? How now, general!

EMILIA

O, are you come, Iago? you have done well,
That men must lay their murders on your neck.

GRATIANO

What is the matter?

EMILIA

Disprove this villain, if thou be'st a man:
He says thou told'st him that his wife was false:
I know thou didst not, thou'rt not such a villain:
Speak, for my heart is full.

IAGO

    I told him what I thought, and told no more

    Than what he found himself was apt and true.

EMILIA

    But did you ever tell him she was false?

IAGO

    I did.

EMILIA

    You told a lie, an odious, damned lie;

    Upon my soul, a lie, a wicked lie.

    She false with Cassio! did you say with Cassio?

IAGO

    With Cassio, mistress. Go to, charm your tongue.

EMILIA

    I will not charm my tongue; I am bound to speak:

    My mistress here lies murder'd in her bed—

ALL

    O heavens forfend!

EMILIA

    And your reports have set the murder on.

OTHELLO

    Nay, stare not, masters: it is true, indeed.

GRATIANO

    'Tis a strange truth.

MONTANO

    O monstrous act!

EMILIA

    Villainy, villainy, villainy!

    I think upon't, I think: I smell't: O villainy!

    I thought so then:—I'll kill myself for grief:—

    O villainy, villainy!

IAGO

    What, are you mad? I charge you, get you home.

EMILIA

    Good gentlemen, let me have leave to speak:

    'Tis proper I obey him, but not now.

    Perchance, Iago, I will ne'er go home.

OTHELLO
O! O! O!

He falls on the bed

EMILIA
Nay, lay thee down and roar;
For thou hast kill'd the sweetest innocent
That e'er did lift up eye.

OTHELLO
[*Rising*] O, she was foul!
I scarce did know you, uncle: there lies your niece,
Whose breath, indeed, these hands have newly stopp'd:
I know this act shows horrible and grim.

GRATIANO
Poor Desdemona! I am glad thy father's dead:
Thy match was mortal to him, and pure grief
Shore his old thread in twain: did he live now,
This sight would make him do a desperate turn,
Yea, curse his better angel from his side,
And fall to reprobation.

OTHELLO
'Tis pitiful; but yet Iago knows
That she with Cassio hath the act of shame
A thousand times committed; Cassio confess'd it:
And she did gratify his amorous works
With that recognizance and pledge of love
Which I first gave her; I saw it in his hand:
It was a handkerchief, an antique token
My father gave my mother.

EMILIA
O heaven! O heavenly powers!

IAGO
Come, hold your peace.

EMILIA
'Twill out, 'twill out: I peace!
No, I will speak as liberal as the north:
Let heaven and men and devils, let them all,
All, all, cry shame against me, yet I'll speak.

IAGO

Be wise, and get you home.

EMILIA

I will not.

IAGO *offers to stab* EMILIA

GRATIANO

Fie!

Your sword upon a woman?

EMILIA

O thou dull Moor! that handkerchief thou speak'st of
I found by fortune and did give my husband;
For often, with a solemn earnestness,
More than indeed belong'd to such a trifle,
He begg'd of me to steal it.

IAGO

Villainous whore!

EMILIA

She give it Cassio! no, alas! I found it,
And I did give't my husband.

IAGO

Filth, thou liest!

EMILIA

By heaven, I do not, I do not, gentlemen.
O murderous coxcomb! what should such a fool
Do with so good a woman?

OTHELLO

Are there no stones in heaven
But what serve for the thunder? Precious villain!

He runs at IAGO; MONTANO *and others disarm him.*
IAGO, *from behind, stabs* EMILIA, *and escapes*

GRATIANO

The woman falls; sure, he hath kill'd his wife.

EMILIA

Ay, ay: O, lay me by my mistress' side.

GRATIANO

He's gone, but his wife's kill'd.

MONTANO
    'Tis a notorious villain. Take you this weapon,
    Which I have here recover'd from the Moor:
    Come, guard the door without; let him not pass,
    But kill him rather. I'll after that same villain,
    For 'tis a damned slave.

Exeunt MONTANO *and*
GRATIANO *and other*

OTHELLO
    I am not valiant neither,
    But ever puny whipster gets my sword:
    But why should honour outlive honesty?
    Let it go all.

EMILIA
    What did thy song bode, lady?
    Hark, canst thou hear me? I will play the swan.
    And die in music.
    Singing
    Willow, willow, willow—
    Moor, she was chaste; she loved thee, cruel Moor;
    So come my soul to bliss, as I speak true;
    So speaking as I think, I die, I die.

She dies

OTHELLO
    I have another weapon in this chamber;
    It is a sword of Spain, the ice-brook's temper:—
    O, here it is. Uncle, I must come forth.

GRATIANO
    [*Within*] If thou attempt it, it will cost thee dear:
    Thou hast no weapon, and perforce must suffer.

OTHELLO
    Look in upon me then and speak with me,
    Or, naked as I am, I will assault thee.
        Re-enter GRATIANO

GRATIANO
    What is the matter?

OTHELLO

> Behold, I have a weapon;
> A better never did itself sustain
> Upon a soldier's thigh: I have seen the day,
> That, with this little arm and this good sword,
> I have made my way through more impediments
> Than twenty times your stop: but, O vain boast!
> Who can control his fate? 'Tis not so now.
> Be not afraid, though you do see me weapon'd;
> Here is my journey's end, here is my butt,
> And very sea-mark of my utmost sail.
> Do you go back dismay'd? 'Tis a lost fear;
> Man but a rush against Othello's breast,
> And he retires. Where should Othello go?
> Now, how dost thou look now? O ill-starr'd wench!
> Pale as thy smock! when we shall meet at compt,
> This look of thine will hurl my soul from heaven,
> And fiends will snatch at it. Cold, cold, my girl!
> Even like thy chastity. O cursed slave!
> Whip me, ye devils,
> From the possession of this heavenly sight!
> Blow me about in winds! roast me in sulphur!
> Wash me in steep-down gulfs of liquid fire!
> O Desdemona! Desdemona! dead!
> Oh! Oh! Oh!

Enter LODOVICO, MONTANO, CASSIO
carried in a chair, and Officers with IAGO, *prisoner*

LODOVICO

> Where is this rash and most unfortunate man?

OTHELLO

> That's he that was Othello: here I am.

LODOVICO

> Where is that viper? Bring the villain forth.

OTHELLO

> I look down towards his feet; but that's a fable.
> If that thou best a devil, I cannot kill thee.

Wounds IAGO

LODOVICO
    Wrench his sword from him.
IAGO
    I bleed, sir; but not kill'd.
OTHELLO
    I am not sorry neither: I'ld have thee live;
    For, in my sense, 'tis happiness to die.
LODOVICO
    O thou Othello, thou wert once so good,
    Fall'n in the practise of a damned slave,
    What shall be said to thee?
OTHELLO
    Why, any thing:
    An honourable murderer, if you will;
    For nought I did in hate, but all in honour.
LODOVICO
    This wretch hath part confess'd his villany:
    Did you and he consent in Cassio's death?
OTHELLO
    Ay.
CASSIO
    Dear general, I never gave you cause.
OTHELLO
    I do believe it, and I ask your pardon.
    Will you, I pray, demand that demi-devil
    Why he hath thus ensnared my soul and body?
IAGO
    Demand me nothing: what you know, you know:
    From this time forth I never will speak word.
LODOVICO
    What, not to pray?
GRATIANO
    Torments will ope your lips.
OTHELLO
    Well, thou dost best.
LODOVICO
    Sir, you shall understand what hath befall'n,

Which, as I think, you know not. Here is a letter
Found in the pocket of the slain Roderigo;
And here another: the one of them imports
The death of Cassio to be undertook
By Roderigo.

OTHELLO

O villain!

CASSIO

Most heathenish and most gross!

LODOVICO

Now here's another discontented paper,
Found in his pocket too; and this, it seems,
Roderigo meant to have sent this damned villain;
But that belike Iago in the nick
Came in and satisfied him.

OTHELLO

O the pernicious caitiff!
How came you, Cassio, by that handkerchief
That was my wife's?

CASSIO

I found it in my chamber:
And he himself confess'd it even now
That there he dropp'd it for a special purpose
Which wrought to his desire.

OTHELLO

O fool! fool! fool!

CASSIO

There is besides in Roderigo's letter,
How he upbraids Iago, that he made him
Brave me upon the watch; whereon it came
That I was cast: and even but now he spake,
After long seeming dead, Iago hurt him,
Iago set him on.

LODOVICO

You must forsake this room, and go with us:
Your power and your command is taken off,
And Cassio rules in Cyprus. For this slave,

If there be any cunning cruelty
That can torment him much and hold him long,
It shall be his. You shall close prisoner rest,
Till that the nature of your fault be known
To the Venetian state. Come, bring him away.

OTHELLO

Soft you; a word or two before you go.
I have done the state some service, and they know't.
No more of that. I pray you, in your letters,
When you shall these unlucky deeds relate,
Speak of me as I am; nothing extenuate,
Nor set down aught in malice: then must you speak
Of one that loved not wisely but too well;
Of one not easily jealous, but being wrought
Perplex'd in the extreme; of one whose hand,
Like the base Indian, threw a pearl away
Richer than all his tribe; of one whose subdued eyes,
Albeit unused to the melting mood,
Drop tears as fast as the Arabian trees
Their medicinal gum. Set you down this;
And say besides, that in Aleppo once,
Where a malignant and a turban'd Turk
Beat a Venetian and traduced the state,
I took by the throat the circumcised dog,
And smote him, thus.

Stabs himself

LODOVICO

O bloody period!

GRATIANO

All that's spoke is marr'd.

OTHELLO

I kiss'd thee ere I kill'd thee: no way but this;
Killing myself, to die upon a kiss.

Falls on the bed, and dies

CASSIO

This did I fear, but thought he had no weapon;
For he was great of heart.

LODOVICO
    [*To* IAGO] O Spartan dog,
    More fell than anguish, hunger, or the sea!
    Look on the tragic loading of this bed;
    This is thy work: the object poisons sight;
    Let it be hid. Gratiano, keep the house,
    And seize upon the fortunes of the Moor,
    For they succeed on you. To you, lord governor,
    Remains the censure of this hellish villain;
    The time, the place, the torture: O, enforce it!
    Myself will straight aboard: and to the state
    This heavy act with heavy heart relate.

                                    Exeunt